Computer Supported Cooperative Work

Springer
London
Berlin
Heidelberg
New York
Barcelona
Budapest
Hong Kong
Milan
Paris
Santa Clara
Singapore
Tokyo

Also in this series

Reza Hazemi, Stephen Hailes and Steve Wilbur (eds)
The Digital University: Reinventing the Academy
1-85233-003-1

Celia T. Romm and Fay Sudweeks (eds)
Doing Business Electronically: A Global Perspective of Electronic Commerce
3-540-76159-4

Gerold Riempp

Wide Area Workflow Management

Creating Partnerships for the 21st Century

With 73 Figures

Springer

Gerold Riempp, Dipl. Wirtschaftsingenieur, PhD
Wittmanstrasse 34, D-64285 Darmstadt, Germany

Series Editors

Dan Diaper, PhD, MBCS
Head, Department of Computing, School of Design, Engineering and Computing, Bournemouth University, Talbot Campus, Fern Barrow, Poole, Dorset BH12 5BB, UK

Colston Sanger
Shottersley Research Limited, Little Shottersley, Farnham Lane
Haselmere, Surrey GU27 1HA, UK

ISBN-13: 978-3-540-76243-0 e-ISBN-13: 978-1-4471-1578-6
DOI: 10.1007/978-1-4471-1578-6

British Library Cataloguing in Publication Data
Riempp, Gerold
Wide area workflow management : creating partnerships for the 21st century. - (Computer supported cooperative work)
1.Teams in the workplace.- Data processing 2.Management information systems 3.Information resources management
I.Title
658'.05'53

Library of Congress Cataloging-in-Publication Data
Riempp, Gerold, 1965-
Wide area workflow management : creating partnerships for the 21st century. / Gerold Riempp.
p. cm. - - (Computer supported cooperative work)
Includes bibliographical references and index.

1. Teams in the workplace.- - Computer networks. 2. Workflow - - Management. I. Title. II. Series.
HD66.2.R54 1998 98-3622
658.4'02'0285- -dc21 CIP

This book is based on a doctoral thesis by the author with the title "Wide Area Workflow Management – Concepts and Solutions for Intra- and Interorganizational Coordination and Interaction of Widely Distributed Workflow Management Systems", submitted to the University of Paderborn, Germany, 1998.

Typesetting: Camera ready by author

34/3830-543210 Printed on acid-free paper

Dedicated to my parents, my wife and my children

Preface

In this book, the results of a three year research and development project on concepts and solutions for Wide Area Workflow Management are presented. This project was carried out at the Groupware Competence Center of the University of Paderborn, Germany, by a team under the direction of the author.

The main goal was to find ways to let the workflow systems of distinct organizations interact in a flexible manner, while preserving the autonomy of the participants. In the course of empirical observations made during case studies, the development of conceptual approaches and the implementation of prototypic software, this goal was refined in many respects which finally led to a *toolbox* of solutions for intra- and interorganizational cooperation allowing companies to network with *varying degrees* of autonomy.

At the time of starting the project in late 1994, there was practically no literature on the topic of Wide Area Workflow Management. The Workflow Management Coalition (WfMC) had recently been founded and had defined a *Reference Model*, which vaguely described a so-called *Interface 4* for the interaction of workflow systems. This was not much more than an early signal that this might become relevant some time in the future.

Writing this preface in spring 1998, the situation looks quite different. With the boom of the Internet and World Wide Web, solutions for interorganizational networking of information systems are discussed everywhere. Developments such as *electronic commerce* are predicted to fundamentally change the way business will be done in the near future. Universities offer lectures and training courses via the World Wide Web. Millions of people worldwide make use of Internet e-mail in companies and at home. An increasing number of banks offer 24-hour electronic banking. "Surfing the Web" has become a popular profession or hobby.

In this scenario, the attention given to methods for connecting business processes across company boundaries along the value-add-chain, such as Wide Area Workflow Management, has increased drastically. Suddenly, the paperless transfer of information among dispersed office workers no longer seems to be an "exotic vision" but starts to become real, promising that companies can achieve significant gains in efficiency.

With respect to workflow management standards, the WfMC specified the *Interface 4* more precisely in 1996. In addition, an increasing number of researchers propose further concepts and solutions for handling *wide area workflows*.

On the part of enabling technologies, such as operating systems, software development frameworks or groupware platforms, many software vendors have updated their products to now support the main standards of the Internet and WWW. The implementation and connection of systems for the flexible and efficient support of *wide area workflows* has thereby been facilitated considerably.

In this scenario, the present book attempts to provide both an overview and detailed information on the topic of interacting workflow systems from different perspectives: from conceptual aspects to practical software systems, from organizational challenges to technological solutions and from empirical observations to managerial recommendations.

The author proposes several possible "workflows" for the readers of this book, which are shown in Figure 1 on page 7. To find an adequate compromise between the basically linear structures of books and the need for context-oriented navigation, extensive cross-references can be found throughout the different chapters. Readers on the "fast track" of the proposed "workflows" can use for instance the summary in Chapter 9 (p. 261) to find relevant information quickly by "cross-reference surfing".

Acknowledgements

A book like this cannot be completed without the help of various persons, whom the author wants to mention here.

In first place, I want to thank the director of the Groupware Competence Center (GCC) at the University of Paderborn, Prof. Dr. Ludwig Nastansky, for giving me the opportunity to spend three very interesting years at his institute. Without the radically practical research approach for which he stands, the valuable discussions with him and the modern infrastructure that his institute provides, the results presented here could not have been achieved.

Colleagues at the GCC have also helped me in many respects to get my work done and therefore are gratefully mentioned here.

The results of the project on Wide Area Workflow Management were developed as part of a joint effort by the "Wide Area Workflow Team". I want to thank all members of this team very much for their dedication, creativity, patience, humor and positive thinking, which led to an outstanding team spirit. In this very positive atmosphere, working on the new challenges of Wide Area Workflow Management was twice as rewarding. I would not want to have missed this time with them.

My friend and former colleague Wolfgang Hilpert has especially contributed to this book, since the initial idea to start a project on Wide Area Workflow Management was born out of discussions with him in 1994. Being an outstanding workflow expert in both conceptual and technical respects, his critical remarks on this work were highly valuable.

Writing this book in the English language was a challenge in itself. Therefore, I am very grateful to Ms. Janith A. Loewen (Ed. M.) from Texas and Ms. Christiane D. Routliffe from Vancouver, B.C. for their valuable corrections and their patience in helping me to find the right words. Since both are North Americans, this book has been written according to US grammar and spelling.

Ms. Rosie Kemp from Springer Verlag London Ltd. did the final proofreading and answered all of my questions concerning the publication of this book. I am very appreciative of her dedicated support.

Prof. Dr. Dan Diaper and Mr. Colston Sanger are gratefully mentioned for their contributions as series editors.

Furthermore, I want to express my deep gratitude to my spiritual teacher, the Zen and Hapkido grandmaster Sonsanim Ko. Myong, for introducing me as one of his students to the philosophy and practice of "Doh" (Tao). I have tried to let this philosophy of balance and clearness inspire me during the writing of this book.

Finally, I am deeply indebted to members of my family, who have helped me in so many respects to write this book.

Darmstadt, April 1998

Gerold Riempp

Availability of the Wide Area GroupFlow System

The Wide Area GroupFlow System (WAGS), which is described in Chapter 6 (p. 179), is available for evaluation purposes via the WWW.

For downloading see:
http://gcc.uni-paderborn.de/wags
http://www.springer.co.uk/comp/support/index.html

WAGS is experimental software that may not function properly. It is not intended for commercial use. The authors of WAGS do not grant any warranty or do accept any liability for results of its use.

Contents

1 Introduction

Everything has been thought of before,
but the problem is to think of it again.
- *Johann Wolfgang von Goethe*

1.1 Scenario

In this book, concepts and solutions for streamlining the flow of information in office work within and between widely dispersed organizations will be proposed. This endeavor is embedded in several major trends:

Globalization: technologies developed in the 20th century, such as cars, airplanes and high-speed trains, have made it possible for persons and goods to travel around the globe within hours, instead of the weeks and months needed in previous centuries. Furthermore, the enormous technological improvements in the fields of telecommunications and computer systems have made it an everyday habit for people all over the world to exchange information with each other within seconds. As a consequence, business is done in a more and more international context and since markets become increasingly transparent through the use of information technology, global competition intensifies.

Companies react in different ways to this development: firstly, they often strive to be present in the major markets of this world by expansion or acquisition. Secondly, they increase their efforts to network with other companies, which are often operating on other stages of the value-add-chain, to improve their goods and services. Both developments require efficient technical support for the communication and interaction of office workers in global intra- and interorganizational business scenarios.

Process orientation: regarding work in offices according to *process* paradigms, rather than *static structures* that dominated former thinking, has fundamentally influenced organizational and technological concepts for the improvement of clerical work. While *process orientation* has long been known in the production sector, the discussion of its application in offices has started to gain popularity since around the 1980s. The enormous attention given to organizational concepts such as Business Process Reengineering in recent years highlights this development. On the part of information technology, various prototypes and products for *workflow management* have been devised in order to actually support the handling of processes in offices. However, the large majority of these *workflow management systems (WFMSs)* have been built for application in one organization at only one location, thereby not yet providing appropriate support for the globalization of business.

It is hoped that the introduction of *process orientation* in offices will lead to comparably high gains in efficiency as could already be realized in the production sector. However, it can be observed that these gains could not yet be achieved by the mere introduction of PCs, local networks and office applications in many organizations [Wesseler 1993], [Herget 1994].

Knowledge management: in the beginning of the use of computer systems, the handling of *data* dominated ("electronic data processing"). With increasing maturity of the related software applications – database management systems – the development efforts turned more in the direction of a representation of *information*. In contrast to *data*, *information* additionally encompasses a semantic context, which makes it easier for human actors to perceive and interpret the underlying facts. *Information* is often represented in electronic documents, which have become very popular in recent years due to the widespread use of PCs, office applications and groupware platforms. The World Wide Web also makes use of electronic documents to present "rich" information to potential readers around the globe. A third step of the "digital revolution" now targets *knowledge* for storage and use in software systems. *Knowledge* describes the ability to handle *information* efficiently in order to achieve a certain goal, the "capacity for effective action" [Senge 1997]. One facet of *knowledge management* is the electronic definition of *office procedure* or *workflow models*, which describe the *knowledge* about the steps necessary for generating and further processing information to achieve a certain result in clerical work.

Environmental protection: the use of paper to handle information in offices has very severe negative consequences on nature. Despite present recycling efforts, there still are large forest areas being cut down in order to produce paper for the single purpose of holding and transferring (office) information often for a very limited amount of time. It was the hope that the *electronic paperless office* would lower paper consumption in clerical work. With the increasing use of PCs in offices, exactly the opposite has happened up until the present. The notion of "what-you-see-is-what-you-get" *on paper* – sometimes called the "WYSIWYG-trap" – has led office employees to use even more paper for letters, memos, protocols, reports etc. Photocopiers and laser printers have led to a significant increase of paper consumption [VDP 1997]. Seen from the environmental perspective, the production and use of photocopiers, PCs and laser printers is also considerably harmful to nature [Reiter 1997d], [Grote/Malley 1997].

The combination of electronic office equipment and increased paper consumption has created a situation calling for rapid and effective measures in office work to protect the environment. If computer systems and electronic networks are to be used in offices – and today's clerical work is hard to imagine without them – a more efficient use of these technologies should now bring a drastic reduction of paper consumption. This is especially true for the interaction of office workers *between* organizations, which today is still mainly supported by paper-based information transfer.

1.2 What is Wide Area Workflow Management (WAWM)?

So what is Wide Area Workflow Management and what does it have to do with the trends described above?

It is widely agreed that *process orientation* in offices should help to streamline formerly inefficient procedures, and that workflow management systems (WFMSs) are appropriate information systems for this purpose. But in a world of increasing globalization, which calls for international business networks within and between organizations, applying the paradigms of *process orientation* in single offices, as done by many of the current WFMSs, does not suffice. The upcoming challenge is to find ways for clerical workers to exchange electronic information in an efficient manner *within and between* offices.

So one might say that local offices should first be targeted for optimization and then the communication between different locations be approached as a next step. This is true to a certain extent, but practical experiences with the implementation of WFMSs show that many of the inefficiencies of today's office processes are induced outside of the organizations attempting to improve their administrative work. Since large organizations receive thousands of documents per day as hard copies from their suppliers and have to send thousands of faxes and letters to their customers, there is limited space for the optimization of internal processes using electronic means. *Structure* and *media breaks* at the boundaries of organizations hinder further gains in efficiency.

This observation is not quite new. Technologies subsumed under the label of *electronic data interchange (EDI)* have been devised to streamline interorganizational cooperation. EDI can be used to efficiently transfer structured *data* in highly standardized processes. However, EDI can only replace a certain percentage of paper-based mail between organizations. In a world of *knowledge management*, where the highly flexible handling of contextual information in "rich" electronic documents is to be supported, EDI is not advanced enough in its current state. Furthermore, empirical studies of EDI use have shown that the application of this technology can create undesirable dependencies between the participants. Finally, EDI concentrates on the interface between organizations, which is only one link in the long chain of activities in business processes across different locations and organizations.

What additionally is needed is an overall *knowledge* about the optimal execution of office procedures, using easily adaptable containers in the form of electronic documents, which are forwarded in a predefined or interactive manner. In order to make this *knowledge* available to software systems, it must be somehow represented. In current workflow management systems for local, intraorganizational use, this is done with *workflow models*.

An upcoming challenge is therefore to define such *workflow models* not only for *local* but *wide area workflows*, which span across different locations of the same or different organizations. In respect to the experiences made with EDI, it is very important to preserve the autonomy of the participants in such a network of dispersed but coordinated activities. Furthermore, intra- and especially interorganizational office procedures cannot in all cases be predefined in *workflow models*. As we all know from our everyday work in offices, the efficient handling of unforeseen situations is an essential challenge as well. Therefore, *flexibility* is a fundamental prerequisite for information systems applied to streamline office work in a globally networked society.

With the aim of flexibly and efficiently connecting formerly disconnected "islands" of information systems in offices, thereby enabling the seamless and streamlined handling of overall business processes along the value-add-chain, WAWM can be defined as follows:

Wide Area Workflow Management deals with flexible planning and execution of office procedures in widely distributed environments, based on the interoperation of distinct workflow management systems in intra- and interorganizational scenarios.

Returning to the trends mentioned above, WAWM is supposed to facilitate the exchange of information in *global business* based on a strict application of the ideas of *process orientation* not only within single offices, but in a network of interacting white collar workers across locations and organizations. The patterns of interaction found by thorough planning of *workflow models* for these *wide area workflows*, or by interactive ad-hoc navigation of information carriers, represent a highly valuable body of *knowledge* to be exploited for gains in efficiency by the organizations involved. Once organizations have switched from paper-based to flexible electronic documents for their everyday information exchange in internal and cross-organizational processes, a significant reduction of paper consumption should be achieved. The author therefore hopes that WAWM can make a considerable contribution to lead office work out of its current environmental crisis.

The necessity of rendering formerly isolated WFMSs capable of interacting with each other across geographical and organizational boundaries has been increasingly discussed in recent times. It can be seen as a logical next step from the local to the global application of the paradigm of *process orientation* in the upcoming "virtual" offices, where participants involved can reside at potentially any place around the globe.

This section concludes with an interesting statement of Adams and Dworkin [1997, p. 213] about the shift from *local* workflow management to *WAWM*:

> "Workflow systems have always shared and distributed work, and therefore information and responsibility, among different workers. These systems have restricted themselves, however, to a single organization with a single set of interests (which all the workers are pledged to serve), and even to a single computer system. Now two or more organizations or individuals, each with their own interests, legal rights, vocabulary, protocols, and computer systems, have to cooperate and share a single process. Organizations have, in fact, always cooperated and "shared a process" by following elaborate protocols. For example, to exchange goods or services between organizations, the protocol involves invoices, terms-of-agreement, and so on. Our job is to take these protocols out of the manual realm and let computers handle the drudge-work of verifying each step in the process."

1.3 Aims of this book

This book attempts to discuss the challenges arising from Wide Area Workflow Management from different perspectives:

- *Empirical perspective*: in order to reflect real-world necessities, the concepts and solutions for WAWM developed in this book are based on the observations made in case studies. After these concepts and solutions have been described in a general manner, they are probed in the concrete scenarios found in the case studies.
- *State-of-the-art perspective*: prior to introducing his own concepts and solutions for WAWM, the author presents conceptual and practical approaches described by others authors to provide an overview of different possible interpretations of the topic.
- *Managerial perspective*: the *strategic and operational implications* of the intra- and interorganizational electronic networking of clerical workers are important aspects of decision making in business. Therefore, methodologies to define goals, plan, implement, maintain and continuously improve systems for WAWM are discussed.
- *Organizational perspective*: different strategies of cooperation within and between organizations can be distinguished according to the fundamental *power relationships* between the potential participants in a WAWM scenario. Hence, a *range* of suitable organizational and technological solutions for different organizational settings will be examined.
- *Technological perspective*: fundamental technological options for WAWM are surveyed to find appropriate base platforms for the development of WFMSs supporting *wide area workflows*.
- *Conceptual perspective*: the description of possible solutions for WAWM is based on a preceding thorough discussion of concepts. For example, different options for *structured* as well as *ad-hoc* WAWM will be presented in order to cover the whole spectrum ranging from *ex ante structured and repetitive* to *unforeseen and unique* office processes.
- *Practical perspective*: to illustrate the concepts discussed, the Wide Area GroupFlow Systems (WAGS) is presented as a prototypic framework for the realization of WAWM. The author uses WAGS to introduce possible solutions for handling *wide area workflows* between the different companies described in the case studies.

The research and development efforts in the field of WAWM can be regarded as being in a rather early stage of development within the lifecycle of technologies. Therefore, the author would like to see the concepts and solutions for WAWM introduced in the course of this book as a contribution to a discussion about possible future ways of building global informational networks among human beings working in offices.

1.4 Structure

The concepts and solutions for WAWM introduced in this book are embedded in and accompanied by observations made in two case studies. Therefore Chapter 2 (p. 9) begins by presenting the circumstances of the companies surveyed. Furthermore, details of office procedures to be optimized by WAWM are described. In the following chapters, recurrent references to these empirical cases help to illustrate the practical relevance of the topics discussed.

In the course of Chapter 3 (p. 23), fundamental concepts and terms relating to office work in widely distributed environments are presented. In the first section, conceptual approaches to the definition, explanation and facilitation of decentralized cooperation among single human actors and entire organizations are introduced. The second section of the chapter examines concepts and techniques for process orientation in offices. The chapter concludes by taking a look at fundamental technological platforms, which are suitable to enable systems for WAWM.

Chapter 4 (p. 73) introduces and discusses state-of-the-art concepts and solutions for WAWM from other sources to the extent that they were available to this author. Based on a classification scheme for workflow management systems presented in the first main section, scientific and conceptual systems and prototypes, which have the aim to support distributed and widely distributed office procedures, are presented in the second main section. In the third part of the chapter, an overview of current commercial workflow systems in respect to their WAWM-related features is given.

In Chapter 5 (p. 103), the author presents his own conceptual thoughts on the possible realization of systems for the flexible and efficient support of *wide area workflows*. The chapter begins by making the important distinction between systems supporting *automation & structure* in contrast to those aimed at *user support & flexibility*. In the second part of the chapter, major challenges of WAWM are structured according to three main dimensions – *organizational integration*, *locations* and *information distribution* – which provide a scheme for the description of different forms and requirements of *wide area workflows*. This is followed by the discussion of possible interaction patterns between distributed workflow parts, building the fundament of WFMS interoperability.

The fourth part of the chapter makes up one of the core elements of this book: the description of three mechanisms for the coordination of WFMSs' interaction, which reflect different power relationships between potential participants in a WAWM scenario. In the following section, options for the flexible planning and execution of WAWM are examined. Based on these thoughts, fundamental concepts for the architecture of systems supporting *wide area workflows* are presented. These architectural concepts focus on the possible structures of three main elements for the connection of WFMSs -- *coordination directories*, *message objects* and *gateways*. In the last part of the chapter, a lifecycle concept for the planning, implementation, maintenance and continuous improvement of systems for WAWM is introduced.

Based on these concepts, Chapter 6 (p. 179) presents the Wide Area GroupFlow System (WAGS) as a prototypic software framework for the illustration and evaluation of different coordination mechanisms for WAWM. The components of the system are explained based on practical examples derived from the case studies.

In Chapter 7 (p. 233), results from the case studies are presented and furthermore the concepts for WAWM and the Wide Area GroupFlow System are applied to propose solutions for the execution of *wide area workflows* in the two scenarios.

The final chapters present conclusions, an outlook on further possible developments and a summary of the main contents of this work.

Figure 1 shows suggested "workflows" for reading this book, illustrated with the help of the WAGS Modeler.

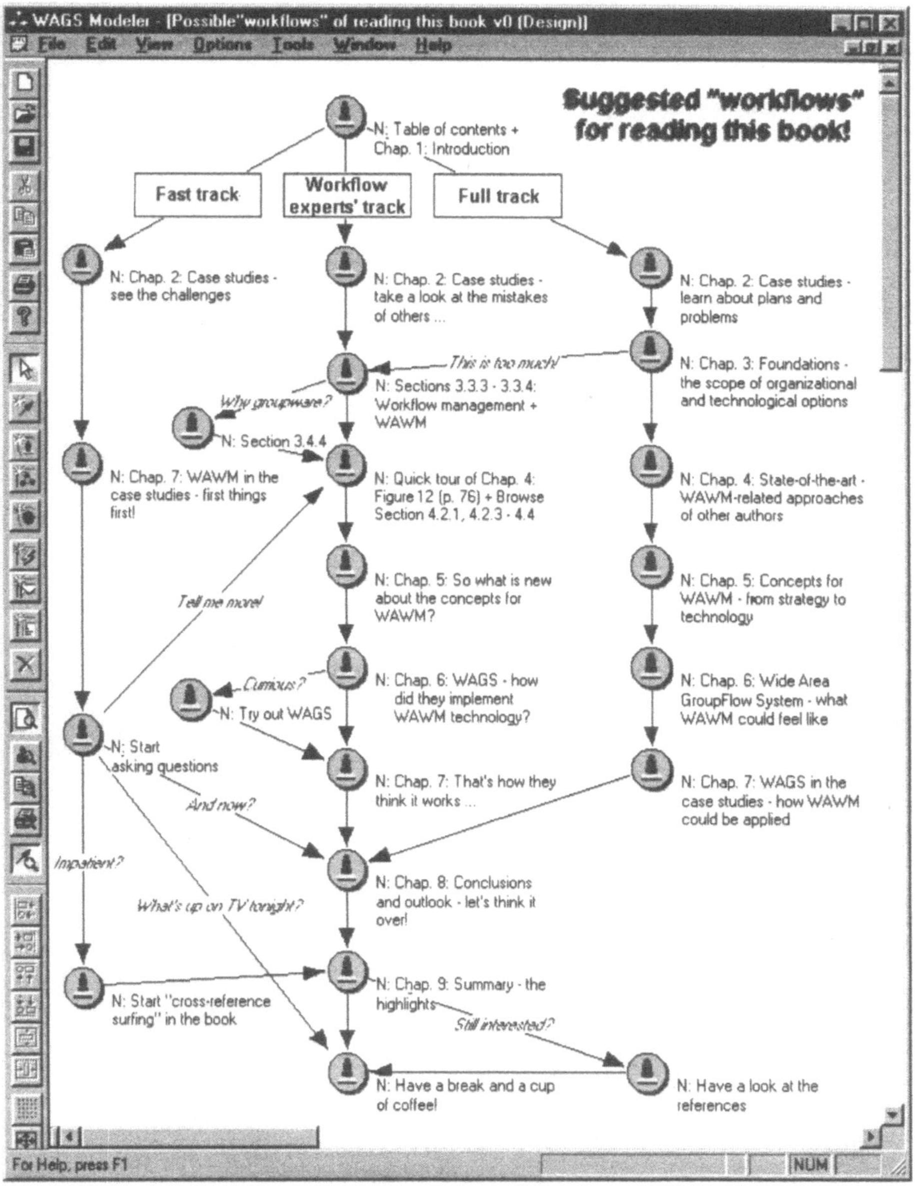

Figure 1: Suggested "workflows" for reading this book

2 Case studies

Wide Area Workflow Management is a relatively new field of research. Case studies can therefore provide important clues to the design of this type of information systems in accordance with real-world requirements.

Empirical studies of workflow management and process-oriented groupware implementations are found for example in [Joosten et al. 1994], [Turrell 1995], [Schmider 1995], several articles in [Oesterle/Vogler 1996], [Prinz/Kolvenbach 1996], [Lloyd/Whitehead 1996], [Zumbach 1996], [Morschheuser/Raufer/Wargitsch 1996], [Kobielus 1997], [Kingsbury 1997]. These studies and others offer relevant insights into "local" workflow management applications. However, many of them do not sufficiently address issues of multiple workflow management systems' interactions within large, distributed organizations or between legally independent organizations.

Case studies of interorganizational information systems as in [Cash/Konsynski 1985], [Hart/Estrin 1990], [Kanter/Myers 1991], [van Koenig/Wijk 1991], [Reekers/Smithson 1994], [Clark/Stoddard 1996], [Oesterwind/ Rohloff 1996], [Finnegan/Galliers/Powell 1997], [Golden/Powell 1997], [Munkvold 1997] are very interesting concerning the design and use of cross-organization IT systems, but often do not provide sufficiently detailed information about workflows *within* the organizations involved. Similarly, case studies on electronic data interchange (EDI) implementations, for example found in [Benjamin/DeLong/Scott Morton 1990], [Krcmar 1993], [Swatman/Swatman 1993], [Eistert 1996], [Chatfield/Murray 1997], concentrate on transfer of data *between* organizations.

Process research in the field of Wide Area Workflow Management must take into account all necessary "local" steps as well as the steps between widely distributed parts of an organization and between organizations. Hence, the initial analysis must be quite extensive and comprehensive. A good example of such an analysis is found in [Wewers/ Wargitsch 1998].

In this chapter, two case studies, which are based on empirical surveys by the author and his research team, will be presented. The cases were chosen because of their special relevance to the topic of Wide Area Workflow Management. They deal with the interaction of widely dispersed office workers in a process occurring internally as well as across the legal boundaries of organizations. At the time of the surveys, management in both organizations was planning to implement a workflow management system.

In order to preserve confidentiality, the organizations are identified only by acronyms. Financial details regarding costs and earnings have also been disguised.

First, a brief introduction to the organizations and their individual circumstances is given. It is followed by a description of the initial objectives of the project, as expressed by management, and the means of achieving them. Furthermore, selected business processes, which were targeted for optimization, are described. The results which were available at the time of writing, and the solutions suggested by the author and his team, are presented in Chapter 7.

The intention of presenting the first part of the case studies at this point is to provide a basis for the discussion of practical solutions in subsequent chapters.

2.1 Case study 1: sales activities in an international brewery

One of the large companies in the European beer market, the "International Brewery" (IB), had revenues of more than 1.2 billion German marks in 1996. Its corporate headquarters lie in Northern Germany with additional production facilities being located in other parts of the country and in South America. There are 1,100 employees in Germany and 200 in the rest of the world. Sales representatives reside in major world markets: Europe, North America, South America, and East Asia.

The International Brewery owns world-known brand names and sells into the high-quality market. Approximately 65% of turnover takes place in Germany, IB's largest market. Until 1995, the company's beer production, sales, and staff were expanding steadily.

Since then, major changes have significantly increased competition in the market place. The most important of these changes are the establishment of the European market and the repeal of the German beer purity law. All European competitors are now able to sell beer in Germany. They are no longer subject to the erstwhile very strict purity law, and its more costly production process. Furthermore, in recent years beer consumption has decreased per capita in Europe. In the high-quality market, differences in taste are not easily detected, thus in an economic downturn even quality-conscious customers tend to purchase lower priced brands. These developments were not anticipated and, consequently, there was an excess capacity on the market. Prices fell and competition became intense. Nevertheless, IB is not willing to either significantly lower quality or prices, thereby preserving the company's good reputation. Instead, strategies have been drawn up to access new markets, do effective marketing, and stress the uniqueness of taste and quality of IB beers. The pressure of shrinking sales has led International Brewery to resolutely streamline sales activities in order to maintain their market share.

IB's sales department is organized by regions:

- Germany, divided into 3 regions (south, north-west, and north-east),
- Europe, with subsidiaries in eight countries,
- Rest-of-the-World with subsidiaries in USA, Canada, Argentina and Singapore.

Each region is led by a sales director (SD) who reports to the group sales director (GSD). There are regional sales managers (RSM) and sales representatives (SR) who travel to contact the customers. IB's sales department has about 140 RSMs and SRs worldwide.

The main market segments are:

- Wholesale,
- Retail,
- Gastronomy (restaurants, fast food chains, bars etc).

Growth in the wholesale and retail trade is very difficult to achieve because of the weak position breweries have in times when overcapacities and economizing customers prevail. Therefore, the areas of gastronomy trade and so-called "experience gastronomy" are targeted for special efforts. In many cases, bars and restaurants have exclusive contracts with breweries that include financing, beer delivery, and so-called "material support". This latter includes for example the provision of glasses, beer dispensing equipment, displays, lighting, and even complete furnishings. Material support is mostly provided on special occasions such as business openings, anniversaries, festivals or events. Since customers in this market are aware of the breweries' efforts to gain new clients and to maintain their established customer base, they can negotiate extensive concessions and material support from their currently contracted brewery. Customer service, quality material and prompt delivery are essential. This requires enormous efforts on the part of supply management and stockkeeping.

An effective logistical system and highly efficient customer service are essential elements for providing timely delivery of beer as well as material support. Therefore, in 1993 IB's management implemented an enterprise-wide "IB Quality Optimization Team" (IBQOT) and an "IB Idea Team" (IBIT) comprising members from all departments of IB. Among the results of the teams' efforts was an ISO 9001 certification in 1995. One main task for the teams was to identify and analyze the main business processes, and to determine ways and means of optimization.

The process of beer delivery is rather simple: customers generally receive fixed monthly quantities of beer and invoices are summarized on a monthly statement. IB's internal management of this process has already been well streamlined. It is supported by a midrange-based warehouse and accounting system.

Auxiliary material support requisition processing

In contrast, the procedure for providing material support to customers has primarily been handled manually and on an individual basis. The diversity of goods supplied, and the fact that much of the material such as lighting and furnishings is custom-built for specific customers, make standard procedures difficult. Therefore, optimization in this area has become the prime focus.

Traditionally, sales representatives negotiate material support with customers. Individualizing the ambience of a bar or restaurant is very important, and the SR must recommend appropriate merchandise. Consequently, catalogue-based or electronic ordering (e.g. via the WWW) is only possible for simple, standard goods. In addition, the hospitality industry in Germany adheres particularly to traditions. Proprietors as well as brewery SRs are quite conservative, lacking familiarity with high technology communications, the Internet and the WWW.

IB's sales force generates an average of approximately 150 material support requisitions per day, at peak times this can double.

Until 1996, the process of material support was mainly paper-based. SRs filled out paper forms at the customer's site and submitted them to the regional subsidiary in person or by mail. Once received, the requisitions were first checked by the RSM in the sales department of the subsidiary. When questions arose, the RSM contacted the initiating SR by phone or fax. Once a requisition was approved by the RSM, it was mailed to the head office. In IB's central sales department, the requisition was again checked by an employee. In certain cases, the sales director had to countersign the requisition. Whether this was necessary, depended on the employee's experience, rather than on the application of fixed rules. If the RSM or the SD decided to reject the requisition, the paperwork was discarded - without informing the initiator.

If the goods were requested for a new customer, the requisition was forwarded for registration and issuing of a welcome letter to another section in the sales department by the in-house mail system. From there, a requisition would be transmitted - again by the in-house mail system - to the warehouse, where a clerk would check what type of material was requested:

- (A) Standard material in stock (e.g. glasses)
- (B) Material to be ordered from other suppliers (e.g. beer dispensing equipment)
- (C) Customized equipment (e.g. neon lights, furnishings).

The warehouse clerk first determined whether all of the requested material was in stock. If not, the employee reserved category A material in the warehouse. He then forwarded procurement requests to the purchasing department. Here, category A and B material was ordered from the respective suppliers. Category C material was treated individually by a purchasing clerk: goods that could be provided by the manufacturer within a short time were scheduled to be shipped with the other material ordered. More complicated and time-consuming requisitions like furnishings were treated separately.

After all material was collected and packaged, the dispatcher would initiate delivery in IB's own trucks or by a forwarding agency. At this point, the documents folder, containing material support requisitions, procurement requests, and delivery documents, was forwarded to the accounting department.

The following Figure 2 illustrates the process of auxiliary material requisition at International Brewery.

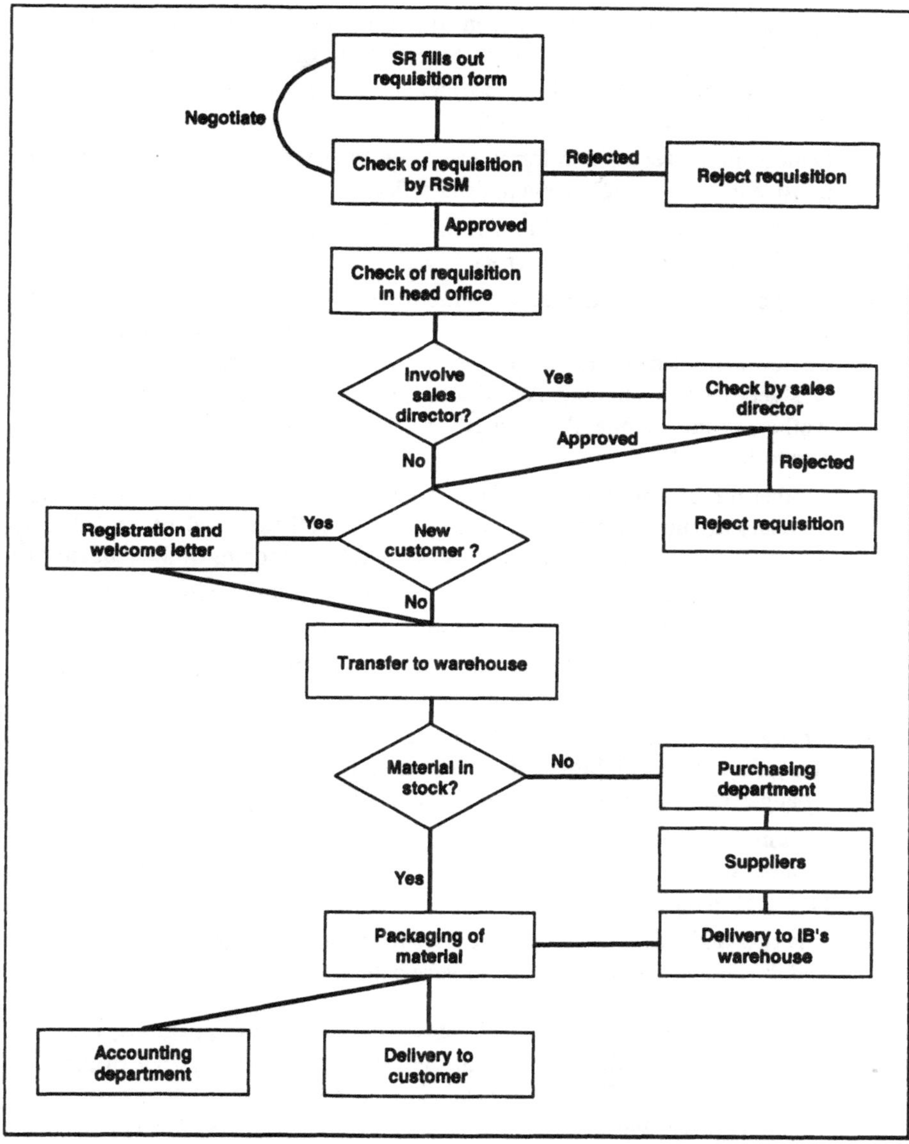

Figure 2: Process of auxiliary material requisition at International Brewery

The following problems were encountered during the processing of auxiliary material support requisition at IB:

- The delay between customer contact and delivery of goods was excessive. On the average, 6 days were needed for a delivery within Germany and 10 days or more outside Germany.
- There was no routine confirmation, either to the initiating SR or to the customer, when a requisition was accepted or rejected.

- A requisition was passed on from the initiating sales representative to the RSM in the subsidiary and from there to head office. If problems were encountered at any stage of processing, the process of finding solutions was time-consuming and complicated.
- Data from the requisition forms had to be transmitted manually to the warehouse and accounting system at head office.
- There were too many different forms for a variety of material requisitions, which resulted in too many errors.
- Category B and C materials were more complicated to handle due to delays when goods had to be ordered from outside suppliers. Transferring of information from a material support requisition into procurement request forms was very time-consuming. Additionally, processing of these orders on IB's as well as on the suppliers' side was very time-consuming due to extensive paperwork.
- Neither the SRs nor the RSMs in the subsidiaries were able to track the status of material support requisitions; they had to call the head office sales department and rely on making hand-written notes on copies of the requisitions.
- The SRs and RSMs had to remember or maintain their own records of what type of material support which customer had received in the past.
- Suppliers could not predict monthly order volumes because IB placed orders upon receipt of material requisitions.
- Changes in customer address, beer quantities or other customer-related data were forwarded to SRs and RSMs in printed lists on a monthly basis. Changes to the data had to be sent to head office on a paper form.
- Information about available material was provided to SRs and RSMs in catalogues and lists. Additions or changes or special occasion offers were also sent in lists.
- The SRs and RSM had no up to date information on goods currently in stock and thus could only estimate a delivery date.

As a result of the complex and complicated processing of requisitions, customer service was seriously curtailed. It was estimated that approximately 25% of the daily working time of SRs and RSM was consumed by paperwork.

A first attempt to solve these problems was undertaken in 1993, when an order for a sales information system was placed with a software business. The following features were implemented:

- electronic completion and printing of forms for beer delivery contracts and material support requisitions;
- database of general customer information;
- databases of available beer brands and support material.

In 1994, after a training phase, all SRs and RSMs were equipped with Penbooks and the sales information software program. The results of this first attempt were disappointing for the following reasons:

- The use of the Penbooks proved to be too complicated for the SRs and RSMs; most of them had had no prior experience with computers.
- In comparison to using printed lists, searching in databases was found to be much too slow.
- Completion and printing of the forms using the Penbooks actually took longer than doing them manually.
- Databases were updated once a month by the head office and thus were not more current than the printed lists. Changes which originated in sales offices could not be electronically transmitted to the head office.
- Printed-out forms were processed exactly the same way as before, with no improvement of overall efficiency.

Consequently, SRs and RSMs objected to using the system after a relatively short period of time. This first optimization attempt cost approximately 4 million German marks and brought no return on investment. Moreover, SRs and RSMs regarded computers with deepened skepticism.

A new project was initiated, aimed at:

- provision of user-friendly software for SRs and RSMs;
- extension of pilot testing and training phases;
- optimization of workflows by reducing duplicate clerical work and removing media breaks;
- seamless integration of data flows to sales department, warehouse, and accounting systems;
- significant reduction in the number of forms;
- reduced administrative tasks for SRs and RSMs, from 25% to 5% of working time;
- increased skills on the part of SRs and RSMs by in-service training;
- enhanced customer satisfaction, by providing up-to-date information to SRs and RSMs at all stages of the process;
- computer-based access and presentation of available auxiliary material;
- reduction of delivery time to 2 days within Germany and 4 days outside of Germany (Europe);
- providing information on the status of various processes to the head office's sales department;
- including all subsidiaries as well as main suppliers in an electronic workflow system;
- including customers into the electronic workflows, e.g. allowing them to initiate processes and receive feedback from IB.

Similar projects with comparable goals are described in [Koepke/Kettler 1997], [Stubner 1997] and [Schugt/Wolf 1997].

In the second project which started in 1996, new notebook computers with up-to-date performance were provided to a pilot group of users. They included color displays, sufficient RAM and hard disk space for modern applications, and a PC-Card modem for connectivity. The selected SRs and RSMs were equipped with a docking station, a 17" monitor, keyboard, mouse, and network adapter in their homes.

The proprietary software was updated and was now based on an SQL database. It supported client/server architecture, user registration, and remote dial-in connectivity with data encryption. Forms could be custom designed with a form generator and transmitted via e-mail. Users could be assigned the right to access folders and to read and edit forms. However, for practical reasons, updates of general customer data could still only be performed once a month. New customer data had to be transmitted on a special form to head office via e-mail. The software did not allow for any other workflow functions apart from one e-mail address for each separate form.

During the pilot testing phase, some improvements were achieved, i.e. a more comprehensive customer database and somewhat more timely communication. However, it was apparent that the application would not serve to achieve the majority of objectives listed above. It was concluded that:

- proprietary software cannot be developed fast enough and is far too expensive compared to its benefits;
- solving the inadequacies of the former procedures with technical measures alone had limited success; the new challenges require a complete rethinking and redesign.
- the social consequences of implementing IT had been underestimated, e.g. the reaction of SRs and RSMs to new technical and organizational measures was negative;
- for the first time, IB's top management was made aware that addressing the optimization of the total marketing and sales process with new IT-systems constituted a major challenge;
- a flexible workflow management system would be a prerequisite for effective and efficient optimization, not merely for streamlining internal processing but requiring the inclusion of suppliers and customers;
- implementation of a groupware platform was taken into consideration by IB's management to facilitate world wide communication.

The author and some of his team members analyzed the case of IB in detail [Ising 1997]. From the perspective of Wide Area Workflow Management, the following aspects were of special interest:

- mobile workers,
- a world wide distributed organization with multiple subsidiaries, and
- the fact that suppliers as well as customers should be included in the workflow.

The results of this project, including a suggested workflow design, are to be found in Chapter 7 (p. 233). The design is based on the concepts discussed in Chapter 5 (p. 103) and the Wide Area GroupFlow System presented in Chapter 6 (p. 179).

2.2 Case study 2: collaboration between a large lighting manufacturer and suppliers

The company in this case will be referred to as "Large Lighting Manufacturer" (LLM). It is one of the largest enterprises of its kind in the world and a major supplier to transportation and building industries. The head office and eight production sites are located in Germany, a further 27 production facilities are situated in 13 different countries, LLM-owned trading companies in over 20 countries, and direct sales offices in 150 countries. LLM has a work force of about 17,500 employees and had a revenue of 3.1 billion German marks in 1997. It has grown from a family-operated business to become one of the global lighting technology and market leaders, offering cutting-edge innovations and high quality standards.

The head office purchasing department handles orders for the production sites in Germany. Branch plants outside Germany have their own purchasing departments which maintain links with the head office to obtain the advantages of larger quantity orders and prime quality for certain goods. Potential suppliers receive the company's "Guideline" which defines detailed quality assurance specifications. ISO 900x certification is a mandatory requirement. LLM purchasing managers visit supplier production facilities prior to signing a contract.

LLM has approximately 2000 different suppliers in Germany. Of these, 800 are the main sources for "principal" or "leading commodities". The others provide "secondary" or "additional goods". LLM has outline agreements and just-in-time delivery contracts with about 200 of the principal suppliers. Weekly requirements of supplies are delivered in accordance with negotiated contracts, and LLM pays weekly without being invoiced. This electronic process is well established and functional. All other suppliers forward individual hard-copy invoices after each delivery.

The procurement process for secondary or additional commodities is complex, time-consuming, and cost-inefficient. *Additional goods* are characterized as:

- not directly used in LLM's products;
- occupying the largest part of LLM's central warehouse (25,000 of 40,000 articles);
- low-cost articles, ordered infrequently, and in low quantities;
- high overhead costs for low-cost goods.

LLM estimates are that a single order for these goods costs on average 150-170 German marks, which is often significantly more than the value of the order. For these reasons, this process has been targeted for optimization.

The following Figure 3 shows the current processing routines for the supply of additional goods at the head office. The right-hand branch of Figure 3 illustrates the processing of goods in stock. While a host-based application for ordering is available, its complicated user interface discourages use. If it is used, inventory status can easily be checked, otherwise a material request card (MRC) is filled out manually and forwarded by an in-house mail system. In either case, the initiator's supervisor/manager has to approve all requests. If the costs appear excessive, a higher level of management must be consulted.

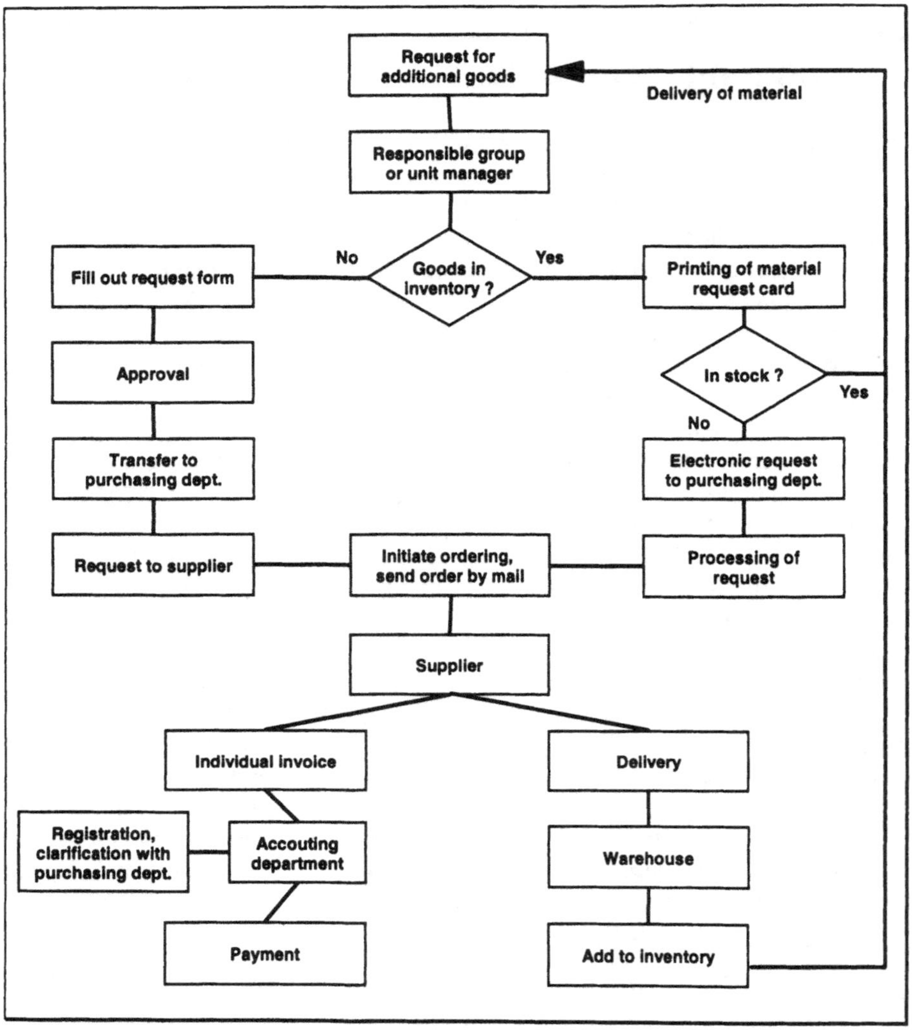

Figure 3: Simplified supply process for additional goods at LLM

After approval, a request is sent to the central warehouse where electronically forwarded MRCs are printed out. The ordered goods are assembled by an issuing clerk and shipped to the initiator of the request. If goods are not in stock, a reservation is entered into the inventory system. Once a week, the inventory system prints out lists of all goods that require ordering or reordering. After these lists have been reviewed and double-checked by a clerk, each individual commodity is entered into the purchasing system. In the purchasing department, the purchasing system prints out another list. It is divided according to material categories and distributed to the appropriate purchasing clerks. They, in turn, generate purchase orders and forward them to the suppliers by mail. LLM's head office purchasing department processes an average of 2000 - 3000 orders per week.

The processing of goods that are not yet in inventory is more complicated. The initiator's department head has to decide whether this new commodity should be added to the range of secondary goods and authorize acquisition. Manually completed MRCs are sent to the purchasing department by in-house mail. There it is determined whether current suppliers are able to provide the goods at reasonable terms and prices. If this is not the case, alternative suppliers are contacted. If, after a routine check, a stable trade relationship has been established with a new supplier, the "LLM Guideline for Suppliers" is sent to the new partner. After potential suppliers for a certain order have been identified, they are asked in a letter to send a quotation. If the goods are needed within a short period of time, quotations or current prices are requested from suppliers in telephone calls. After purchasing clerks have decided which supplier should deliver the goods, an order is placed by mail.

The subsequent procedures are the same for both inventory goods and new goods. They are delivered to the central warehouse where the shipments are checked for completeness and correctness, and a goods received number (GRN) is generated by the purchasing system. Then goods are recorded in the inventory system and forwarded to the initiator. There they are checked again. Problems may arise if the initiator is not satisfied with the goods. Since invoices are paid by the accounting department without delay if the purchasing system has confirmed receipt, payments are sometimes made before the initiator of a request is able to communicate objections to or rejection of received goods.

LLM's accounting department receives about 1000 invoices on an average working day. Some suppliers of secondary goods submit 10 or more invoices per day. On receipt, invoices are separated into original and copy. The copy is sent to the initiator. Then relevant data from the original is entered into the invoice registration system. LLM purchase order numbers are matched with the corresponding number on the invoices, and thus can be found in the order system. Clerks compare invoice data with purchase order data and data from receiving reports. If everything seems to be correct, a receipt is printed out, attached to the original invoice, and forwarded to Accounting. If there are discrepancies between order and receiving report, or between order and invoice, they have to be clarified by phone. LLM's accounting department estimates that approximately 30% of all invoices require such individual clarification. This often takes too long so that early payment discounts are lost. After discrepancies have been resolved, the accounting department processes payment, crediting the appropriate accounts.

The process described so far has many media breaks, unnecessary pauses and is quite complicated. The handling of exceptions poses enormous problems, especially when requisitions originate in a German production site outside of the head office. If additional goods are ordered by a production site, it is first determined whether they are in stock locally. If they are neither in the production site's nor in the head office's warehouse, the head office purchasing department does the ordering, but the goods are shipped directly to the production site's warehouse. Accounting procedures, as described above, are done at the head office. The paperwork process becomes very time-consuming. Processing of orders becomes even more complex if LLM subsidiaries outside Germany want to consolidate their purchasing activities of primary or secondary goods with those at head office, to obtain more favorable terms or conditions for bulk orders.

A good example of the occurrence of potential problems when secondary goods are purchased is the acquisition of new desktop computers. In Germany alone, LLM bought more than 3000 new PCs in 1997. PCs are generally not in stock and therefore always need special handling such as consolidating orders from several LLM locations so as to obtain better terms and conditions. Quality assurance procedures in the case of PC deliveries are not possible in so far as the receiving clerks in the warehouse do not have the necessary qualifications for this task. Even initiators are often not capable of ensuring that the merchandise received is in accordance with orders. Almost all PC orders require clarification from Accounting, Purchasing, initiators, and suppliers before payment is made.

On account of these experiences, LLM's management formed a project group with the mandate of analyzing and optimizing the purchasing of secondary goods. Members of the group came from all departments involved, and the author's team was included [Marr 1997].

After detailed analysis of the process, including especially the numerous exceptions and encountered problems, the following objectives were defined:

- simplification of the overall process, for example, by delegating more authority to process participants;
- significant reduction of processing time by removing media breaks;
- significant reduction of the number of different commodities with similar uses;
- consolidation of purchasing processes concerning respective suppliers;
- elimination of verification procedures in the warehouses, and their replacement to be performed by initiators instead;
- significant reduction in numbers of secondary goods suppliers and enhancement of relationships with remaining suppliers;
- electronic exchange of information with suppliers concerning deliverable products and services, ordering, and consolidated invoices;
- coordination of processes between various locations of LLM;
- explicit attention and support for handling of exceptions or special orders within the company, and in communications with suppliers;
- enhanced user-friendliness of software systems.

On the more technical side, the following goals were agreed upon:

- implementation of a integrated business software system, to seamlessly combine purchasing, warehouse, accounting, and related functions;
- standard purchasing procedures for additional goods (either in stock or inventory) to be handled primarily by the integrated business software system.
- purchase orders requiring special procedures (goods not in stock and exceptional orders) to be processed by a dedicated workflow management system;
- transparent connection of integrated business software system and workflow management system at the requisite processing steps;
- workflows to include all of the various locations of the company;

- workflows to include suppliers;
- implementation of a groupware platform to facilitate communication within LLM.

After an agreement on these objectives had been reached within the project group and with LLM's management, the project was divided into several sub-projects. The following will focus on the workflow management system (WFMS) sub-project, dealing with purchasing procedures for orders that require special treatment, the linkage of the corresponding workflows between various locations, and communications with suppliers.

The purchasing of PCs will serve as a reference workflow. The PC market changes very rapidly and, therefore, the ordering process is fairly difficult. In a first step, LLM's IT department was assigned to establish and regularly update specifications for three PC classifications: standard, intermediate, and high-end. These specifications were intended to serve as means of determining which kind of configuration a user needed and was entitled to order. In a second step, potential suppliers were contacted to ascertain whether they could provide electronic product specifications, quotations, and consolidated invoices via online transmission. It was found that none of the selected suppliers was capable of providing all of the requested information electronically. Furthermore, each supplier suggested the use of a different system for information transfer. Similar problems were encountered with suppliers of other secondary goods, which required special treatment.

An IT task force at LLM was assigned the task of developing a proprietary workflow management system (WFMS), based on a relational database management system. Transfer of data between LLM and suppliers should be handled EDIFACT-based, using standardized document types for quotations, orders and invoices. Suppliers were requested to devise and implement their own systems, which would be able to process such incoming and outgoing documentation.

The task force invested one year into this task, but the results were not satisfactory for the following reasons:

- Development of the proprietary WFMS did not proceed fast enough and it was also found to be much too expensive.
- The WFMS lacked a graphical modeling tool and all settings had to be coded manually. With the number of workflow models increasing, maintenance costs also increased. In addition, it was found to be more and more difficult to keep track of different workflow models and thus avoid duplicated work.
- Setup of equipment, protocols, and software systems at LLM as well as at the suppliers' site was time-consuming and expensive. Any change or addition of suppliers, therefore, became too complicated and thus the solution was not flexible enough.
- Handling of exceptions was difficult to implement.
- Technical problems arose when the task force undertook to initiate the cooperative functionality with other LLM locations.

After pilot testing of the workflow management software, as far as it was developed at that point, the project was halted by LLM's management. Further work was postponed while implementation of the chosen integrated business software system was carried out and given top priority.

Subsequently in early 1997, the top management decided to implement the groupware platform Lotus Notes as the strategic information backbone for LLM's worldwide activities. Installation proceeded quickly, and within a short period of time, more than 2,000 head office employees were ready to use e-mail and shared document databases on this basis. Installation of the groupware system in all LLM's foreign and domestic facilities is in progress and is expected to be completed in the near future.

The workflow management system project for optimization of special orders purchasing processes was reinstituted with the provision that the groupware platform be used as a foundation, and seamless transfer of data between the groupware-based workflow management system and the integrated business software system would be enabled.

A case like LLM's is of interest for empirical studies of Wide Area Workflow Management on account of the company's extensive worldwide operations and the required interaction and collaboration between and among multiple corporate locations. In addition, the inclusion of suppliers in interorganizational workflows, allowing for flexibility and adaptability in the special goods purchasing process, is a practical illustration of the importance of effective and efficient interactions of widely-distributed office workers within and between organizations.

Results of this project, as far as available at the present time, and a workflow model recommended by the author and his team will be described in Chapter 7 (p. 233).

3 Foundations of computer-aided interaction among widely dispersed office workers

Today there is no longer any question that widely dispersed office workers need efficient technical support by telecommunication and computer technology in order to meet the challenges of fast and flexible performance. They have to achieve high quality results at adequate costs, which cannot be obtained without electronic support today. For synchronous cooperation and communication between widely dispersed office workers various solutions, such as video-conferencing, electronic meeting rooms, and other means have been devised. Wide Area Workflow Management addresses the requirement of supporting asynchronous interactions between office workers who are dispersed globally and often are also separated by the legal boundaries of autonomous organizations.

This chapter intends to introduce topics and research related to Wide Area Workflow Management. The author wants to locate WAWM in the fields of computer science, business computing, information systems, and organizational theory. Definitions for important terms used in subsequent chapters, and a brief introduction to related technologies, are given.

The sections of this chapter are structured as follows: first, substantial characteristics of the respective topic are outlined and relevant literature is cited; secondly, its contribution to the field of Wide Area Workflow Management is discussed.

Many publications explain various aspects of *workflow management (WFM)*. The author does not intend to recapitulate all of these works but rather to focus on those highlights that lead towards Wide Area Workflow Management. In this chapter, WFM is discussed from a more general viewpoint. Further details and works of other authors concerning WFM are found in Chapter 4.

3.1 Developments in the application of computer systems

The meaning of the terms *data*, *information* or *knowledge* is discussed frequently. To define *information* in the context of WAWM and to differentiate it from *data*, the following distinction of terms will be used (see also [Date 1990], [Senge 1990], [Senge 1997], [Hansen 1992]):

- *Data* is a fact that is expressed in a machine-readable (digital) form.
- *Information* is data that is made meaningful to a person by a semantic context.
- *Knowledge* is the ability to use information to solve a certain problem, or as Peter Senge puts it, "Knowledge is the capacity for effective action" [Senge 1997]. It is acquired over time in a process of learning.
- *Wisdom* is the ability to correctly assess in advance the short- and long-term consequences of actions taken by a person, based on prior experiences. Wisdom is often the result of cumulative, lifetime experiences in comparable situations.

Data, information, knowledge and wisdom are ways in which mankind collects, reflects on, and "stores" events they observe in their environment. In the course of the development of computer systems, more and more of these mental structures are made explicit in digital representations.

One can draw a matrix with the described terms depicted on a time axis and the development from intraorganizational to interorganizational and extra-organizational computing on the other axis (Figure 4).

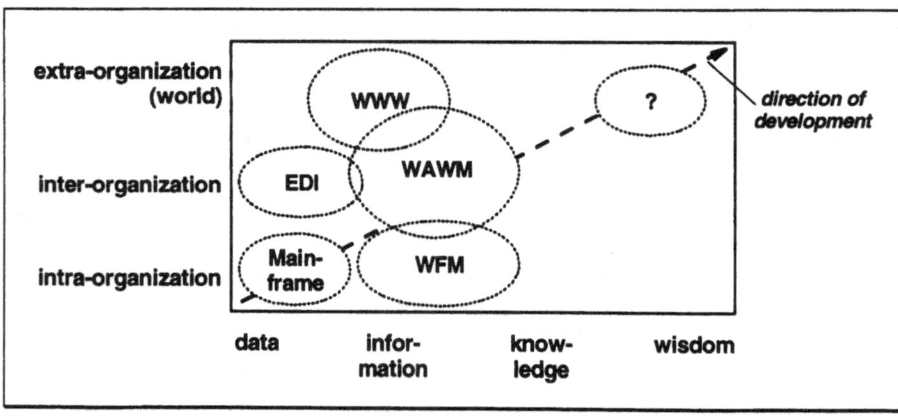

Figure 4: From local data processing to worldwide knowledge sharing - shifts in the application of computer systems in business

In the early stages of computer applications, sometimes also called electronic *data* processing, handling of data was dominant. With increasing experience and advances in hard- and software, not only data but also relevant semantic contexts can be handled leading to *information* processing. Data is typically stored in records of databases and presented to users in text-based forms. Increasingly, information is stored in structures of hyperlink-enabled documents and is presented in graphical environments. These documents are often called *semi-structured* or *compound documents* because they contain highly structured field-based data as well as less structured contextual parts that can hold formatted text, graphics, videos, speech annotations etc., to build user-oriented *information* [Malone et al. 1987], [Kawell et al. 1992]. Known standards for semi-structured, hyperlink-enabled document representations are SGML with its descendants HTML and XML, or HyTime [Reich 1997]. The enormous potential and impact of documents as information representation items is obvious considering the fact that millions of people are now using wordprocessor software along with drawing, charting and other software to generate compound documents.

Pfeiffer [1996] estimates that of the total amount of information in businesses:

- 10-20% is "typical data" such as accounting records or addresses, stored in (relational) databases,
- while 80-90% is stored in documents, to a large degree still as hard copy.

Models for data structuring such as the Entity-Relationship Model (ERM) [Chen 1976], [Date 1990] or models for information representation like the above-mentioned document standards (SGML, HTML, XML, HyTime) do not have explicit arguments to represent changes to data or information over time.

With the focus now shifting from these more static models towards *process orientation*, *knowledge* about the consecutive modification of data and information across the diverse steps of a (business) process is also modeled and stored in computer systems. One known descriptive language for processes is Petri-nets [Petri 1974].

Process orientation has a long tradition in the systematization of production lines. In recent years, this focus on processes rather than on static competencies has also greatly influenced office systematization. One outcome of this paradigm shift is the development of *workflow management systems (WFMSs)* that facilitate the handling of business processes.

There are certainly many other conceivable ways to express human *knowledge* in digital systems, apart from business process modeling. In general, the representation of *knowledge* in computer systems can be regarded as being in an early phase. Furthermore, the structures of *wisdom* seem to be very complex and thus are very difficult to comprehend. Research in artificial intelligence (AI) addresses the challenge of analyzing and representing intelligent behavior, which is the basis of *knowledge* and *wisdom*. The question of whether the digital representation of such intelligence in the form of *knowledge* or *wisdom* is ethically justifiable is the subject of controversial discussions.

Another trend has been apparent in recent years. Intraorganizational use of computers has become commonplace, and highly integrated business applications such as the SAP R/3 system provide advanced control of internal information. Once internal information is computerized efficiently, the next logical step is to electronically connect the internal information systems of divers organizations. This leads to interorganizational links among organizations (e.g. electronic data interchange (EDI)) and extraorganizational connections with, potentially, anyone in the world. The enormously rapid growth of the Internet and the World Wide Web (WWW) in relatively few years illustrates this shift.

Depicting these two developments graphically shows the position of various computer-based applications and their relationships to each other (Figure 4). Beginning with the initial centralized data processing systems (*mainframes*), distinct steps have led towards global availability of information, even *knowledge*. Although further developments will no doubt follow, a definitive direction is not yet apparent.

In Figure 4, some examples of computer applications and their differences, based on the chosen categories, are illustrated. For example, current approaches to workflow management (WFM) focus primarily on support of intraorganizational business processes and combine information handling with knowledge of such processes. Wide Area Workflow Management (WAWM) aims to make parts of this information and process knowledge accessible to other organizations or even the anonymous global marketplace.

3.2 Decentralized collaboration

In the past decade, computer-based applications to effect collaboration among people have increased in importance, especially where personnel is geographically dispersed. In the following brief overview of several different areas of research into the support of decentralized cooperation, each respective topic's relevance to Wide Area Workflow Management is shown.

3.2.1 Computer-Supported Cooperative Work (CSCW)

CSCW is an interdisciplinary field of research, comprised for example of computer science, sociology, psychology, organizational theory, systems theory, ergonomics, and statistics. Briefly stated, CSCW research attempts to devise organizational and technical solutions which assist people in working together with more efficiency, flexibility, and comfort while at the same time taking into account the social and emotional concerns of users. A basic premise in CSCW is the differentiation between situations where participants of a group interaction:

- are either in the same or in different locations,
- communicate with each other at the same time (synchronously) or at different times (asynchronously).

These distinctions can be depicted on two axes of the so-called "CSCW matrix" which is one of the best-known illustrations concerning CSCW [Engelbart 1970]. Different CSCW applications can be sorted into this matrix. For instance, electronic meeting rooms facilitate cooperation at the same time and in the same place, videoconferencing serves synchronous interaction in different locations whereas e-mail or workflow management can be used asynchronously in different locations.

There is no commonly accepted definition of CSCW yet. Greenberg [1991] has stated that "Computer-Supported Cooperative Work is not particularly well defined, a consequence of its youth and multi-disciplinary nature".

Important milestones in CSCW research are the CSCW conferences in Austin 1986, Portland 1988, Los Angeles 1990, Toronto 1992, Chapel Hill 1994, Boston 1996, and Seattle 1998, as well as the European CSCW conferences in Gatwick 1989, Amsterdam 1991, Milan 1993, Stockholm 1995 and Lancaster 1997. Apart from the conference proceedings (see references), a multitude of books and articles on CSCW have been published. They treat various aspects of this wide research field (for example [Greif 1988], [Bowers/Benford 1991], [Grudin 1994], [Hasenkamp/Kirn/Syring 1994], [Khoshafian/Buckiewicz 1995], [Borghoff/Schlichter 1995], [Krcmar et al. 1996], [Reichwald et al. 1998], and the CSCW Journal [JCSCW 1996]).

Another central focus in CSCW research is the characterization of applications according to the "3Cs": communication, coordination, and cooperation. Teufel et al. developed the illustration below to categorize different CSCW applications in a "3Cs" triangle [Teufel et al. 1995, p. 27].

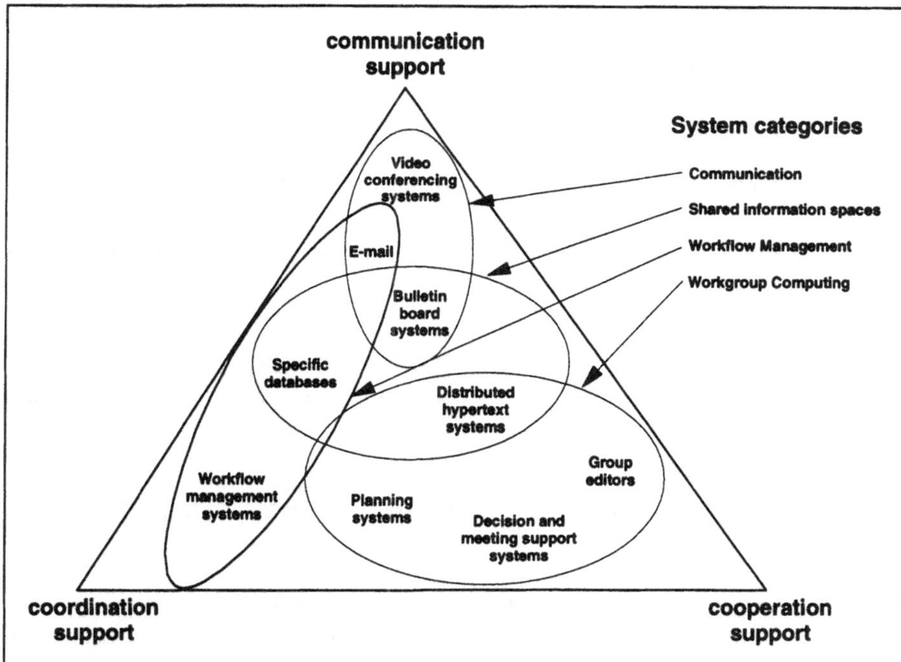

Figure 5: Classification of CSCW applications (based on [Teufel et al. 1995], reproduced with permission)

In addition to positioning a variety of CSCW applications in a triangle built by the "3Cs", Teufel et al. distinguish between four system categories (Figure 5). Applications can belong to several system categories simultaneously. For example, e-mail can be used for communication purposes as well as within workflow management systems.

Other terms often used in the context of CSCW are "groupware" and "workgroup computing". Groupware is often understood as the software enabling CSCW concepts or, more narrowly defined, the commercial software with CSCW features. "Groupware is software that supports and augments group work. It is a technical oriented label meant to differentiate "group-oriented" products, explicitly designed to assist groups of people working together, from "single-user" products that help people pursue only their isolated tasks" [Greenberg 1991].

Other authors use groupware and CSCW de facto as synonyms. Ellis, Gibbs and Rein do not limit groupware to software itself, broadening the definition to: "Specifically, we define groupware as computer-based systems that support groups of people engaged in a common task (or goal) and that provide an interface to a shared environment" [Ellis/Gibbs/Rein 1991]. So defined, there appears virtually no difference between CSCW and groupware.

These authors classify groupware systems according to their functions [Ellis/Gibbs/Rein 1991]:

- message systems, e.g. e-mail, bulletin board systems or message-based computer conferencing;
- multi-user editors, facilitating either real-time or asynchronous, joint writing;
- group decision support systems and electronic meeting rooms for support of synchronous group interaction;
- real-time video conferencing, computer teleconferencing, and desktop conferencing.
- intelligent agents that enable groups to navigate in complex information structures;
- coordination systems, divided into:
  - Form-oriented systems that route forms based on process models,
  - Procedure-oriented systems that integrate processes through programming techniques,
  - Conversation-oriented systems based on speech act theory [Searle 1969],
  - Communication structure-oriented systems describing organizational activities on role relationships.

Workflow management systems belong to the group of coordination systems. They can be simultaneously form-oriented, procedure-oriented, conversation-oriented and role-based or only have parts of these features.

Workgroup computing is usually defined as providing basic technical support for computer-based group interaction, without necessarily being oriented towards a specific form of cooperation [Nastansky 1993]. This includes PCs or workstations equipped with sound- and video-devices. They are connected to a network that allows access to shared resources such as file servers, print servers, e-mail-servers, shared databases, bulletin boards, online-libraries, and groupware-servers. Connectivity to the Internet and World Wide Web is nowadays also regarded as an essential feature in workgroup computing environments. In contrast to this discernment of workgroup computing, Teufel et al. (Figure 5) use the term for a specific category of CSCW applications, which includes group decision support systems and group editors.

As shown here, terminology and definitions in the fields of CSCW, groupware, and workgroup computing vary considerably among authors. This is due to the relatively short time which has elapsed since such research was first undertaken, as well as the dynamic proliferation of concepts and applications, which thus complicate the formation of a coherent, widely accepted body of theory, with consistent terminology.

Undoubtedly, workflow management is a part of CSCW research. Wide Area Workflow Management (WAWM), in addition to "local" workflow management, explicitly stresses the coordination efforts between planners and users in different workflow management domains that are willing to connect their systems. These efforts are necessary so that independent workgroups are able to efficiently communicate and cooperate by workflow means. Therefore, the author proposes that WAWM be considered to be an area of CSCW research.

3.2.2 Coordination science

The terms *coordination theory* and *coordination science* were introduced by Thomas Malone and his team at the Center for Coordination Science, Massachusetts Institute of Technology (MIT) in Cambridge, Massachusetts. According to Malone and Crowston [1990, p. 358] this means:

"We define *coordination theory* as a body of principles about how activities can be coordinated, that is, about how actors can work together harmoniously. ... In coordination theory, the common problems have to do with coordination: How can overall goals be subdivided into actions? How can actions be assigned to groups or to individual actors? How can resources be allocated among different actors? How can information be shared among different actors to help achieve the overall goal?"

The approach of coordination theory and coordination science is very fundamental and extensive. It tries to incorporate ideas from several other disciplines such as organizational theory, sociology, social psychology, anthropology, linguistics, systems theory, cybernetics, law, and political science. Consequently, Malone et al. try to narrow the framework by emphasizing the aspect of several people *working together*, and the definition of basic components of coordination. These components and the associated coordination processes (in brackets) are:

- goals (identifying goals);
- activities (mapping goals to activities, e.g. goal decomposition);
- actors (selecting actors; assigning activities to actors);
- interdependencies ("managing" interdependencies).

Based on these components, coordination is defined as "the act of managing interdependencies between activities performed to achieve a goal" [Malone/Crowston 1990, p. 361]. The interdependencies of two or more activities can be determined by looking at *common objects* that are involved in some way in both actions. These common objects constrain how each activity is performed. Different patterns in the use of the common objects can be classified according to different types of constraints. For example, a *prerequisite interdependency* means that one task, e.g. the creation of an object, has to be completed before the next task. A *shared resource interdependency* means that a common object is needed in two activities and therefore some agreement has to be found on the use of the object. *Simultaneous interdependency* refers to the fact that two activities have to occur at the same time and hence have to be synchronized. For example, goods produced in a manufacturing process or documents in workflows can be regarded as *common goods*, requiring certain strategies to manage interdependencies within and between various processing steps.

A fundamental question here is what strategies can be used to manage the interdependencies and thereby solve potential conflicts. The following strategies for coordination are suggested in coordination theory [Malone/Crowston 1994]:

- One of the participants decides how the interdependencies are managed and has the power to convince other participants to accept this solution. This strategy is termed *hierarchy* by the author of this book.
- Participants can negotiate how interdependencies are to be managed. This may be an iterative process supported by joint meetings. The author wants to label this solution strategy *equal partnership*.
- One of the participants, who knows how to manage interdependencies, makes this knowledge available to other participants. If they agree on the suggested approach, they can accept. This strategy can eliminate the need for explicit negotiation. This is a familiar business strategy, and shall be labeled *offer and acceptance* or simply *market*.
- The participants agree on that a superior they have in common is responsible for finding an appropriate solution. This will be called *broker*.

Coordination strategies can be employed to describe a range of possibilities where a vendor and a potential customer have to agree on a common object, a product. If a vendor wants to make a specific sale and has no real alternative, he will accept the customer's condition (*hierarchy*). One well-known example of such a hierarchical relationship can be found between automobile manufacturers and their suppliers.

If a vendor has a comparably strong position and a customer is interested in dealing with this vendor, the vendor can negotiate with the customer. Only if both sides are satisfied with the conditions, will they accept them (*equal partnership*). If a vendor has an independent position concerning customers, he can offer his product to many potential buyers, e.g. in a catalogue or via the WWW. Customers can check out all of the conditions of several vendors beforehand and then decide which offer to accept (*market*). A consultant could play the role of a *broker* who brings vendor and customer together, providing that both parties consider the consultant trustworthy and are willing to pay his fees (*broker*).

Equal partnership and *market* are primarily distinguished by freedom of choice. For example, two office colleagues who have to achieve a common goal have no alternative but to work as a team, more or less harmoniously, in an *equal partnership*. In an ideal *market* situation, multiple sellers and prospective buyers have free choice whether or not they deal with each other. The *broker's* role does not essentially change the relationship between the participants and, therefore, does not really constitute a coordination strategy of its own. It is a special negotiation technique in the case of *equal partnership* or *market*. Basically, the three strategies of *hierarchy*, *equal partnership* and *market* reflect the balance of power between the participants and have previously been discussed in other contexts.

The process of coordination can be divided into several layers or *process levels*:

- At the top level, the coordination of goals, activities, actors, resources, and interdependencies must be achieved. This involves identifying goals, deriving and ordering activities and assigning them to actors.
- Prior to this, investigations and negotiations about different alternatives and (group) decisions about choosing between these alternatives are necessary.
- To enable all that, it is important that participants communicate with each other. They use messages that are transferred between sender and recipient and can only be understood if everyone comprehends a common language.
- Finally, participants need things to communicate about and therefore have to perceive common objects, such as physical objects or information.

The coordination theory approach is of crucial importance in all designs of CSCW applications. Still in its generality, it is not simply transferable into the specification of a cooperative information system. Malone et al. suggest an application of coordination theory in a *handbook of organizational processes* [Malone et al. 1997]. It will be described in Section 4.2.2.1 (p. 83).

In the conceptual approach to WAWM, introduced in Chapter 5, coordination science and coordination theory can be regarded as a fundamental cornerstone. If different parts of widely distributed organizations or different organizations want to cooperate using workflow management systems, they first have to agree on common *goals*. Then they have to coordinate their *activities* to achieve these goals. This requires planning, i.e. which *actors* should handle which *common objects*, e.g. workflow documents exchanged between them, and will most likely have to *negotiate* about that. Finally they have to agree on how to manage *interdependencies* between their workflows, for example when to exchange workflow documents and what information they should contain.

To realize these coordination efforts, the author uses the coordination mechanisms of *hierarchy*, *equal partnership* and *market* and has implemented derived techniques together with his team in the Wide Area GroupFlow System introduced in Chapter 6.

3.2.3 Transaction cost theory

Transaction cost theory tries to explain why individuals and companies prefer certain ways of conducting business compared to others. According to Williamson, different ways of doing business can be described with the following institutional arrangements [Williamson 1985], that are similar to the coordination strategies in coordination science (see Section 3.2.2):

- coordination through command or hierarchy (firm),
- coordination through the pricing mechanism (market),
- coordination through hybrid forms between firm and market (cooperation or relational contracting)

Based on this typology, Williamson looks at the factors that lead to a certain choice of one of the institutional arrangements. Alternatives which carry the lowest transaction costs, i.e. where the least efforts in the exchange of goods or services are required, will be chosen. Consequently, organizations will attempt to reduce transaction costs as far as possible: "The modern corporation is to be understood as the product of a series of organizational innovations that have had the purpose and effect of economizing on transaction costs" [Williamson 1981]. Transaction costs are defined as:

- all ex ante costs incurred in developing and securing of contracts, such as search for potential partners, search for information, initiation of contact, negotiations, etc., and
- all ex post costs incurred if initial contract agreements are not met and either expectations must be adjusted or deliverables corrected.

It is assumed that the participants perceive all of these efforts or costs as such and are able to adapt their behavior accordingly.

Similar to transaction costs, Malone defines coordination costs: "Production costs include the physical or other primary processes necessary to create and distribute the goods or services being produced. Coordination costs include the transaction (or governance) costs of all the information processing necessary to coordinate the work of people and machines that perform the primary processes. For example, coordination costs include determining the design, price, quantity, delivery schedule, and similar factors for products transferred between adjacent steps on a value chain" [Malone/Yates/Benjamin 1987, p. 299].

Various coordination strategies, such as *hierarchy* or *market*, affect coordination, or as a synonym, transaction costs: "Markets have been characterized by low production costs and high coordination costs, and hierarchies by high production costs and low coordination costs" [Benjamin/Wigand 1995, p. 65].

Transaction cost theory does not (merely) use pricing mechanisms to explain economic behavior, but also emphasizes the influence of efforts needed to obtain a desired result. Williamson supposes that progress in technology leads to:

- uncertainty associated with the impossibility and cost of enumerating all of the possible contingencies and appropriate adaptations, and
- greater asset specificity, meaning that durable investments that are transaction specific have certain "lock in" effects on future relations between participating firms.

Consequently, coordination of activities can decreasingly be achieved through pricing mechanism. He concludes from these observations that hybrid forms of coordination, such as strategic alliances, will gain importance in economic behavior because they allow for a reduction of transaction costs compared to market coordination. If negotiation efforts in such an arrangement become too dominant and result in excessive transaction, one of the parties may resort to a buy-out of the previous partner, thus creating a *hierarchical* arrangement. Williamson concludes that vertical integration and concentration of firms is the consequence of rising transaction costs caused by advances in technology.

This trend can indeed be observed in some markets, whereas in other markets quite the opposite occurs. Especially in high technology industrial sectors with fast progress in technology, outsourcing of activities has become a dominant trend in the past decade. A number of authors attribute this to the fact that activities coordinated by means of flexible adaptation, communication and information exchange between partners are favored by players in the marketplace [Johanson/Mattsson 1987], [Powell 1990], [Backhaus/Meyer 1993].

Therefore, hybrid forms of collaboration with a more market-like character, such as strategic networks, are seen as preferred options. These flexible arrangements are assumed to be more vital and better able to react to rapidly changing market conditions. Large organizations are viewed as having high internal coordination costs due to inefficient structures, making them less able to adapt to quickly changing customer's needs caused by rapid progress in technology.

Explanations of economic strategies, based on transaction cost theory, such as those proposed by Williamson, are not universally accepted. Reekers and Smithson state: "However, transaction cost theory has a number of limitations. Firstly, it does not make any universal claims that are applicable to all organizations, nor does it accurately predict what will happen in a specific situation. Secondly, it takes little or no account of organizations' strategic choices, their abilities to adopt particular technologies (e.g. EDI) or the complex interdependencies that comprise the structure of an industry. Its preoccupation with the economic dimension means that transaction cost theory tends to neglect the political aspects of interorganizational relationships. Thirdly, there are weaknesses in operationalizing the concepts of transaction and transaction costs. Finally, it fails to consider the transition costs that may render suboptimal structures cheaper than the optimum" [Reekers/Smithson 1995]. Nevertheless, the basic idea of analyzing coordination and transaction costs within and between organizations, and taking them into account when trying to explain economic behavior, is certainly beneficial.

With regard to Wide Area Workflow Management, transaction theory provides another theoretical foundation for explaining the choice of different cooperation strategies between organizations that are the basis for interaction patterns of different workflow management systems in these organizations.

Other authors also stress the role of transaction cost theory for examining *interorganizational information systems (IOS).* Hart and Estrin state: "Since interorganizational networks (IONs) provide the means to exchange data quickly between geographically distant locations, we would expect that their use would improve the ability of partners to address contingencies when they occur, and eliminate or reduce certain asset investments. In these respects, IONs would contribute to reducing transaction costs." [Hart/Estrin 1990, p. 134]. IOSs and IONs are addressed in the following section.

3.2.4 Interorganizational information systems

Wide Area Workflow Management (WAWM) can be considered to be a component in the research on *interorganizational information systems (IOS).* Although IOSs focus in particular on the aspect of *inter*organizational information transfers while

WAWM also includes the support of widely dispersed office workers within single, widely distributed organizations, the basic technological and organizational challenges are virtually the same.

Interorganizational information systems (IOSs), sometimes also referred to as *interorganizational networks (IONs)*, are aimed at achieving seamless transfers of data or information between legally separate organizations by avoiding structural and media breaks. Golden and Powell define an IOS as "... a computer based information system that facilitates the exchange of information electronically using telecommunications between different organisations' computer systems" [Golden/Powell 1997, p. 267].

IOSs can support different kinds of interorganizational processes [Gulledge/Hirschmann/Scheer 1997]:

- logistics processes like purchasing, sales (including shipment) or customer service;
- integrated product development processes such as research, development or product design;
- information and coordination processes such as invoicing and payment procedures or treasury/funds management.

In many cases logistics and product development involve information and coordination processes. An IOS must provide a range of different functions, depending on the kind of interorganizational processes they are meant to support. For example, in Case Study 2, an IOS between PC suppliers and LLM has to provide information about the availability of the merchandise, transmit orders and invoices, and allow for clarification of exceptions. Hence, certain agreements about the structuring of the information exchange must be reached.

The topic of IOS has a longer history. While early publications focussed mainly on technical aspects [Kaufman 1966], in times of global availability of the Internet and World Wide Web, concerns have shifted to legal, organizational, and economic questions.

IOSs are likely to change the way goods are exchanged in the market place because they allow for new forms of cooperation. Caused by the use of IOS, the coordination efforts between participants can be reduced. "We conclude that significant improvements in inter-organization coordination result when IONs support exchanges between internally integrated firms." [Hart/Estrin 1990, p.131]. On the basis of transaction cost theory, Clark and Schiano expect the emergence of new economic strategies in IOSs: "Transaction cost economics theory predicts that significant reductions in transaction costs should enable new organizational and channel structures" [Clark/Schiano 1996, p. 281].

The IOS label can apply to a variety of technologies. *Electronic Data Interchange (EDI)* is one of the well-known terms. It serves to connect data systems between organizations for the exchange of mass data such as inventory levels, freight bills, etc. [Swatman/Swatman 1991]. EDI and EDIFACT will be addressed in detail in Section 3.4.1 (p. 59).

Quick Response (QR) refers to interorganizational streamlining of the supply channel using EDI technology [Hammond 1993]. By accelerating the transmission of purchasing data between manufacturers and their suppliers, manufacturing cycles have been significantly shortened. "Quick Response has been called the retail industry's version of just-in-time (JIT) manufacturing because it seeks to manage and move inventory better through the supply-chain. In a QR arrangement, a supplier sends stock to a retailer to replace what has been sold, automatically and quickly" [McMichael/Mackay/Altmann 1997, p. 296]. Both QR and JIT aim to keep inventories as low as possible without creating shortages, and to quickly re-supply goods as they are needed. QR extends to all levels of the supply-chain and aims to include all of the organizations involved. Especially in markets influenced by frequently changing fashions, e.g. the clothing and footwear manufacturing and retail sectors, QR serves to prevent retailers from having outdated merchandise in stock. By assuring flexible and swift re-supply, inventory levels can be kept low during all phases of the manufacturing and marketing processes.

Continuous Replenishment (CRP) specifically focuses on a distinct aspect of the supply chain. Suppliers are responsible for checking the stock of goods they deliver to customers in the customers' warehouse system. Upon request, they receive the relevant data from customers via EDI. If the stock falls below an agreed level, it is the supplier's responsibility to refill immediately without having to wait for an order from the customer. Suppliers are paid routinely for goods delivered. CRP is characterized by stable relationships and outline agreements between parties and the assurance of automatic replenishment of inventory for customers and reliable, regular payment for suppliers [Clark/Stoddard 1996]. CRP can significantly reduce coordination costs by avoiding the frequent exchange of orders and invoices. For instance, North American superstore chains use CRP extensively.

Supply Chain Management (SCM) has essentially the same objectives as QR, may include CRP, but is used in a wider sense. Often described from a manufacturer's viewpoint, SCM aims to remove media breaks and inefficiency in the supply chain as well as in the marketing channel by using IOSs [Mertens 1995]. SCM includes automated planning, control, and administration of all goods and information along the entire value chain. A basic premise of SCM, QR and CRP is that all economic activity is driven by customers' needs and therefore only those goods should be produced that are demanded by customers, and as rapidly as possible. This is often called "build-to-customer" and marks the fundamental change from a seller's market to a buyer's market [Oliver/Webber 1992]. Software vendors also use the term SCM. The widely known SAP R/3 system, for example, has recently been expanded to support SCM. This allows direct connections of SAP R/3 systems between enterprises, using the so-called IDOC interface [Killer 1997]. Electronic connections enable seamless transfer of data along the supply chain, thus – as mentioned previously - shortening manufacturing cycles significantly.

The importance of SCM is underscored by the founding of the "Supply Chain Council (SCC)", comprising over 70 companies. In 1996, the SCC introduced the "Supply Chain Operations Reference (SCOR)" as a standardized model for electronic interactions along the supply chain [Berglund 1997].

In contrast to EDI's focus, which is mainly technical, QR, CRP and SCM also include organizational measures.

The German term *Zwischenbetriebliche Integration (ZBI)* translates as *interenterprise integration*. Various books and articles describe the technical and organizational aspects of integrating information systems across organization's boundaries, for example [Mertens 1966], [Mertens 1985], [Scheer 1987], [Schumann 1992], [Fischer 1993], [Rupprecht-Daeullary 1994] or [Alt 1997]. ZBI can be understood as a synonym for IOS [Simon 1998].

In the course of finding more powerful technical solutions and a wider availability of computers and networks, IOSs have become more flexible and, as a consequence, their implementation has become easier and more cost-effective. Benjamin and Wigand mention an important aspect in the development of IOSs: "Electronic ... channels will evolve from separate databases within the firm, to linked databases between firms (EDI) to shared databases between firms" [Benjamin/Wigand 1995, p. 65]. This enhanced technical functionality also means a notable shift in the balance of power between market partners. Companies that maintain IOS linkages with each other have an "insider"-advantage over their competitors. On the other hand, changing partners becomes more difficult because the investment costs of IOSs are still relatively high [Cash/Konsynski 1985], [Kanter/Myers 1991], [Golden/Powell 1996]. One drawback in the use of IOSs is that companies are more enmeshed with each other and dependent on this technology. An empirical study of 100 large IOS users asked for the potential consequences if an IOS connection were unavailable. Seventy-six percent of the respondents stated that an interruption of one day would cause moderate to major problems; one week without IOS connection would lead to major problems, even to closure in 73% of the surveyed companies [Finnegan/Galliers/Powell 1997].

Balance of power issues a consequential role in the establishment and use of IOS-mediated interactions [Premkumar/Ramamurthy 1995]. It has been reported from the automobile industry that large companies force their suppliers into using IOSs. Golden and Powell have surveyed IOS implementations in Ireland and UK with the following conclusions [Golden/Powell 1997]:

- large companies gain more flexibility from IOSs than smaller ones;
- initiators benefit more from IOSs, and larger companies are more often the initiators.

This study also found that electronic mail (e-mail) is the IOS application that is most used (59%), followed by EDI connections (57%) and Internet/WWW usage (43%) [Finnegan/Galliers/Powell 1997].
Other authors have pointed out that trust is a prerequisite of successful IOS implementations [van Koenig/Wijk 1991], [Clark/Schiano 1996]. Because IOSs tie companies more closely to each other, the parties must trust their partners more so than in conventional business relationships.

With the growth of the Internet and WWW, it is expected that Electronic Commerce (see below) will become an important form of IOSs in the future.

3.2.5 Electronic commerce

Electronic commerce (EC) is the electronic trading of commodities and money exchange between companies or between vendor and public. It constitutes the economic interface between the parties, and nowadays uses primarily the Internet and

WWW as platforms. Many books and articles on the subject have been published on the subject lately [Adam/Yesha 1996], [Alpar 1996], [Hansen 1996], [Kurbel 1997]. Analysts predict enormous future growth of this new kind of trade. According to a study by the European Information Technology Observatory, in Europe alone the total value of goods traded via *EC* is estimated to be 3.7 billion German marks (DM) in 1997. Predictions are, that it will rise dramatically to some DM 13 billion (1998), DM 36 billion (1999), DM 73 billion (2000), and to DM 110 billion by 2001 [Grund-Ludwig 1997].

Reliable standards for the secure transfer of financial data (electronic cash transactions) and the acceptance of contracts with digital signatures are fundamental prerequisites for *EC*. Various standards are evolving currently, and a reliable and commonly accepted technical basis for secure financial transactions should soon be available. Another element in EC is the consumer acceptance of this innovation. Consumers need a computer, a connection to the Internet, the ability to use EC features and have to trust this new way of buying goods.

Benjamin and Wigand have found that specific goods are especially suitable for *EC*. From a transaction cost theory perspective, they conclude that for certain types of products, i.e. where asset specificity is low and products are easily described, the electronic marketplace is a more efficient form of transaction coordination than the traditional way of trading. They expect a proportional shift from traditional sales channels to their electronic counterparts [Benjamin/Wigand 1995].

Electronic commerce, as it is understood by many authors, does not explicitly include the business processes inside the organizations that lie before and behind the electronic interface. Wide Area Workflow Management (WAWM) tries to cover the overall business process across different organizations and also covers information that does not deal with trade or payment. Although WAWM focuses on the connection of larger organizations, it can include users working at home (so-called teleworking). *Electronic commerce* and Wide Area Workflow Management can be seen as complimentary elements of new forms of electronic interaction between distributed users, regardless of whether they work in organizations or at home.

3.2.6 Types of cooperation among organizations

Apart from the technological elements described so far, Wide Area Workflow Management has major organizational aspects. Organizations will be amenable to connecting their workflow management systems only if they are basically willing to cooperate with each other.

Different types of cooperation among legally independent organizations can be distinguished according to the proximity of the participants [Hirschmann 1996]. Based on coordination science and transaction cost theory concepts, the different degrees of nearness are located between the coordination strategies of market and hierarchy. Examples of cooperation are listed below according to increasing intensity:

- conventional interaction between buyers and sellers;
- closer relations between organizations, e.g. supported by outline agreements for delivery;

- close relations, e.g. supported by electronic supply chain management;
- strategic alliances or strategic networks, formed to achieve common objectives;
- virtual organizations (described below);
- establishment of a commonly owned, new enterprise (joint venture);
- exchange of shares;
- mergers or take-overs, effectively terminating legal autonomy.

Cooperation between organizations can also be classified according to the "direction" of working together. *Horizontal cooperation* describes the joining of forces between partners who have equal status on a value-add-chain. In distinction to this, *vertical cooperation* connects firms that undertake concatenated steps along a value-add-chain. *Heterogeneous cooperation* is established by companies operating in different market sectors [Power 1993], [Klein 1996].

The ways in which organizations cooperate determine the legal and organizational foundation for IOS applications. Many authors predict that changes in market behavior, and the radically new functions of IOSs, will create new modes of cooperation such as *value-adding partnerships* [Johnston/Lawrence 1988], *networking of organizations* [Powell 1990], *value constellation* [Norman/Ramirez 1993] and *strategic partnerships* or *strategic networks* [Backhaus/Meyer 1993]. One particular means of cooperation between organizations that has been discussed at length in recent years is *virtual organizations*. Therefore, the primary characteristics of such organizations are detailed below.

The term *Virtual Organization (VO)*, also called *virtual corporation* or *virtual enterprise*, is applied to a temporary coalition of several, legally independent organizations, with the purpose of offering a jointly manufactured product or jointly provided service to a customer who perceives the VO as a singular entity. A VO may be defined as a "... temporary network of independent companies – suppliers, customers, even competitors – linked by information technology to share [resources such as], skills, costs, and access to one another's markets" [Byrne/Brand/Port 1993]. Traditional boundaries of organizations dissolve in favor of faster reaction to customer needs.

In other words, in VOs several specialized organizations join forces in order to attain a common goal much more effectively and promptly than it would be possible for each individual company [Davidow/Malone 1992]. By contributing their core competencies, each of the participating organizations concentrates on specific steps in the fabrication and marketing process of a product or service, e.g. research and development, production, distribution or sales. The fields of competencies of the participants may also be distinguished according to other categories such as technical components of a product or geographical regions.

By leaving other functions to their partner organizations and concentrating on those for which a contributor is especially qualified, a high level of proficiency is attained within each participating organization. The synergistic combining of these "lean" organizations can result in adaptable teams of specialists, enabling them to exploit market opportunities much faster than a single organization, which would need to develop all of the required expertise in-house. With less bureaucratic overhead and more extensive use of modern information technology to share and pool know-how, VOs are seen as a promising means to maintain the leading edge in response to ever shorter product life cycles in technology-intensive markets [Miller/Clemons/Row 1993], [Semich 1994], [Mertens/Faisst 1995].

In the language of coordination science, VOs belong to the *equal partnership* scheme rather than into the *market* or *hierarchy* classification (see Section 3.2.2, p. 29). While strategic alliances or partnerships also aim at consolidating core competencies of the partners, VOs differ in that their objective is to appear to customers and in the market place as a singular entity. In strategic alliances or partnerships, the participating companies are identifiable. The alliance of IBM, Motorola, and Apple which develops, produces, and markets the PowerPC processor, is a prominent example of this case. Although these companies have joined forces to supply a single product, they remain visible as distinct organizations to customers. A traditional way of building a single interface towards customers would have been to found a joint venture as a new legal entity. VOs thus are positioned between strategic alliances and joint ventures.

VOs are often considered as short-lived and mission-oriented, existing only as long as the partnership provides higher profits than any one of the participants could achieve on its own. Therefore, the development of VOs is often described in lifecycle models of formation, existence, and dissolution [Faisst 1997].

Trust plays an important role in the formation of and the cooperation within VOs [Handy 1997]. Since flexibility and swift response to a "window of opportunity" are essential, contract negotiations between the partners cannot be as extensive nor take into account every potential contingency, some parts or even entire contracts have to be replaced by mutual trust.

Some examples of VOs are described in [Byrne/Brand/Port 1993], [Mertens 1994], [Sieber 1997]. It is interesting that in many cases found to have characteristics of VOs, partnerships of organizations do not call themselves *virtual organizations* and sometimes are even not aware of the existence of the VO concept.

Some authors are enthusiastic about the potential inherent in VOs and predict enormous growth in this kind of cooperative behavior. Others mention the potential for problems and contradictions, that can also be observed in practical scenarios [Introna/Tiow 1997], [Hirschmann/Scheer 1997]:

- Trust is regarded as an important foundation for VOs. The establishment of trust-based relationships, however, requires an extended period of interaction between partners. This is contradictory to the short-lived nature of VOs.
- If not all details are stated in contracts, responsibilities that arise in the case of a failure may not be clear.
- VOs cannot dissolve until the guarantee/warranty period for the product has expired. Consequently, a quick termination in case of falling profit margins poses problems.
- Enterprises may participate in several VOs, and it is likely that situations arise where there is a conflict of interests.

- It has not yet been proven that coordination costs within VOs are lower than in other forms of cooperation, such as strategic networks or joint ventures.
- If VOs do not have independent legal status, as is the case in joint ventures, customers may force participants in a VO to give up "virtuality". Powerful customers may want one or several of the participating companies to sign contracts directly and thus take on full responsibility.
- The nature of VOs makes it difficult for employees to identify themselves with the VO's brand name. It is not likely that a stable and reliable corporate culture can develop in a short-lived collection of companies such as a VO.
- Customers will be unable to form an impression of the quality of products, nor gain confidence in a relationship with a VO that appears and disappears within a short period of time.
- Many human relationships are subject to power plays. The notion of equality in a virtual organization probably applies only to limited number of situations or for a limited time. For example, it is quite possible that a larger partner in a VO might try to dominate others or, if a product strategy has been successful, one of the partners might try to buy out other partners.
- Norms and rules governing social interactions have to evolve over time. There can be no guarantee that partners in a VO will develop synergy; in fact, their behavior may become destructive. In other words, the whole is not always superior to its parts.
- The objective of a VO is the pooling of core competencies in order to achieve a common goal. A basic problem is that many companies are not really certain what all of their core competencies are. Furthermore, these capabilities are not static; they are constantly evolving and changing. In many cases, the competencies of an organization exist in a tacit, unconscious and not easy re-locatable way. Therefore it is difficult to quickly pool them with others in VOs.

Based on these thoughts it seems more likely that existing types of cooperation among organizations will over time take on some characteristics of VOs. This assumption is based on the fact that new opportunities of information technology are likely to change the cooperative behavior of organizations because information has become easier to move. This movement towards "virtuality" is more likely to occur in an evolutionary process rather than in a widespread, revolutionary shift towards VOs.

The concept of VOs, seen as an extreme form of cooperative behavior between organizations, is nevertheless a challenge for the application of Wide Area Workflow Management. Since VOs consist of several autonomous organizations, they are likely to have distinct workflow management systems with a strong need for interoperability. This will be true also for other forms of cooperation among legally separate organizations.

3.3 Process orientation in office work within and between organizations

A process can be described as a goal-oriented sequence of activities that are connected to each other by a logical context, which as a whole allow for the completion of a certain task. During a process, either material, information or both are transformed [Gaitanides 1983], [Harrington 1991], [Elgass/Krcmar 1994]. Process orientation entails organizing activities and the common objects they require along a defined path so that a desired goal is reached efficiently.

Process orientation has a long tradition in the design of production lines, and significant improvements in productivity have been achieved in this field. The application of the paradigms of process orientation also in office work has been extensively discussed in recent years. Traditional organizational structures, such as strict hierarchies and functional division of organizations into departments, do not appear to be appropriate any longer as product lifecycles become shorter and customers expect increased flexibility and quality of products and services.

The promise is that process orientation in office work can achieve improved administrative efficiency by organizing the relevant parts of enterprises according to processes rather than static functions.

Before such improvements can be realized, a dramatic change in the social configuration of offices has to occur [Hirschheim 1985], [Hirschheim 1986]. Hierarchies and status symbols such as titles have to be (at least partly) removed, and employees have to get used to project-oriented work and quickly changing responsibilities. Adaptability and a high educational level of the personnel are prerequisites for this shift.

Figure 6 illustrates the paradigms of functional and process-oriented organizations. On the left side, the complicated paths of "horizontal" business processes through "vertically" oriented organizational structures are sketched. Applying process orientation means to structure organizations along the main business processes, thereby removing inefficiencies (right side).

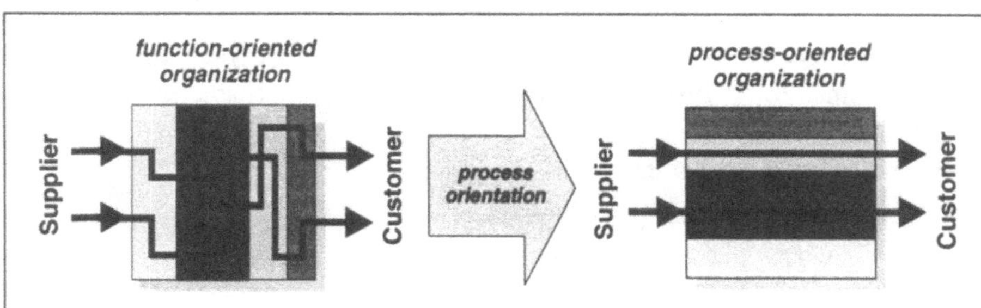

Figure 6: Paradigms of function-oriented and process-oriented organizations

Function-oriented organizations aim at providing as much internal stability as possible through processing similar activities within specialized organizational entities (e.g. departments). Activities handled in such an entity, however, often belong to different overall processes. Advantages of function-oriented organizations are a stable and reliable environment for employees, as well as acquisition and maintenance of expertise for certain process steps. Process-oriented organizations on the other hand establish temporary organizational entities (e.g. project groups), that manage entire processes and their required steps within an organization. In these circumstances, aptitude in performing certain steps is likely to be lower than in function-oriented departments, but overall processing time will probably be shortened significantly. The majority of employees in a process-oriented organization will belong to several project groups and may have different tasks in each of these.

An attempt to combine function-oriented and process-oriented organizational forms is found in *product managers*. They are responsible for guiding certain operations through a function-oriented organization in a process-oriented manner [Law 1974], [Gemmill/Wilemon 1980], [Dibb et al. 1991].

Benefits expected from process-oriented office work not only require a change in social structures and behaviors of employees. Additionally, information technology must support process-oriented organizational forms. Workflow management systems hold the promise of providing this enabling technology.

3.3.1 Office work

According to Weick, organizations can be defined as information processing systems. Tasks performed by individuals in organizations are comprised of acquiring, interpreting, generating, assessing, distributing, and storing information [Weick 1979]. This applies especially to offices where large quantities of information are handled while the amount of physical goods dealt with is low, in contrast to production processes. Due to division of labor, the need for coordination by communication in offices is high [Reichwald 1984].

In *office work*, the transfer of information items can be regarded as messages or speech acts with different characteristics [Searle 1969]. Messages can be transmitted between sender and recipient either verbally or in documents. Frequently, messages are initially verbal and then confirmed in written form for the purpose of legal documentation (e.g. meeting protocols, contracts).

Different tasks in office work can be categorized in different ways [Rathgeb 1994], [Krcmar/Zerbe 1996]. One category is the repetitive character of work that can be:

- repetitive at regular intervals,
- repetitive but occurring irregularly,
- unique tasks that occur only once in a specific form.

Another category is the degree to which tasks in office work can be structured and planned in advance [Nastansky/Hilpert 1994], [Rathgeb 1994], [Picot/Rohrbach 1995]:

- completely structured,
- partially structured (also called semi-structured),
- unstructured.

Partially structured and unstructured tasks complicate an ex ante planning of business processes.

In the following matrix, repetitiveness is depicted on one axis and structure on the other. This allows for a classification of different kinds of office work (Table 1). Repetitive and structured processes are especially suited to being handled by workflow management systems (WFMS). However, workflows with unique and less structured tasks should also be supported by advanced, flexible WFMSs.

Office Work	Structured	Semi-structured	Unstructured
Repetitive, regular	Weekly accounting report; Annual balance sheet	Monthly sales report; Annual report for shareholders	Analysis of deviations between inventory and actual stocks
Repetitive, irregular	Registration of goods received; Update of inventory	Order process for exceptional goods (Case study 2)	R & D report; Design of new furnishing (Case study 1)
Unique	Change of legal form	Building of a new production site	Research for a new product category

Table 1: Examples of a categorization of office work according to structure and repetitiveness

The total time required for any particular office process can be divided into actual working hours of employees, transportation time and time for temporary storage. The working hours of employees can be further split up into time used for information retrieval and actual time worked on the respective task.

Empirical studies in office environments have proven that only a small fraction of the time needed to complete an entire process is actual working time of employees. Average numbers for time fractions in office processes are [Peters 1995], [Schmider 1995], [Iten 1996], [Vogedes 1997], [Beyer 1997]:

- actual processing: 10-15%
- transport: 10-15%
- temporary storage: 60-80%.

A major challenge in process-oriented office work is the substantial reduction of total processing time. This can be achieved mainly by reducing time fractions of temporary storage and transport. Workflow management systems target precisely these aspects by reducing transport times to a minimum. WFMS can reduce temporary storage times further by better organization of the overall workflow (e.g. elimination of extraneous tasks), parallel execution of independent activities, and also by balancing the load between several workers who can perform the same task.

Schmider reports the following time fractions from a case study of a manually executed quotation process for fabricating machine parts according to customer specifications: actual processing 20%, transport 16%, and temporary storage 64%. After implementation of a WFMS, time fractions were 24% (actual processing), almost 0% (transport) and 76% (temporary storage). The overall processing time was reduced on average from 55 to 35 working days [Schmider 1995].

3.3.2 Business process reengineering

The term *Business Process Reengineering (BPR)* has been made popular by Michael Hammer and James Champy [Hammer 1990], [Hammer/Champy 1993]. The principal ideas in BPR are similar to those in process orientation. Hammer and Champy especially stress complete rethinking and redesigning of business processes, starting at 'square one' rather than attempting to optimize existing processes: "At the heart of reengineering is the notion of discontinuous thinking - of recognizing and breaking away from the outdated rules and fundamental assumptions that underlie operations. Unless we change these rules, we are merely rearranging the deck chairs on the Titanic. We cannot achieve breakthroughs in performance by cutting fat or automating existing processes. Rather, we must challenge old assumptions and shed the old rules that made the business underperform in the first place" [Hammer 1990, p. 108].

Information technology is seen as a key enabler for successful BPR [Davenport 1993]. Processes can be fundamentally altered with a radical use of modern IT. Hence, all existing processes have to be completely re-thought. This opinion is also expressed in the advice "Don't pave cow paths" [Hammer 1990]. In other words, merely automating existing processes with information technology will not achieve meaningful gains in efficiency. BPR is a fundamental approach that tries to reorganize a whole company in all aspects and not just limited parts of it.

All efforts of BPR should be led by customer's needs. Companies are supposed to concentrate on their core competencies in order to satisfy customers' needs in an efficient way. All other activities apart from the core competencies should be outsourced. To achieve *process orientation*, existing hierarchies have to be reconceptualized and are apt to be flattened in the course of a BPR process.

The strategy of *Continuous Process Improvement (CPI)* [Robson 1991] is sometimes considered the opposite of BPR because it constantly evaluates and optimizes existing processes. However, CPI can also be the logical consequence of BPR since completely reengineered processes subsequently have to be adapted regularly to changing circumstances and requirements.

Various books and articles have been written on BPR (e.g. [Andrews/Stalick 1994], [Johansson et al. 1994], [Manganelli/Klein 1994], [Morris/Brandon 1994]). The ideas of BPR initiated a major wave of reengineering projects. Not all of these projects were successful. Critics remark that BPR ruins the social environment of workers and, therefore, is rejected by them. Hammer admits that the social consequences of BPR projects have been underestimated [Hammer/Stanton 1995]. Willcocks et al. report on a extensive BPR project that failed in an initial attempt at radical reengineering. A subsequent endeavor was successful because a well-planned, evolutionary approach was taken, with early user involvement, and limited changes that employees could accept more readily [Willcocks/Currie/Jackson 1997].

Hohberger surveyed members of middle and upper management of European companies about expectations and outcomes of BPR projects [Hohberger 1995]. Only 27% of the respondents stated that BPR projects were initiated on account of a severe crisis in their organization. The remaining respondents were planning to improve current, well-functioning business methods. Asked to rank their expectations before the project started, on a scale from 1 (very low) to 5 (very high), managers expected significantly reduced costs (3.72), shortened processing times (4.12), improved quality (3.90), and greater customer satisfaction (3.99). After projects were completed, the results were found to be much less positive. On a scale of 1 (result not achieved), 2 (results achieved) and 3 (results better than expected) all of the mentioned aspects were rated considerably below 2, except customer satisfaction (2.05). Asked why employees and managers are apprehensive of BPR, the following factors were cited as important: loss of power, feeling threatened by new situations, the potential of additional work, and fear of job loss.

In light of similar experiences in many organizations, the euphoric BPR wave has been replaced by a more rational attitude towards the possibility of success in reengineering projects.

It is commonly agreed that workflow management systems are a key enabler for implementation of BPR projects in office environments [Derungs/Vogler/Oesterle 1997]. Following an analysis of current business procedures, processes should be reconceptualized and reorganized fundamentally in accordance with the BPR approach, incorporating the new possibilities offered by WFMSs. Only after a completed reengineering effort, streamlined workflow models should be designed [Oesterle 1996]. According to Erdl and Schoenecker, WFMS implementations without prior revision of processes achieve only very moderate improvements in overall processing time and personnel costs. However, such savings can be doubled or tripled if processes are radically redesigned before a WFMS is introduced [Erdl/Schoenecker 1995].

Seen from the perspective of IOSs and WAWM, BPR projects gain the additional dimension of not only "reengineering *the* corporation" [Hammer/Champy 1993], but reengineering processes across *several* organizations [Hundehege 1997]. Based on case studies, Clark and Stoddard conclude that implementations of IOSs can only be successful if preceded by interorganizational BPR [Clark/Stoddard 1996].

3.3.3 Workflow management

In this section *workflow management (WFM)*, as related to process orientation, will be discussed from a conceptual perspective. Starting with definitions of the term, principal considerations in WFM approaches in general as well as different interpretations and classifications of WFM will be addressed subsequently. More detailed information about scientific and commercial approaches to the development of workflow management systems will be presented in Chapter 4.

Workflow management has evolved from miscellaneous technological and organizational sources. On the organizational side, major contribution came from circulation folders transferred internally via in-house mail, and the writing of handbooks aiming to standardize processes within organizations. The technological foundations of WFM are, amongst other things, electronic mail, (active) database management systems, document management systems, business process modeling tools, and groupware systems. So-called *office procedure* or *office automation systems* can be regarded as forerunners of workflow management systems. Many authors see Zisman's work on office automation as the first approach of this kind [Zisman 1977].

Other known sources on office automation are [Bracchi/Pernici 1984], [Hasenkamp 1987] and descriptions of OfficeTalk [Ellis 1979], [Ellis/Nutt 1980], [Ellis 1983] and DOMINO [Kreifelts et al. 1984], [Kreifelts et al. 1991]. Jablonski and Bussler provide a detailed introduction to the technical forerunners of workflow management, including an overview of a selection of such systems [Jablonski/Bussler 1996].

In the following paragraphs, the terms *workflow*, *workflow management* and *workflow management systems* will be briefly introduced.

A *workflow* can be described as "1. the flow or progress of work done by a company, an industry, a department, or a person. 2. the rate at which such flow or progress takes place" [American Heritage Dict. 1994]. This non-technical definition emphasizes the process orientation of workflow. Today, the term *workflow* is practically synonymous with computerization. The Workflow Management Coalition (WfMC) states: "Workflow is concerned with the automation of procedures where documents, information or tasks are passed between participants according to a defined set of rules to achieve, or contribute to, an overall business goal. Whilst workflow may be manually organised, in practice most workflow is normally organised within the context of an IT system to provide computerised support for the procedural automation" [WfMC Ref. Mod. 1994, p. 6]. Therefore the WfMC defines workflow as "... computerised facilitation or automation of a business process, in whole or part" [WfMC Ref. Mod. 1994, p. 6]. The Workflow Management Coalition and its reference model will be introduced in Section 4.2.1.

Workflow management aims to find appropriate ways and means to optimize workflows according to given objectives. Frequently stated goals are for example (see also [Marshak 1992], [Hasenkamp/Syring 1993], [Galler/Scheer/Peter 1995], [Black Forest Group 1996], [Jablonski/Bussler 1996], [Kingsbury 1997], [Kobielus 1997] and others):

- reduction of overall processing time for the supported business processes, e.g. by drastically shortening times for transport and temporary storage (see Section 3.3.1, p. 42) through better planning, parallel execution of independent activities, elimination of media breaks, etc.;
- reduction of administrative costs, e.g. by avoiding needless and duplicated work, and thus improving productivity of workers;
- improvement in quality of work, e.g. by automatically providing comprehensive information required for the accomplishment of a task. An often mentioned example of this is an improved customer service which is achieved by making all relevant data and related workflows readily accessible;
- better balancing of workload between workers, e.g. by flexible task assignment and automatic substitution of performers in case of staff absence;
- enhanced flexibility through workflow models which anticipate exceptions during workflow run-time and offer various alternatives;
- improved control over workflows and their associated costs and benefits, e.g. by status management, monitoring, analysis and controlling tools;
- continuous learning and improving of business processes by analyzing inefficiencies in completed workflows;

- job enrichment and increased user competency. Elimination of superfluous, fatiguing, and time-consuming routine work such as searching through paper-based archives, etc.

However, workflow management is not exclusively seen in an optimistic light. Some of the apprehensions are (see also [Jablonski/Bussler 1996, p. 31]:

- Total control of users through status management, monitoring, and analysis of workflows.
- Loss of competence and flexibility through overplanned workflows; employees fear being downgraded to computer operators.
- Social isolation of users.

These anxieties cannot be ignored and thus it is the responsibility of system designers as well as managers to take these concerns into account and avoid such effects.

Workflow management systems (WFMSs) facilitate the execution of workflows with information technology, or more narrowly stated, with computer systems. There are many different definitions of the term WFMS (for example [Hasenkamp/Syring 1993], [Elgass/Krcmar 1994], [WfMC Ref. Mod. 1994], [Koulopoulos 1995]) that will not be repeated here. Components of WFMSs will be described in Section 4.2.1 (p. 77).

The literature on workflow management reveals clearly that the term encompasses technical, organizational, sociological, and business aspects. Authors differ in their emphasis on these aspects and, therefore, their perceptions of the overall workflow management topic vary astonishingly. Researchers in the field of computer science focus strongly on technical aspects [Jablonski/Bussler 1996], [Oberweis et al. 1997] and often only loosely discuss the social and financial impact of their systems' designs. On the other hand, authors with a background in business management and economics stress the organizational, social, and financial aspects of workflow management [Carlsen 1995], [Koulopoulos 1995], [Fischer 1995], but rarely offer concrete recommendations for an effective WFMSs' design. Lastly, WFMS vendors focus on business aspects such as return on investment, claiming that their respective system is superior to others, but often do not take the organizational and social implications of the implementation into account. These divergent interests and attitudes can be seen as one explanation for the fact that workflow management systems have not yet achieved market breakthrough. Much interdisciplinary research must still be conducted so that satisfactory trade-offs between the various aspects of workflow management can be established.

Paradigms of workflow management

How then can workflow management achieve all of the above-mentioned objectives, i.e. improved performance, while reducing processing time and costs?

There are many possible answers to this question, but foremost among them is *thorough assessment and planning* of workflows prior to implementation. It is hoped that, once a workflow has been planned and optimized, it can be repeated often enough so that the efforts that were invested in planning will be rewarded.

As a first step in the planning procedure, existing business processes should be analyzed. Subsequently, the major ones should then be selected for optimization. Business process modeling languages, mainly *directed graphs*, are often used to represent the results of this initial analysis.

Through optimization or complete redesign, planners strive to remove inefficiencies in the selected business processes. For each of the processes, a *workflow model* is then derived. First these workflow models (sometimes also referred to as a workflow class or workflow type) are freed of obvious errors and subsequently are tested and optimized, for example by simulation techniques. Then they are converted into *process definitions* that a WFMS can execute. At this point, *workflow instances* can be initiated in the WFMS, allowing users to actually perform the necessary work as it was planned.

The approach of precisely planning *workflow models* and executing *workflow instances* according to these models is often termed *structured workflow management*.

Figure 7 illustrates the described steps, that can be called *levels* of workflow management (similar levels are found with other authors, for example [Jablonski/Bussler 1996], [Dourish et al. 1996]).

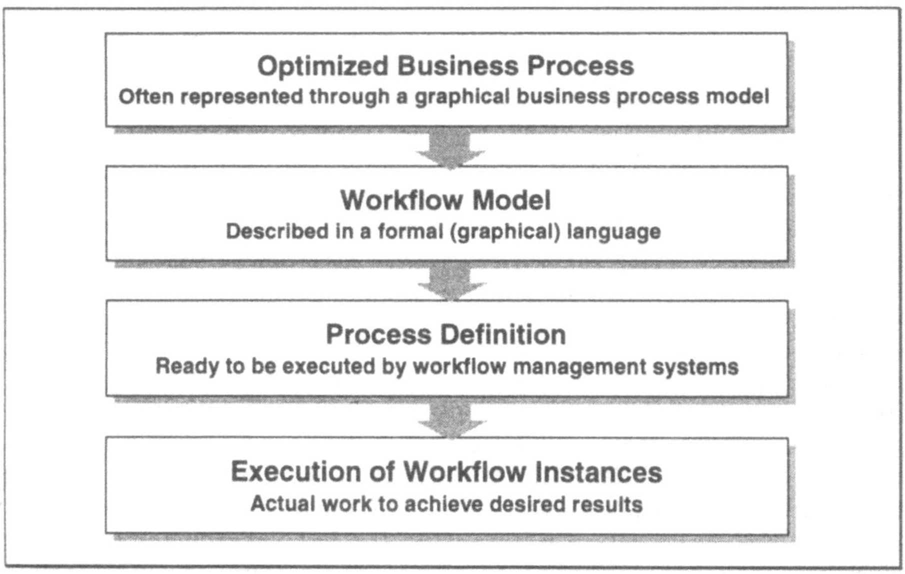

Figure 7: Steps from optimized business processes to executed workflow instances in structured workflow management

In order to model business processes and to define derived workflows, a basic set of descriptive elements is needed. For example, activities can be illustrated by a certain symbol and the transitions in-between activities by an arrow. Each of the descriptive elements has certain properties, e.g. a performer assigned to an activity or a condition for a transition.

Taken as a whole, the descriptive elements construct a language, which allows for representation of business processes or workflow models. This language is often labeled *workflow meta-model* [Galler 1995], [zur Muehlen/Rosemann 1997]. The various elements of such *meta-models* and their specific properties determine the scope of workflows that can be described. Although the main elements of *meta-models* are similar for most of the known WFMS prototypes and commercial systems, they differ in certain aspects. This makes it difficult to compare workflow models of unlike systems. A further challenge lies in the matching of divers *meta-models* of business process modeling tools and workflow management systems. For a further discussion of *meta-models* see Sections 5.3 (p. 117) and 5.4 (p. 125).

A one-time effort to analyze business processes and derive optimized process and workflow models is not sufficient. In order to keep the models factual and adequate for the problems they are meant to solve, analysis and optimization should be performed in a continuous process of improvement. This notion is illustrated in workflow life cycles that can for example be found in [Deiters/Gruhn/Striemer 1995], [Heilmann 1996], [Krallmann/Derszteler 1996]. The workflow life cycle described in [Hilpert 1994] shows that first, the existing business processes need to be analyzed, e.g. with respect to the way documents are treated and routed through an organization (Figure 8). Subsequent steps required to arrive at a workflow model have already been described in Figure 7. After the model has been tested by simulation, and flaws within it have been removed, workflow instances can be processed. Finally, the executed workflow instances are analyzed again to improve the workflow model, thus entering a new loop in the workflow life cycle.

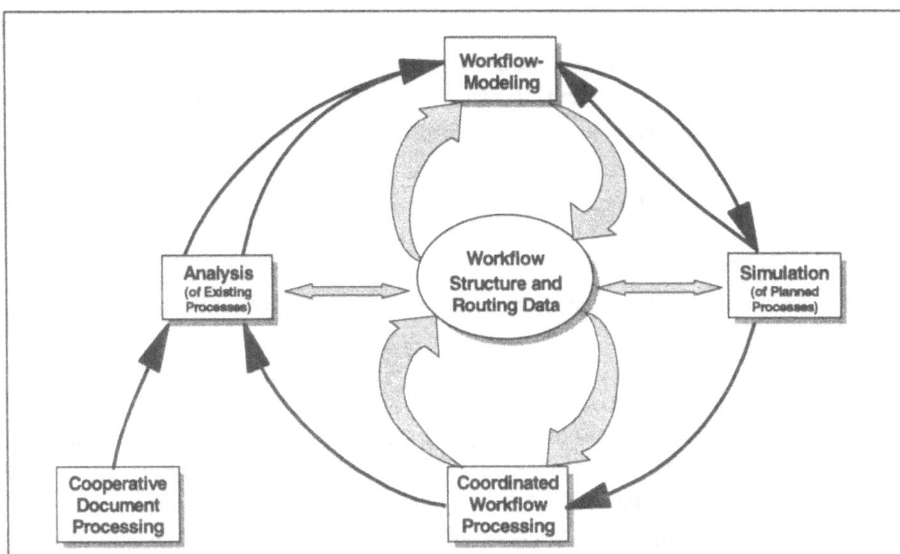

Figure 8: Workflow life cycle concept [Hilpert 1994, all rights reserved]

In an office without computers, business processes could also be planned thoroughly, and subsequently executed according to these plans, similar to the steps in Figure 7. This was attempted in *organizational handbooks*, which provide detailed descriptions of how certain processes are to be handled. However, a major problem with *organizational handbooks* was that too much time was taken from the analysis of a problem until the availability of solutions. Many rules were already obsolete before they could be made available to the workers concerned. Therefore, ad-hoc solutions were often found without allowing users an overview of the entire process. This may be the reason that business processes observed in case studies sometimes show very inefficient and illogical structures (see Chapter 2, p. 9). In addition, reading and applying solutions contained in an *organizational handbook* is still complicated and time-consuming for workers.

Many of these problems can be eliminated with workflow management systems. Graphical modeling tools allow for a fast description of optimized business processes, thus shortening the time needed between analysis of a problem and implementation of optimized procedures. Many WFMSs permit partly or fully automatic conversion of *workflow models* into *process definitions* so that the WFMS is enabled to execute workflow instances. Furthermore, a WFMS helps office workers to actually use the workflow models without having to apply or even to know complicated rules. Tools for monitoring and analysis enable comparison of a workflow model and resultant actual workflow instances, to determine deviations.

Implementation of WFMSs requires an infrastructure of networked computers and people who are qualified to use these computers. While both of these prerequisites exist in most organizations today, nonetheless numerous problems of workflow management remain (see also [Abbott/Sarin 1994], [Bowers/Button/Sharrock 1995]):

- There is still a time gap between analysis of business process and construction of a workflow model on the one hand, and the execution of workflow instances on the other hand. In rapidly changing business cycles, this gap may still produce inappropriate workflow models.
- As is the case with all planning efforts, much of the required knowledge base is experiential, held by the people who actually apply the processes. It is difficult and costly for planners to collect all this knowledge and to transfer it into workflow models.
- Users may need or want to have the ability to change workflows during runtime.
- A considerable percentage of business processes cannot be planned in detail in advance because their structures are not predictable (see Section 3.3.1, p. 42). It may only be possible to plan milestones or it may even be impossible to plan at all. Therefore ex ante structured processes must be handled differently from processes that are ex ante unstructured.
- Even if a business procedure can be planned in detail, it may not be worth doing so because the process does not occur often enough. In other words, highly repetitive processes are better suited to structured workflow management than unique ones. Nonetheless, infrequent or unique processes constitute an important portion of office work and, therefore, should be somehow supported by computer systems.
- Implementation of WFMSs leads to fundamental changes in the working culture and social structure of organizations. The initial costs of transferring

business from manual operations to computer-based workflow management are very high in relation to the costs of WFMS software itself.

- Once an organization is committed to a WFMS, it is utterly dependent on the system. Any disruption or malfunction can halt work completely.

These may be some of the reasons why workflow management has been discussed for a long time, but has not yet been used significantly in companies. According to a representative opinion poll of over 300 German IT managers in July 1997, only 6% of the companies used WFMSs at that time. Asked for the reasons why they have not implemented WFMSs, they responded *lack of mature products* (57%), *lack of money* (28%) and *no need for a WFMS* (15%) [Heinrich 1997].

Of the above-named problems, the last two - high transition costs and vulnerability to malfunction – can be approached by making WFMSs technically more robust and simplifying implementation procedures. Most of the other challenges mentioned, which are mainly of organizational nature, however will remain.

Many researchers and WFMS designers have addressed the problems inherent in the gap between planning efforts and actual application. The different solutions can be summarized under the label of *flexible workflow management*.

As a basic possibility for enhancing flexibility, numerous WFMS prototypes and commercial systems already allow for controlled exceptions from the workflow model during run-time. Additional flexibility is achieved by leaving parts of the workflow model open for decisions that can be made during run-time of workflows. Since only major steps are planned, this is called "milestone modeling", "semi-structured modeling", "late modeling" or "modeling of coarse workflow phases" [Nastansky/Hilpert 1994], [Nastansky/Hilpert 1996], [Deiters et al. 1996], [Wargitsch/Wewers/Theisinger 1998]. Where business processes are long-term (several months or years), "milestone modeling" has a long tradition in the form of project management [Ehlers 1997]. Workflow management, as distinct from project management, mainly deals with short-term business processes of several days or weeks.

An early attempt to increase flexibility in workflow management was made by Hilpert and Nastansky [Hilpert 1993a], [Nastansky/Hilpert 1994]. In their so-called *Workflow Continuum*, they distinguish workflows from each other by discerning how much structure can be imposed in advance. The continuum shows structured workflow management (ex ante completely structured) at one end and flexible group interaction (ex ante unstructured) at the other end (see also Section 4.2.3.1, p. 85). In between these two extremes, the so-called semi-structured workflow is built using different combinations of structured and flexible elements. Deiters et al. discern in further detail whether work order, participants, and the information base can be planned in advance or not [Deiters et al. 1996].

A very high degree of flexibility is achieved by not planning a workflow model at all. Here, during run-time of a workflow, users are able to define a routing path interactively. They thus navigate the workflow according to their respective needs, but are supported by a WFMS. This is often called *ad-hoc* or *instance-based workflow management* [Nastansky/Hilpert 1994], [Wargitsch/Wewers/Theisinger 1998]. Still work is *pushed* from one performer to the next (for the distinction of *push* and *pull*, see also Section 5.2.2.1, p. 113).

Maximum flexibility is achieved by neither planning a workflow model nor defining a routing path during run-time. Users interact in a common environment based on individual agreements. They *pull* shared objects from a shared database as required and based on their own decisions. This is the paradigm of *groupware*.

Depicting the categories of structured versus unstructured processes on one axis and repetitive versus unique tasks on another (see Table 1, p. 43), the different kinds of workflow management discussed so far can be placed in a matrix (Figure 9).

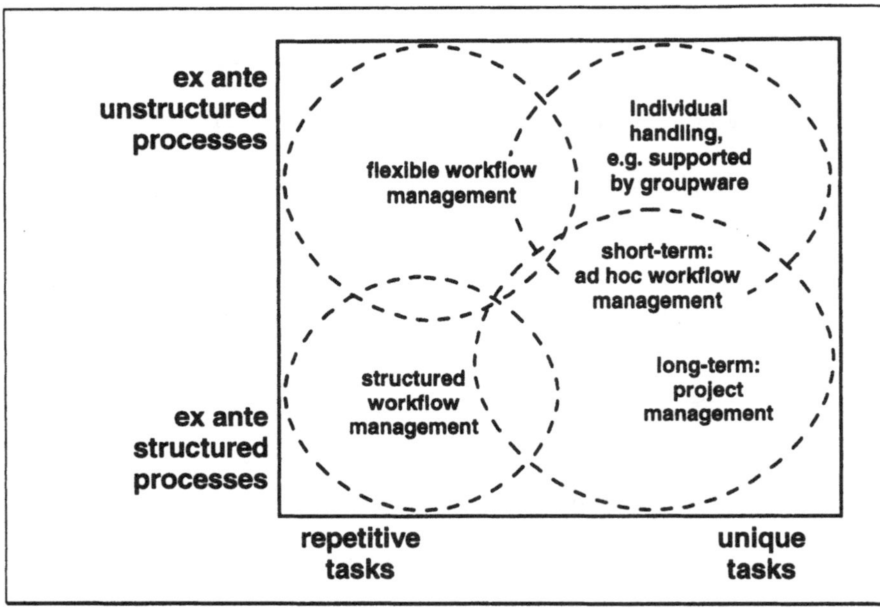

Figure 9: Classification of diverse workflow management approaches and project management based on process structure and repetitiveness of tasks

Approaches for structured workflow management have been discussed in detail in literature (see [Georgakopoulos/Hornick/Sheth 1995], [Jablonski/Bussler 1996] and others) and therefore will not be examined further here. Some WFM approaches that fall into the category of *flexible* and *ad-hoc workflow management* and the derived WFMSs will be discussed in Section 4.2.3 (p. 85). Fundamental aspects of *groupware* systems will be addressed in Section 3.4.4 (p. 65).

Apart from the above attempt to classify different WFM approaches (Figure 9), many other classification schemes for WFM and WFMSs can be found in literature (e.g. [Schulze/Boehm 1996]). Some of these will be presented in Section 4.1 (p. 73) as a basis for the introduction of scientific and commercial workflow management systems.

3.3.4 Distributed and Wide Area Workflow Management

How was office work performed and interconnected between various departments or organizations in the days of paper-based information handling?

The answer to this question provides important insights into the discussion of distributed and Wide Area Workflow Management: they used a multitude of different documents (written messages) to transfer information, meaning data *and* semantic context (see Section 3.1, p. 23). Letters, memos, sales reports, meeting protocols, orders, invoices, price lists, catalogues, brochures and many other documents served and still serve the information exchange between different workers in intra- and interorganizational settings. If workflow management systems are to improve efficiency in the handling of business processes, they have to reconstruct this manifold structure of information carriers and their dissemination among users. This is especially true if the persons involved are geographically dispersed.

Therefore, a major goal of workflow management is to seamlessly connect office workers who work for example in different rooms or floors of an office building. Transmitting common objects of workflows – mostly electronic documents – with the help of a computer network reduces the time needed for transportation (see p. 43) to a minimum. Participants in workflows can also be located in a number of buildings, branches or even countries. The workflow-oriented, computer-based support of these distributed and widely distributed office workers will be discussed in this section from a conceptual viewpoint.

There are two ways of implementing workflow support in distributed and widely distributed environments: on the one hand, existing WFMSs can be enlarged to include all participants in various locations. On the other hand, interoperability between different WFMSs at different locations can be achieved. In reality, it can often be observed that distinct organizations and even different departments within a single organization start to apply different WFMSs for limited purposes. Once they have gained some experience, they try to enlarge the use of their WFMS and soon realize that interoperability with other WFMSs is necessary.

An increasing number of authors emphasize the importance of WFMS interoperability [Abbott/Sarin 1994], [Vogler 1996], [Wewers/Faisst 1996], [WfMC, IF 4 1996a]. The Black Forest Group, a consortium of major multi-national corporations, states: "The simplest implementation of a workflow application will have all users locally. They then can all be connected to a central scheduler; administration and monitoring facilities can encompass the entire system, and so on. But that may not be what is needed. There may be a number of offices, each with independent workflow requirements as well as the requirement to participate in a cross-organization workflow. Items of work may need to be passed from one office to another. And what about inter-organization workflow? Support for mobile users? What if cross-site monitoring is needed?" [Black Forest Group 1996, p. 95].

Williams concurs: "Today few vendors offer true multi-departmental or even multi-site workflow systems but in the future your company may need to handle processes that cross departments and go beyond the company's boundary. As companies rethink their business processes they will discover new roles for other companies to play in the chain of actions that runs from the perception of market need to its successful exploitation in the form of goods and services, paid for by customers. Using technology to support these new networks of companies will become a core competency for tomorrow's organizations" [Williams 1997, p. 205].

Many authors perceive WFMS interoperability across several locations as a mere technical problem. Most of them suggest distributing workflow instances across several workflow servers by using different technologies such as messaging or replication [WfMC Ref. Mod. 1994], [Reinwald 1995], [Casati et al. 1996], [Jablonski/Böhm/Schulze 1997].

The author is convinced that technical issues are important for WFMS interoperability and there are still many problems to be solved on this level. He additionally wants to emphasize the important role of strategic and organizational aspects of cooperation and interaction between distributed workflow management systems. According to Williams, the approaching challenge will be to connect WFMSs along the value chain, which will primarily require ways and means of *coordinating* the efforts of participating firms. First, coordination strategies among the partners such as *hierarchy*, *equal partnership* and *market* (see Section 3.2.2, p. 29) must be determined to fit the respective cooperative situations, before technical measures can be applied efficiently.

In the following paragraphs, fundamental terms in the context of Wide Area Workflow Management (WAWM) are explained. Subsequently levels of distribution of WFMSs are discussed, and the term WAWM is further elucidated.

In a workflow, all participants can belong to one organization and hence respective applications shall be called *intra*organizational. This is distinguished from the case of workflow participants belonging to legally separated organizations which will be termed *inter*organizational workflow management. Further on, workflows which connect different users at one location (mostly using one LAN) will be called *distributed.* If several locations, connected by WANs or mobile computing, are concerned, workflow management will be labeled *widely distributed.* The following combinations are possible (Table 2):

Forms of workflow management	***Single organization***	***Several, legally separate organizations***
One location (LAN)	*Intra*organizational, distributed workflow management ("standard" WFM). Example: Application for credit in a bank.	*Inter*organizational, distributed workflow management. Example: Quotation workflow within a virtual organization with member firms in one office building.
Several locations (WAN & mobile)	*Intra*organizational, widely distributed workflow management. Example: Material support request of IB (Case study 1), before redesign.	*Inter*organizational, widely distributed workflow management. Example: Purchasing process for additional goods of LLM including suppliers (Case study 2).

Table 2: Different forms of workflow management depending on location and organizational integration

For all forms of workflow management described above (Table 2), either one distributed WFMS or several interoperating WFMSs can be appropriate.

A basic question is, which components of WFMSs have to be distributed in order to achieve adequate support for distributed and widely distributed workflows within one homogeneous system environment. Another basic question is how several different WFMSs can interoperate to achieve a seamless network of cooperating, heterogeneous systems.

A fundamental method to characterize interoperability is to identify distinct levels within systems. A well-known example of this is the ISO/OSI model of system connectivity comprised of seven levels. Clark and Schiano have adapted the concept of the ISO/OSI model and transferred it to a model, which describes the variety of possible levels of interorganizational connectivity [Clark/Schiano 1996]. Using grocery distribution channels in the USA as examples, their descriptions of levels of integration range from *physical data transfer* to *electronic data interchange*, *new policies and integrated operations*, *joint channel optimization* and, finally, *virtual channel integration*. This allows distinctions to be made between various interorganizational cooperation models according to the intensity of common, integrated activities.

WFMSs are usually divided into levels, e.g. modeling tools, run-time environment and networked computer systems [WfMC Ref. Mod. 1994]. Some authors divide these general levels into further layers [Jablonski/Böhm/Schulze 1997, p. 241]. Others emphasize the levels between hardware and user interfaces and create technically oriented level models for distributed WFMSs [Reinwald 1995, p. 91] that do not encompass modeling tools. In contrast to the model of Clark and Schiano, these models do not include aspects of coordination of different organizations.

To describe the different technical and organizational aspects involved in the distribution of WFMSs as well as of the interoperability of several WFMSs, the following *level model* (Figure 10) is introduced.

Workflow management is the goal-oriented coordination of different actors in a business process. According to the BPR approach, business processes should be derived from the strategic aims of an organization. Therefore, the top level of the model in Figure 10 represents strategic and organizational conditions. If implementation of a WFMS in an organization is planned, e.g. across several departments, then the basic objectives of cooperation must be defined and the efforts of the participants coordinated. Where workflows are to include several organizations, it can be assumed that different workflow management systems exist. Depending on the proximity of the organizations involved (see Section 3.2.6, p. 37), those forms of cooperation will be chosen, which will lead to the achievement of a common goal. In cases of a strong organizational integration, the WFMSs concerned will have to interoperate closely, thus most likely making it necessary to invest in expensive technical measures. In rather loose forms of cooperation between the participating organizations, technical measures are likely to be much less sophisticated and costly. The degree of organizational integration will determine the scope and extent of technical measures that can then be justified on the basis of cost/benefit calculations.

The strategic and organizational level (4th level) influences the design of workflow models. These models are developed according to the steps introduced in Figure 7 (p. 48). The general goals of cooperation, described in the 4th level, should be reflected in the workflow models.

For *intraorganizational, distributed* workflows, most of the known *meta-models* are appropriate. It is likely that workflow *meta-models* need to be extended in order to allow for the design of *interorganizational, widely distributed* workflows (see

Section 5.4, p. 125). Based on the chosen meta-model, a set of workflow models will be designed to achieve strategic goals in a given organizational scenario (3rd level).

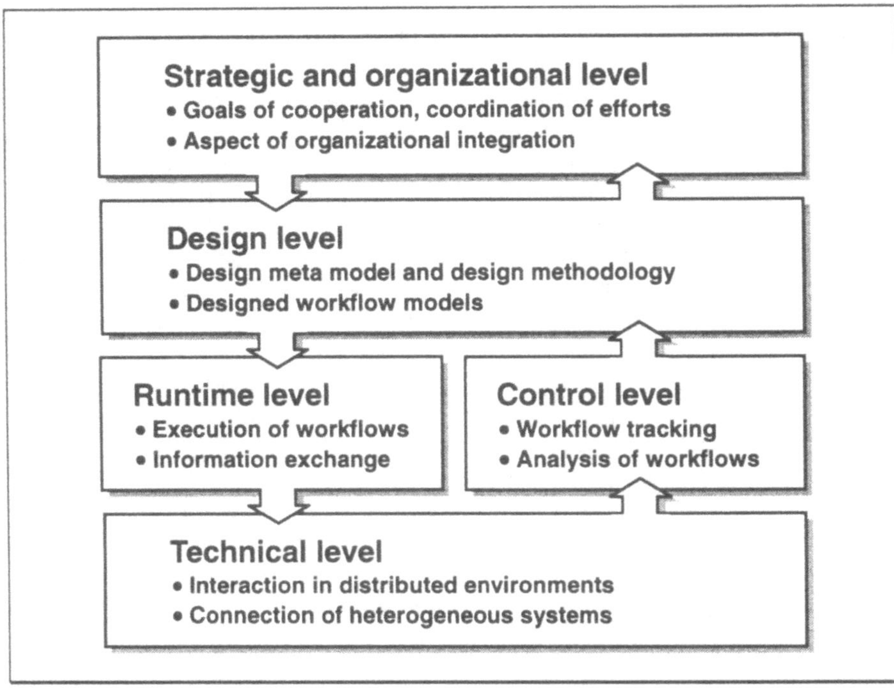

Figure 10: Levels of distributed and widely distributed workflow management

Workflow instances derived from workflow models are executed in a run-time environment (2nd level). Execution may be either *distributed* or *widely distributed*. If several WFMSs are involved, a structured information exchange must be enabled. On the technical side (1st level), all essential hard- and software has to be adapted for a seamless interaction in homogeneous and heterogeneous environments during workflow run-time.

During run-time operation, and especially after workflows have been completed, tracking protocols are analyzed, providing data on the actual workflow performance as compared to the planned workflow model. If no workflow models have been planned beforehand, then an analysis of ad-hoc workflows can be used to identify process structures and inefficiencies. Results of an analysis will also serve to influence the strategic and organizational levels, e.g. by enhancing a successful relationship with a cooperating partner or by changing partners in the case of failures. Therefore, a loop of top-down *and* bottom-up relations is depicted in Figure 10. As will be described later (see Section 4.2.3, p. 85), there is an ongoing discussion as to whether one should start with a bottom-up approach of first performing exploratory workflows and developing the structure from there, or start with top-down planning activities. The answer to this question will largely depend on the specific situation in which workflow management is applied.

Based on these levels of distributed and widely distributed workflow management (Figure 10), a developmental path of workflow management systems can be observed (Figure 11). Each item in the bulleted lists in the lower part of Figure 11 represents one level of the model in Figure 10.

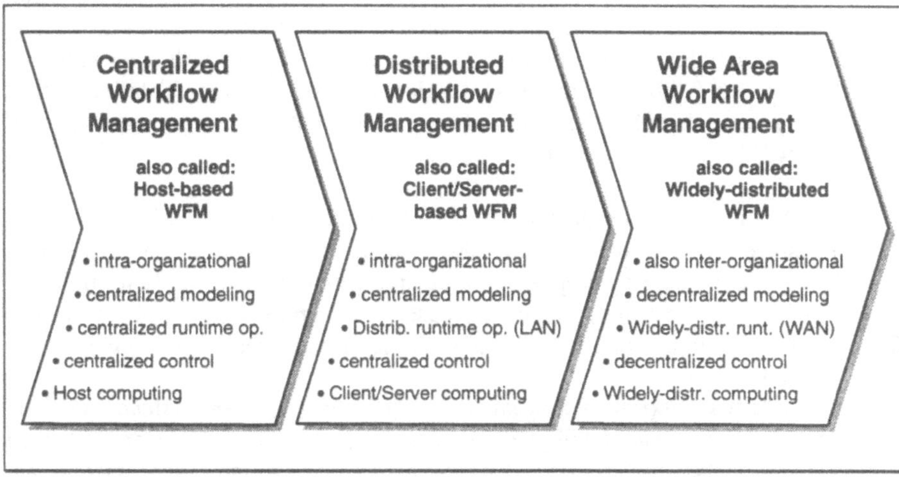

Figure 11: Steps towards Wide Area Workflow Management

The initial approaches to WFM were centralistic at all levels (left side of Figure 11). They only focused on *intra*organizational WFM with centralized modeling, run-time, and control architecture. With the second generation of WFM, a certain measure of distributability was achieved (middle part of Figure 11). Most of the currently available WFMSs are second generation, mainly built on client/server architecture. They allow workflow instances to be spread across several servers, which are connected by a local area network (LAN). They are still primarily supporting *intra*organizational workflows with a centralized modeling and control architecture. Some of the current WFMSs already provide connection of workflow servers by means of *wide area networks* (WANs), to enable widely distributed workflows. As such, they already have one characteristic of the third generation of WFMSs, which supports *Wide Area Workflow Management.* The description of concepts and solutions for a third generation of workflow management systems (right part of Figure 11) is the principal objective of this book.

It is anticipated that third generation WFM can also be applied to *inter*organizational workflows by supporting different coordination strategies for more or less autonomous participants. A most important feature of third generation WFMSs is decentralized modeling. It is not plausible, for example, that widely distributed, *inter*organizational workflows are planned centrally by one of the participating organizations. This would presuppose extensive knowledge of the internal operations of all partners, and would be unacceptable in many situations. Only in strictly hierarchical scenarios would centralized modeling of *inter*organizational workflows be likely to occur. Even within a single, large organization, a centralized modeling approach poses enormous problems because of the balance of power among different departments. Consequently, decentralized modeling can also be advantageous in *intra*organizational workflows. The same holds true for the control of *intra-* and *inter*organizational workflows, which needs to be decentralized in many cases.

The underlying technical platform for third generation workflow management should support the connection of widely distributed WFMSs. It can be expected that the Internet and WWW will have an important role as enabling technologies.

Various authors have also described generations of WFMSs with somewhat different focal points [Abbott/Sarin 1994], [Jablonski/Bussler 1996], [Schulze/Boehm 1996]. Many agree though that support of widely distributed and *inter*organizational workflows will be an essential feature of the future.

The author and his colleagues have used the term "*Wide Area Workflow Management*" since 1993. It originated in discussions about ways in which different WFMSs can interoperate by employing wide area networks and was first published in [Riempp 1994]. Other authors have also used the term recently [Williams 1997], [Kozlowski 1997] indicating that it intuitively describes a particular technical and organizational approach.

Now, the terms *workflow management*, *workflow management system*, and *Wide Area Workflow Management* will be defined as a basis for the subsequent discussion of various approaches to these topics by other authors, and to introduce conceptional and practical solutions developed by the author and his team.

> *Workflow Management (WFM)* describes the analysis, modeling, use, control, and optimization of computer-based support for – predefined or ad-hoc – goal-driven information exchange and improvement processes between multiple agents in office work, including all required communication.
>
> *Workflow Management Systems (WFMSs)* are able to coordinate the participants in serial or parallel working order, route information to the next agents according to predefined rules or flexible interactive control, provide all information required, control timely completion of tasks, and monitor the current status of workflows.
>
> In addition, *Wide Area Workflow Management (WAWM)* aims at the planning and execution of workflows that exchange workflow-related information with other workflows controlled by distinct workflow management systems at least once during run-time phase. WAWM thus connects two or more workflow parts to an overall process, which is called *intra*organizational if all involved WFMSs are controlled by one legal entity and *inter*organizational if the WFMSs are controlled by several, legally distinct entities. Although other technical measures are feasible, the WFMSs involved are mostly connected by wide area network technology including mobile telecommunication systems.
>
> In short:
> *Wide Area Workflow Management* deals with flexible planning and execution of office procedures in widely distributed environments, based on the interoperation of distinct workflow management systems in intra- and interorganizational scenarios.

3.4 Technological fundaments

In this section, selected technologies and their relevance to the topic of Wide Area Workflow Management are discussed.
It is not possible to give a detailed description here of all technologies that have influenced this work. Terms such as distributed computing, client/server architecture, local area network, wide area network, object orientation, relational databases and other terms are explained in literature (e.g. in [Hansen 1992], [Laudon/Laudon 1996]), and are thus regarded to be known.

3.4.1 EDI and EDIFACT

Electronic Data Interchange (EDI) refers to the automated, standardized exchange of structured data between computer systems of cooperating organizations, using common communication networks [Emmelhainz 1993]. EDI mainly uses standardized document types for business purposes, such as orders and invoices as data carriers. Other types of data, such as CAD drawings, technical descriptions or pictures can also be transferred via EDI as long as a standardized format is used enabling all participants to integrate such files seamlessly into their existing software systems [Picot/Neuburger/Niggl 1991].

There are several national standards for general purpose EDI (e.g. ANSI X.12 or TRADACOMS) as well as a number of industry-specific standards such as ODETTE (European automobile industry) or SWIFT (European banking sector).

Electronic Data Interchange for Administration, Commerce and Transport (EDIFACT) is a international standard for EDI that is independent of industrial sectors. It was passed by the United Nations in 1987 and standardized by the ISO. EDIFACT comprises more than 25 standardized document types for trade, transport, customs, and banking. Document types used in trading are, for example, price lists, requests for quotations, quotations, orders, order confirmations, and invoices. There is a distinction between UNSMs (United Nations Standard Message) which are standardized internationally, so-called *subsets* containing a part of UNSMs, and industry-specific *adaptations* of UNSMs.

EDIFACT document types (also called "messages") are based on the ASCII character set. They consist of standardized elements and a fixed syntax. An EDIFACT session starts by establishing a connection between the systems involved. Then several data files can be transferred. Each data file has a header segment that for example defines a delimiter for the data that follow, and is terminated by an end segment. The actual data may consist of groups of concatenated messages and is identified by a second type of header and end segment. Each separate message is again delimited by a third type of header and end segments and consists of actual data segments containing data such as values, names, addresses, etc. Service segments transfer data such as sender, date/time or priority. A segment tag consisting of 3 capital letters (e.g. DTM for the date segment) identifies each data or service segment. This allows for the dropping of segments that are not used and the repeating of other segments, e.g. for a list different goods in an order. The basic components of

EDIFACT messages are data elements such as order number, amount, price etc. that are separated by a delimiter.

The EDIFACT standard is very detailed and, therefore, requires voluminous instructions for use. Specific software was developed to support the exchange of EDIFACT messages (so-called EDIFACT converters) and to translate data from business software systems to EDIFACT messages and vice versa.

Like many extensive, detailed standards, EDIFACT is inflexible. It is difficult and time-consuming to adapt it to new needs and the adaptation of the respective software systems is costly.

In the beginning, many authors predicted that EDI technology would deliver enormous cost savings and significant competitive advantages by eliminating most, if not all, paperwork and accelerating document transfer. This highly optimistic forecast was not borne out – as analysis of initial EDI implementations has revealed. Wallace conducted a survey of EDI benefits and found that 95% of the respondents could not cite any advantages or benefits of EDI [Wallace 1988]. Reekers and Smithson carried out an empirical study of EDI use in the European car industry. They found that although manufacturers judged EDI effects positive, they were not able to quantify the return on investment. Suppliers frequently complained that additional costs incurred by EDI implementation were not compensated for by additional turnover. They also claimed that EDI had adversely affected the ordering process: "However, since the introduction of EDI, suppliers have noted significant variances of up to +/-15 per cent between initial orders and actual quantities delivered. In many cases EDI data insufficiently reflects reality. Typical problems reported by interviewees are: lack of manufacturer's input control, double ordering, use of similar older parts or lost products. Instead of trying to make a few exact forecasts, manufacturers simply make frequent changes without considering the confusion these changes might cause for their suppliers" [Reekers/Smithson 1994, p. 9]. Eistert concludes from case studies in Germany and Spain that EDI reality has significantly fallen behind expectations [Eistert 1996]. Benjamin, de Long and Scott Morton studied eight EDI implementations and reported that "gaining competitive advantage from EDI applications is much more difficult than it might appear. ... The desire for strategic advantage remains the most commonly espoused reason for implementing EDI systems. But of eight different applications only one system ... showed the potential of providing significant competitive advantage by gaining first-mover benefits. ... One of the most striking aspects of the eight different systems in our sample was how little change they had created in the supplier's organization. ... Along with the few staff reduction, there was very little change in the tasks performed by those using the system" [Benjamin/DeLong/Scott Morton 1990, pp. 35, 36].

A main reason for EDI's failure to meet expectations is seen in the fact that the mere electronic transfer of documents does not affect the overall process. Clark and Stoddard conclude that only interorganizational BPR can achieve considerable gains in efficiency for the participating companies [Clark/Stoddard 1996]. Brousseau states that EDI would only be successful if business processes were standardized along with EDI, and "the payoff of EDI is not due to EDI itself, but rather to the implementation of new coordinating techniques" [Brousseau 1994, p. 333].

Recent publications raise the possibility of using the Internet and World Wide Web as technological bases of EDI [Karszt 1996], [Tuunainen/Saarinen 1997], [Lindemann/Klein 1997]. If the remaining technological problems and security concerns can be addressed [Ottomeier 1996], Internet- and Web-EDI can offer access to the world of EDI to smaller companies as well because of lower initial costs. However, the problem remains that a mere electronic data transfer itself will not lead to a marked improvement of efficiency, unless the underlying processes are reconceptualized.

With regard to devising concepts and solutions for Wide Area Workflow Management, the following conclusions can be drawn from the experience with EDI implementations:

- Standardization of message types is beneficial for frequently used document categories. It is helpful if these standards are extensible, allowing for supplementation on an individual basis.
- Flexible mechanisms are required which allow for an expeditious definition of those individual document structures that are not covered by standards. Software systems designs must be able to handle both standardized and individual messages.
- Systems have to explicitly provide flexibility, not only for document structures but also for selection and change of partner organizations. Consequently, the costs of any changes should be kept to a minimum. If systems are inflexible and expensive, they can easily be abused as instruments of power because transition costs are too high.
- Overall processes must be taken into consideration. In WAWM, the electronic transfer of *information* (not only *data*) between WFMSs should not be more than one step within a *wide area workflow*.
- EDI is a point-to-point technology. WAWM has to route information carriers flexibly between various partners. Therefore, routing schemes have to be made explicit, e.g. by using modeling tools. Routing schemes should be stored separately from actual workflow information.
- Electronic documents should have an embedded representation (as found in HTML, for example) which can be viewed with standard tools. This allows senders to determine the appearance of their messages and recipients to check documents individually.

In an article on workflow interoperability, Adams and Dworkin point out differences between EDI and WAWM. Regarding the information necessary for interoperation of WFMSs, they state: "Different systems must therefore exchange messages concerning the detailed content of the process, and this detailed content will be different for each domain from car parts to college courses. Therefore, they have to share common vocabularies in each specific domain. We see this problem in EDI (Electronic Data Interchange), where committees have worked out elaborate standards covering the meaning of each piece of each exchange document. Even so, these standards must work out another elaborate, ad hoc agreement to cover the processing of the document ("Company A will cancel the order if it does not get a response to document 123 from Company B within 10 business days"). A shared workflow would automate this processing, rather than rely on written agreements. But a shared workflow requires a shared domain-specific vocabulary to describe the process details" [Adams/Dworkin 1997, p. 214].

3.4.2 Internet and World Wide Web

The *Internet* and *World Wide Web (WWW)* are important platforms for the enabling of Wide Area Workflow Management because they are based on open standards and are available worldwide. The technologies underlying the Internet and WWW are explained in literature (e.g. [Scheller et al. 1994]) or in the WWW itself (for example http://www.w3.org). Some technological aspects are of special interest when it comes to the enabling of *wide area workflows* with the help of the Internet and WWW and therefore will be discussed in the following paragraphs.

The Internet can be used to transfer electronic mail. Standards often used are *Simple Mail Transfer Protocol (SMTP)* or *X.400*. Both are based on the ASCII character set and have a limited number of fields for sender, recipient, date, message text (so-called "body" field) etc. The *Multipurpose Internet Mail Extension (MIME)* standard extends Internet e-mail with country specific character sets and the ability to transfer more than mere textual data (e.g. attached files).

The "body"-field of an Internet e-mail can be used to store workflow data. This kind of data is mostly field-based (e.g. text, number, date fields etc.). Structuring of data in the body field therefore requires a syntax for field-based elements similar to EDIFACT. The *Workflow Management Coalition* (WfMC) has defined such a syntax [WfMC MIME 1996] that will be discussed in Section 4.2.1.2 (p. 78).

A basic problem with transferring workflow information this way is that it cannot be properly read by the recipient before it is decoded. Additionally, the sender cannot influence the appearance of the message. WAWM not only covers automated procedures such as EDIFACT, but must also allow for human interaction in all stages of a workflow. If WAWM wants to replace the manifold structures of letters or brochures, it needs information carriers with embedded representation.

With the spreading of WWW browsers, HTML-Mail has become popular. It allows users to format e-mails and thus the sender can influence the way the recipient will see the message. This is achieved by so-called *tags* that are set in the text of the body field. HTML-mail also needs additional structures to define field-based data in the body field of an e-mail.

What is necessary for WAWM is a message format based on the notion of *compound documents* [Malone et al. 1987]. This would allow for the transportation of highly structured field-based data as well as a presentation defined by the sender. Additionally, the inclusion of object technology for documents such as OLE or OpenDoc would enable users to send *contextual information* (e.g. spreadsheet calculation, drawings, speech annotations) that is becoming more and more important in business life. Proprietary groupware platforms such as Lotus Notes or Microsoft Exchange (see Section 3.4.4, p. 65) incorporate e-mail systems that fulfill these requirements. These e-mails can be sent via the Internet, but they are not based on open standards and need proprietary software to be received, read and processed.

The WWW has more characteristics of compound documents than Internet e-mail. The presentation of pages in the WWW is based on HTML (Hypertext Markup Language). HTML is a subset of SGML (Standard Generalized Markup Language) and is currently used in Version 3.2. Version 4.0 is being released by the W3C (World Wide Web Consortium) at the time of writing this book. Modern Web browsers use proprietary extensions to HTML for advanced layout features.

HTML consists of text with embedded *tags* for formatting and layout purposes as well as the inclusion of pictures etc. The FIELD tag allows HTML to present forms to the users with fields that can be filled out. Therefore HTML allows designers to define field-based structures for workflow information. The FIELD tag is limited to the definition of text fields. A severe problem with HTML with regard to the transfer of workflow information is that textual information, fields, and representation are not separated. It is not intended to divide HTML documents into form and content (or record), as it is known from databases. Hence, representation must always be transferred despite the fact that it would suffice to send the representation for a certain document type once and re-use it in order to make future messages smaller.

WWW pages can be made interactive by using CGI scripts. These scripts are processed on the server that provides the accompanying pages. Another possibility for embedding functionality in WWW pages is the use of the object-oriented programming language *Java*. It is processed on the client computer. Java was developed by Sun Microsystems and was accepted for standardization by the ISO [Reiter 1997b]. In the context of WAWM, Java can, for example, support the design of WWW pages that allow for the remote participation of users in workflows with all features of proprietary WFMSs front-ends. It is not generally accepted that Java code should also be embedded in messages that are sent from one WFMS to another because of security concerns.

A basic approach of workflow management is that workflow information is *pushed* from one actor to the next. The technology of the WWW is, in contrast, *pull*-oriented. It is impossible to send (or push) a WWW page to a specific recipient. The so-called push-technology of WWW browsers is really only a predefined pulling of pages. The only way to make someone aware of a WWW page is to send an e-mail containing the URL-address of the page. This is sometimes called push-pull approach, but does not guarantee that the recipient really reads the page.

Workflow information is mostly confidential and must be protected from unauthorized access during transfer via the Internet. Different security mechanisms, such as *Secure Socket Layer (SSL)*, can be used to encrypt information with safe methods like *public key encryption*. Nevertheless, many companies are concerned about security problems and therefore refrain from a mission-critical use of the Internet.

A promising new standard for the WWW is the *Extensible Markup Language (XML)* [Light 1997], [WWWJ 1997], [http://www.w3.org/XML/]. It is derived from SGML and can be used to transfer structured data that for example stems from a relational database. XML is not completely defined, but can be extended by own definitions. It is divided into sections for *content*, *layout* and *structure* that are clearly separated. Therefore, it is ideal for transferring workflow information. A content section can contain different field types such as text, date, number, picture, etc. The structure of a XML document is described in the so-called *document type definition (DTD)*. Various DTDs will have to be developed, for different industrial sectors or educational purposes for example. XML is more complicated to handle than HTML. Additionally, the processing of XML pages needs significantly more processor power than is necessary for HTML pages. Thus, it is likely that HTML will dominate representation-oriented WWW pages for a certain period of time. Nevertheless, the W3C has announced that HTML 4.0 is the last release of this language [Reiter 1997a]. For business applications with a strong need for structuring of data, it is expected that XML will be the future standard.

The processing of an XML document can be done by a client as well as a server. In the latter case, only the results are transferred to the client. XML can be combined with Java to build truly platform-independent business solutions. One possible application could be WAWM-enabled workflow management systems.

3.4.3 Object management standards

An important characteristic of large computer networks such as the Internet, WWW and also large corporate networks is that they are heterogeneous in regard to computer systems, network protocols and software applications. Hence, workflow management systems and particularly wide area workflow-oriented systems must adapt to a great variety of standards.

To facilitate the development of (object-oriented) software applications that can interact in heterogeneous environments and across networks, object management standards have been invented. An important milestone in these efforts was the foundation of the *Object Management Group (OMG)* in 1989 whose task it is to develop, adopt and promote standards for the development and deployment of applications in distributed heterogeneous environments. Since that time, the OMG has grown to become the world's largest software consortium with over 700 developers, vendors and end users in its membership roster. These members contribute technology and ideas in response to *Requests for Proposal* issued by the OMG [Vinoski 1997], [http://www.omg.org]. The OMG has had the status of an ISO PAS-submitter since 1997. Thus OMG proposals can be standardized within a short period of time [CZ 1997a].

The OMG has developed the *Object Management Architecture (OMA)* that defines *Object Services*, *Common Facilities*, *Domain Interfaces* and *Application Interfaces* that are connected by an *Object Request Broker (ORB)*. An ORB can be described as a *software bus* connecting objects between different software applications. The platform-independent ORB standard defined by the OMG is called *Common Object Request Broker Architecture (CORBA)* and has been available in Version 2.0 since 1995. An ORB delivers requests from client programs to objects handled by server programs and returns any responses to the clients making the requests. An essential feature of an ORB is the transparency of communication between client and target object. The client does not have to know where an object is located, in what language it is implemented, in which state the object currently is or what communication mechanism is used to deliver requests and return responses. This is achieved by defining an implementation-independent object interface with a standardized *Interface Definition Language (IDL)* and identifying an object with a unique *Object-ID*. Both the ID and the interface of an object are made available to potential clients via repositories.

The communication of clients and objects is basically bi-directional and synchronous. The client program issues a request to an object and waits for the return of a response with the desired answer or an error report. Other possibilities are *one-way-requests* that do not wait for a response, and *deferred-synchronous-requests* that allow client programs to proceed and include responses later. These mechanisms can for example be used for the communication between workflow parts (see Section 5.3, p. 117).

Common Facilities are oriented towards end-user applications. An example of such a facility is the *Distributed Document Component Facility (DDCF)*, a compound document *Common Facility* based on *OpenDoc*. With the help of DDCF, compound documents for workflow purposes can be defined within the OMA architecture.

Since the invention of the CORBA standard, several companies have developed CORBA-compliant ORBs. To enable the interaction of different ORBs, two protocols are defined in CORBA 2.0: *General Inter-ORB Protocol (GIOP)* and *Internet Inter-ORB Protocol (IIOP)*. The latter is TCP/IP-based and allows the use of the Internet or corporate Intranets to connect multiple WFMSs [Schwarz 1997].

The OMG has announced its intention to develop a standard set of interfaces and a specialized semantic that enables WFMSs to exchange objects and meta data for the purpose of Wide Area Workflow Management [CZ 1997b]. Several research groups have already built WFMSs on the basis of CORBA (see Section 4.2.4).

Another object management standard is the *Distributed System Object Model (DSOM)* by IBM that, for example, uses the OpenDoc standard for compound documents. DSOM is an extension of CORBA.

Microsoft has developed the *Distributed Component Object Model (DCOM)* that (among other things) builds the basis for the compound document technology of *Object Linking and Embedding (OLE)*. OLE has been further developed to become ActiveX and recently Win-DNA [Reiter 1997c]. DCOM is not CORBA-compliant, but interface products linking both have been announced or already made available.

Despite the enormous efforts to develop object management standards, analysts remark that none of the available standards is yet robust enough to be used for large-scale, mission-critical software applications. The writing of applications based on the different standards is described as very complicated [Ottomeier 1997].

In the context of this book, object management standards form a promising technical solution for the exchange of information between distributed and widely distributed WFMSs. In the level model of Figure 10 (p. 56), object management standards are located in the *technical level*.

3.4.4 Groupware platforms

The term *groupware* has already been described in Section 3.2.1 (p. 26). In this section, some characteristics of commercial groupware platforms will be discussed. In addition, the groupware product Lotus Notes will be explained in further detail since it serves as the development platform for the prototypic Wide Area GroupFlow System (WAGS) that will be introduced in Chapter 6.

Examples of widely known commercial groupware platforms are Microsoft Exchange, Novell GroupWise, DEC LinkWorks, Netscape SuiteSpot or Lotus Notes. By the year 2000, it is expected that more than 70 million people will work with commercial groupware systems, not including Internet and Intranet use [Peters 1997]. Many articles have been written with the purpose of comparing available groupware products (for example [Lyons 1996], [Roberts 1996], [Willis 1997], [Hayes/MacLeish 1997]).

It is not intended to conduct a further comparative study here, but to look at common characteristics of commercial groupware products in general. Hereby, the ability to provide basic support for WAWM is of special interest.

3.4.4.1 General characteristics

Groupware platforms aim to help people working together in teams using computers. In literature, there are many descriptions of the possible components of groupware platforms [Johansen 1991], [Nastansky 1993], [Joosten/ Ploeger/Brinkkemper 1995], [Khoshafian/ Buckiewicz 1995]. The following main elements are found in many of the commercial products, although not every product contains all of the characteristics mentioned:

- Groupware platforms use *compound documents* as information containers. These types of electronic documents integrate field-based data, formatted text and embedded multimedia objects such as graphics, videos or speech annotations.
- Compound documents are stored in *shared document databases* that are available to multiple users (so-called *Share Model*). List views sorted by various, user-definable categories are used to navigate through databases. To prevent "information overflow", filters can be defined for these list views. Users themselves are responsible for *pulling* documents from databases.
- Powerful retrieval functions such as field search or full text search facilitate the handling of large document databases.
- Context-oriented navigation between compound documents is enabled by user-definable *hyperlink structures.*
- *Integrated messaging* allows users to *push* compound documents to other users or shared databases via e-mail (so-called *Send Model*). The complete structure of the compound document is preserved during transfer.
- Shared databases can be distributed and synchronized with the help of *replication technology.* So-called "optimistic algorithms" save all versions in case of conflicting changes. Replicas can contain only defined fractions of the original database which is achieved by filters for *selective replication.*
- *User registration and authentication* provides basic information on participants and is needed for security mechanisms.

- Powerful and reliable *security mechanisms* allow administrators to define different access rights (such as reader, editor, designer or manager) for servers, databases and documents.
- Reliable *encryption methods* (e.g. public key encryption) prevent information from unauthorized access; *digital signatures* are used for proof of authenticity.
- *Mobile offline and online work* is supported by different mechanisms including messaging, replication and support for remote dial-in.
- *Integration of standard office applications* such as wordprocessors, spreadsheets or presentation graphics into compound documents by mechanisms such as attachments, im-/export, object embedding or in-place object activation.
- Support for *joined writing* of documents and *document versioning* allow teams to synchronously and asynchronously edit shared documents.
- Inclusion of *desktop video-conferencing* for synchronous, real-time communication allows for direct communication among group members.
- *Calendar tools* with group scheduling features facilitate the planning of activities between several participants.
- *Basic support for workflow management*, for example by defining next editors for a document in a shared database or preparing e-mails with a list of consecutive recipients.
- *Integrated development environment* aimed at rapid design of GUI-based applications.
- *Cross-platform availability* bridging heterogeneous hardware, operating systems and network protocols including the use of wide area networks.
- *Integration with Internet and WWW standards* for sending and receiving e-mails via the Internet or publication of documents on the WWW.

With the help of these different elements, groupware platforms allow for new forms of cooperation among office workers [Orlikowski 1992], [Orlikowski 1995]. Team collaboration supported by groupware can take place in a group of workers that is controlled centrally as well as in widely distributed, completely decentralized groups. By the use of shared document databases and integrated messaging, globally dispersed intra- and interorganizational teams can work on *common objects* [Malone/Crowston 1990] or *shared material* [Schwarzer/Zerbe/Krcmar 1997] in a transparent way at any time. An example of new forms of cooperation enabled by groupware are so-called 24-hour-teams where 3 or more teams at three different places around the world can combine their eight hours working time to a full-time service around the clock by the use of commonly available material. Another example is that groupware allows services such as programming or desktop publishing to be outsourced to a partner who can reside in any place in the world.

More and more of the outstanding features of groupware platforms have been implemented in the WWW over the last few years. Therefore, the question arose as to whether so-called Intranets based on pure WWW technology would edge out groupware products. Groupware vendors reacted to this development by adopting the main parts of WWW technology, thereby blending the two technologies. Some authors even expect that groupware functionality will become so omnipresent in all kinds of software applications that it will disappear as a separate product category [Gagne 1997].

Many of the features of groupware listed above can build a basis for the development of workflow management systems. WFMSs can, for example, make use of document management features, user authentication, security mechanisms, integrated development environments and integration of standard applications. Additionally messaging, replication, Internet/WWW integration and cross-platform architecture are very well suited to supporting WAWM.

However the working paradigms inherent to groupware platforms and WFMSs differ from each other. Groupware supports open interaction in teams, whereas workflow management aims at the handling of (more or less) structured business processes. By synergistically combining them, WFMSs can become more flexible and groupware more structured [Nastansky/Hilpert 1994], [van Leuwen 1997].

Based on the awareness of this synergetic potential, several scientific and commercial WFMSs have been built on groupware platforms, some of which are Action Technologies ActionWorkflow, Pavone GroupFlow or Onestone ProZessware [Marshak 1993], [Marshak 1995], [Weber 1997a]. All of the above-mentioned WFMSs own a workflow run-time engine based on a groupware platform, and feature additional modeling and analysis tools as separate software applications.

3.4.4.2 Lotus Notes

Lotus Notes was one of the first commercial products called "groupware". At the time of writing this book, it has the largest share of the groupware market and has developed into a mainstream software. Small firms with regional markets as well as very large, global companies with installations of several tens of thousands of clients use Lotus Notes as a corporate information backbone [McCready et al. 1994], [Thompson/Chapman-Pincher 1994], [Turrell 1995]. Some of the early adopters were, for example, global consulting companies that have a special need for sharing information world wide in order to exploit existing organizational knowledge as quickly and efficiently as possible.

Lotus Notes owns almost all of the general characteristics of groupware platforms (see list above) and can be seen as one of the most complete (and therefore complex) products of its kind.

At the time of writing this book, Lotus Notes has reached Version 4.6 and is available for almost all relevant operating system platforms as server software (called Lotus Domino) and also as client software. It represents a true cross-platform environment since it builds a consistent groupware layer above operating systems. Lotus Notes and Lotus Domino cover all major network protocols and allow for the development of applications regardless of the specifics of different operating environments. The availability of Lotus Domino server software for different UNIX platforms, AS/400 and OS/390 allows companies to handle large scale, mission-critical installations of Lotus Notes [Weber 1997b].

The architecture of Lotus Notes is client/server-based. Servers are responsible for user registration and authentication, security mechanisms and communication with clients and other servers. They store shared document databases and allow clients to access these databases according to defined access rights (depositor, reader, author, editor, designer and manager).

Lotus Notes databases consist of compound documents that are formed by fields of different types (e.g. text, number, date, keywords, access control, etc.). Additionally, so-called *richtext fields* can contain:

- formatted text,
- hyperlinks,
- embedded objects like drawings, spreadsheets or presentation graphics,
- multimedia elements such as speech annotations or videos, and
- file attachments.

Therefore, documents in Lotus Notes are a symbiosis of field-oriented database structures ("records"), documents known from wordprocessors and multimedia containers. Internally, a document is made up of a so-called *note* holding the content and a *form* that defines the appearance of a document. *Notes* can be combined with different *forms* to display different fractions of the content. Documents are stored flat in the databases. By default, they have no relation to each other. Designers can implement relations between fields in different documents with the help of integrated programming languages using lookup and write-back operations.

Users can define hyperlinks between elements in documents, whole documents, views and databases to facilitate navigation and build context-oriented informational networks. Documents in Lotus Notes have a unique number for worldwide use (called DocumentUniqueID) to identify them which is for example used for hyperlinks. Hence, documents containing hyperlinks can be moved to other databases. Hyperlinks will continue to work as long as the referenced document is available somewhere in the network. Another feature of Lotus Notes documents is *versioning* which means that several versions of a document can be kept. This is very helpful, especially in office work, and is also used by modern wordprocessor software.

Documents are organized in list views (simply called *views*) that can display contents of document fields in tables with one row for each document. Default fields storing previous editors, dates of changes and other information can always be used for views categorized by "last editor", "last update" etc. *Views* can be used like tables in other database systems. They can be accessed for programming purposes by so-called *lookups* inside of Lotus Notes. If external applications need to get data from Lotus Notes databases, *views* can be accessed for example via ODBC drivers. Apart from this, there are various other possibilities for connecting Lotus Notes databases with relational databases, e.g. through im-/export filters, so-called datalense drivers or third party software. In the context of workflow management, views are very helpful for any kind of navigation, programming and legacy system connectivity.

Various search mechanisms facilitate document retrieval within Lotus Notes. Especially helpful is multi-database *fulltext search* which includes all fields and embedded objects (such as OLE-embedded wordprocessor documents) and thereby allows users to browse efficiently in very large document archives.

The messaging architecture of Lotus Notes is set up to send all kinds of documents to and from every database in form of e-mails. Sending documents as e-mails does not affect their structure or content, apart from some e-mail related fields which are added. The users' mail files are also databases that can therefore receive any kind of Lotus Notes documents as well as e-mails in many other relevant formats. The ability of Lotus Notes to send electronic mail containing any kind of highly structured, field-based information can very well be used to connect different workflow management systems based on Lotus Notes.

A very powerful feature of Lotus Notes is *replication* between databases. With the help of replication, full or partial copies of databases (called *replicas* that are identified by a unique *replicaID*) can be placed on different servers, and also client computers. Changes in the respective replicas are synchronized on an individual or regular basis [Kawell et al. 1992]. Partial copies can be generated with the help of filter formulas for *selective replication*. Since Notes 4.0, *field-level replication* improves replication efficiency by only transferring changed fields instead of entire documents. An optimistic conflict algorithm allows Lotus Notes to keep different, concurrent changes to documents in different replicas until conflicts have been resolved by user interaction. As long as changes in the same document, placed in different replicas of a database, apply to different fields, field-based replication can merge the different changes without user interaction. Replication is a very powerful means of building systems for Wide Area Workflow Management. It allows companies to (selectively) distribute information needed by different, widely distributed WFMSs in a simple and efficient way.

Seen from a technical point of view, there is no difference in Lotus Notes between moving a document from one database to another by e-mail or via replication. If a document with the same DocumentUniqueID already exists in the target database, conflict handling is activated as described above.

Replication also allows Lotus Notes clients to store (partial) replicas locally. Together with messaging and remote dial-in, this allows for a flexible support of mobile offline and online work. Different location setups facilitate switching between appropriate settings for different environments.

Databases not only contain documents, but can also be used to develop complex applications independent of the specifics of underlying operating systems. Lotus Notes offers different possibilities for customizing databases derived from templates, or for developing databases from scratch. *Forms* and *views* are designed with a GUI-based development environment. Programs embedded in the databases (also called *agents*) can be realized with so-called *simple functions* (for end-users), a *formula* language (for advanced users), an object-oriented programming language called *Lotus Script* (for developers) or with *Java*. User-oriented *agents* can be activated via buttons in documents, view headers or via menus. *Agents* also allow developers to prepare automated tasks as background programs on servers.

Databases can inherit all or parts of their design elements from so-called *templates*. Design elements can be changed centrally in the template and subsequently all derived databases can be upgraded manually or automatically. With the help of this feature, organizations can maintain and upgrade Lotus Notes applications worldwide from a central location.

The security mechanisms of Lotus Notes are very sophisticated and powerful. Reliable user authentication, various possibilities for limiting access to servers, databases, views, documents and fields with different rights, public key encryption (RSA) and digital signatures make Lotus Notes a well-suited platform for mission-critical, highly confidential information.

Realtime Notes is an add-on to Lotus Notes that allows for desktop video conferencing and joint editing of documents.

Lotus Notes is well integrated with Internet and WWW standards. Users can browse WWW pages with the Lotus Notes client software, send and receive e-mail via the Internet and easily publish databases and, therefore, documents on the WWW. Published databases preserve their hyperlink structure and can be fulltext searched from a WWW browser. The programming environment of Lotus Notes allows developers to generate interactive applications including the use of *Java*. These applications can be accessed simultaneously with a Lotus Notes client and a WWW browser. WFMSs based on Lotus Notes can thus be easily upgraded to be used via the WWW as a first step towards Wide Area Workflow Management.

For the upcoming Version 5.0, Lotus has announced a further integration with Internet and WWW technology. The implementation of the CORBA-compliant *Internet Inter-ORB Protocol (IIOP)* is of special interest in the context of this book. It will allow for a standardized exchange of objects with other applications using the Internet.

Further explanations about the architecture of Lotus Notes are found for example in [Calabria/Plumley 1997], [Dierker/Sander 1997], [Richards 1997].

Many conservative IT professionals considered the early versions of Lotus Notes to be a "toy" rather than a serious product because of its heavy reliance on PCs and client/server architecture. Lotus Notes also does not make use of relational database technology but has its own kind of distributed document-oriented databases. This architecture is different from relational databases and therefore was often considered to be "non-professional" and "chaotic", not deserving the right to be called a real database.

A main characteristic of Lotus Notes' database architecture is the fact that each single document is complete in itself. This causes enormous redundancy, but allows each document to have an individual set of fields. Changing the design of a database does not automatically mean the addition or deletion of fields from existing documents, as would be the case in relational databases. Only new documents will have the new structure. Existing documents can be upgraded to fit the new structure when needed. This may seem complicated on first sight, but allows documents of very different structure and content to exist in one database. An additional advantage is that each single document can be transferred to another database and will not lose its content and context. If a recipient is not expected to have an appropriate *form* to display the document, *forms* can be embedded into documents by the sender, rendering them completely self-contained. Hence, this architecture is very well suited to communication based on documents.

In contrast, the paradigm of relational databases is to avoid redundancy by all means. Therefore, forms or lists displayed on screen are usually a combination of fields from records of different tables connected to each other by relations. These relations are implemented with the help of unique keys. The content of a form, e.g. a letter, thus does not exist as a single entity but as a combination of records linked by keys. It cannot be easily moved to another relational database by replication or e-mail. The content of the letter could be collected and put in an e-mail to be sent to another relational database. This would only be reasonable if the receiving database had a similar structure that can handle letters. This e-mail would nevertheless have to be converted into a different set of fields to fit into the receiving database. Therefore, messaging between relational databases is quite complicated. This is also true for replication between relational databases, which is possible as long as the structures are identical. However, enormous problems, such as concerning conflict handling, arise. The existence of several states of the same data is basically forbidden in relational databases.

With the enormous growth of the Internet and WWW, many IT professionals became aware of the potential of semi-structured compound documents with hyperlink architecture. It became obvious that when it comes to information presentation and communication, classic paradigms such as safe database transactions and avoidance of redundancy are of minor importance. User-orientation through document design, ease-of-use, powerful search mechanisms and context-oriented navigation with hyperlinks are increasingly perceived to be important characteristics of information systems. It also became obvious that groupware platforms such as Lotus Notes have all these feature as well as reliable security mechanisms, replication technology, rapid application development and more to build powerful information backbones.

It was already mentioned that (an estimated) 10-20% of the overall information owned by organizations is of structured nature and therefore can be well handled by relational databases. A large part of the remaining 80-90% consists of less structured contextual information stored in documents [Pfeiffer 1996]. Groupware platforms are designed to manage these documents. The question is not *whether* relational databases or shared document database systems such as Lotus Notes should be used. Rather it is important to assign certain types of information to the appropriate database system and to exploit the *synergetic potential* of both worlds.

For example, many companies use SAP R/3, which is based on relational databases, and Lotus Notes in synergetic coexistence. Often SAP R/3 data is exported to Lotus Notes for use in sales departments and mobile sales forces. Results from sales activities are given back from Lotus Notes to SAP R/3.

The need for a coexistence of relational databases and shared databases storing compound documents can also be observed when designing flexible WFMSs. In particular systems for Wide Area Workflow Management must support structured, internal data as well as flexible, mobile information carriers based on compound documents. These information carriers, called *message objects* (see Section 5.6.2, p. 153), are supposed to replace things like orders, invoices, letters, faxes, brochure or catalogues which are used in today's world to transfer information between different organizations.

4 Workflow management related approaches under aspects of distribution

In this chapter, conceptual approaches for workflow management as well as existing scientific and commercial workflow management systems (WFMSs) will be introduced and discussed with respect to the topic of Wide Area Workflow Management.

Firstly, different classification schemes for the description and distinction of workflow management approaches are presented. Subsequently, conceptual approaches for workflow management and scientific WFMS prototypes are introduced. They were selected according to concrete features that support the interaction of widely distributed WFMSs or because they own certain characteristics that point towards Wide Area Workflow Management in other respects. Further on, selected commercial WFMSs with functionalities supporting cross-system interaction are examined. Due to limited space, only important characteristics and features of the respective scientific and commercial systems will be presented. Finally, the approaches, prototypes and products presented are discussed in respect to the different levels of Wide Area Workflow Management, as have been identified by the author.

4.1 Classification of workflow management systems

Various different interpretations and perceptions of the overall topic of workflow management led to the development of a large variety of systems with a wide scope of different functionalities. Therefore authors with scientific and commercial backgrounds have defined classification schemes in order to differentiate between the basic characteristics of different workflow management systems.

A general approach for describing different kinds of *workflow* categories based on structure and repetitiveness of the underlying business processes has already been introduced in Figure 9 (p. 52). In this section, characteristics of *workflow management systems* will be discussed.

An often-cited attempt to categorize WFMSs is described in Palermo/McCready [1992]:

- *Production workflow systems* with high transaction rates and customized applications (e.g. order management).
- *Administrative workflow systems* with lower transaction rates and form-based, recurrent processes. They replace manual systems and have a high level of user interaction.
- *Ad-hoc workflow systems* that are people centric and support ad-hoc and unplanned work.

This classification is based on different characteristics such as repetitiveness and predictability of tasks (see Figure 9, p. 52), how the workflow is initiated and controlled (e.g. human-controlled or automated) or the requirements for WFMS functionality. The Black Forest Group identifies similar categories of workflow systems but has defined three additional kinds of coordination based systems aside from ad-hoc workflow systems [Black Forest Group 1996].

Other authors distinguish between *workflow management* with a high degree of user interaction and *workflow automation*, which is mainly software-controlled [Joosten/Brinkkemper 1995]. Georgakopoulos et al. extend this notion with a scale ranging from *system-oriented WFMS* to *human-oriented WFMS* with different system approaches located in-between. They especially stress the role of *transaction-oriented systems* that are necessary to support production-oriented workflows with high volume. These are placed more on the system-oriented side whereas CSCW applications are located more on the side of human-oriented applications [Georgakopoulos/Hornick/Sheth 1995]. A similar categorization between *transaction-oriented* and *ad-hoc-oriented WFMSs* is described by Picot and Rohrbach [Picot/Rohrbach 1995].

An interesting approach to classifying WFMSs and an overview on existing classification schemes is presented by Weiss and Krcmar [1996]. According to this article different "characters" of WFMSs with increasing capabilities can be distinguished:

- *Traffic policemen* only control the routing of workflow objects.
- *Helmsmen* control the flow of documents and activities according to rules. They allow for exceptions and they report on steps that have been processed.
- *Assistants* support an organization's management in the analysis of business processes and allow for modeling and simulation of workflow models. Additionally they have all features of *helmsmen* and *traffic policemen*.

Schwab analyses coordination mechanisms and meta models that underlie workflow management products. He discriminates between *process-oriented* systems, *object migration* systems (focussing on the consecutive change of workflow objects), *conversation oriented* systems (e.g. based on speech act theory) and *information sharing* systems (following the groupware paradigm) [Schwab 1996].

Stark focuses on technical aspects and thereby identifies systems which support *form-based workflow* on the basis of messaging, *engine-based workflow* that is driven by a routing engine on top of databases and *embedded workflow* that is part of e.g. business software systems [Stark 1997]. Often the platforms on which WFMSs were developed are used as a criteria for classification [Erdl/ Schoenecker 1993]. These are, for example, business software systems, document management systems, imaging systems, e-mail systems and groupware platforms. Workflow systems that have been designed from scratch are sometimes called "genuine" WFMSs.

A very detailed classification scheme for workflow management systems is proposed by Schulze and Boehm [1996]. According to this model, the basis of all workflow-related efforts can be seen in the attempt to support business processes by *office automation*. Tools for office automation are further divided into *document-oriented* and *process-oriented* systems; the distinction between the two is based on major characteristics neglecting details that may fall into both categories. Process-oriented systems are divided into groupware, process-oriented office systems, "hard-wired" applications (where processes are built into programs) and workflow management systems that are further classified as:

- control & transport oriented systems,
- integrated WFMSs and
- flexible development systems.

The author has listed this variety of classification approaches in order to demonstrate the many different concepts and perceptions concerning workflow management.

Some tendencies can be found in all of the classification schemes mentioned. A first dimension can be seen in the distinction between *automation & structure* on the one hand and *user support & flexibility* on the other hand.

Looking at the above-mentioned terms, *automation & structure*-oriented systems are comprised of *production workflow systems* [Palermo/McCready 1992], *system-oriented WFMSs* [Georgakopoulos/Hornick/Sheth 1995], *transaction-oriented systems* [Picot/Rohrbach 1995] and *control & transport oriented WFMSs* [Schulze/ Boehm 1996].

Ad-hoc workflow systems [Palermo/McCready 1992; Picot/Rohrbach 1995], *human-oriented WFMSs* [Georgakopoulos/Hornick/Sheth 1995], *information sharing systems* [Schwab 1996] and *flexible development systems* [Schulze/Boehm 1996] belong to the group of *user support & flexibility* oriented workflow systems. Other categories like *administrative workflow systems* [Palermo/McCready 1992] can be located between *automation & structure* and *user support & flexibility*.

Another dimension is the technological basis on which WFMSs are built. Here a fundamental distinction can be made between systems based on relational or object-oriented databases with transaction concepts on the one hand. This group will be called *database & transaction* oriented systems. On the other hand, there are systems that focus on documents, forms and messages. They will be gathered in a group labeled *document & communication* oriented systems. The author is aware of the fact that documents can also be handled by databases. Here the "traditional" notion of databases with tables and data records is meant.

A third dimension for a classification of workflow management systems is derived from the generation model in Figure 11 (p. 57). It was chosen to describe systems according to their ability to support Wide Area Workflow Management.

Figure 12 illustrates these three dimensions of classification.

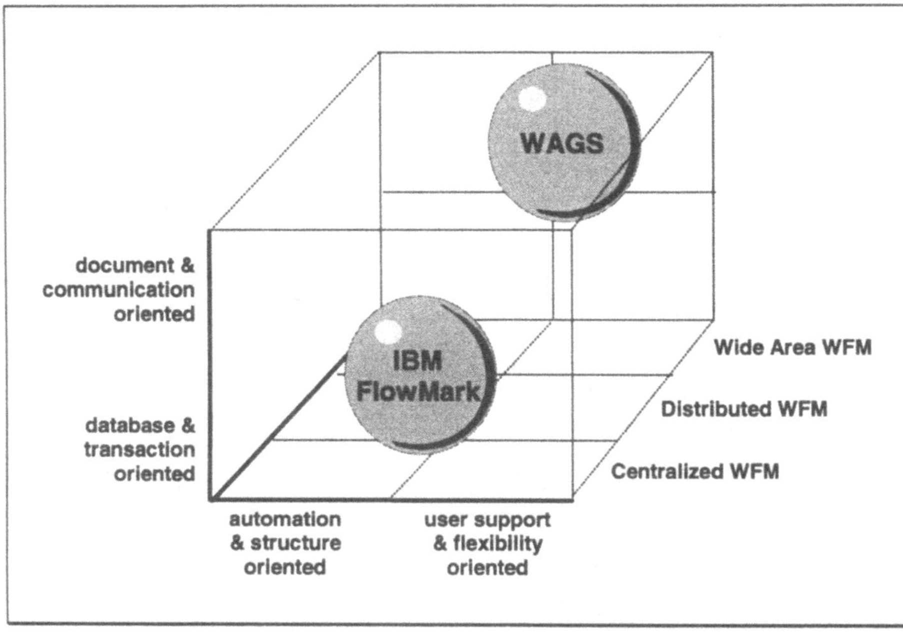

Figure 12: Classification scheme for workflow management systems with two examples

Two WFMSs have been placed into Figure 12 as examples. The form of round clouds is used to illustrate that classification into these qualitative categories cannot be exact. IBM FlowMark [Leymann/Altenhuber 1994], [Leymann 1995], [Roller 1996] is a *database & transaction*-oriented system that allows the handling and also automation of well-structured workflows. A certain flexibility is achieved for example through exceptions [Leymann 1996], [Leymann 1997]. Therefore, IBM FlowMark is located between *automation & structure* and *user support & flexibility.* It allows for the spreading of workflow instances across several servers and thus supports distributed run-time operation. IBM FlowMark focuses on intraorganizational workflows and has a centralized architecture for modeling and control of workflows. Hence, it belongs to the group of systems that support *distributed WFM*. Another example is the *Wide Area GroupFlow System (WAGS)* that will be introduced in Chapter 6. It is located in the category of *document & communication* orientation and between the categories of *automation & structure* and *user support & flexibility.* *WAGS* supports *WAWM* on all levels.

Workflow management systems discussed in the following will be classified according to Figure 12 where possible. The following scheme will be used:

Classification of "*System X*":

1. *database & transaction - document & communication,*
2. *automation & structure - user support & flexibility,*
3. *distributed WFM - WAWM (... on what levels of* Figure 10, *p.56).*

Only major characteristics of the respective systems will be used for classification, thereby simplifying the complexity of the systems to a certain extent.

4.2 Conceptual approaches

4.2.1 Reference Model of the Workflow Management Coalition

The *Workflow Management Coalition (WfMC)* is a non-profit, international organization of workflow vendors, users and analysts. It was founded in August 1993 and now has over 100 members [http://www.aiim.org/wfmc/].

The WfMC wants to promote the use of workflow through the establishment of standards for software terminology, interoperability and connectivity between workflow products. It is divided into two major committees, the Technical Committee and the Steering Committee. Small working groups exist within each committee for the purpose of defining workflow terminology, interoperability and connectivity standards.

To describe different elements of workflow management systems and the interfaces between them, the WfMC has defined the so-called *Reference Model.*

4.2.1.1 Basic concept of the WfMC Reference Model

The aim of the *WfMC Reference Model* is to promote a standardized interaction of different components of WFMSs. The focus is particularly on the integration of components from different workflow products [WfMC Ref. Mod. 1994].
The *Reference Model* has been largely discussed in literature (for example [Jablonski 1997], [Kobielus 1997]) and therefore will only be briefly introduced. It identifies a *workflow enactment service* as a central element of WFMSs. The enactment service creates, manages and executes workflow instances with the help of one or several *workflow engines*. It is connected to other components via five interfaces that are described in the so-called WAPI (Workflow Application Programming Interface).

Interface 1 connects the enactment service with process definition tools that prepare and provide process specifications for the execution of workflow instances [WfMC IF1 1995]. Connections to workflow client applications responsible for interaction with users are defined in Interface 2. External applications (e.g. for document handling) are invoked via Interface 3. Administration and monitoring tools exchange data with an enactment service via Interface 5.

Interface 4 is of special interest for WAWM because it specifies techniques for interoperability between different enactment services. Therefore it is surrounded by a dotted line in Figure 13 and will be discussed in further detail here.

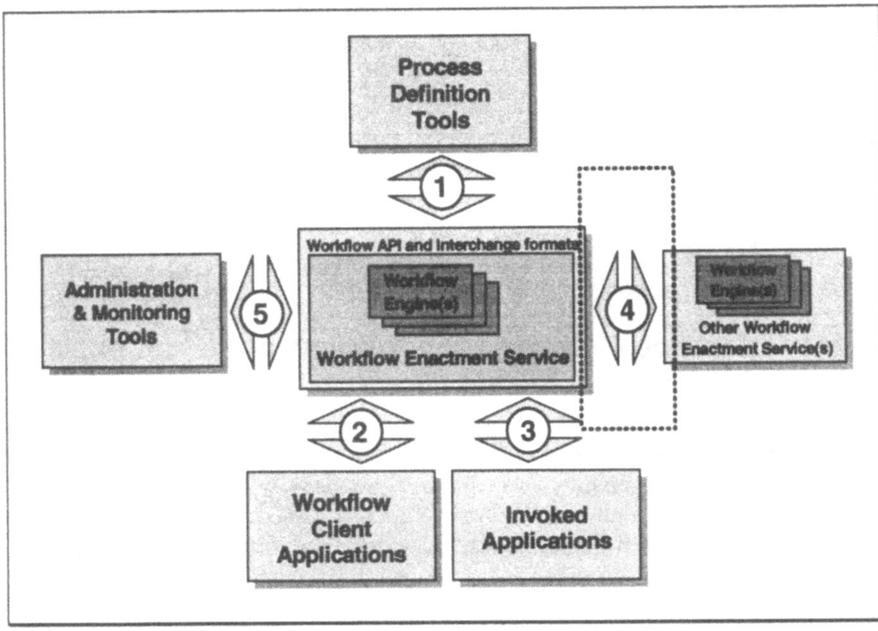

Figure 13: Reference Model of the Workflow Management Coalition (based on [WfMC Ref. Mod. 1994], reproduced with permission)

4.2.1.2 Interface 4: interoperability between workflow engines

"A key objective of the coalition is to define standards that will allow workflow systems produced by different vendors to pass work items seamlessly between one another" [WfMC Ref. Mod. 1994]. In order to achieve this connection of WFMS the WfMC has released an Interoperability Abstract Specification [WfMC IF4 Abstr. 1996] describing further details of Interface 4. According to this specification, workflow interoperability means "... the ability of two or more workflow engines to communicate and interoperate in order to coordinate and execute workflow process instances across those engines". The workflow engines concerned can belong to a single or different enactment services.

The WfMC very loosely describes that interoperating workflow engines and enactment services need some organizational context in the form of business agreements. A distinction is made between *closed workflow domains* where all workflow engines are trusted and *open workflow domains* where an identification is necessary. No further details are provided on this topic.

Interoperability can be realized by different technical measures [WfMC IF4 Abstr. 1996]:

- *Direct interaction* of WFMSs.
- *Message passing* between WFMSs.
- *Bridging* of systems, for example using *gateways* to connect different protocols and formats.
- Use of *shared data stores*, realized for example by commonly accessible repositories. This possibility is not further addressed by the WfMC.

Different levels of interoperability are defined in the Interface 4 specifications with an increasing proximity of workflow systems. The description starts with *no interoperability* (level 1) and *coexistence* (level 2) where interoperability is handled individually. *Unique gateways* (level 3) route operations between engines and translate workflow and application data. *Common gateway APIs* (level 3a) simplify the interaction of *gateways* by a normalized set of instructions. *Limited common API subsets* (level 4) allow for a direct interaction of workflow engines based on a shared API. In case of a *complete workflow API* (level 5), all operations of a WFMS can be directly accessed by another system. Using *shared definition formats* (level 6), different workflow systems can execute instances based on the same process definitions. The WfMC has proposed a vendor-independent *workflow process definition language (WPDL)* for this purpose. *Protocol compatibility* (level 7) allows workflow systems to exchange process definitions, workflow and control data seamlessly. Finally, a standardization of user interfaces is achieved with *common look and feel utilities* (level 8).

A discussion about which cooperative settings would be best supported by which "level" is not yet included. Furthermore, there is no explanation or comparison of the advantages and disadvantages of the different levels.

For the connection of workflows between different WFMS, four interoperability models are defined by the WfMC:

- *Chained process*: A process instance in one workflow engine triggers the creation and enactment of a sub-process instance in another workflow engine. No data is transferred back to the initiating process instance.
- *Nested subprocess*: In this model a process instance in one workflow engine invokes a sub-process instance in a second workflow engine and then waits for its termination before carrying on with its own enactment.
- *Parallel synchronized*: Two workflow engines simultaneously enact process instances and at some point in each instance a rendezvous with mutual data interchange is performed. This model is not further defined by the WfMC yet.
- *Peer-to peer:* This model allows a fully mixed environment where two or more workflow engines execute different steps of a commonly controlled process instance. This model was mentioned in the *Reference Model* but has been dropped in [WfMC IF4 Abstr. 1996].

Thus, only the *chained process* and *nested subprocess* models are covered by the WfMC at the time of writing this book. These models are well known from programming techniques or object management standards (see Section 3.4.3, p. 64). The author has adopted the idea of process interoperability models and will discuss his findings in Section 5.3 (p. 117).

In order to execute process instances and invoke sub-process instances, workflow engines need access to process definitions. According to the WfMC this can be achieved through passing on process definitions between engines or through common access to shared repositories storing these definitions.

The WfMC further defines how two or more workflow engines can communicate with each other in order to select, instantiate and enact process instances based on known process definitions. For example, with the help of requests and responses the following actions are defined: *create process instance, set process instance attributes, get process instance attributes, start process enactment, get process instance state, list process instances, abort process instance*. Each of these actions is further described through an abstract specification of a syntax containing structure, parameters and values of calls between workflow engines. Practical solutions based on different techniques are realized with so-called "bindings" based on the abstract specification.

The WfMC has defined a binding for Internet e-mail based on the MIME standard [WfMC IF4 MIME 1996]. With the help of this specification, workflow data can be transferred in the body of Internet e-mail. Messages are identified as workflow carriers by a specific MIME header and thus can be recognized by applications. The body contains requests and responses using the encoding concepts of CGI (Common Gateway Interface).

Several demonstrations of commercial WFMSs, which were interoperating based on the MIME binding specification, were conducted during public events. More than 20 members of the WfMC are currently validating the Interface 4 specification (see [http://www.aiim.org/wfmc/faq.html]).

Discussion of the WfMC specification on WFMSs interoperability

Regarded to be in a preliminary state of development, the Interface 4 specification serves as "a basis for early experimentation by workflow product vendors to provide informed feedback, leading to the production of a ratified standard in the fullness of time" [WfMC IF4 Abstr. 1996].

Based on the level model for distributed and widely distributed workflow management (Figure 10, p. 56) the WfMC approach is located on the second level of run-time and control operations. Not covered by the WfMC specifications are:

- aspects of distributed and decentralized modeling of workflows,
- organizational and strategic implications of the techniques used.

In the WfMC Interface 4 specification, it is assumed that different workflow engines use a shared process definition or pass on process definitions to each other. In other words, invoking workflow engines obtain complete knowledge of the process definition of the sub-processes they call up. In scenarios of interorganizational cooperation, one partner organization would have to provide complete process definitions to another in order to allow WFMSs to interoperate.

While conducting the case studies described in Chapter 2 and other practically applied workflow management systems elsewhere, the author has observed that organizations and even departments within organizations regard process definitions as highly confidential. They have laid down much of their knowledge in these process definitions and are, even within organizations, not willing to disclose them to others without strong reasons. Similarly, in cases where processes are carried out manually, organizations do not usually disclose information on how they handle their internal procedures to other organizations. It is, for example, very common to keep internal details confidential when providing quotations, orders, letters, price lists, catalogues etc. to other organizations.

In the opinion of the author, the WfMC interoperability specification is only applicable within organizations in its current state. Additionally, in interorganizational settings where one organization has the power to "convince" another organization to provide complete process definitions, the model of the WfMC is applicable. This can be the case in coordinative settings of *hierarchy*. Cases of *equal partnership* and *market* (see Section 3.2.2, p. 29) require mechanisms for WFMSs interoperation where internal details about process handling can be kept confidential. Even in hierarchical settings among the owners of different WFMSs, it is not necessary that participants share process definitions with each other. A method for workflow interoperability, which respects the need for confidentiality of internal process definitions, is introduced in Chapter 5 (p. 103).

Moreover, the WfMC authors assume the existence of complete process definitions that are centrally specified for all WFMSs involved. Based on the experiences gained in the case studies, this is not likely to be applicable in many situations. If the execution of workflow instances is handled by different WFMSs, which are for example owned by legally separate organizations, it is likely that the process owners will want to design their workflow parts independently but still find ways to coordinate their efforts. Therefore, during the build-time of wide area workflows, concepts to connect independent workflow-part models are needed before process instances can be started. Proposals for decentralized, coordinated modeling of process definitions will be introduced in Chapter 5.

The handling or transfer of *information* in documents as opposed to mere *data* (see Section 3.1, p.23 for definitions) is not (yet) covered by the WfMC specifications. Now, early in 1998, no bindings for the known compound document standards such as SGML, HTML, XML or HyTime have been included in the specifications. It has already been stated that a large part of the information within organizations is stored in documents (see p. 25). Today, the largest part of interorganizational information transfer is also document-based. Therefore, Wide Area Workflow Management needs information carriers with document character that are able to transfer structured data along with contextual information.

The WfMC approach only covers structured workflow management (see Section 3.3.3, p. 45). Aspects of flexible workflow management are not discussed.

The model of eight levels of WFMS interoperability introduced by the WfMC does not include a discussion of which "level" would be appropriate for what organizational scenario. The term "level" implies a vertical arrangement and an upward direction of development. The author would propose not to term these as "levels" but "technical options", arranged horizontally on a continuum between *completely separate WFMSs* and *fully integrated WFMSs*. A strong tendency towards modularized information systems (e.g. object orientation, componentware, object management standards) in recent years indicates that "technical options" on the side of *fully integrated WFMSs* (levels 6-8) are unlikely to be primary choices for system vendors and customers in near future. Based on accounts in the case studies (see Chapter 2), the author assumes that completely distinct WFMSs interoperating by *gateways* ("level 3") will usually be chosen, especially in interorganizational settings. Workflow management systems will continue to develop rapidly. Thus, the definition of common APIs will most likely be partially outdated at the time of its release.

In order to standardize common APIs for WFMSs, precise specifications are necessary. However, in recent years, it has become evident that precise specifications have of been edged out by more practically oriented "industry standards".

In fast evolving markets, there is no alternative to variety and change. In such situations, standards can provide a certain stability as long as they are extensible, adaptable, and are constantly updated.

In the judgement of the author, the interoperability specifications of the WfMC do not yet allow for a complete realization of Wide Area Workflow Management. According to levels of distributed and widely distributed workflow management introduced in Figure 10 (p. 56) and the generation model in Figure 11 (p. 57), only a widely distributed run-time operation in hierarchical settings has been specified. The author therefore proposes to look at the WfMC *Reference Model* in a different way (Figure 14). An additional "Interface 6" or an enlargement of Interface 4, which covers the interaction and coordination of workflow designers during build-time, would allow the necessary structures to plan information exchange between WFMSs in advance in a de-centralized manner.

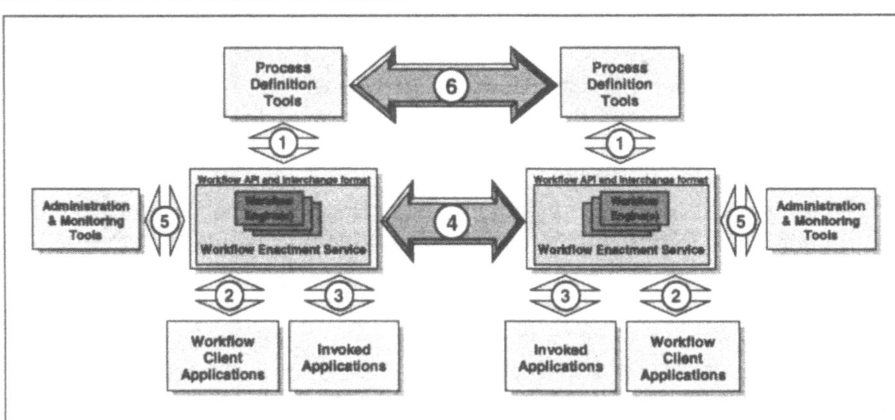

Figure 14: A different way to see the WfMC Reference Model

Despite the preceding propositions for further refinement of the WfMC interoperability specification, it remains an important milestone on the way towards coordination of different WFMSs. With this book, the author would like to contribute to a discussion about the further development of WFMS interoperability strategies and techniques.

4.2.2 Business process oriented approaches

Analysis, modeling and optimization of business processes are an important prerequisite for the definition of workflow models (see Figure 7, p. 48). In the following sections, selected approaches, which deal with the handling of interorganizational business processes, will be discussed.

4.2.2.1 Handbook of organizational processes

Malone et al. from the Center for Coordination Science at MIT, Cambridge, propose the building of an electronic handbook of organizational processes [Malone et al. 1993], [Malone et al. 1997]. Its aim is to store definitions of business processes, for example for the following purposes:

- Imagining new organizations through invention of new processes.
- Redesigning existing organizations through redesign of processes.
- Sharing ideas and "best practices" about organizational processes among different organizations.
- Generating software for supporting and analyzing processes, e.g. workflow management systems.

In a first step, a technique for representing organizational processes is described. Organizational processes can be organized in a hierarchical tree similar to object-oriented programming. Root processes (e.g. "Sell something") can be used as a basis for specializations on several levels. For example "Sell how?" is a specialization of the root process and can be further divided into "Sell by direct sales", "Sell by retail store" etc. On this level, concrete business processes are stored which consist of different activities. Each activity can be inherited without change from the level above or can contain individually different characteristics.

A further step is to define dependencies among activities and ways to manage these dependencies by the use of coordination strategies based on *coordination theory* (see Section 3.2.2, p. 29). A basic set of dependencies is identified which are termed *flow*, *sharing* and *fit*.

Finally, Malone et al. introduce software tools that support the formation of handbooks of organizational processes. This software is capable of displaying and managing hierarchical specialization trees of organizational processes.

The concept described for a handbook of organizational processes does not cover mechanisms for a continuous improvement of stored processes. One could image that a lifecycle concept of definition, simulation, use, analysis and optimization of processes (similar to Figure 8, p. 49) would be helpful in enhancing the quality of handbooks of organizational processes.

In the context of Wide Area Workflow Management, several things are remarkable. Storing business processes in a hierarchical tree similar to object-oriented programming can also be used for workflow models. It helps to form a knowledge base for learning organizations. Duplicated work can be avoided through the derivation of new workflow models from existing and well-tried templates. Making parts of workflow models, which are stored in such a repository, available to other organizations can be a powerful method for decentralized, coordinated planning of interorganizational workflows. For example, standardized *interfaces* for workflow models such as those used in object management standards (see Section 3.4.3, p. 64) could be used to invoke workflow instances in other organizations without having to know internal details. If organizations cooperate closely, shared repositories of workflow models could be used for a more intensive knowledge exchange, for example in virtual organizations.

4.2.2.2 PRINCESS

The acronym *PRINCESS* stands for *Process Management with Intelligent Cooperating Information Systems* and describes a research project conducted by Scheer and Hirschmann at the University of Saarbruecken, Germany [http://www.iwi.uni-sb.de/research/princess/dfg_spp.html].

The project deals with identification, modeling, optimization and monitoring of interorganizational business processes. A special focus is on the costs involved and the revenues gained when organizations connect their business processes. Process-oriented accounting methods for process cost evaluation are used for example in a case study which takes a look at financial results of the cooperation of different firms within a multi-national holding [Gulledge/Hirschmann/Scheer 1997].

To describe business processes, the language of *extended event-controlled process chains (eEPC)* is used. It is part of the methodology of the *architecture of integrated information systems (ARIS)* developed by Scheer et al. [Scheer 1992], [Scheer 1994]. The *PRINCESS* prototype uses the eEPC notation to allow for the modeling of interorganizational business processes during the analysis phase. Subsequently knowledge-based methods support users in finding inefficiencies and help to derive and evaluate measures for optimization. The system is based on distributed agents residing in the different member organizations, which participate in a cooperative scenario [Hirschmann 1996].

The implementation of *PRINCESS* necessitates the building of a complete and detailed model of the overall business processes that covers all participating organizations. This requires confidential information on internal processes to be exchanged between the partner firms. The case study presented describes a hierarchical cooperation scenario within a holding. Here the notion of sharing knowledge of the complete process can be justified. It is not likely that this approach would be accepted in rather loose cooperative settings, for instance *equal partnership* and *market* (see Section 3.2.2, p. 29).

The aspect of value-based controlling of interorganizational processes developed in the *PRINCESS* project is of importance to Wide Area Workflow Management. It is not enough to provide techniques for the interoperation of WFMSs. Controlling mechanisms, based on cost/revenue calculations, have to assure that the application of these techniques is truly efficient.

4.2.3 Flexibility oriented approaches

Providing flexibility in workflow management systems is one of the key focuses in the recent developments in scientific and commercial systems. Wide Area Workflow Management needs to be especially flexible in order to adjust to the constant changes that occur when independent partners in dynamic markets cooperate with each other.

Fundamental thoughts on flexibility in WFM have already been discussed in Section 3.3.3 (e.g. Figure 9, p. 52). Further conceptual aspects about the flexibility of WFMS are found for example in [Carlsen et al. 1997], Section 5.1 (p. 104) and Section 5.5 (p. 139). In the following sections, different approaches for gaining flexibility within workflow management will be introduced.

4.2.3.1 Workflow Continuum and GroupFlow

The *Workflow Continuum* was developed in 1993 by Hilpert and Nastansky at the University of Paderborn, Germany [http://gcc.uni-paderborn.de]. It shows different types of workflow management on a scale between *structure* and *flexibility* (Figure 15).

On the left side of the *Workflow Continuum*, flexible group interaction patterns are described. The so-called *ad-hoc workflow* uses e-mail as an information carrier whereas *autonomous workgroups* make use of shared databases. These interaction patterns can be supported by groupware platforms (see Section 3.4.4, p. 65). Structured workflow management, as was already explained in Section 3.3.3 (p. 45), is placed on the other side of the *Workflow Continuum*. The so-called *semi-structured workflow* is located in-between these two extremes. It is made up of different combinations of structured and flexible elements [Nastansky/Hilpert 1994].

Ad-hoc Workflow	Autonomous Workgroup	Semi-structured Workflow			Structured Workflow
	Open team task	Open team task within structured workflow	Controlled team task within struct. workflow	Ad hoc modification of structured workflow	
E-mail, store and forward	One-step next agent, shared databases	Combination of pre-determined and open tasks within a workflow	Partially unspecified elements within pre-determined workflow	Completely pre-determined workflow allowing for exceptions	Completely pre-determined workflow, shared databases
- urgent - short-lived - exceptional - confidential	- shared access - common tasks - "Pull" approach	- completely open as well as standardized tasks - intersection of both	- preset number of group members - regardless of sequence	- highly recurrent - pre-determined - easy-to-apply ad-hoc modification/re-routing	- highly recurrent - well structured - pre-defined
e.g. new type of request	e.g. co-authoring of publication	e.g. co-editing of annual report	e.g. counter-signature	e.g. consumer credit application with particular conditions	e.g. consumer credit application

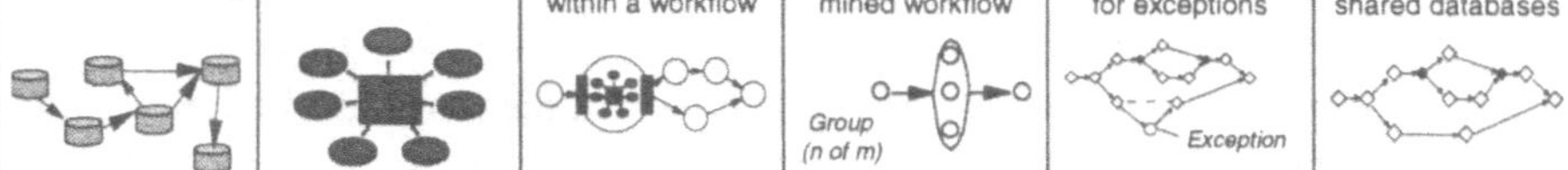

flexible, changeable, unique ⟷ determined, structured, recurrent

Figure 15: Workflow Continuum ([Nastansky/Hilpert 1994], all rights reserved)

This model's contribution to research on flexible WFM lies in different combinations between the flexible world of *open group interaction* on the one hand and the world of *structured workflow management* on the other hand. For example, by including so-called *open team tasks*, only milestones of workflows are planned ("milestone modeling"). The handling of single activities within these *open team tasks* is organized by a team according to actual needs which arise during workflow run-time. The activities, however, are still supported by a WFMS and can be analyzed afterwards. One or two persons in the team are responsible for collecting the results of an open team task. These results are then forwarded to the next workflow step according to the respective workflow model [Nastansky/Hilpert 1995], [Nastansky/Hilpert 1996].

Since its first publication in 1993, many authors have discussed and used the *Workflow Continuum* (for example [Marshak 1995], [Weiss/Krcmar 1996], [Deiters et al. 1996]).

Based on the notion of the *Workflow Continuum*, the *GroupFlow System* (see for example [Marshak 1995], [Nastansky/Hilpert 1996]) was developed as scientific prototype of a groupware-based workflow management system. The *GroupFlow* methodology of workflow management is based on the workflow lifecycle shown in Figure 8 (p. 49). After analyzing existing business processes, workflows are rather roughly planned using open team tasks as self-organized milestones. After run-time operation, an analysis identifies successful workflow modules, which have for instance been developed by users within open team tasks. These can be stored within a so-called workflow library for reuse in similar situations.

The complete workflow engine of *GroupFlow* was build on top of Lotus Notes Version 3.x allowing for highly flexible workflow execution. Graphical tools for modeling, simulation, monitoring and analysis of workflows were added. They were developed as independent software tools using an interface library to access data in the workflow repository stored in Lotus Notes databases. A complete prototype version of *GroupFlow* was presented in 1994. It was evaluated by various scientific institutes and commercial users. Based on these tests it was decided to make *GroupFlow* a commercial product. Version 1.0 was launched in 1995 and became a widely known WFMS.

With the release of Lotus Notes Version 4.x, a completely new programming language, *Lotus Script*, was available that offered significantly more flexibility and performance for application development based on Lotus Notes. It promised a drastically optimized workflow engine of *GroupFlow* and the removal of all major limitations of Version 1.0. At that time, the developer team of *GroupFlow* founded a new company and started with a completely new workflow product on the basis of the *Workflow Continuum* and Lotus Notes 4.x. This product, called *Onestone ProZessware* [Weber 1997a], is now a successful WFMS used by major companies worldwide. The commercial *GroupFlow* System was further developed based on Lotus Notes 4.x for a new product called *Pavone Espresso*. It is an office management system with strong workflow features, which has also become very successful on the market place.

Scientific research on flexible workflow management was carried on at the University of Paderborn. Results of this research are the concepts for Wide Area Workflow Management discussed in this book and the *Wide Area GroupFlow Sys-*

tem (WAGS) presented in Chapter 6 (p. 179). *WAGS* is based on the concepts of the *Workflow Continuum* and allows for intra- and interorganizational, flexible WAWM. From a technological viewpoint, *WAGS* has been completely rebuilt to overcome several limitations of the original *GroupFlow* prototype.

Classification of *GroupFlow*:

1. *document & communication,*
2. from *automation & structure* towards *user support & flexibility,*
3. *distributed WFM.*

4.2.3.2 FlexWare

FlexWare is a research prototype developed in 1997 by Wargitsch, Wewers and Mertens at the University of Erlangen [http://www.wi1.wiso.uni-erlangen.de/wi1wiso.html]. It has been built on top of the commercial WFMS COI Business-Flow. The authors of *FlexWare* propose an initial phase in which workflows are drawn up on a rather coarse milestone level, assuring stable, long-life models. Then workflow instances are initiated and users are supported while using the milestones in a self-organized "learning by doing" phase. Periodical supervision of actual work structures within the milestones allows for a continuous improvement of business processes over time [Wargitsch/Wewers 1997].

FlexWare tries to remove the distinction between workflow models (process definitions) and workflow instances (process instances). Workflows can be designed using a combination of workflow building blocks stored in a workflow catalogue. Workflow planners are supported by case-based reasoning tools, which search for workflow building blocks that are applicable to the new situation. During workflow run-time, users are free to change to proposed structures (if any exist) in the workflow building blocks according to their needs. Each single workflow building block within each workflow instance is regarded as being independent of a workflow model. Therefore, it can be changed when needed with the help of a graphical modeling tool. This methodology is called *instance-based modeling* and allows for a flexible workflow execution [Wargitsch/Wewers/Theisinger 1998].

The approach of leaving parts of workflow models open until decision-making during run-time has already been developed within the *Workflow Continuum* and *GroupFlow* (see Section 4.2.3.1, p. 85). Storing workflow modules in a workflow library and reusing them has already been realized in *GroupFlow*, but *FlexWare* goes one step further to add a helpful case-based reasoning tool. While *GroupFlow* still relies on ex ante designed workflow models, the *FlexWare* approach goes one step beyond. The notion of instance-based modeling allows for high flexibility in workflow execution. However, the information overhead for all instance-based models is significantly higher than with *structured* workflow management (see Section 3.3.3, p. 45).

Classification of *FlexWare*:

1. between *database & transaction* and *document & communication,*
2. from *automation & structure* towards *user support & flexibility,*
3. *distributed WFM.*

4.2.3.3 FreeFlow

FreeFlow is a prototype developed by members of Apple Research Laboratories, Rank Xerox Research Center Cambridge Lab (EuroPARC) and Department of Information Science, Aarhus University. It was presented at the CSCW '96 conference [Dourish et al. 1996].

Activities in *FreeFlow* can have different *states* (e.g. inactive, active, enabled, pending) and *dependencies* with other activities. These *dependencies* are defined in workflow models with the help of *constraints* (activity B should not be performed until activity A has been completed) rather than sequential relations (perform activity A, then activity B etc.). Thus, workflows are not defined in a forward-oriented manner, but backwards from the desired results. Predefined *constraints* between activities can be changed by users so that workflows can be influenced during work itself. Users can thus actively mediate between process descriptions and process execution.

FreeFlow has been developed using WWW technology like HTML forms and CGI scripts. It consists of a *process manager* responsible for the execution of process instances and *interactors* responsible for presenting work to users. Both are linked by *events* managed by an *interest manager*. This architecture allows for a flexible connection between system components.

The design of *FreeFlow* is another example of the flexibility that comes with the possibility of changing process instances during run-time operation depending upon users' needs. The notion of defining workflow in a backward manner resembles the KANBAN system, which is successfully used in organizing production processes, and presents a new way of workflow definition.

Classification of *FreeFlow* (as far as possible based on available material):

1. *document & communication,*
2. *user support & flexibility,*
3. (not described).

4.2.3.4 MOVE

MOVE is a project which draws its members from several scientific institutes and commercial enterprises [Goesmann et al. 1997]. It was started in 1996 and is supported by the German Federal Ministry for Education, Science, Research and Technology [http://www.do.isst.fhg.de/move]. The project goal is to do research and empirical evaluation of methodologies to support business processes with flexible WFMSs [Herrmann/Scheer/Weber 1998].

Flexibility is achieved through several methods [Hagemeyer et al. 1997]. The concept of *late modeling* allows for the inclusion of undefined workflow parts ("black boxes") into workflow models. During run-time operation, these undefined parts can be defined in an ad-hoc modeling process. First a model is proposed by a designer and all participants can negotiate on it. After agreement of terms and finalizing of this model, it can be used for the specific workflow instance it was designed for. Additionally it can build the basis for a new general element in workflow models [Deiters et al. 1996].

A second concept is called *workflow adaptation* and describes possibilities for changing workflow instances during run-time. Users can include or leave out steps, change pre-defined applications or assign activities to other persons, thereby creating workflow variations. They can be analyzed in order to extract workflow parts that can then be generalized.

Workflow steps are classified according to "change authorizations": *static steps* can only be changed by a workflow supervisor, *conditional steps* can be changed upon negotiation and *flexible steps* can be changed by all assigned users. Persons that are affected by a change are notified and can react differently according to their rights regarding changes; the scale reaches from *being informed* to *right to negotiate* to *right to appeal* [Herrmann/Walter 1997].

The concepts of *late modeling* and *workflow adaptation* are similar to those developed within the *Workflow Continuum, GroupFlow, FlexWare* and *FreeFlow*. The aspect of negotiation on proposed "late models" and adaptations of workflow instances is a valuable contribution to flexible workflow management.

Krcmar and Zerbe also propose negotiation as a way to achieve more flexibility within workflow management [Krcmar/Zerbe 1996].

Classification of *MOVE*:

1. (not described),
2. from *automation & structure* until *user support & flexibility*,
3. *distributed WFM*.

4.2.4 Distribution oriented approaches

Various publications deal with aspects of distribution in workflow management. Based on the level model introduced in Figure 10 (p. 56), different approaches are introduced and classified in the following sections.

4.2.4.1 ActMan

ActMan (Activity Management) was designed in 1992 by Reinwald at the University of Erlangen and is described in his doctoral thesis [Reinwald/Wedekind 1992], [Reinwald 1995]. It is a prototype for transaction-oriented, structured workflow management on the basis of relational databases.

Activity nets are built with a verbal activity definition language (ADL). The assignment of data to activities is defined by a data definition language (DDL). Finally, the exchange of data between distributed nodes in a network is defined in a data interchange definition language (DIDL).

Distribution is achieved through transferring and synchronizing data among distributed, interoperable databases with the help of replication. Activity nets are centralized and assume a completely definable workflow including knowledge about all actors and necessary data.

ActMan is a technical approach to distributed workflow management. No models for distributed design of workflow models or coordination mechanisms in interorganizational scenarios are discussed. *ActMan* covers the technical layer of the level model (Figure 10, p. 56) and the run-time level.

Classification of *ActMan*:
1. *database & transaction,*
2. *automation & structure,*
3. *WAWM (lower two levels).*

4.2.4.2 Exotica/FMQM

Exotica/FMQM was developed at the IBM Almaden Research Center in cooperation with scientists from UC Santa Barbara and UM at Amherst. The preceding *Exotica* project aimed to incorporate advanced transaction management in IBM's products and prototypes. *FMQM* means *FlowMark on Message Queue Manager* and describes research efforts to use products of the IBM Message Queue Series (*MQSeries*) to build a distributed, message-based workflow engine for IBM FlowMark [Mohan et al. 1995]. IBM FlowMark originally has a centralized architecture based on relational databases which handle the *flow of data* that is modeled separately from the *flow of control.*

The *Exotica/FMQM* project focuses on distribution, scalability and fault-tolerance by minimizing the need for central control structures. Persistent message queues placed at each *run-time node* of a network involved in a workflow allow for a distributed, transaction-based and thus persistent storage of all relevant data. Furthermore, a specific *process definition node* is responsible for providing details about workflow models (called *process definitions*) to involved *run-time nodes.* Workflow models are designed centrally, necessitating a complete knowledge of all participants involved in workflows. In each run-time node, a *node manager* builds a *process table* that contains static information related to the execution of process instances. Workflow data is transferred from *output containers* of finished run-time nodes to *input containers* of next run-time nodes with the help of messages [Alonso et al. 1995].

Methods for the tracking of distributed workflows have been envisioned in the form of an audit queue. Structures of messages for the transfer of process descriptions and workflow data are not explained in detail. Aspects of flexibility such as exception handling or milestone modeling are not discussed. Publications concerning Exotica/FMQM do not cover aspects of WFMS interoperability in intra- or interorganizational settings.

An extension to *Exotica/FMQM* uses distributed, replicated Lotus Notes databases to provide for a decentralized data flow [Alonso/Reinwald/Mohan 1997]. This technique is similar to that of *ActMan* (Section 4.2.4.1, p. 89).

Exotica/FMQM is a technically oriented research prototype addressing the technical and run-time layer of the level model shown in Figure 10 (p. 56). The design and control architecture follows a centralized paradigm. The idea of a completely distributed workflow execution with the help of messages or in conjunction with replication technology is important to Wide Area Workflow Management (WAWM).

Classification of *Exotica/FMQM*:
1. *database & transaction* and *(document) & communication,*
2. *automation & structure,*
3. *WAWM (lower two levels).*

4.2.4.3 POLIKOM

The goal of the *POLIKOM* project is to research and evaluate methods and systems supporting cooperation between public authorities and commercial enterprises in widely distributed scenarios. It was started in 1994 and is supported by the German Federal Ministry for Education, Science, Research and Technology together with system vendors and scientific institutes [http://www.ba.dlr.de/md/it/iv/tk/polikom/index.html].

POLIKOM consists of four sub-projects:

- *POLITeam* deals with the support of widely distributed workgroups. Electronic circulation folders and shared workspaces allow for document handling between participants at different locations [Kloeckner et al. 1995], [Prinz/Kolvenbach 1996], [Pankoke-Babatz/Syri 1996]. A field study demonstrates how approximately 50 persons are supported by respective applications based on DEC LinkWorks [http://orgwis.gmd.de/projects/POLITeam/].
- *POLIFlow* provides solutions based on workflow management, groupware and synchronous telecooperation to facilitate the relocation of a specific public authority from Bonn to Berlin [http://www.ba.dlr.de/md/it/iv/tk/polikom/index.html], [http://poliflow.hewlett-packard.de/index.html]. Particular emphasis is placed on the integration of synchronous and asynchronous forms of cooperation [Petrovic/Kopperger 1997], [Siebert/Kindler/Soyez 1997].
- *POLIWork* focuses on methods to facilitate unplanned, ad-hoc work of different public authorities. Techniques for synchronous and asynchronous cooperation and document management solutions are evaluated.
- *POLIVest's* aim is to develop a document management system for the Upper House of the German Parliament based on Intranet-technology. Additionally a WFMS has been invented for use by an administrative body. Both projects include support of ad-hoc workflow management and synchronous telecooperation.

The entire scope of different approaches, solutions and experiences found in the different sub-projects of *POLIKOM* cannot be described here. A strong focus is placed on integration of groupware, workflow management and synchronous telecooperation. According to available literature, the different sub-projects can be located in the lower two layers of the level model (Figure 10, p. 56).

POLIKOM and its sub-projects cannot be consistently classified in the scheme of Figure 12 (p. 76) due to the variety of different approaches.

4.2.4.4 FUNSOFT nets

Modeling and enactment of interorganizational workflows with *FUNSOFT nets* is proposed by Gruhn et al. [Gruhn/Kampmann 1996], [Gruhn 1997]. *FUNSOFT nets* are abstract Petri Nets for workflow modeling with *instances* representing activities and *channels* standing for temporary storage of objects and documents associated with activities. Objects and documents are defined with extended Entity Relationship Models [Deiters/Gruhn/Striemer 1995]. Based on the observation that many business processes within organizations have interfaces with other organizations, the modeling language of *FUNSOFT nets* is extended with so-called *interface channels*. These are included in several interoperating business process models. Interface channels are *opened* during run-time and can be kept constantly open for an ongoing exchange. Information in *interface channels* is exchanged with documents based on the EDIFACT standard (see Section 3.4.1, p. 59).

Two methods for the coordination of different workflow parts are described. When a hierarchical structure between organizations exists, one of them is likely to define the terms of cooperation and thus would define *interface channels*. This approach is not pursued further. The second method makes use of a *business process broker* who coordinates offers and demand for services. The broker maintains a directory with specifications for interorganizational workflows describing the workflow parts involved in the form of *roles*. Additionally the directory contains specifications for the necessary *interface channels* associated with these *roles*. A second directory lists internal workflows offered to the broker. It contains information about 1) organizations which offer workflow services, 2) specification of input which their internal workflows need to be started and 3) description of the information they will deliver as results. A *yellow page service* can be used to find similar offers.

The workflow management system *LEU* [Dinkhoff et al. 1994] is used as the basis for implementing these concepts. With the help of *LEU*, a system has been devised which coordinates apartment repairs done by independent repair services.

The *FUNSOFT* approach presented by Gruhn et al. allows for Wide Area Workflow Management. It encompasses the lower three layers of the level model shown in Figure 10 (p. 56). The proposed coordination mechanism is similar to the concept of a *broker* in coordination science (Section 3.2.2, p. 29). The modeling of workflow parts is decentralized, but a central instance (the *business process broker*) is necessary to store specifications of overall, interorganizational workflows. The use of EDIFACT messages does not allow for transfer of compound documents.

Classification of *FUNSOFT nets*:

1. *database & transaction,*
2. *automation & structure,*
3. *WAWM (lower three levels).*

4.2.4.5 Workonnector

Workonnector is a prototype developed by Wewers, Wargitsch and Mertens at the University of Erlangen [http://www.wi1.wiso.uni-erlangen.de/wi1wiso.html]. It is designed to handle workflows that deal with the disposal of hazardous waste in Bavaria. Disposal documents have to be routed between companies and legal authorities.

The WFMSs of the participants are connected with messages handled by *Workonnector*. Messages are based on Internet/MIME e-mails. *Workonnector* uses its own structure of transferring field-based data within the body of an e-mail, which is similar to the WfMC specification, but not compliant with it (see Section 4.2.1.2, p. 78). Messages can additionally contain attached files, which can for instance be used to transfer images, CAD drawings etc. [Wewers/Faisst 1996].

Sending messages between different workflows can be planned by using a specific type of node (called *remote action*) within a workflow model. This node type was added to *Workonnector* in 1997 and is similar to methods described in [Riempp 1994], [Hilpert/Riempp/Nastansky 1994], and [Riempp/Nastansky 1996a].

During run-time, workflow instances are processed internally until they reach a *remote action*. There, a message is sent via the *Workonnector* invoking a workflow instance in the receiving WFMS with the data provided in the message. The WFMS, which has been called up, can send back messages with status information, synchronization data and termination notifications. Upon completion of the called workflow instance, a message with resulting data is transferred back to the initiating WFMS. Consequently, the calling workflow instance is resumed and processed further [Wewers/Wargitsch 1998].

Workonnector was specifically developed for application within the given scenario of a disposal company and two public authorities. It is connected to an installation of the commercial workflow management system COI BusinessFlow in one of the organizations. A second *Workonnector* is interoperating with a prototypic Lotus Notes database with basic workflow features in another organization.

No mechanisms are described for a systematic exchange of *interface specifications* of workflows between organizations. The mapping of internal data to fields in messages is hard-coded on the sending as well as on the receiving side. It is not mentioned how the terms of cooperation between the participating organizations are negotiated. Additionally, no exception handling, inclusion of flexible workflow parts or ad-hoc invocation of external workflows is described. In the case study, only structured and completely standardized interorganizational workflows are supported within proprietary system environments.

The approach of *Workonnector* is an example of a prototypic installation of WAWM. Although it is limited to a specific case, it shows characteristics that can be generalized. One important feature is the use of messages transferred with the help of a *gateway* (the *Workonnector*). Another is the inclusion of a specific node type (*remote action*) into workflow models allowing for the planning of external workflow connections. However, this planning is limited to hierarchical relations between *main processes* and *subprocesses*.

Workonnector is located in the lower two layers of the level model shown in Figure 10 (p. 56). The third level of planning wide area workflows is also covered partially, but features for the negotiation and coordination with other workflow designers of cooperating WFMSs are not offered within the system.

Classification of *Workonnector*:

1. between *database & transaction* and *document & communication,*
2. *automation & structure,*
3. *WAWM (lower three levels).*

4.2.4.6 ORBWork

ORBWork is a research prototype of Sheth, Miller, and Kochut et al. at the University of Georgia [http://www.cs.uga.edu/LSDIS]. It uses CORBA technology to build a distributed workflow run-time environment. *ORBWork* is based on research concerning transactional workflow management presented in the METEOR and $METEOR_2$ projects [Miller et al. 1996], [Das et al. 1997].

A main focus of *ORBWork* is to assure reliability and error recovery in the execution of workflows across different workflow engines connected via CORBA-compliant Object Request Brokers (ORBs) (see Section 3.4.3, p. 64).

Distribution is discussed concerning technical, run-time and control layer of the level model (Figure 10, p. 56). Aspects of decentralized modeling or interorganizational workflow management are not mentioned.

A further project on CORBA-based WFM started at the University of Dresden in 1997 is called WorCOS [http://wwwdb.inf.tu-dresden.de/~schulze/worcos/].

Classification of *ORBWork*:

1. *database & transaction,*
2. *automation & structure,*
3. *WAWM (lower two levels).*

4.2.4.7 VORTEL

VORTEL is a project dealing with interoperability issues of WFMSs [http://www.deteberkom.de/projekte/texte/VORTEL_engl.html]. Within the project, a fundamental architecture of WFMSs with 5 interfaces connecting different components was defined [Deiters/Lindert et al. 1996]. This interface model is similar to, but not compliant with, the *WfMC Reference Model* (see Section 4.2.1, p. 77). *Interface 5* is responsible for bridging different workflow engines [Deiters/Lindert/Friedrich 1996].

Several models for the connection of workflow engines are described: *vertical/tightly-linked/isolated* is similar to *nested subprocess* of the WfMC *Interface 4* specifications (4.2.1.2, p. 78). *Vertical/tightly-linked/non-isolated* adds requests and feedback from the currently executed subprocess. *Horizontal/loosely-linked* is similar to *chained processes* of the WfMC. Sub-processes are called up by messages for the purposes of control, document exchange and status requests based on CORBA technology. In the *VORTEL* project, it is assumed that all WFMSs involved can understand one kind of process definition. Methods for decentralized modeling or flexible workflow management are not discussed [Deiters/Lindert 1996].

A *VORTEL demonstrator* was set up connecting three systems: CORMAN (a WFMS developed by Fraunhofer Institute, Berlin), DEC LinkWorks and IBM FlowMark. The *VORTEL* project describes concepts and solutions for the two lower layers of the level model shown in Figure 10 (p. 56).

Classification of *VORTEL:*

1. *database & transaction,*
2. *automation & structure,*
3. *WAWM (lower two levels).*

4.2.4.8 ContAct

ContAct was developed by Galler, Hagemeyer and Scheer at the University of Saarbruecken in cooperation with IDS Prof. Scheer GmbH and IBM German Software Development Laboratory [http://www.iwi.uni-sb.de/contact/]. It deals with the coordination of distributed designers who want to design business process models and derived workflow models jointly. Designers can share data about models and communicate with each other using structured messages. They mark certain objects within models and are subsequently informed when changes to these objects occur [Galler/Hagemeyer/Scheer 1995], [Galler/Hagemeyer/Scheer 1996].

A *ContAct* prototype has been developed in the form of a *cooperation service software* connected with IDS ARIS Toolset for business process modeling and IBM FlowMark for workflow modeling and execution. Both ARIS Toolset and IBM FlowMark support business processes models and derived workflows models with centralized process definitions. Thus, *ContAct* allows for a decentralized modeling of centralized models. It is located in the design layer of the level model shown in Figure 10 (p. 56).

4.2.5 WWW oriented approaches

With the enormous growth of the Internet and WWW, many authors have started to use these platforms to enhance their WFMSs. Functionalities provided via a WWW-based interface can range from simple user interfaces for workflow participants to complete modeling environments programmed in Java.

WAWM needs mutual exchange of workflow information between two or more WFMSs. At some point within workflow instances, information must be "pushed" to different workflow instances, which may be executed in different organizations. This is often done with the help of a message (e.g. Internet e-mail) as described earlier in this chapter. A problem with WWW technology is that it was originally designed to support information "pull". Web-based interfaces for modeling or workflow participation are often used for *remote access* rather than actual information exchange between widely-distributed, heterogeneous WFMSs.

In the following section, selected approaches for realizing WFMSs with WWW technology are presented.

4.2.5.1 WebWork

WebWork is a WFMS prototype developed at the University of Georgia [http://www.cs.uga.edu/LSDIS]. It is based on the same conceptional framework as *ORBWork* (see Section 4.2.4.6, p. 94), but is implemented on the basis of WWW technology only. The different components of *WebWork* have been realized using Web browsers, Web servers, HTML, JavaScript and CGI scripts. This allows for a distributed run-time operation in Intranets or in the Internet [Miller et al. 1997a], [Miller et al. 1997b].

WebWork uses centralized workflow models and control tools. It covers the lower two layers of the level model shown in Figure 10 (p. 56).

Classification of *WebWork*:
1. *database & transaction,*
2. *automation & structure,*
3. *WAWM (lower two levels).*

4.2.5.2 WAX

WAX (Web-AXessed Workflow Management) is another part of the prototypic WFMS framework developed at the University of Erlangen [http://www.wi1.wiso.uni-erlangen.de/wi1wiso.html] and builds a Web-frontend to a WFMS based on the prototypes *FlexWare* (4.2.3.2, p. 87) and *Workonnector* (4.2.4.5, p. 92).

WAX builds a client interface for a proprietary document management and workflow system (COI Business Flow), which underlies *FlexWare* and *Workonnector*, and allows for search, download and upload of documents with the help of a Web browser. Furthermore, it can display worklists for specific users. An interesting part of *WAX* is a modeling tool developed using Java. It can be used to design workflow models for general use as well as to alter running workflow instances with a method called *instance-based modeling*.

A combination of the prototypes *WAX*, *FlexWare* and *Workonnector* enables flexible Wide Area Workflow Management with WWW access. Even though the underlying platform is proprietary, some of the concepts can be generalized and encompass main aspects of the lower three layers of the level model shown in Figure 10 (p. 56). However, the framework only supports hierarchical coordination between WAWM participants and has no explicit mechanisms for negotiations among distributed workflow designers or the exchange of interface specifications. Features for flexible workflow management are only applied internally, while settings for WFMSs' interoperation are strictly predefined and cannot be adapted during runtime operation.

Classification of *WAX:* see *FlexWare* and *Workonnector*.

4.2.5.3 Phanta Rhei

Phanta Rhei (Heraklit: "everything flows") is a WFMS prototype developed by Eder and Groiss at the University of Klagenfurt, Austria [http://www.ifi.uni-klu.ac.at/~herb/Overview.html]. Like many other WWW-oriented workflow systems, *Phanta Rhei* offers a Web-frontend to internal users. External persons like customers can initiate workflows via Web browsers.

An interesting aspect is the ability of *Phanta Rhei* to exchange EDIFACT-based documents with other WFMSs using HTML pages. These pages are transferred via HTML-Mail.

Workflow models are defined with the help of a text-based workflow definition language (WDL). By using specific statements ("remote *taskname(send_forms*, receive_forms*)*") connections to other WFMSs can be defined. "*send_forms*" contains addresses of recipients and outgoing workflow data. "*receive_forms*" specifies desired results. "Every workflow system provides a description of the forms it can receive, which process will be started on receiving, and whether it answers with a form and of which type this answer form is. Each form has a type, which is member in a type hierarchy. The root of this type hierarchy is the general message type. Every document type is a subtype of it" [Groiss/Eder 1997].

The *Phanta Rhei* prototype shows some interesting characteristics. The approach of publishing interfaces of externally available workflows to other organizations helps to realize decentralized modeling of interoperating workflows. However, the run-time operation relies on the methodology of *main processes*, which invoke and control *subprocesses* in a strictly hierarchical manner. This way, the autonomy of the participating organizations, which is gained by decentralized modeling, is "lost" again during run-time operation.

Organizing documents in document hierarchy reduces specification efforts and allows for re-use in similar situations. The lack of a graphical workflow modeling tool and the use of EDIFACT documents limits the applicability of the system. Aspects of flexible workflow management are not discussed and there are no reports on a practical evaluation of the system.

Phanta Rhei encompasses the lower three layers of the level model shown in Figure 10 (p. 56) and allows for Wide Area Workflow Management.

Classification of *Phanta Rhei*:

1. between *database & transaction* and *document & communication,*
2. *automation & structure,*
3. *WAWM (lower three levels).*

4.2.5.4 WorldFlow

WorldFlow is a Web-based WFMS prototype developed at the University of Massachusetts at Amherst [http://www-ccs.cs.umass.edu/kamath/hpts97.html]. It focuses on transactional, structured workflow management using WWW technology. Workflow engines are realized on top of Web servers and can be accessed via Web browsers. Additionally different workflow engines can interoperate by transferring control over parts of workflow instances in a hierarchical manner [Kamath et al. 1997].

According to the literature, *WorldFlow* is located in the lower two layers of the level model shown in Figure 10 (p. 56).

Classification of *WorldFlow*:

1. *database & transaction,*
2. *automation & structure,*
3. *WAWM (lower two levels).*

4.3 Commercial systems

This book cannot possibly give an overview of the vast variety of commercial WFMSs that are available. Therefore, only general characteristics that point in the direction of WAWM will be presented here.

The market for commercial WFMSs has grown from a global expenditure on workflow products of US $518 million in 1993 to around US $1.000 million in 1997. Additionally, services in this market had an estimated volume of US $2.905 million in 1997 [Stark 1997], [Kozlowski 1997b]. Compared to other segments of the software market, e.g. office suites or groupware products, workflow software is still a rather small market.

A large number of vendors offers products with significantly different scopes. Various product overviews and comparisons have been published in the past (for example [Hales/Lavery 1991], [BIFOA 1993], [Bragen 1994], [Karl/Deiters 1994], [Sodan 1994], [Erdl/Schoenecker 1995], [Mummert 1996], [Weiss/Krcmar 1996], [Goetzer 1997], [Hales 1997], [Hofland/Utsler 1997], [Kobielus 1997], [Lawrence 1997], [Mummert 1997], [Karl 1997/1998]). It is interesting to note that aspects of interoperability among WFMSs are only covered by some of the newer studies. Recently, features such as the use of Internet e-mail or access via the WWW are also taken into consideration. This development can be understood as a growing awareness of the necessary use of open standards to build the basis of interoperable products.

Many of the currently available workflow products have parts or all of the following features which lend support to distributed work (see the newer product comparisons listed above and [Frappaolo 1997], [Hofland/Utsler 1997]):

- They are based on client/server architecture.
- Workflow instances can be executed across several servers of a specific product. These servers can by connected by LANs and in many cases also by WANs (e.g. by using TCP/IP protocol).
- Web browsers can be used as alternative client frontends for internal workflow participants. Functionalities offered this way differ largely between products.
- Web browsers allow external users (e.g. customers) to initiate workflow instances and to receive feedback from the workflows they started.

These features allow for a distributed and in many cases a widely-distributed run-time operation and thus cover the technical and run-time level of Figure 10, p.56. As most of these WFMSs require centralized workflow models, they are mainly used in *intra*organizational settings. Initiation of workflow instances via a Web browser allows for *remote access* but control over workflow execution is not handed over from one organization to another.

Some WFMS vendors have implemented functions into their products that allow the exchange of workflow information according to the WfMC Interface 4 (see Section 4.2.1.2, p. 78). Products that offer Interface 4 connectivity are, for example, Computron Workflow, CSE Workflow, DEC LinkWorks, DOMUS Software, DST

Systems, IBM FlowMark, ICL RoleModel, InConcert, Software AG Entire Workflow, Software Ley COSA Workflow, Staffware and WANG OPEN/workflow [Ueberhorst 1996], [Goetzer 1997], [http://www.aiim.org/wfmc/faq.html]. Further companies are validating Interface 4 [http://www.aiim.org/wfmc/validation.html]. The WfMC standard allows for interoperability of workflow engines during execution of workflow instances. Coordination of decentralized workflow designers in independent companies is not covered within the WfMC standard. Further limitations of this approach have already been discussed in Section 4.2.1.2 (p. 78).

Microsoft has defined a standard for e-mail based interaction of WFMSs called *Workflow MAPI* [Kaneshige 1995], [Microsoft WF MAPI 1996]. It can be used to connect workflow engines to MAPI-compliant message transfer agents (MTAs). MAPI (Messaging Application Programming Interface) is a widely used industry standard for messaging. The Workflow MAPI specification can be used to connect heterogeneous workflow engines via structured and formatted messages. It supports sequential, parallel and conditional routing of work items. The Workflow MAPI standard comprises features for the tracking of message locations and status as well as the consolidation of recipient responses into the original message or public folders [Kobielus 1997]. In the level model of Figure 10 (p.56), the Workflow MAPI encompasses the lower two layers.

Microsoft is a funding member of the WfMC and has implemented key Interface 4 commands, such as *Create*, *Get Process Instance Data*, and *Set Process Instance Data* in the *MAPI Workflow Framework Command Message Interface, Version 2.0* [Microsoft WF MAPI 1996]. The Workflow MAPI is used for example to enable basic workflow features within Microsoft's groupware platform *Exchange*.

In general, groupware platforms are well suited to the support of WAWM because of their ability to hold documents in shared databases. At the same time, they can transfer these documents via messaging to other databases that may reside in other organizations. Replication technology can be used to seamlessly integrate remote locations (e.g. subsidiaries) and mobile workers into workflows.

Groupware platforms use document types that consist of structured field-based data as well as contextual information and do not have to be converted in order to be sent via e-mail. Therefore, they build ideal information containers to transfer rich workflow information between (groupware-based) WFMSs with no need of conversion or other additional technical measures. As groupware platforms can transfer these e-mails via the Internet and additionally are well integrated with the WWW, they build a powerful basis for the development of WFMSs that are *document & communication* and *user support & flexibility* oriented and allow for Wide Area Workflow Management. With the help of specialized workflow products, groupware platforms can also be used to support *automation & structure* oriented workflows.

An example of a successful WFMS based on groupware platforms is Onestone ProZessware [Weber 1997a], [Weber 1997c]. It is used by major financial institutions and insurance companies to support extensive workflow applications. For instance, a large European bank is in the process of installing 25.000 units of ProZessware for workflow management facilitating customers' credit applications.

Additionally, ProZessware it is one of the few workflow systems that do not only support distributed and widely-distributed execution of workflow instances across several servers. During build-time, sub-workflows can be included into workflow models that will be filled out by different workflow designers (e.g. working in other organizations) and thus allow for a decentralized approach to model workflows. During run-time operation, workflow instances can be exchanged between different workflow engines via replication or messaging. Mobile users can participate in workflows by means of replication or by remote access based on the Internet and WWW. In the current version, these features, as with most other WFMSs, can only be used in homogeneous system environments.

Another WFMS enabling the planning of wide area workflows was *LEU* (see Section 4.2.4.4, p. 91), but its further development has been halted and the product is no longer offered.

4.4 Discussion of the approaches presented in respect to Wide Area Workflow Management

Looking at the conceptual and scientific approaches to distributed and widely distributed workflow management, which have been presented in Section 4.2, the discussion of technical challenges is by far dominant in comparison to organizational aspects. The majority of the concepts and prototypic systems presented focuses on the lower two layers of the level model introduced in Figure 10 (p. 56). In these layers, the authors describe aspects of the interaction of dispersed information systems in general and, more specifically, they discuss measures to enable the execution of workflows in these distributed environments.

Some authors also present possible solutions for the third layer, which deals with the design of workflow models for WAWM. All of the approaches that include concepts for the purpose of planning distributed workflow execution, such as *FUNSOFT Nets*, *Workonnector* and *Phanta Rhei*, adhere to mechanisms of centralized or hierarchical coordination of the participants.

Similar observations can be made of commercial workflow management systems: most of the products allow for distributed and widely distributed execution of workflow instances in homogeneous and sometimes also in heterogeneous environments. Some systems additionally provide tools for the planning of this distribution based on the notion of *main processes*, which invoke and control remote *subprocesses* in a hierarchical manner.

However, none of the prototypes or products allows workflow designers to plan *wide area workflows* in a *flexible* manner. Furthermore, no concepts for *flexibility* during run-time operation of workflow instances, which connect several WFMSs, are discussed. The paradigm of *structured workflow management*, where run-time operation is predefined as far as possible during build-time, is predominantly discussed. It has been stated earlier that this paradigm is only applicable for a limited percentage of office procedures, while the structure of a considerable fraction of processes is partially or entirely unforeseeable during the planning phase. Thus, workflows systems for WAWM have to provide options for undefined parts in workflow models, where workflow paths are defined by users during run-time operation.

Most scientific authors and commercial WFMS vendors do not approach the important challenge of devising *meta-models* for the design of *wide area workflows*.

The building of such descriptive languages, which contain elements for the development of models for WFMSs' interaction, is an important prerequisite for an efficient connection of isolated business processes fragments to overall process networks along value-add chains. Based on meta-models for WAWM, the next logical step would be to devise different *design methodologies*, which reflect the variety of ways how WAWM participants in intra- and interorganizational can collaborate. Apart from the notion of *main processes* and *subprocesses*, no further *design methodologies* could be found in products or literature.

None of the approaches presented provides concepts or solutions for the fourth layer, where the fundamental goals of cooperation and the organizational settings are reflected. Some of the questions that should be answered in this layer are: "What are the differences in the handling of *wide area workflows* between intra- and interorganizational collaboration?", "How do the terms and conditions of business influence the interaction patterns of workflow management systems?", "What does the existence of different coordination strategies in actual settings, such as *hierarchy*, *equal partnership* and *market*, mean for WFMSs' interoperability?", "Who is allowed to define the interfaces between the workflow systems?" and "What are the (transaction) costs of different interoperation modes of workflow systems?".

Questions like this fall into the discipline of *business computing*, where academic and business professionals try to describe the *organizational* and *financial* consequences of the application of information technology.

In the following chapters, the author will attempt to find answers to the above questions by discussing concepts and solutions for <u>all</u> of the four levels of Wide Area Workflow Management, which he regards as important for the interaction of workflow systems in times of global communication networks.

Taking the terms of real life business into account, the following points are of special interest:

- Are there methods for the interaction of WFMSs between autonomous organizations, where no centralized or hierarchical coordination instance is welcome?
- How can Wide Area Workflow Management be planned reflecting different power relationships?
- How can the planning and execution of *wide area workflows* be kept flexible?
- How can not only the data, but also the competencies, be distributed?

Hoping to have made the reader as currious as possible, the author will address these points in the next chapter introducing concepts and solutions for *structured* and *flexible* WAWM in intra- and interorganizational settings.

5 Concepts for Wide Area Workflow Management (WAWM)

In this chapter, fundamental characteristics of systems for the realization of Wide Area Workflow Management (WAWM) will be discussed.

First, the author will look at the kind of information which is exchanged between widely-distributed office workers. Based on this initial analysis, the two paradigms of *automation & structure* and *user support & flexibility* are discussed concerning their relevance to the exchange of this information within WAWM.

Subsequently, new dimensions distinguishing WAWM from local workflow management will be introduced. This is followed by a more technical view on how workflow parts can interoperate in general and how this can be planned in workflow models.

Based on these fundamental considerations, a methodology of three *coordination mechanisms* for the interoperation of distributed workflow parts is developed. These *coordination mechanisms* take the *power relationships* between participants explicitly into account. It is further discussed how planning and execution of wide area workflows can be performed in a flexible way, based on the three *coordination mechanisms*.

Following these principal thoughts on the realization of WAWM, concrete architectures for systems supporting wide area workflows will be introduced. Elements such as *coordination directories* and mobile information containers (called *message objects*) are targeted as elements of such architectures. Aspects of bridging heterogeneous systems in WAWM with the help of *gateways* then follow.

Since it is not enough to know in principle how WAWM should be supported in a conceptual and technical way, this chapter ends with the introduction of a life cycle model for implementation and maintenance of Wide Area Workflow Management.

In this chapter, the author wants to emphasize the importance of organizational aspects to workflow management and especially WAWM. The intention is to develop concepts based on real-life situations rather than first developing an elaborate technical solution for which the problems must then be devised. Therefore, the following concepts are based on the case studies presented in Chapter 2 (p. 9) and explicitly take organizational implications of technical measures into consideration.

The concepts which are presented in the following sections build the basis for the prototypic framework of the Wide Area GroupFlow System (WAGS) described in Chapter 6 (p. 179).

5.1 Fundamentals

How should widely distributed office work be supported by Wide Area Workflow Management?

There are certainly many imaginable responses to this question. A possible strategy to find appropriate answers is to first look at what kind of interaction actually takes place between distributed and widely distributed office workers in today's organizations: when office work is compared to production processes, one finds that the involvement of human actors is significantly higher. Consequently, communication between office workers is very important. Communication processes can be oral or based on written communication carriers in the form of documents. In many cases both forms of communication are used simultaneously and consecutively, for example: first a meeting takes place in which certain documents are used and then a meeting protocol is written, serving as material for further documents and meetings, and so on.

What kind of information is transferred in these communication processes? The following list gives some examples:

- *Functional* or *factual information* covers information that is supposed to lead to a certain result. Examples are product numbers and names, amounts, prices, signatures, terms and conditions. In general, this is mainly perceived as *the* information or data and is the main target for technical measures;
- *Contextual information* is intended to further describe factual information and make them easier to understand for recipients. Examples are pictures or descriptions of goods;
- *Meta information* is used to enable communication, e.g. sender, addressee, dates and references;
- *Feelings* and *judgements* express emotions that come with the communication processes and the topics discussed. They are, for example, expressed through body gestures, facial expressions and emphasis on certain words in oral and written communication. Feelings and judgements play an important role in communication processes.

Technical measures should take all of these information types into account in order to simulate "natural interaction" as closely as possible. This is one of the aims of CSCW research (see Section 3.2.1, p. 26). In the following, only asynchronous CSCW techniques will be further regarded.

Increasing the distance between office workers in many cases will call for increasing the use of written documents versus oral communication. It can be observed that widely-distributed office workers make extensive use of all kinds of documents in order to exchange all of the above-mentioned types of *information* (not only *data*: see Section 3.1, p. 23). Often used document types for this kind of information exchange are letters, memos, protocols, brochures, catalogues etc. Letters can be further categorized into *general purpose letters* (e.g. welcome letters) and *specific purpose letters* (e.g. requisitions, quotations, orders, confirmations, delivery notes, invoices etc.).

Office workers have a common knowledge of how to interpret the *syntax* of these documents, allowing recipients to *decode* the contained information. For example, letters usually start with information about the senders' company and the address. On the left side below one can find the addressee and on the right side, more detailed information about the sender, date of writing, customer number etc. is provided. Even when people send messages which are not compliant with certain standards, recipients are often able to understand these documents. This allows for an enormous flexibility in office work.

There are extensive logistical systems which were devised to transfer documents between senders and recipients. Major elements are, for example, systems for document printing, enveloping, payment, distribution and delivery, returning receipts etc. For many years, technical measures are used and further developed to facilitate communication using paper-based or electronic documents. Parts of the electronic measures have been described in earlier chapters of this book, for example electronic mail or shared document databases.

The different types of information described above can be fully or partially represented and transferred between widely-distributed office workers by these techniques, for example

- *Field-based data* (e.g. in field types of text, number, date) can be used for *factual information.*
- *Compound documents* are able to represent *factual* and *contextual information* with the help of formatted text, images, spreadsheet calculations, charts, speech annotations or videos.
- Standards for *electronic mail* (e.g. X.400, SMTP, MAPI, VIM) or *compound documents* (e.g. SGML, HTML, XML, HyTime, OLE, OpenDoc) have specific sets of fields for *meta information.*
- *Emoticons* or *mood stamps* (e.g. ☺, ☹) as well as speech and video objects allow users to express feelings and judgements.

This list shows that technology is mature enough to represent major elements of information handled in offices. One can observe two fundamentally different strategies for applying these increasingly mature options of computer and telecommunication technology to workflow management:

A first paradigm is to use technical measures to *automate* business processes in office work. For example, Schulze and Boehm [1996] use the term *office automation* as the basis for a classification of groupware and workflow systems. The underlying notion is that manual office work is inefficient and can be streamlined with *automation* methods similar to production processes. This is a fundamental thought of BPR (see Section 3.3.2, p. 44).

For WAWM, this means that systems would automate workflows between widely distributed office workers as much as possible (Figure 16).

Automation implies that users are not confronted with routing tasks and would perhaps not be aware that the next step in a workflow will be performed in another organization or that work just arrived from outside. Comparable approaches for interorganizational information systems are described in EDI literature (see Section 3.4.1, p. 59).

Also the WfMC mainly focuses on the paradigm of *automation* in the definition of its Interface 4 specifications for the interoperability of WFMSs (see Section 4.2.1.2, p. 78).

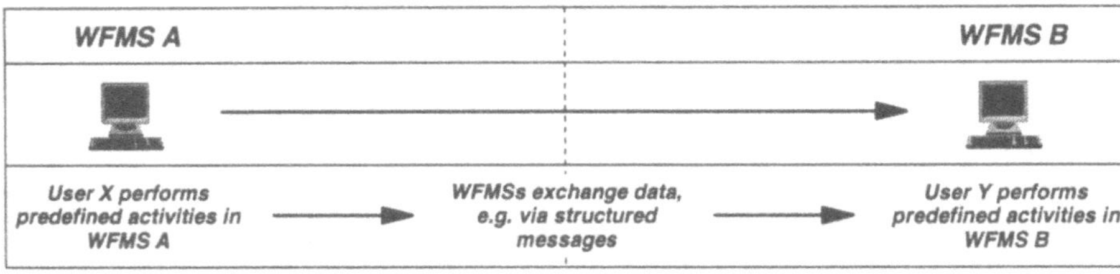

Figure 16: Paradigm of automation & structure in Wide Area Workflow Management

Attempts to fully automate production lines, as were discussed in conjunction with *CIM (Computer Integrated Manufacturing)*, failed in many cases because of very high costs, lacking flexibility and rejection by workers. This has led to insights that an optimal degree of automation is far below the maximal level of automation. A new paradigm in production processes is to form small groups of workers who are equipped with multi-purpose, easily adjustable machines. These groups are easier to coordinate, flexible, less costly and help to motivate workers due to increased competence. Even in car manufacturing, once a domain of highly tayloristic assembly lines, flexible group production has proven to be successful.

Therefore, another paradigm is to *support users* with *flexible tools* while they handle office processes (Figure 17). A distinction between *automation & structure* and *user support & flexibility* in respect to workflow management systems has already been discussed in conjunction with the classification scheme in Figure 12 (p. 76).

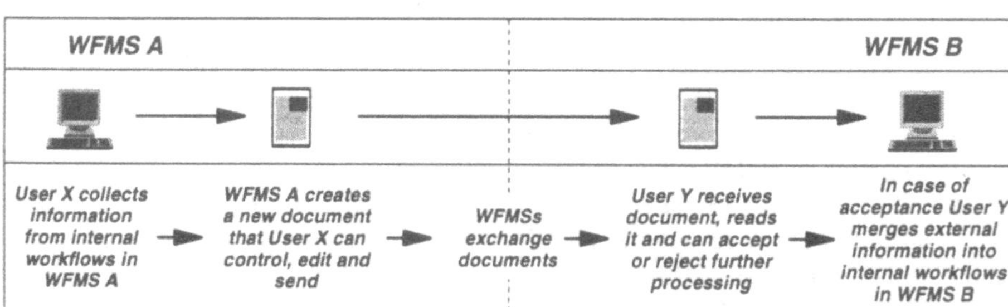

Figure 17: Paradigm of user support & flexibility in Wide Area Workflow Management

In the context of Wide Area Workflow Management, *user support & flexibility* would allow for more influence of involved human actors (Figure 17). Information from an internal workflow is collected in a new document which can be monitored and altered before sending. On the recipients' side, incoming documents would be presented to users, allowing them to accept or reject tasks that are requested from the outside. If accepted, flexible tools help to incorporate information from incoming documents into internal workflows of the recipients for further treatment (Figure 17).

Excursus on *automation & structure* versus *user support & flexibility*

Discussions on whether *automation & structure* or *user support & flexibility* are desirable have strong ethical aspects. At the heart of *automation*, which essentially means extensive replacement of human labor by machines, is the assumption that human beings are inefficient, costly and hard to predict. It therefore seems to be efficient to replace parts of their work with automated machinery that run 24 hours a day at low cost, do what they are told and are easy to predict. The notion that people are expensive and machines are cheap is based on a very shortsighted way of calculating costs. Natural resources can be easily exploited to produce and run machines at supposedly low costs. So far, the consequences of environmental pollution are not included into their prices. On the other hand, a large percentage of internal revenue is comprised of the taxes waged on human labor, which thereby becomes expensive. Based on this simplistic illusion, shortsighted attempts at rationalization aimed at laying off human beings and replacing them with machines, are often made. Thereby work is only shifted from one organization to others, e.g. machine vendors, consultants, programmers etc. Shifting taxation from labor to consumption of energy and resources would immediately thrust rationalization efforts into the exact opposite direction. The "oil crisis" in the 1970's is a good example to support this hypothesis. The "oil crisis" was caused by the fear that a primary energy source could be in short supply and that energy prices would continue to rise dangerously; drastic changes in economic behavior ensued, aimed at measures to economize on energy intensive production processes.

At the heart the concept of *user support & flexibility* is the assumption that human beings are not obstacles in working environments, but rather are the reason why work is done at all. This applies to human beings who perform specific tasks as well as to those who have induced this work by their needs (e.g. customers). Therefore, supporting human beings in their attempts to accomplish work with high quality results within a reasonable period of time (and thus appropriate costs) is seen as a primary goal of this paradigm.

A very fundamental way to think of human collaboration, as found in offices, is the comparison with living organisms. Using this perspective, certain structures are only snapshots of systems in constant change. A basic principle of living organisms is the adaptation to new circumstances to ensure survival. Nothing is permanent in nature – everything flows. Transferred to the sphere of workflow management, not the (static) *definition of structures* but rather the enabling and guiding of *constant change of structures* should be given first priority. Since human beings are far more intelligent and flexible than any computer system today, it seems much more promising to provide users with flexible tools than to struggle for the automation of structures with the help of machines, thereby increasing inflexibility.

At the heart of this discussion are philosophic questions about order and chaos. In many situations human beings fear constant change (perceived as chaos) and struggle for order – this is a basic principle of automation. "We finally have this process under control..." is a widespread, but very static way of thinking. The Eastern philosophy of contemplation would perhaps suggest that we watch and enjoy constant change, and adapt flexibly.

Several observations provide further arguments that benefits of *automation* have been largely overestimated in the past. For example, many attempts to prove a significant increase of productivity by the use of computers in office work have failed (see for example [Herget 1994]). Furthermore, the use of EDI in interorganizational cooperation has not led to significant improvements (see Section 3.4.1, p. 59). In the judgement of the author, this is also due to the fact that aspects of *user support & flexibility* have not been sufficiently taken into account; this is especially true for first and second generation WFMSs and many EDI implementations. When viewing the processes of manual office work, it is obvious that a high proportion of unplanned, ad-hoc work takes place (see case studies in Chapter 2, p. 9). This is reflected in the high percentage of low structured information that needs flexible handling by human beings (see p. 25). Therefore, supporting users in a flexible manner is a must when trying to implement computer systems in office environments.

It can be further observed that the use of groupware platforms is one of the first examples of significantly increased performance and efficiency in office work [McCready et al. 1994] due to their explicit support of flexible forms of work. The enormous success of the WWW has proven that flexible information systems that are easy to understand, helping users instead of replacing them, are essential elements in the improvement of office work. It has been stated earlier that the underlying principles of information presentation and handling in groupware platforms and the WWW are similar.

Finally, it can be proven with the first and second principle of thermodynamics that natural processes of energy transformation as found in plants, animals and also in human beings cause the lowest possible increase in entropy. In other words, seen from an energetical point of view, human beings can work very efficiently compared to machines which were built by human beings. To restate this concept, the notion that human beings are expensive and inefficient in comparison to machines, which are supposed to be cheaper and more efficient, is based on a very questionable way to calculate costs and judge benefits. This notion misleads efforts to improve efficiency in office work into the direction of *automation*.

End of excursus.

The author does not want to deny the need for structure and the unquestionable success of automation in certain areas, like mass production. However, in the field of workflow management that attempts to support office work, the potential benefits of automation have been overestimated in the past. The discussion of general models, scientific prototypes and commercial WFMSs in Chapter 4 (p. 73) shows that the majority of authors adheres to the paradigm of *automation & structure*. In the opinion of the author, it is not enough to enable flexibility by allowing *exceptions* from structure, but *user support & flexibility* is at the heart of workflow management because it is at the heart of office work. This is especially true of Wide Area Workflow Management because participants, in interorganizational settings for example, are largely independent and therefore need to be coordinated flexibly. It is difficult, costly and thus inefficient to force them into systems which mainly support *automa-*

tion & structure (see for example case studies in Chapter 2, p. 9) because *coordination* or *transaction costs* are too high (see Section 3.2.3, p. 31).

The concepts of Wide Area Workflow Management presented in this chapter follow the paradigm that a balance between *automation & structure* and *user support & flexibility* must be struck for each specific situation according to the following principle:

Use only as much *automation & structure* as necessary while at the same time allow for as much *user support & flexibility* as possible.

Since in the past, research and development in the field of workflow management and WAWM has largely focused on *automation & structure*, the author wants to emphasize the paradigm of *user support & flexibility* shown in Figure 17 (p. 106) in the subsequent discussion of concepts.

5.2 General characteristics and requirements

The term of Wide Area Workflow Management has already been defined in Section 3.3.4 (p. 52). In the following sections, fundamental organizational and technical challenges of WAWM will be discussed.

5.2.1 Challenges of coordinating the collaboration of widely distributed workflow participants

How can widely-distributed office workers in intra- and interorganizational settings cooperate by means of workflow management?

A fundamental answer is that their efforts have to be *coordinated*. First of all, this is an organizational challenge where aspects of *needs*, *goals* and *power* come into play. In order for people to cooperate, they must have a *common goal* that is mutually agreed upon (e.g. the delivery of goods). A certain *need* will drive them to struggle in order to reach this *goal* (e.g. the will to earn money). Multiple efforts by different persons have to be *coordinated* so that the common goal is actually achieved. Basic strategies of coordination such as *hierarchy*, *equal partnership* and *market* have already been discussed (see Section 3.2.2, p. 29). Coordination strategies chosen for certain situations depend on the relations of *power* among the participants.

An additional element in the coordination of collaboration is *trust* [Senge 1997]. It builds the foundation for the realization of coordination strategies, especially in settings of *equal partnership* and *market*.

These fundamental thoughts can build the basis for this book's topic: Wide Area Workflow Management is about the collaboration of office workers in distinct, widely-distributed WFMSs. First of all, the participants must agree on *common goals* that should be achieved. Subsequently, they will negotiate on what coordination strategy is appropriate in a given situation. Finally, they will implement or adapt certain technical measures to enable cooperation.

This means that users in different WFMSs do not collaborate because interoperability of their WFMSs has been achieved on a technical level. They will work together because of *common goals*, whether they can make use of interoperable WFMSs or not.

The primary challenge of Wide Area Workflow Management is therefore ***not*** to connect WFMSs with technical measures, but to allow for a *flexible coordination* of participants. Flexibility is a primary prerequisite because goals and therefore coordination strategies may change in the course of a cooperation, especially in interorganizational settings. Flexible coordination is necessary during the planning of WAWM (build-time) as well as during execution of wide area workflows (run-time).

These dependencies between different levels of WAWM – coordination of goals, negotiation, planning, execution and control – can also be found in Figure 10 (p. 56).

In the following section, the author will first look at organizational and technical dimensions of WAWM. Subsequently, fundamental interaction patterns for independent, distributed workflow parts will be discussed (Section 5.3, p. 117).

Based on these fundaments, the author will come back to the challenge of flexible coordination within WAWM in Section 5.4 (p. 125) and Section 5.5 (p. 139).

5.2.2 Three dimensions of Wide Area Workflow Management

Workflow management within a single organization at one location is based on the following fundamental prerequisites:

- Within most organizations, a *hierarchical* coordination strategy is applied. This means that all legal and organizational aspects of workflow management are under the control of a single management and can thus be influenced centrally.
- The persons and groups who are involved in workflows as well as their competencies, user rights and addresses in an organizational network are known in advance. This information is mostly stored in *directory services* (e.g. X.500) or similar structures.
- Possible routing paths of workflows and storage locations of workflow information are also known. It is thereby possible to display the status of workflows, to remind actors of tasks which are due or to carry out statistic evaluations .
- Security aspects are under the control of a single organization. The actors who can read or change certain information, and those who are explicitly excluded from access, can be described within a consistent environment.
- Technical aspects such as hardware, operating systems and workflow management applications are known and can be influenced. WFMS environments are mostly homogeneous, or in case of heterogeneity, can be integrated. Transfer rates in local area networks are mostly high.

As we enlarge the scope of workflow management and try to connect several internal workflow parts across the boundaries of distributed, independent WFMSs in the sense of Wide Area Workflow Management, the prerequisites described above are no longer given. For WAWM the following can be stated:

- Possibilities for influencing legal and organizational aspects in partner organizations differ largely depending on respective coordination strategies (e.g. *hierarchy, equal partnership and market*). It may not be possible to influence them at all, necessitating decentralized approaches to the planning and execution of wide area workflows.
- The persons or groups participating in parts of workflows executed in partner organizations are partially or completely unknown.
- Routing paths and storage locations of external workflow parts may be unknown, too. Workflow tracking or reminding of actors can only be realized if allowed by partner organizations.
- Ensuring the security of workflow information is more complex. The information leaving an organization has to be actively filtered. In general, unauthorized access to information is more likely during a transfer by WANs.
- Hardware, operating systems as well as WFMSs used are often heterogeneous. Transfer rates in WANs are mostly low compared to LANs.

In WAWM one faces a variety of new challenges to be mastered in order to plan and execute workflows across distributed, independent WFMSs in a seamless and sound manner. These new aspects can be summarized within three orthogonal *Dimensions of Wide Area Workflow Management* (Figure 18).

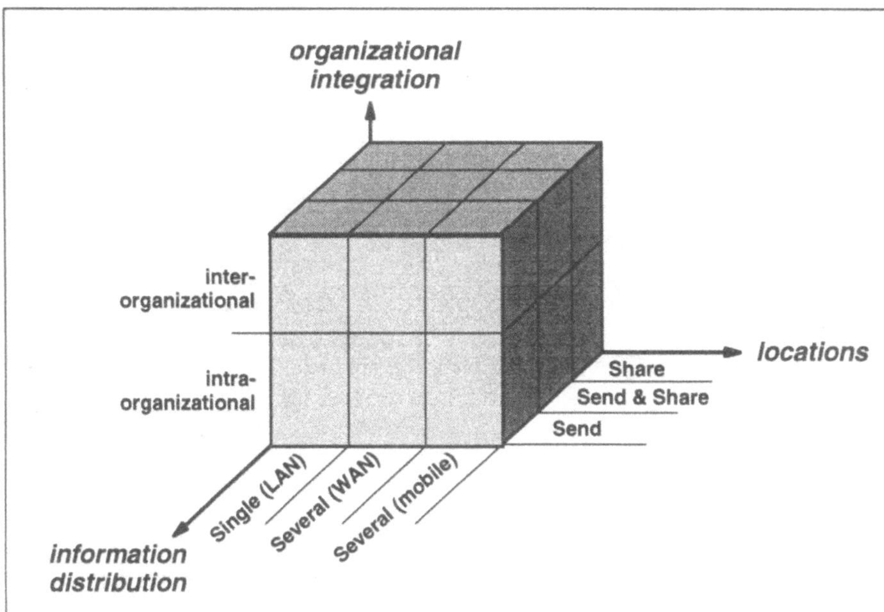

Figure 18: Three dimensions of Wide Area Workflow Management

The cube built by these dimensions of WAWM can be used to line out technical solutions for different organizational and geographical settings in 18 segments. Each segment describes a certain constellation that requires special measures to enable the connection of workflow parts between the partners involved. The arrows at the axes indicate increasing complexity for the respective dimension.

To further illustrate this classification of WAWM, the case of a sales engineer will be used as an example. Whilst at a construction site, this engineer wants to request a quotation for a machine from a partner company. He would probably use a notebook, modem and cellular phone as technical equipment. With the help of a local replica of his company's WFMS, he would start a request workflow. After typing in information about the necessary machine, his WFMS would connect to the partner company's WFMS through the modem and cellular phone and allow for the selection of an appropriate workflow "hook" from a shared database. Subsequently, the engineer would tell his WFMS to transfer a structured message to the partner company. There a quotation engineer would check the incoming request and start a quotation workflow. After a few hours, a message containing a quotation would be sent back to the initiating WFMS and thus to the sales engineer at the construction site. He can then make an offer to his customer as a result of the workflow he started.

In this example, members of two autonomous organizations connect workflow parts across several locations. They make use of shared databases and send messages for workflow purposes, communicating via mobile systems (Figure 19).

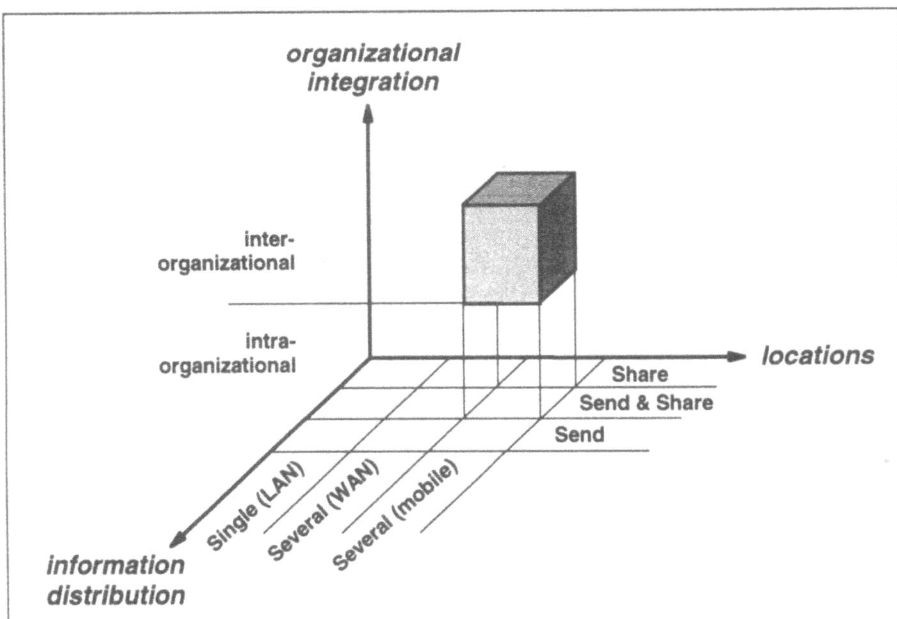

Figure 19: Example of a segment: Sales engineer requesting quotations from partner companies whilst at construction sites

The author has helped to implement a similar application for a paper machinery manufacturer in the USA. With the help of an interorganizational WFM solution and a layout and quotation program for the respective machines, the duration for delivery of quotations to independent sales engineers was reduced from several weeks to less than one day. The ROI for this WAWM system was significantly higher than 100% in the first year of use. Customers of the sales engineers were impressed by the speed and accuracy of quotations, leading to a real competitive advantage for the sales engineers and the paper machinery manufacturer.

WAWM solutions provided for a case such as shown in Figure 19 can be applied to similar situations as well. They thus form a distinguished class of technical measures for certain organizational and geographical settings within Wide Area Workflow Management.

The three dimensions of WAWM shown in Figure 18 and Figure 19 will be further explained in the following sections. Two of them have already been briefly introduced in Table 2 (p. 54).

5.2.2.1 Information distribution

Generally speaking, the access and transfer of information within a group of persons can be achieved in two different ways: all pieces of information can be routed from one person or group to another by sending messages (*Send Model*) or by giving access to common information (*Share Model*). In paper-based office environments, we know the *Send Model* from letters or faxes and the *Share Model* from black boards or libraries.

The *Send Model* is realized through routing (or *pushing*) of information from one point to the next in a store-and-forward manner. Electronic mail is a well-known example. It is for instance applicable to support ad hoc workflow with a minimum of planning necessary (see also Figure 15, p. 85). In the context of WAWM, the *Send Model* can be used to transfer information between independent, distributed WFMSs. A major advantage is that information within the participating WFMSs remains completely separate. This is especially helpful in interorganizational settings. The efforts for structuring messages and tracking their workflow paths are comparably high.

The basic principle of the *Share Model* is to give a group of persons access to a shared database environment, where they can *pull* information at their own discretion. Information processed in local WFMSs is mostly handled in such a shared database environment because of powerful programming features, adaptable access rights and simple tracking.

In addition, open team tasks within self-managing workgroups, which may be included as a non-regulated step within a predefined workflows, can be very well managed within shared databases (see Figure 15, p. 85). The possibility of reacting flexibly when solving problems and dealing with exceptions due a larger pool of actors who check regularly for pending tasks in a common work environment has proven to be one of the biggest advantages of the *Share Model*. Within this model, the distribution of information across different locations can be realized by placing (partial) copies of the databases at the sites involved and regularly synchronizing them by means of *replication*. A certain level of trust between the participants of a wide area workflow is implied because they work in a common "virtual" workflow sphere.

Send and *Share Model* are complementary building blocks for the realization of flexible WAWM across several locations and organizations.

5.2.2.2 Locations

Connecting multiple workflow management systems across several locations has various aspects. A first and important one is the coordination of distributed organizational units or organizations that will be discussed in the next section and in Section 5.4 (p. 125).

On the more technical side, solutions that bridge heterogeneous systems and allow for the exchange of dedicated information carriers between WFMSs must be available. Various technical solutions for this purpose, e.g. EDI, Internet/WWW, CORBA or groupware platforms, have already been introduced in Section 3.4 (p. 59).

A basic characteristic of WAWM is the use of WANs or mobile communication to connect widely-distributed workflow participants. The use of WAN carriers usually allows for much lower transfer rates than in LANs and includes the danger of unauthorized access to information. These limitations are especially true of mobile connections via wireless communication systems.

When planning systems for WAWM, the frequency of information exchange must be taken into account as well. Intensive cooperation implicates high frequency and volume of information exchange. Therefore, higher setup costs for stable and powerful communication channels can be justified.

Systems for WAWM have to adapt to these limitations and requirements by choosing different channels according to the actual communication load or because of varying costs at different times of the day. In addition, the reliable encryption of information (e.g. using public key encryption methods like RSA) is very important because information transferred between WFMSs is mostly confidential.

5.2.2.3 Organizational integration

The distinction between intra- and interorganizational workflows has already been introduced in Section 3.3.4 (p. 52). In this chapter, the author wants to further differentiate between various degrees of organizational integration and their effects on the realization of WAWM.

Different forms of cooperation among organizations have been discussed in Section 3.2.6 (p. 37). WAWM also covers cooperation within organizations, for instance between distributed subsidiaries and head offices as in Case Study 1 and 2 (p. 9). In the following, the author wants to define a simplified working model in form of the *continuum of organizational integration.* It shows different examples of organizational integration in intra-and interorganizational settings and allows requirements for WAWM to be derived (Figure 20).

On the left of Figure 20, highly integrated organizational settings, for example centrally controlled companies with distributed subsidiaries, are found. One can assume a high level of trust between participants in a *wide area workflow* and a strong obligation to cooperate. The dominant coordination strategy in this kind of setting will be *hierarchy* (see Section 3.2.2, p. 29). Hence, the interaction of WFMSs can be largely influenced by a central management in regard to build-time and run-time operation. More to the middle of the continuum, there are intraorganizational settings with more independence of the participants, such as trusts or profit center oriented organizations. Still, *hierarchy* will be a widely found coordination strategy, but *equal partnership* and even *market* are also possible.

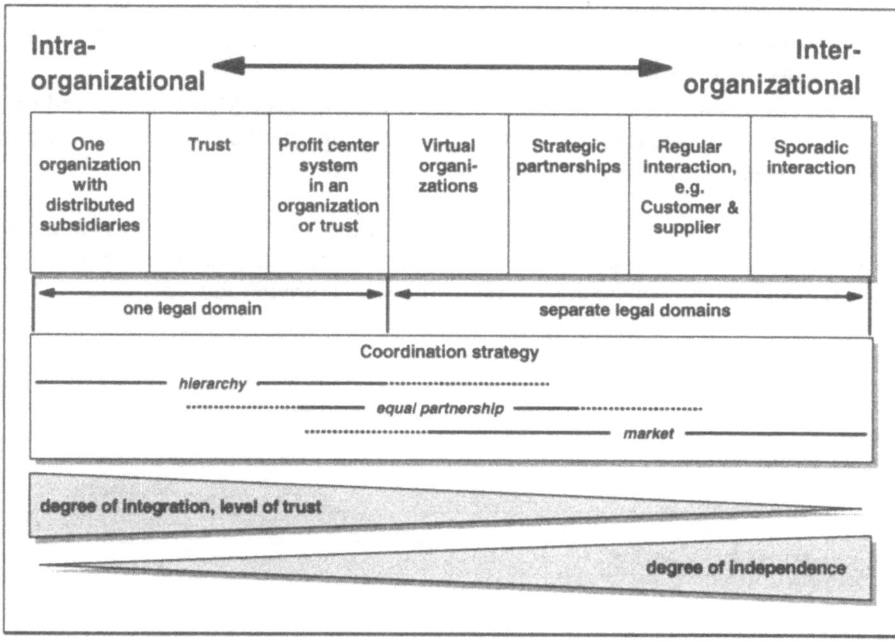

Figure 20: Continuum of organizational integration in Wide Area Workflow Management

Cooperation of separate organizations on the right side of the continuum is characterized by a comparably high degree of independence of the participants. Within this *inter*organizational collaboration, virtual organizations (VOs) would be a form of close networking (see Section 3.2.6, p. 37). A comparably high level of trust can be assumed in VOs, but as participants are autonomous, *equal partnership* will be the coordination strategy mostly found. In addition, *market*-like coordination and maybe sometimes *hierarchy* are possible. Going to the right of the continuum, integration and trust decrease and independence further increases. Therefore coordination according to the *market* paradigm will be dominant and *equal partnership* may be a good choice for certain situations. *Hierarchy* may also be found in cases of strategic partnerships, for example in Case Study 2 (p. 9) between LLM and certain suppliers.

As a first approach towards useful combinations of the dimensions of *organizational integration* and *information distribution* (Figure 18, p. 111), the following statements can be seen as "rules of thumb":

- In cases of a high integration and a high level of trust, Wide Area Workflow Management can very well be handled by using the *Share Model*. With the help of this model, a seamless "virtual" workflow sphere can be formed across multiple locations, e.g. with the help of replication technology.

- In cases of less integrated organizational parts or organizations, a combination of *Share Model* within areas of high trust (e.g. within profit centers or single members of VOs) and exchange of workflow information between these areas according to the *Send Model* can be chosen. Setting up a shared workflow sphere may then not be worth the costs or may be rejected by participants because of lack of trust.
- In cases of rather low integration and low trust, WAWM is best realized using the *Send Model* because of its simple setup and the complete separation of the respective internal workflow information.

In addition, aspects of geographical distribution of the involved locations and intensity of cooperation influence the choice of information distribution techniques. In Table 3, examples of combinations of these dimensions are introduced.

Organizational integration	***Intra-organizational***		***Inter-organizational***	
Intensity of cooperation	Low	High	Low	High
Information distribution	Generally: *Share Model* with adaptable selective replication; Exceptions handling: *Send Model*	Generally: *Share Model* with predefined selective replication; Exceptions handling: *Send Model*	Only *Send Model*	Exchange between WFMS: *Send Model*; Coordinative information (e.g. available workflow types): *Share Model*
Autonomy of interacting WFMSs	Integrated WFMSs; Shared computing, identical access in distributed „virtual offices"	Integrated WFMSs; Shared computing, identical access in distributed „virtual offices"	Autonomous WFMSs; protected computing; exchange of well-defined information items via e-mail	Autonomous WFMSs; protected computing; exchange of information via gateways
Security	Encryption	Encryption	Encryption, Explicit content filtering	Encryption, Explicit content filtering
Technology	WAN or mobile	Mostly WAN, mobile when needed	WAN or mobile	Mostly WAN, mobile when needed
Sample scenarios	Sales force	Subsidiaries	Customer & suppliers	Strategic partnerships, virtual organizations
Case studies (Chapter 2)	Mobile sales force of IB	Cooperation between different locations of LLM	Cooperation of IB with suppliers of auxiliary material	Cooperation of LLM with main suppliers

Table 3: Examples of different combinations of the dimensions of location and organizational integration in cases of low or high intensity of cooperation

5.3 Interaction and synchronization of distributed workflow parts

In the preceding sections, fundamental challenges and different dimensions of WAWM have been discussed in a general perspective. Now further details will be provided concerning the technical realization of WAWM based on what has been stated before. In this section, possibilities for connecting distributed workflow parts between independent WFMSs will be looked at.

First, a short introduction to a workflow *meta-model* will be given, laying the foundation for a graphical description of workflow parts later on.

Existing *meta-models* (see p. 48) for the design of workflow types mostly have *nodes* for activities and *arrows* for transitions between activities. Sometimes dedicated *split* or *join nodes* are used to handle parallel branches. In other models, regular *nodes* can incorporate *split* and *join* operations. Conditions for transitions are sometimes directly assigned to *arrows* (e.g. in IBM FlowMark, GroupFlow and others) or are symbolized by *dedicated nodes* (e.g. OR, XOR etc.).

The following *meta-model* will be used to describe workflow parts (Figure 21).

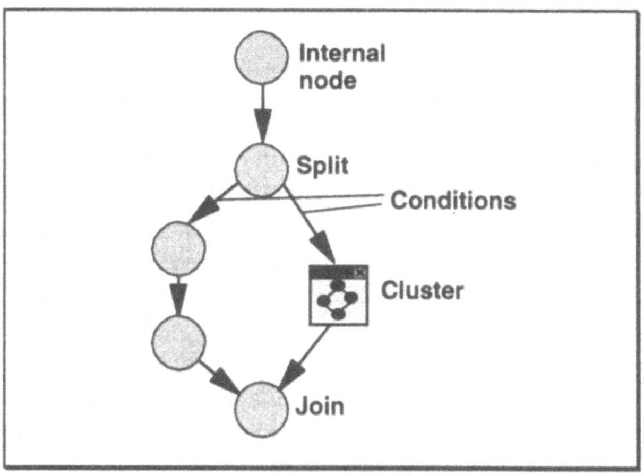

Figure 21: Basic meta-model for workflow parts

Activities performed within workflow parts are symbolized by so-called *internal nodes*. They are called "*internal*" to distinguish them from nodes for *external* activities that will be introduced later. *Internal nodes* can be followed by *split* operations. Conditions for split operations are assigned to arrows. *Join* operations are performed within regular *internal nodes*. Therefore, special *split* or *join* symbols are not necessary.

Several internal nodes can be gathered in so-called *clusters* that require exactly one incoming and one outgoing arrow. *Clusters* serve to make large workflow models easier to understand by aggregating certain parts of already designed models bottom-up. Additionally, they can be used to start workflow modeling in a top-down manner by first using empty *clusters* for major steps and later filling these *clusters* with *internal nodes* and *arrows*. Since these kind of *clusters* only contains internal nodes, they can also be called *internal clusters*.

This meta-model is based on the methodology of *GroupFlow* (see Section 4.2.3.1, p. 85), where activities in *internal nodes* can be assigned to persons, roles, groups or departments. Additionally, *internal nodes* can be used to symbolize *open team tasks* and *controlled team tasks* in the sense of the *Workflow Continuum* (Figure 15, p. 85). They thus can build segments in workflow models where the actual working order is not predefined and will be developed by users during run-time operation.

The author now wants to look at interaction patterns to connect several independent workflow parts. There is a strong similarity between the patterns described below and programming techniques for distributed programs [Andrews 1991]. In the CORBA specification of the OMG (see Section 3.4.3, p. 64), three interaction patterns between client programs and targeted objects are described:

- *One-way requests*: a client programs "fires" a message to a remote object and does not expect a response;
- *Synchronous requests*: a client programs issues a request to an object and waits until the return of a response;
- *Deferred synchronous requests*: client programs can proceed while waiting for the return of responses from objects they contacted.

These patterns can be adapted for the interaction of workflow parts.

The WfMC describes four interaction patterns [WfMC IF4 Abstr. 1996], [WfMC Ref. Mod. 1994] that have already been introduced in Section 4.2.1.2 (p. 78). The current specification of the WfMC goes in further details for so-called *chained processes* that are similar to *one-way requests*, and *nested subprocesses* that are the same as *synchronous requests*. Further patterns only mentioned are *parallel synchronized* and *peer-to-peer*.

In the following section, the approach of interaction patterns between distributed workflow parts will be further developed. First, some terms will be defined to facilitate the subsequent presentation and discussion:

- WFMSs starting interaction with other WFMSs will be called *initiators*. Targeted WFMSs are labeled as *addressees*.
- Workflow parts are illustrated with *internal nodes* for activities and *straight arrows* for transitions between these activities. They are limited by surrounding rectangles. Each workflow part is controlled by a single WFMS.
- Interactions with other workflow parts are symbolized by *curved arrows*. The start of an interaction will be called *exit* on the side of an *initiator*. The receipt on the side of the *addressee* will be called *entry*.

In the following Table 4, different interaction patterns will be described and illustrated with examples. These examples are partially taken from the case studies of IB and LLM presented in Chapter 2 (p. 9).

Interaction pattern	*Examples and synchronization strategies*	*Visualization*
1. Sequential workflow parts (SWP)	Examples: - Enrollment of new software from head office to distributed subsidiaries (LLM) - Release of new accounting regulations to different departments - Distribution of new product information and prices to sales representatives (IB) Synchronization: - By sequence	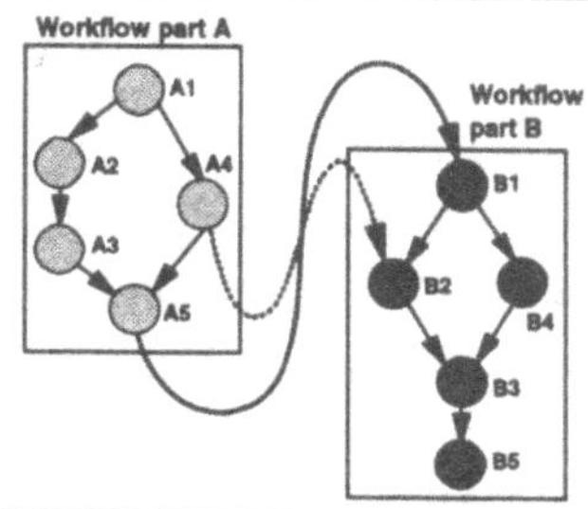
2. Nested workflow parts (NWP)	Examples: - Request for an offer from supplier during provision of auxiliary material (IB) - Request to sales force for sales forecasts within IB's budget planning - Delegation of work to a partner company within a virtual corporation Synchronization: - By sequence	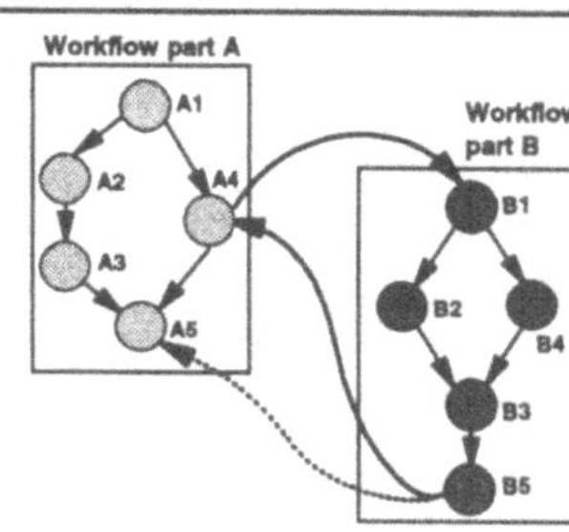
3. Parallel workflow parts with synchronization (PWPS)	Examples: - Distributed product development between LLM and supplier(s). - Preparation of a trade show with several departments - Evaluation of different financing strategies for a company merger by several teams Synchronization: - By "virtual" start node and synchronization nodes (also possible: "virtual" end node)	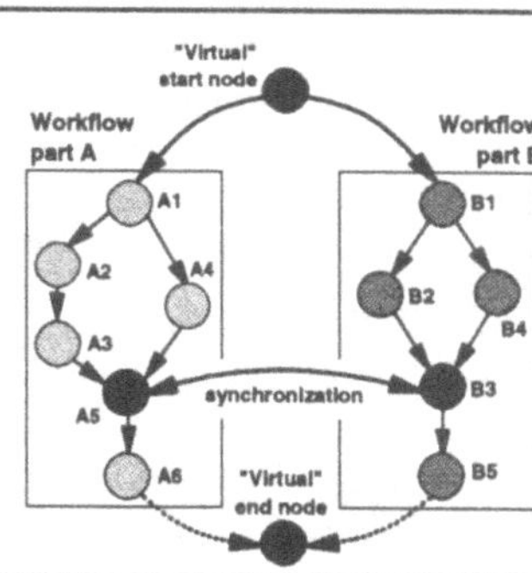
4. Complete integration of workflow parts (CIWP)	Examples: - Cooperation in virtual organizations - Common project work among distributed subsidiaries - Development of new sales methods between subsidiaries and members of mobile sales force Synchronization: - By "virtual" start node and sequence	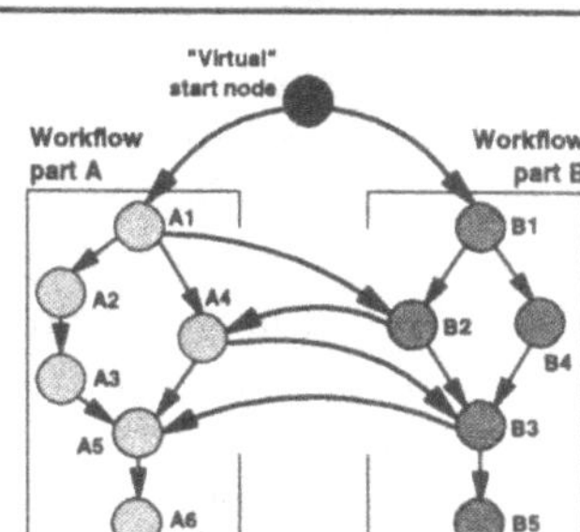

Table 4: Interaction patterns for distributed independent workflow parts

A first pattern is called *sequential workflow parts (SWP)* and is similar to *chained processes* of the WfMC. In an *SWP* interaction, workflow part A of an *initiator* terminates and hands over workflow information to an *addressee*. There, workflow part

B is started. One can also imagine an *exit* from a running workflow part A (e.g. from node A4) that targets an activity in a running workflow part B (e.g. node B2). This possibility is indicated by a dotted curved arrow in Table 4. *Exits* from running workflow parts do not pose synchronization problems. However, *entries* into running workflow parts require that, in the example of Table 4, workflow part B has been started in time and activity B2 waits for information coming from workflow part A.

For reasons of simplification, the following limitations will be stated:

- *SWP* patterns allow for *exits* at any point of workflow parts.
- Additionally, internal processing in other branches of the same workflow part can continue.
- An *addressee* is always required to start a new workflow part, though, when called by an *initiator* with a *SWP* interaction.

In other words, firing at running workflow parts is not allowed within *SWP* interactions. This is not a major limitation because the *addressee* can define rather small, elementary workflow parts that do not need *entries* except in the start node. *Entries* and *re-entries* into running workflow parts will be covered by the following patterns.

Nested workflow parts (NWP) are similar to *nested subprocesses* of the WfMC. The basic model of an *exit* and *re-entry* in a single activity (e.g. A4) is the same in both models. Additionally *NWP* describes *re-entries* in different nodes of the *initiators'* workflow part than where the *exit* was initially performed. This is the model of *deferred synchronous requests* within the CORBA specification. In both cases of combined and split *exit/re-entry* nodes, other branches of the same workflow part can be continued. As with *SWP*, *NWP* also requires the *addressee* to start a new workflow part. *SWPs* and *NWPs* can also be embedded in *addressees'* workflow parts, thereby allowing that for instance workflow part B could call a third workflow part C etc.

A third method is called *parallel workflow parts with synchronization (PWPS)* and describes two workflow parts being executed at the same time. To assure a joint start of both workflow parts, a *"virtual" start node* is necessary that belongs to neither of the workflow parts (therefore, it is "virtual"). Telephone calls between administrators of the WFMSs involved are a simple form of realizing *"virtual" start nodes*. During workflow run-time, contents handled in both workflow parts are synchronized at certain *synchronization nodes*. All parallel branches within workflow parts must be joined before synchronization can take place. Within the *PWPS* pattern, the roles of *initiator* and *addressee* can alternate frequently. In both *start* and *synchronization nodes*, one side initiates a negotiation to find out if the other side is ready to do a joint operation, e.g. starting workflow parts or synchronizing contents during workflows. One can also imagine that both sides agree to inform each other upon termination of their workflow parts with the help of a *"virtual" end node*. This can also be realized with the help of an *uncoupling statement* at the end of the last synchronization process, allowing both sides to terminate workflow parts at their own discretion.

The fourth interaction pattern, called *complete integration of workflow parts (CIWP)*, aims at an intense exchange of information. It also needs a *"virtual" start node* in order to synchronize the initiation of workflow parts. From then on, synchronization is achieved through sequence. Therefore, a *"virtual" end node* or an *uncoupling statement* is not necessary. As contents are not synchronized, the parallel execution of additional internal branches is allowed. A *token system* with a *counter* is necessary to realize *CIWP*, so that for example A4 knows that an *entry* coming from B2 is a response to an *exit* from A1 issued earlier. *Entries* coming from other workflow parts can be requests, answers, or answers including new requests.

It will be shown later that an *addressee* can connect several workflow parts to an overall workflow. Thereby, each workflow part has exactly one *entry* from an *initiator* and one corresponding *exit* with a response to this *initiator*. Thus several *concatenated NWP* interactions allow for similar interactions as within *CIWP*.

All of the four interaction patterns can also be used with more than two workflow parts, but complexity increases rapidly. To handle *exits*, *entries* and *re-entries* among several workflow parts, a unique identification of workflow parts must at the very least be exchanged between respective *initiators* and *addressees*. For the realization of *"virtual" start* and *end nodes* as well as *synchronization nodes*, an elaborate negotiation protocol is necessary to ensure that all involved workflow parts are ready to do a joint operation.

Basically, all of the interaction patterns can be realized with both *Send* and *Share Model* (see Section 5.2.2.1, p. 113). Regarding *PWPS* and *CIWP*, it can be stated that run-time operation is easier to handle with the *Share Model* because dependencies among workflow parts are easier to control compared to the *Send Model*.

A result of the discussion of interaction patterns is a necessary enlargement of the basic *meta-model* (Figure 21, p. 117) with the following elements:

- *OUT-nodes* for *exits* and *IN-nodes* for *entries*. These can be separate, but also combined *IN/OUT-nodes* or *OUT/IN-nodes* are possible. Special *IN-nodes* mark points in workflows where *entries* from outside are expected, but the time of arrival cannot be predicted. Likewise, dedicated *OUT-nodes* are necessary to indicate that an *exit* takes place and the further control over the workflow information is outside of the respective WFMS.
- *"Virtual" start nodes* are used to synchronize the joint initiation of distributed workflow parts.
- *Synchronization nodes* indicate that all workflow parts involved wait until a joint synchronization of workflow information can take place. This can be achieved by a *synchronization protocol*. Basically, *synchronization nodes* are an aggregation of multiple *IN/OUT-nodes* simultaneously used in both workflow parts during a synchronization process.
- *"Virtual" end nodes* are used to confirm the termination of all workflow parts involved. They can be replaced by *uncoupling statements* at the end of the last *synchronization* process.

A fundamental question is how *IN-* and *OUT-nodes* can be connected to each other within one workflow part, e.g. in case of *NWP* interactions. It is possible to have several *OUT-nodes* (*exits* for requests) and *IN-nodes* (*re-entries* with related answers) within a workflow part of an *initiator*. Hence, an identification is necessary within an *(re-) entry* to mark it as an answer and to show what prior *exit* it is connected to. On the side of an *addressee*, there must be a connection between *IN-nodes* receiving *requests* from an *initiator* and *OUT-nodes* sending the related answer.

The following notation will be used (see also Figure 22):

- OUT indicates a node for an *exit* and IN a node for an *entry* or *re-entry*.
- These words are followed by a subscript letter indicating whether a node belongs to a specific *initiator* (e.g. $_I$) or a specific *addressee* (e.g. $_A$). For example, OUT_I sends a request to IN_A and subsequently OUT_A responds to IN_I.
- A second subscript letter indicates a unique identifier for each interaction. For example $OUT_{I,X}$ is an *OUT-node* from a requesting *initiator I* for *interaction X* and $IN_{A,X}$ is the corresponding *IN-node* on the *addressee's* side. An interaction is seen as the whole process of, for instance, request and answer in the case of *NWP* patterns. In the example of an *NWP-interaction X* mentioned above, the *addressee A* would send a response from $OUT_{A,X}$ to $IN_{I,X}$.
- Combined IN/OUT-nodes are described by a concatenated notation. For example an $IN_{A,X}$ /$OUT_{A,X}$ node would be used in case an *addressee* can respond to a request within an *interaction X* in one step, such as shown in the illustration of the *CIWP* interaction pattern in Table 4 (p. 119).

In Figure 22, a system with two workflow parts M, N and two *NWP* interactions X, Y is illustrated.

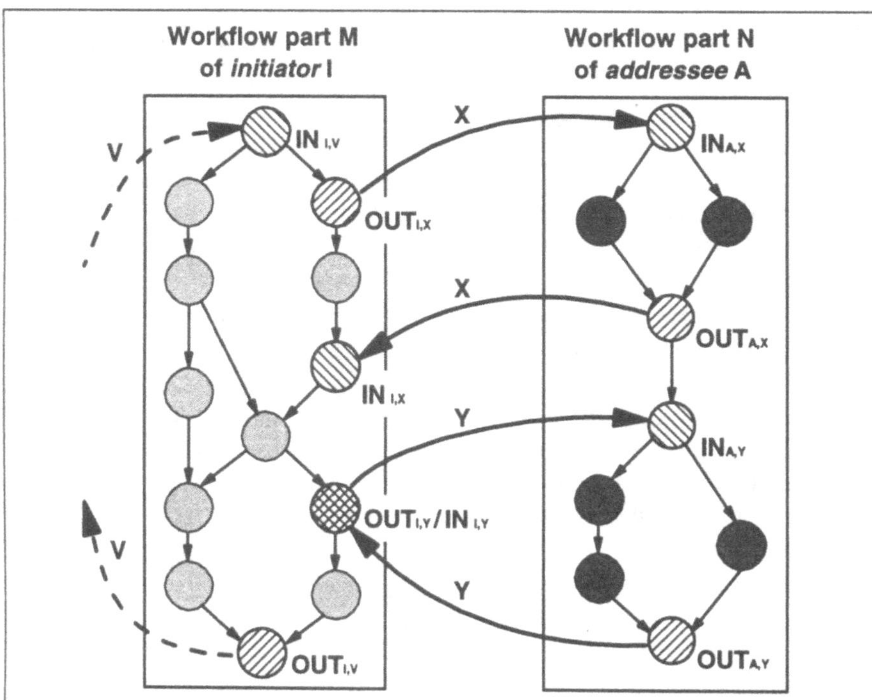

Figure 22: Extended meta-model for WAWM with OUT-, IN- and combined OUT/IN-nodes for interaction between independent workflow parts

For the purpose of a clear arrangement, corresponding *IN-* and *OUT-nodes* within workflow parts only have internal nodes between them. It would also be possible that, for instance, $IN_{A,Y}$ comes before $OUT_{A,X}$ in workflow part N (Figure 22).

A connection between corresponding nodes in workflow parts (e.g. between $OUT_{I,X}$ and $IN_{I,X}$) is necessary in order to detect incoming answers to previously issued requests. Therefore, the *meta-model* has to provide *connections* between *OUT-* and *IN-nodes* that can be used during planning of workflow types. During run-time, *connections* can be checked with the help of unique identifiers for each interaction.

OUT- and *IN-nodes*, as shown in Figure 22, can have both internal and external predecessors and successors. Because they represent normal activities in workflow parts, persons, roles, groups or departments are assigned to such nodes.

During the development of the *Wide Area GroupFlow System (WAGS)* (see Chapter 6, p. 179) the author found that larger workflow models with multiple *OUT-* and *IN-nodes* become very difficult to handle. This is especially true if workflow parts issue various requests in the role of *initiators,* and receive other requests in the role of *addressees* at the same time. This is illustrated in Figure 22 with *interaction V* that invokes workflow *part M* of the *initiator I,* who is thus also *addressee* of another *initiator.*

To simplify the use of *connections* between *OUT-* and *IN-nodes*, the *meta-model* can be enlarged with an additional node called *external task.* It is only used to symbolize *connections* between *OUT-* and *IN-nodes, or IN-* and *OUT-nodes.* No persons, roles, groups etc. are assigned to *external tasks.*

In order to make a clear distinction between corresponding *OUT-* and *IN-nodes* of *initiators* and corresponding *IN-* and *OUT-nodes* of *addressees* (that may occur in a single workflow part), the following rules for a *meta-model* facilitate the understanding of workflow models for Wide Area Workflow Management:

- Corresponding *OUT-* and *IN-nodes* of *initiators* are replaced by *external tasks.* Thereby a *connection* between them is automatically achieved. External tasks are symbolized by a rectangle (notation: $EXT_{I,X}$).
- On the side of *addressees*, corresponding *IN-* and *OUT-nodes* are left separate. Explicit connections between them are only necessary if more than one pair of these nodes are included in one workflow part. In practical application, this can be avoided in nearly all situations by defining small workflow parts with only one pair of corresponding *IN-* and *OUT-nodes.* Afterwards these distinct workflow parts are concatenated to an overall workflow model.
- Combined *IN/OUT-nodes* on the *addressees'* side are dissolved into *IN-nodes* directly followed by *OUT-nodes.* On the side of *initiators*, combined *OUT/IN-nodes* are symbolized with *external tasks.*

These measures have proven to make larger workflow models with various external interactions much easier to handle. The following Figure 23 illustrates these simplifications based on the example introduced in Figure 22.

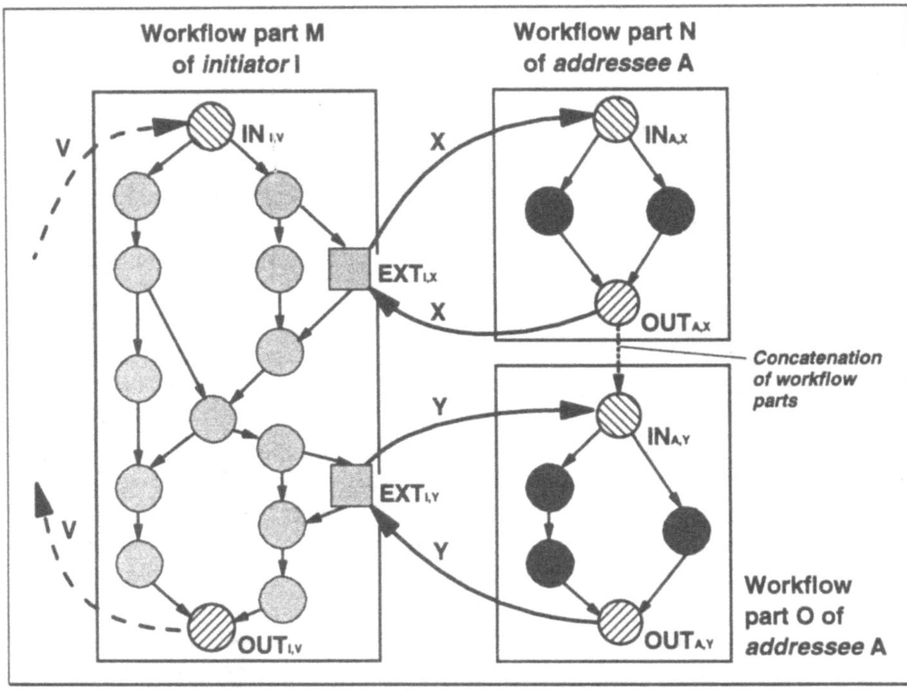

Figure 23: Simplification of the meta-model for wide area workflows with "external tasks (EXT)" and dissolution of combined OUT/IN-nodes

The use of *external tasks* and dissolution of combined *IN/OUT-nodes* is only meant to make models for WAWM easier to understand. Run-time operation is exactly the same with or without these simplifications.

The former *IN-* and *OUT-nodes* (Figure 22) in workflow part M are now regular *internal nodes* in Figure 23. This is necessary because *exits* have to be controlled in the preceding activity. Likewise, *entries* have to be checked before workflows can continue.

As we will see later, designers of workflow models may only see their own workflow part. In this case, other workflow parts are no more than "black boxes" with defined interfaces. Therefore, *external tasks* additionally help to symbolize workflow parts of *addressees* as "black boxes" on the side of *initiators*.

The four interaction patterns presented up to here are neutral regarding the control of interactions between workflow parts. Not discussed here is whether *initiators* or *addressees* specify the interfaces that connect workflow parts.

As described in conjunction with Figure 20 (p. 115), the *balance of power* among owners of connected information systems is of high importance to the form of cooperation. Therefore, in the following sections the author will look at different *coordination mechanisms* reflecting different power relationships.

5.4 Coordination of WFMSs' interaction - three different mechanisms

So far, general characteristics of Wide Area Workflow Management (WAWM) have been discussed in the form of fundamental thoughts on *automation & structure* versus *user support & flexibility*, followed by the introduction of *three dimensions of WAWM*. Basic patterns for the interaction of workflow parts were then presented in the last section, thereby concluding the introduction of essential organizational and technical aspects of WAWM.

The author now wants to focus the attention on a further important question concerning the connection of workflow management systems (WFMSs):

How can an interaction between
independent, distributed WFMSs be coordinated?
In other words, how can the will of widely-distributed office workers to collaborate by workflow means be realized across several WFMSs?

The need to find flexible coordination strategies for this purpose has already been discussed in Section 5.2.1 (p. 109). Additionally, fundamental coordination strategies have been presented based on *coordination science* (Section 3.2.2, p. 29). Now, these thoughts are combined to build *three coordination mechanisms* for WFMSs' interaction as answers to the above questions. These *mechanisms* are based on another important question:

Who defines and controls the interfaces between interacting WFMSs?

Responses to this question have to reflect the *power relationships* among the participating organizational units or organizations. Based on the notion of *initiators* and *addressees* introduced in the last section, three basic possibilities can be distinguished:

- *Initiators* define and control interfaces. Since they need the power to convince *addressees* to accept the defined interfaces, this mechanism is called *hierarchy.*
- *Addressees* are in charge of interfaces. They offer services with defined interfaces to *initiators*, who can then subscribe to these offers. Since this strategy is often used in commercial life, for example with catalogue-based ordering or opening of bank accounts, this mechanism will be called *publication & subscription* or simply *market.*
- Both sides jointly agree on the definition and further control of interfaces. This scenario is mainly applicable in cases where participants have approximately the same power and therefore will be called *equal partnership.*

A fundamental difference between the mechanisms of *hierarchy* and *market* is that in *market* arrangements *initiators* have choices between several offers. Besides having this choice, they can also give up plans to interact, if none of the offers is adequate. *Hierarchy* implies that there are few or no choices and that participants are obliged to cooperate in most cases.

As with all models, these three *mechanisms* simplify the complexity of coordination strategies for interaction among departments or firms. In reality, the actual strategy often lies in between these *mechanisms* or shifts from one to the other during collaboration. For example: the *initiator* of a workflow connection between two firms wants to take an offer made by a large *addressee* (e.g. a powerful bank), following the model of *market*. The *initiator* agrees to most of the terms, but would like the *addressee* to change some of them. If the *initiator* has got the power to convince the *addressee* of his purpose, the underlying *coordination mechanism* would shift towards (a more or less) *equal partnership*.

According to the level model of Wide Area Workflow Management (Figure 10, p. 56), *coordination mechanisms* must reflect different levels and related phases during WFMSs interaction:

- First, an agreement on fundamental goals of cooperation must be made during initial negotiations. Subsequently, aspects of *organizational integration* (see Section 5.2.2.3, p. 114) and the *balance of power* among the participants influence the choice of a certain *coordination mechanism*. In *intra*organizational settings, goals are often obvious (e.g. contribution to a product) and do not need further negotiation. As shown in Figure 20 (p. 115), participants within organizations are often coordinated by *hierarchy*. In contrast, *inter*organizational cooperation among owners of WFMSs often calls for initial clarification of goals and terms of collaboration. In many cases, *coordination mechanisms* such as *equal partnership* or *market* are applied in these settings.
- Subsequently, workflow models must be planned that allow for an interaction of involved WFMSs. Interfaces between the workflow models of the different, interacting workflow parts have to be synchronized *before* workflow instances can be executed.
- After workflow part models have been coordinated, workflow instances can be started. With the help of the interfaces defined earlier, workflow information is exchanged during run-time. Often the complete control of workflow information is handed over between WFMSs involved.

In the following sections, build-time of workflow part models and subsequent run-time operation will be discussed for the three *coordination mechanisms* of *hierarchy*, *market* and *equal partnership*.

5.4.1 Hierarchy

In hierarchical settings, *initiators* define whole workflow models for all participants or at least define interfaces between different workflow parts. In principle, three different degrees of autonomy in hierarchical settings can be distinguished:

A) Build-time centralized – run-time across several WFMSs

In this method, central workflow models are planned that cover all involved WFMSs. This implies that designers know all participating persons, groups, departments and organizations and that WFMSs can exchange workflow part models.

During build-time, workflow designers have to decide where certain workflow parts will be executed. Therefore, the basic meta-model introduced in Figure 21 (p. 117) can be enlarged to include a specific *cluster* that describes workflow parts and the WFMSs that executes them. This type of cluster will be called $\text{CLUSTER}_{\text{CEN,WAW}}$ because it is designed *centrally*, but run-time operation is based on *wide area workflows* among several WFMSs. It has the same symbol as an internal cluster, but an additional flash indicates that models for workflow parts are transmitted to other sites.

Figure 24 illustrates this modeling approach for two workflow parts M, N that are designed by an *initiator I*.

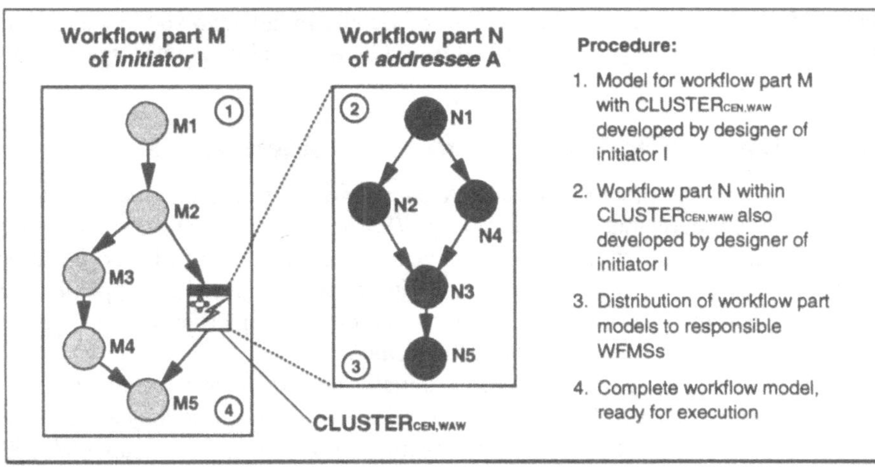

Figure 24: Hierarchy, method A:
build-time centralized – run-time across several WFMSs

Interfaces between workflow parts can be completely defined from a central point. Therefore, all interaction patterns between workflow parts (see Table 4, p. 119) can be realized. Figure 24 shows the example of a *NWP* interaction. It can modified as a *SWP* pattern by removing the arrow from the $\text{CLUSTER}_{\text{CEN,WAW}}$ to node M5.

To design parallel workflow parts with synchronization (*PWPS*), other elements of a meta-model would be necessary, as described in conjunction with Table 4 (p. 119). These elements will be further discussed in Section 5.4.3 (p. 134). A complete integration of workflow parts (*CIWP*) can be realized by centrally planning the workflow parts involved accordingly.

Since workflow models can be designed for all workflow parts involved, they only have to be distributed to all WFMSs involved and derived workflow instances can be started immediately. The distribution of workflow part models is best achieved with the *Share Model* (see Section 5.2.2.1, p. 113). All WFMSs involved would make use of a shared database with workflow models that is distributed and synchronized by replication. The *Send Model* is also applicable, but information distribution and synchronization is more complicated when several workflow designers are involved in different locations.

Run-time operation can also be handled with *Share* or *Send Model.* Using the *Share Model*, workflow repositories holding workflow information and related organizational information (e.g. persons, roles, groups, departments etc.) would be replicated among the involved sites. With the help of selective replication, each WFMS would only receive the information necessary to execute its workflow parts. The actual transfer of workflow information at the interfaces would also be handled by replication. If the *Send Model* is applied, workflow repositories remain separate and messages with predefined contents are exchanged at the interfaces, as for example proposed by the WfMC (see Section 4.2.1.2, p. 78). Aspects of run-time operation will be further discussed beginning with Section 5.6 (p. 143).

The application of this method is limited to intraorganizational settings because a central designer has to have knowledge of details of all involved organizational units. It is very unlikely that this method would be accepted in an interorganizational cooperation.

B) Build time participative – run-time across several WFMSs

In distinction to the previous method A, workflow designers of *initiators* do not define workflow parts that are executed by WFMSs other than their own. They plan which external workflow parts will be included at certain stages of workflows and assign responsible WFMSs. They further define what is supposed to happen in these workflow parts and determine the incoming and outgoing interfaces. These persons or groups will therefore be called *master designers.*

To implement this planning method, initially empty *clusters* are included into workflow models. They will be called $\text{CLUSTER}_{\text{PAR,WAW}}$ because they are designed in a *participative* way and are used for *wide area workflows* among distinct WFMSs. They are symbolized by an empty *cluster* icon, containing a "flash" for transmission (Figure 25).

After this initial design phase, workflow models containing $\text{CLUSTER}_{\text{PAR,WAW}}$ (status: *empty*) are distributed to the involved WFMSs. Workflow *part designers* fill empty *clusters* that will be performed in their WFMS and thereby contribute to overall workflow models with local expertise. After completion of the subordinated workflow parts (status: *completed*), the involved sites submit their design to the *master designers.* Submitted $\text{CLUSTER}_{\text{PAR,WAW}}$ are checked by *master designers* and are given the status *approved.* As a result, an overall workflow model describing all workflow parts has been accomplished. Finally, master designers switch workflow models to the status *operative*, allowing the execution of workflow instances.

This process of participative workflow design can be very well supported by *selective replication* of workflow model databases among the involved sites (*Share Model*). Run-time operation is handled the same as within the method A.

Figure 25 summarizes the approach of method B.

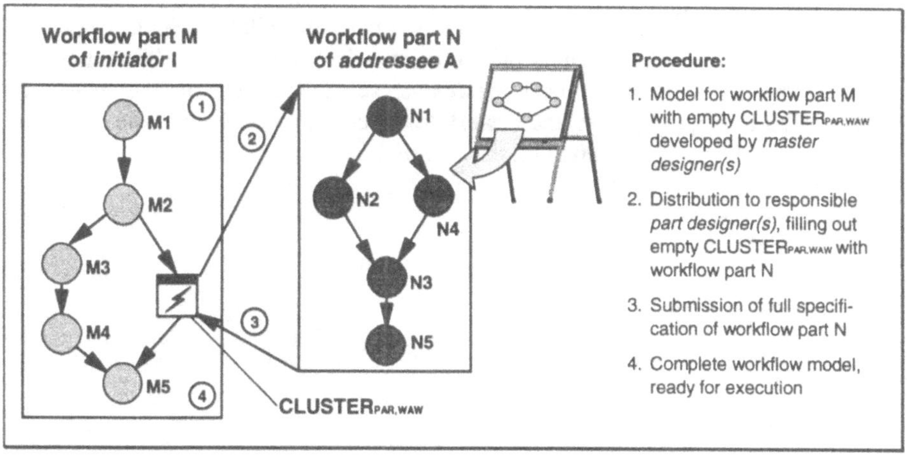

Figure 25: Hierarchy, method B: build-time participative – run-time across several WFMSs

As with method A, method B can also be used for all interaction patterns introduced in Table 4 (p. 119). Figure 25 shows *NWP* interaction that includes the possibility of *SWP* patterns.

Master designers need complete knowledge of the developed workflow models and the persons, roles, groups or departments involved in order to control the final workflow models. Therefore, method B of the hierarchical *coordination mechanisms* is mainly applicable in intraorganizational settings, but subordinate workflow parts have more autonomy when compared to method A.

C) Build time decentralized – run-time across several WFMSs

A further degree of autonomy can be achieved by not sending the specification of subordinate workflow part models back to *initiators*, as done in the previous method B. *Master designers* on the side of *initiators* develop their workflow part and include specific symbols for other workflow parts to be invoked during run-time. Subsequently, *part designers* model their workflow parts, but do not have to submit these models to *master designers*.

Since *master designers* no longer know details about these external workflow parts, they can not be seen as a variation of *internal clusters* (Figure 21, p. 117). Therefore, this new element of the *meta-model* for WAWM will be called *subworkflows* with the notation $\text{SUBWORKFLOW}_{\text{DEC,WAW}}$ *(decentralized, wide area workflow)*. A rectangular icon containing a closed envelope was chosen as the symbol for $\text{SUBWORKFLOW}_{\text{DEC,WAW}}$ (Figure 26).

Similar to method B, *master designers* describe the general purpose of *subworkflows*, define incoming and outgoing interfaces and the WFMSs responsible for execution (status: *empty*). Afterwards they send this information about the included $\text{SUBWORKFLOW}_{\text{DEC,WAW}}$ to the responsible *part designers*. There, workflow parts are developed according to the *interface specifications* provided.

Upon completion of the design of workflow parts in $SUBWORKFLOW_{DEC,WAW}$ (status: *completed*), *part designers* inform *master designers* that workflow parts are ready to be instantiated. *Master designers* set the status of the respective $SUBWORKFLOW_{DEC,WAW}$ in their workflow parts to *confirmed*. Subsequently, workflow instances can be started on the side of *initiators*.

Figure 26 illustrates this method.

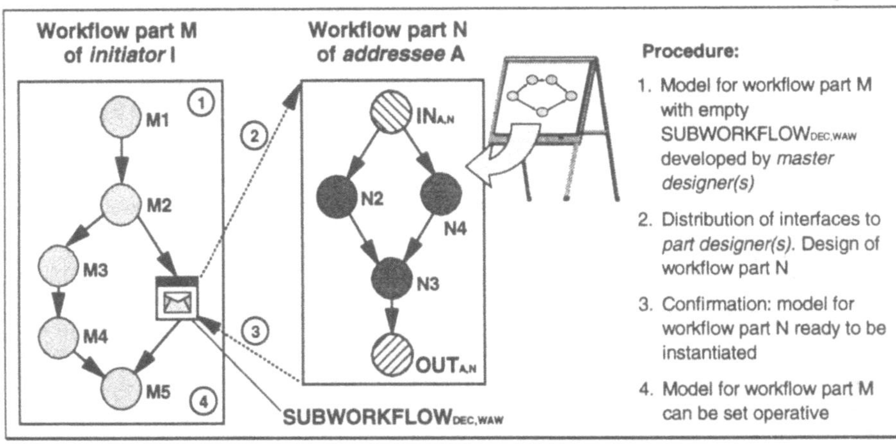

Figure 26: Hierarchy, method C:
build-time decentralized – run-time across several WFMSs

While *clusters* in method A and B contain a fully specified workflow part on the side of *initiators*, *subworkflows* are only *black boxes* with defined interfaces. This possibility has already been mentioned in conjunction with Figure 23 (p. 124). It illustrates a certain degree of autonomy between *initiators* and *addressees*.

Workflow parts of *initiators* and *addressees* have autonomous workflow models and are controlled by independent WFMSs. Hence, they can no longer be seen as distributed parts of one centrally controlled workflow. *Initiators* do not have control over workflow information leaving their workflow parts during the invocation of $SUBWORKFLOW_{DEC,WAW}$. *Addressees* take over control of *entries* and process incoming workflow information independently until they give back results in *exits*. Hence, workflow parts of *addressees* need dedicated *IN*- and *OUT-nodes*, as has been introduced in conjunction with Figure 22 (p. 122).

Since participants are more autonomous, method C is best suited to support *SWP* and *NWP* interaction patterns (see Table 4, p. 119) as shown in the example of Figure 26. *PWPS* patterns are difficult to realize because each designer can only see the internal structures of his/her own workflow part, while details of other workflow parts are inaccessible. For that reason, *PWPS* patterns are excluded for method C in the following discussions. The use of *CIWP* patterns can be substituted by concatenating several workflow parts on the side of *addressees*, as shown in Figure 23 (p. 124).

One can imagine that despite a certain autonomy, *master* and *part designers* may have to communicate informally to solve problems arising during the procedure of method C. For this purpose, they can use all kinds of technical support from telephone calls to e-mail or video-conferencing.

To support decentralized modeling according to method C, the *Share Model* can be applied again. Shared databases containing *interface specifications* of *sub-workflows* would be distributed and synchronized among participants with the help of selective replication. The *Share Model* can also be implemented with the help of shared *coordination directories* (e.g. according to X.500) to distribute interface definitions. Further details on *coordination directories* will be discussed in Section 5.6.1 (p. 145).

It is also possible to use the *Send Model* for transfer of *interface specifications* and confirmations among *master* and *part designers*.

Run-time operation can be supported by the *Share Model*, but it is also possible to apply the *Send Model* in order to keep workflow repositories of the WFMSs involved separate. Structured messages would be exchanged between workflow parts at the respective workflow steps, according to the *interface specifications* predefined by *master designers* of *initiators*. Since *addressees* have been informed in time about what information they will receive as input for a certain workflow part, invocation of respective workflow instances (e.g. based on models of workflow part N in Figure 26) can be prepared. In the case of an interaction between heterogeneous WFMSs, participants would have to agree on common exchange formats.

Since only interfaces of workflow parts – not complete process descriptions – are exchanged between designers, method C is well suited to application within intra- *and* interorganizational cooperative settings.

5.4.2 Market

Within the *coordination mechanism* called *market*, *addressees* define and control interfaces between workflow parts. They offer workflow services to *initiators* who can subscribe to these offers during planning of their workflow parts.

The respective purposes of workflow parts can be based on initial negotiations among partners. For example, an automobile manufacturer can make an agreement with lighting manufacturers that the latter offer workflow parts for the design of automobile and truck headlights. Workflow parts which are offered can also be derived from the general business goals of the organizations offering, e.g. allowing partners to request product information, quotations or sales forecasts.

Based on an initial agreement to cooperate, *addressees* start to design workflow models for the workflow parts they want to offer. They define the interfaces of these workflow parts by specifying the following:

- A general description of the results that can be expected when subscribing to an offer and subsequently invoking the respective workflow part.
- An exact definition of the required incoming information from *initiators*, specified on field-level. This definition can be based on standardized document types (e.g. EDIFACT-based) or can be specified individually.
- Likewise, an exact description of the outgoing information delivered, that will be send back to *initiators*.

- A list of formats *addressees* can deal with for incoming and outgoing information (e.g. WfMC-compliant Internet/MIME e-mail, HTML, XML etc.).
- Optionally, a predicted maximum processing time from invocation until delivery of results.

These *interface specifications* can be published for three groups of recipients:

- only for specific partners, where publication of selected workflow parts was agreed upon;
- for all partners an organization currently cooperates with;
- for potentially everyone, for example through catalogues or via the WWW.

After potential *initiators* have been informed about the *interface specifications* of workflow parts being offered, they can include them into their workflow models by a method called *subscription*. Because the interfaces of subscribed workflow parts are not controlled by *initiators* but by *addressees*, they cannot be compared to *subworkflows* within the *coordination mechanism* of *hierarchy*. To reflect the independence of subscribed workflow parts, they will be called $\text{WORKFLOW}_{\text{SUB,WAW}}$ (*subscribed, wide area workflow*). They are symbolized by rectangular icons as shown in Figure 27. Subscribed $\text{WORKFLOW}_{\text{SUB,WAW}}$ are "black boxes" on the side of *initiators*.

After initiators have subscribed to workflow parts being offered, they must then map internal workflow information to the required fields defined in the respective *interface specification*. An example illustrates this: an *initiator* designs a workflow for ordering parts in his PC maintenance department. The number of components needed will be stored in the internal workflow field called "parts_amount". *Interface specifications* of a subscribed ordering workflow of a reseller requires that the ordered quantity is provided in the field "order_quantity". Therefore, during run-time operation the content of the field "parts_amount" must be transferred to the field "order_quantity" before the subscribed workflow part can be invoked. The filtering and mapping of internal workflow information to *interface specifications* is called *content management* and will be further discussed in Section 5.6.3 (p. 162).

Within the *coordination mechanisms* of *hierarchy* (see previous section), *initiators* define the *interface specifications*. Therefore, *content management* has to be performed on the side of *addressees*. Since *addressees* design workflow parts at the request of *initiators*, they can adapt to the field structures defined in *interface specifications* sent by *initiators* in most cases. Hence, explicit field mappings are usually not required.

In the *coordination mechanism* of *market*, *addressees* start offered workflow parts with a single *IN-node* and terminate them with a single *OUT-node*. Several workflow parts, each with a single pair of *IN-* and *OUT-nodes*, can be concatenated according to Figure 23 (p. 124). Thereby, several *entries* and *exits* can be realized on the side of the *addressees*.

Since the publishers of *interface specifications* for $\text{WORKFLOW}_{\text{SUB,WAW}}$ can set the respective workflow part models to status *operative* before publication, *initiators* can invoke subscribed workflow parts immediately after *content management* has been set.

To distribute *interface specifications* of WORKFLOW$_{SUB,WAW}$ among interacting WFMSs, *directory services* can be used (e.g. based on X.500). Because they are set up to coordinate workflow parts in different WFMSs, they will be termed *coordination directories*. These *directories* can be distributed and synchronized with the help of selective replication (*Share Model*) or by exchanging messages (*Send Model*). Further characteristics of *coordination directories* will be discussed in Section 5.6.1 (p. 145).

Run-time operation is best supported by sending structured messages (*Send Model*), reflecting the autonomy of the involved WFMSs. This approach will be further discussed in Section 5.6.2 (p. 153).

Figure 27 summarizes the design methodology of the *coordination mechanism* termed *market*.

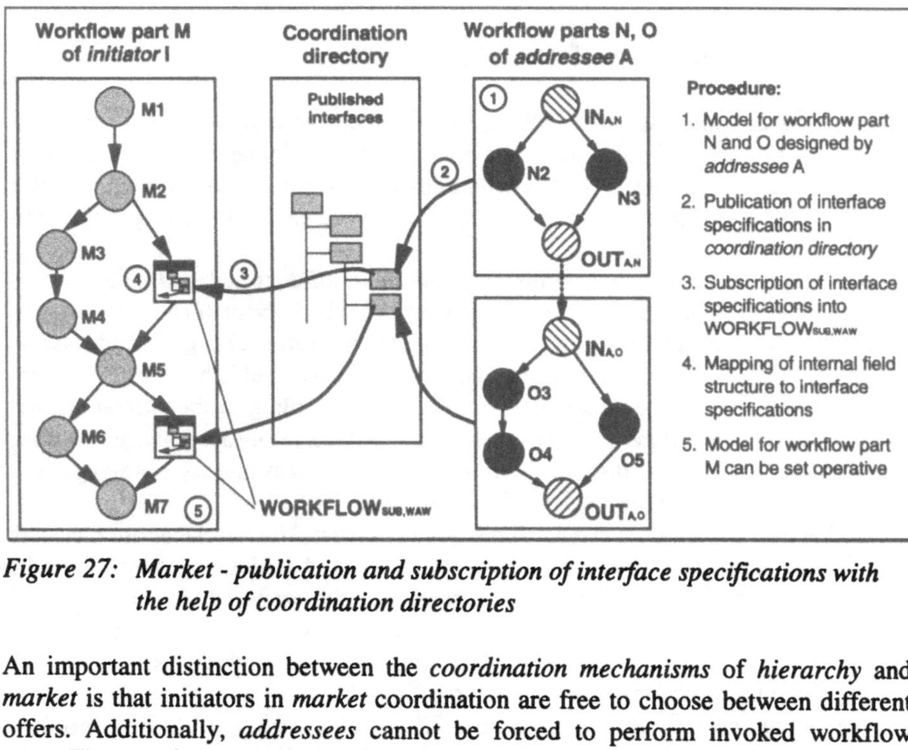

Figure 27: Market - publication and subscription of interface specifications with the help of coordination directories

An important distinction between the *coordination mechanisms* of *hierarchy* and *market* is that initiators in *market* coordination are free to choose between different offers. Additionally, *addressees* cannot be forced to perform invoked workflow parts. They are free to reject incoming requests for services they offered.

Since *initiators* and *addressees* can act autonomously, *addressees* do not necessarily know who has subscribed to the services they have offered and hence cannot predict the actual number of workflow instances invoked from outside. It is therefore helpful in certain situations that *initiators* can inform *addressees* of the fact that they have subscribed to certain offers and give an estimate of how many respective invocations they plan for a certain period of time. This feedback can also be given with the help of *coordination directories*.

The *market coordination mechanism* can be used to support *SWP* and *NWP* interactions (see Table 4, p. 119). Because workflow parts are largely autonomous,

PWPS interactions are not possible in this mechanism. Again, *CIWP* interaction can be substituted by concatenation of workflow parts on the side of *addressees*, as shown in Figure 27. For example, workflow part N could deliver a quotation for goods offered by *addressee A*. After *initiator I* has checked this quotation in node M5, he can decide to order the goods being offered in the next WORK-FLOW$_{SUB,WAW}$. Thereby, workflow part O for order processing is invoked. *Addressee A* can concatenate workflow part N and O with the help of a quotation number, for example.

Coordination of interacting WFMSs according to the *market mechanism* is well suited to supporting interorganizational collaboration because of the comparably high autonomy of participants. It can also be used in intraorganizational settings, e.g. among profit centers or distributed subsidiaries. Coordination efforts and costs are higher than within hierarchical mechanisms.

5.4.3 Cooperation of equal partners

In the practical application of WAWM, situations will arise in which neither *initiators* nor *addressees* should solely have the right to define interfaces between workflow parts. Therefore, a third *coordination mechanism* called *equal partnership* describes methods for allowing *initiators* and *addressees* to jointly specify interfaces.

A first step towards *equal partnership* between *initiators* and *addressees* would be an agreement to use one of the mechanisms described above (*hierarchy or market*). In advance, negotiations on the terms of information exchange would have to take place. For example, one can imagine that *addressees* publish *interface specifications* based on these negotiations with *initiators*, according to the *market mechanism*. Nevertheless, *addressees* maintain their privilege to always change *interface specifications* afterwards. *Initiators* can reject these changes and try to re-negotiate, however this possibility lies outside of software systems.

Within the *coordination mechanism* of *equal partnership*, interfaces are therefore specified by all partners involved right from the start. Additionally, they cannot be altered without both sides reaching an agreement on the proposed changes. This can be achieved through legal contracts, but here the author wants to look at possibilities for designing WFMSs in order to support *equal partnership* in this sense.

Negotiations usually take place in live meetings, be they face to face or supported by video-conferencing etc. (see Section 3.2.1, p. 26). A way to design workflow models synchronously would be to let several workflow designers work together in one modeling software, bridging geographical distance. This will be called *joint modeling*. Each designer of the involved WFMSs has his/her own cursor and toolbar in a joint drawing area. Designers can communicate with each other by voice and possibly also by desktop conferencing (video and voice).

In this scenario all designers involved can develop one large workflow model together. This approach will not be further pursued, because it is largely covered by method A and method B of the *hierarchical coordination mechanism*. The following discussions will deal with how independent workflow parts can be connected by *joint modeling*.

In this approach, each workflow part is shown in a *private drawing area*. Designers can agree to let other designers see all of their workflow parts or only interfaces, for example represented by *IN-nodes*, *OUT-nodes* and *external tasks* (Figure 23, p. 124). Workflow parts are separated by *boundary lines* that can be used to place interface elements.

An offer for a negotiation would start by for instance placing an *external task* on a *boundary line* and announcing this to other, concerned designers. The designer making the offer would explain the purpose of the interface being offered. Other designers might propose changes or start to adapt their workflow models according to the offer. At one point, all designers involved in an interaction between workflow parts would have to agree on the mapping of fields between *exits* and *entries*. This procedure is called *content management* (see also Section 5.6.3, p. 162). In the case of *NWP* interactions, designers would additionally have to agree on field mappings for *re-entries*, symbolized by an *OUT-node* at the end of the workflow part invoked and an external task on the side of the invoking workflow part.

If all involved designers start to develop their workflow part models from scratch, they would first roughly sketch the purpose and structures of their respective workflow part. After broadcasting these basics to other designers, they would next negotiate on the interfaces between workflow parts. After interfaces have been specified, all designers could use the agreed field specifications internally, too. Thereby, explicit field mappings would not be necessary.

Joint modeling can be used for the realization of *SWP* and *NWP* interactions (see Table 4, p. 119). Additionally, it is well suited for realizing *PWPS and CIWP* interaction patterns that are more difficult to cover within *coordination mechanisms* of *hierarchy* and *market*. To enable synchronization within *PWPS* interactions, *synchronization nodes (SYNC)* are included in the involved workflow parts and are connected with bi-directional *synchronization arrows (S_ARROW)* across *boundary lines*. The definition and structures of contents to be exchanged during synchronization has to be agreed upon in negotiations among designers.

The *meta-model* for *joint modeling* needs *internal arrows* to connect *internal nodes*, and *interaction arrows* to realize connections between different workflow parts. These arrow types are distinguished by straight lines for *internal arrows* and *curved lines* for *interaction arrows* in the following Figure 28. *"Virtual" start nodes (VSTART)* are represented by arrow-symbols directed downwards. Other symbols used in Figure 28 have already been introduced in Figure 23 (p. 124).

The notation for these elements of the WAWM meta-model is:

- *"Virtual" start nodes* are termed VSTART, followed by subscript letters indicating the workflow parts that are supposed to be start (e.g. $VSTART_{M,N}$).
- *Synchronization nodes* are labeled SYNC. The first subscript letters are a list of the involved workflow parts, with the own workflow part in first place. The second subscript letter after the comma identifies the synchronization process (e.g. $SYNC_{MN,U}$).
- Notation for *synchronization arrows* is S_ARROW. As with SYNC nodes, first the involved workflow parts (with no regard to order) and then the identification of the synchronization process follows in the subscript letters.

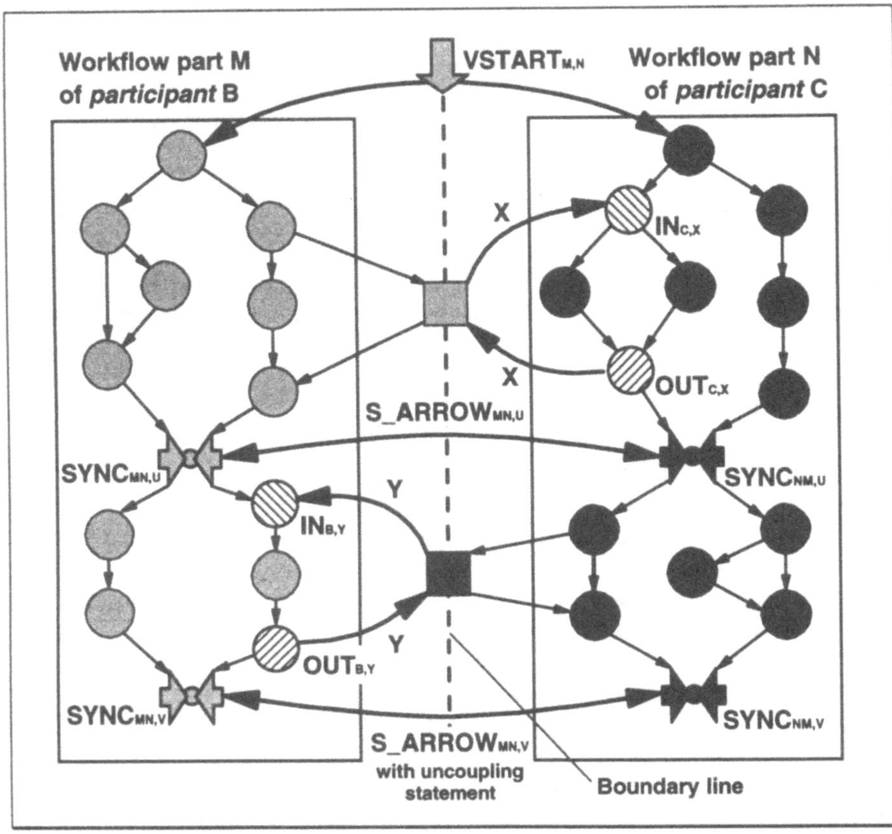

Figure 28: Equal partnership – realization of PWPS and CIWP interaction patterns through joint modeling

Since interfaces between workflow parts can be defined in a negotiation process, mixed *PWPS* and *CIWP* interactions can be realized with *joint modeling* as shown in Figure 28. The owners of different workflow parts are called *participants*, because the roles of *initiators* and *addressees* can change frequently within the mechanism of *equal partnership*.

The exchange of *interface specifications* during build-time can be realized with the help of a shared *coordination directory* (*Share Model*), as it is also used for the realization of *market coordination*. Workflow parts are stored in separate workflow repositories of the respective WFMSs. Run-time operation can be supported by both *Share* and *Send Model*.

The *coordination mechanism* of *equal partnership* can be applied in both intra- and interorganizational cooperation. It allows for more autonomy than mechanisms of *hierarchy*, but requires participants to collaborate more closely than within the *market mechanism*.

5.4.4 Continuum of coordination mechanisms

In this section, the three coordination mechanisms of *hierarchy*, *market* and *equal partnership* will be summarized. Based on the *continuum of organizational integration* (Figure 20, p. 115), a more detailed *continuum of coordination mechanisms* is presented in Figure 29.

Different levels of distributed and widely distributed workflow management, as introduced in Figure 10 (p. 56), are depicted in the outmost right column of Figure 29. These levels are combined with the *coordination mechanisms* described in the preceding sections. A scale ranging intra- and interorganizational settings builds the basis for the location of the different ways of coordinating participants in Wide Area Workflow Management (WAWM) collaboration (see top row of Figure 29).

<table>
<tr><td colspan="6">Inter-organizational ⟵⟶ Intra-organizational</td><td>Organizational integration</td></tr>
<tr><td>Ad-hoc</td><td>Market</td><td>Equal partnership</td><td>Hierarchy, method C</td><td>Hierarchy, method B</td><td>Hierarchy, method A</td><td>Coordination mechanism</td></tr>
<tr><td>---</td><td>publication & subscription</td><td>joint modeling</td><td>decentralized modeling</td><td>participative modeling</td><td>centralized modeling</td><td>Design methodology</td></tr>
<tr><td>---</td><td colspan="5"></td><td rowspan="2">Extensions to workflow meta-model</td></tr>
<tr><td>---</td><td>$\text{WORKFLOW}_{SUB,WAW}$</td><td>VSTART, SYNC, S_ARROW</td><td>$\text{SUBWORKFLOW}_{DEC,WAW}$</td><td>$\text{CLUSTER}_{PAR,WAW}$</td><td>$\text{CLUSTER}_{CEN,WAW}$</td></tr>
<tr><td colspan="2">decentralized autonomous WAWM</td><td>decentral. synchronized WAWM</td><td>decentral. controlled WAWM</td><td colspan="2">centralized controlled WAWM</td><td>Run-time operation</td></tr>
<tr><td colspan="2">decentralized</td><td colspan="2">partly decentralized</td><td colspan="2">centralized</td><td>Control</td></tr>
<tr><td>e-mail</td><td colspan="3">coordination directories, gateways, message objects</td><td colspan="2">shared databases</td><td>Technology</td></tr>
<tr><td colspan="6">Send Model ⟵⟶ Share Model</td><td>Information distribution</td></tr>
<tr><td colspan="6">autonomous, loose cooperation ⟵⟶ dependent, close cooperation</td><td>Autonomy, cooperation</td></tr>
</table>

Figure 29: Continuum of coordination mechanisms for Wide Area Workflow Management

Within the mechanism of *hierarchy – method A* (second column to the right), a *centralized modeling* with the help of $\text{CLUSTER}_{CEN,WAW}$ is used to plan for *centralized, controlled WAWM* that will be realized in most cases on the basis of *shared databases*. This mechanism is geared for settings of rather low autonomy where close cooperation is practiced. Going to the left, autonomy increases calling for a term of cooperation which must be based on mechanisms that allow for more independence in less close cooperative settings. *Hierarchy – method C* is the first *coordination mechanism* that can make use of *coordination directories, gateways and message objects*. It therefore supports *decentralized WAWM* during run-time operation, but still relies on hierarchical design and control of interfaces. It is the first mechanism that can be applied to both intra- and interorganizational collaboration. Within the *market* mechanism, the design and coordination of workflow models are as independent as possible through the use the *publication & subscription* method realized on the basis of *coordination directories*. During run-time operation, WFMSs will exchange *message objects* that can be converted by *gateways* in the case of heterogeneous systems. The upmost flexibility and autonomy is achieved through the realization of WAWM using e-mail only. Since there is no planning, this can mainly be used for ad-hoc processes to manage exceptional situations.

The *continuum of coordination mechanisms for WAWM* (Figure 29) can be understood as a toolbox providing solutions for the realization of Wide Area Workflow Management in different organizational settings. By taking all layers of the level model introduced in Figure 10 (p. 56) into account, the *continuum* allows for the selection of appropriate technical measures for different constellations between WAWM participants concerning important factors of real-life cooperation, such as *balance of power* and *autonomy*.

Most of the approaches to distributed and widely distributed workflow management presented in Chapter 4 focus on technical aspects of widely distributed run-time operation and thereby are limited to the lower two layers of the level model (Figure 10, p. 56), neglecting the important role of organizational factors in WAWM. Some scientific and commercial WFMSs also present methods for the planning of WAWM, but mainly adhere to *hierarchical* or *centralized* coordination of participants.

With the *continuum of coordination mechanisms for WAWM*, the author wants to emphasize the important role of *coordination mechanisms* other than *hierarchy* to allow for a flexible interaction of partners in *inter*organizational collaboration. In particular the methods of *equal partnership* and *market* promise a much higher applicability and acceptance in cases where WAWM participants would – for many reasons – reject being pressed into subordinate relations, induced by a lack of flexibility in the technical measures.

When departments or whole organizations plan to collaborate, managers involved will intuitively make use of different *coordination mechanisms* – such as *hierarchy*, *equal partnership* and *market* – to find appropriate terms and conditions for the respective situations they are in. The intention of the *continuum of coordination mechanisms for WAWM*, and seen in a wider perspective, the intention of this book, is to discuss appropriate measures for the relevant levels of Wide Area Workflow Management – from meta-models to technical measures – to allow for the use of all of these *coordination mechanisms* with as few technically induced limitations as possible.

Seen from a philosophical perspective, the *continuum* first looks at the extremes at each end of the scale, and then tries to identify useful combinations in-between – in the tradition of Aristotle who recommends to always search for a balance between extremes, or the very similar East Asian philosophy of Ying and Yang.

5.5 Aspects of flexibility

Principle ideas of flexible workflow management (see Section 3.3.3, p. 45) and practical solutions (see Section 4.2.3, p. 85) have already been introduced. Here, these approaches will be applied to the topic of Wide Area Workflow Management.

Flexibility in WAWM can be achieved in two phases:

- During the planning phase, workflow models can be made flexible by anticipating several possible workflow paths and planning accordingly. Further on, certain elements of workflow models can be left open for decisions that will be made during the run-time phase. This can be achieved, for instance, by predefining milestones only rather than all single activities, or by leaving the details of connections to other WFMSs open.
- During run-time phase, users can navigate workflows freely within the milestones depending on their needs. Additionally, they can be entitled to change predefined elements of underlying workflow models, such as routing paths, performers or external partners in unforeseen situations.

The necessary degree of flexibility in WAWM is determined by the *transaction* or *coordination costs* (see Section 3.2.3, p. 31) induced during the planning and run-time phase of business processes. If procedures can be planned exactly and are likely to be frequently executed without significant exceptions, then rather high coordination costs during the planning phase can be justified. It has already has been pointed out that this will only apply to a rather small fraction of office processes. The more variations, exceptions and new solutions are necessary during the run-time phase, the less planning efforts can be justified based on a cost/benefit calculation. In these cases, coordination has to be achieved mainly during run-time operation, necessitating an appropriate support by workflow management systems.

Based on the principle distinction between *ex ante structured*, *semi-structured* and *unstructured* processes introduced in Table 1 (p. 43), Table 5 shows the connection of process structure and coordination costs during planning and run-time phase.

Processes, that are ex ante ...	*Coordination costs during planning phase*	*Coordination costs during run-time phase*
structured	High	Low
semi-structured	Medium	Medium
unstructured	Low	High

Table 5: Connections between process structure and coordination costs

Systems supporting Wide Area Workflow Management have to facilitate the coordination of activities during planning as well as the run-time phase and should support structured, semi-structured and widely unstructured processes. This is necessary for internal workflow steps as well as interactions with external WFMSs.

5.5.1 Flexible planning

Mechanisms for planning the coordination of several, autonomous WFMSs have been introduced in Section 5.4 (p. 125). When comparing these mechanisms regarding aspects of flexible planning, one finds that mechanisms of *hierarchy*, especially *method A* and *B*, are in principle better suited to support *ex ante structured* processes. It is in the nature of these methods that one organization defines and controls the interfaces between the workflow parts involved. Only the dominant organization can plan flexibly while subordinate organizations have limited or no influence on the planning process. Invoked subprocesses have to be performed by subordinate WFMSs in the way they were planned, at least in regard to the results they have to deliver to main processes.

The mechanism of *hierarchy* allows for example for the following possibilities for *flexible planning* of workflow models:

- Designers can make use of *milestone modeling* in main processes as well as subprocesses, thereby only doing basic planning. Users are required to achieve certain goals at the end of the *milestones*, but can make decisions on the necessary activities, choice of performers and resources themselves.
- Designers of main processes can prepare the simultaneous or alternative invocation of several subprocesses. They can thereby give users the opportunity to chose between multiple subprocesses during run-time operation according to actual needs.
- In the case of *method C*, *addressees* are free to plan their workflow parts according to their needs. This in principle allows for a higher degree of flexibility than within *methods A* and *B*.
- Designers can entitle users to change predefined workflow models by executing *exceptions*. This usually excludes interfaces between workflow parts that have to be kept stable in order to assure WFMSs interoperability.

Within the mechanism of *equal partnership*, flexibility during the planning phase can be achieved by negotiations between the participants. They can agree on leaving models fairly open for decisions that will later be made during run-time operation. Nevertheless, *joint modeling* requires participants to specify things like *synchronization nodes* in advance in order to plan how the information needed for synchronization can be prepared internally.

The following options for flexible planning of workflow models are available within *equal partnership*:

- Again, all participants can make use of *milestone modeling* within their internal workflow parts.
- The definition of multiple interfaces between workflow parts allows users to make choices during the run-time operation. Nevertheless, workflow parts must be jointly initiated.
- *Exceptions* can be executed within internal workflow parts. Additionally, participants can agree to allow for variation of terms of synchronization based on preceding *ad-hoc negotiations* during run-time operation.

The *market* mechanism as such provides for a high degree of flexibility. Since interface definitions are completely defined before they are offered, they can be included in workflow models very flexibly. Therefore, as distinct from the mechanisms of *hierarchy* and *equal partnership*, the *market* approach allows for a free choice of partner organizations during the planning *and* run-time phase by simply selecting and invoking workflow services which are offered.

Within the *market* mechanism, the following flexibility features are feasible:

- *Milestone modeling* within internal workflow parts can be applied.
- *Initiators'* designers can pre-select various comparable offers (by using several, alternative $\text{WORKFLOW}_{\text{SUB,WAW}}$) and leave choices to users during the run-time phase.
- Additionally, *initiators'* workflow designers can include "empty" $\text{WORKFLOW}_{\text{SUB,WAW}}$ nodes, only defining the goal of an external workflow connection. For instance, in Case Study 2 (p. 17), this could mean prompting users with the message "Please request quotations for the PCs described below from listed external suppliers" and displaying all services offered by PC vendors. Users can decide which of the actually offered workflow service(s) they want to choose.
- Since workflow parts of *initiators* and *addressees* are as independent as possible, both sides can plan flexibly according to their needs. For example, *addressees* can change the design of their workflow parts at any time as long as the *interface specifications* are kept stable.
- Designers can allow for *exceptions* during run-time operation including also the possibility of changing the selection of an offer assigned to a $\text{WORKFLOW}_{\text{SUB,WAW}}$ elements.

Possibilities for a practical realization of these flexible planning mechanisms will be introduced in Chapter 6, where the Wide Area GroupFlow System will be described.

5.5.2 Flexible run-time operation

A flexible execution of wide area workflows can be achieved by providing principle support for *exceptions* from the predefined workflow models. For example, the following types of *exceptions* can be granted to users within internal workflow tasks:

- *Involvement* of other than the predefined users while performing an activity may be reasonable if the actual performer needs help. This can be achieved by asking other persons to comment on or contribute to a certain task. Nevertheless, work is mainly carried out by the persons originally assigned.
- *Partial delegation* of an activity means to assign work to other users but to control their results before the workflow instance is continued.
- *Complete delegation* of an activity shifts work to other persons as whole. The new performers can continue the workflow instance when they have finished the predefined activities.

- *Inclusion of a new activity* that has not been predefined. Unlike the above exceptions, not only different performers but also new actions are included into workflow instances.
- *Pull-back* of workflow instances by the last performers can be desirable, for example, if they realize that they have forgotten something. A *pull-back* operation can be executed as long as the succeeding performers have not started to work on their activities.
- *Route-back* operations allow users to reassign work to previous performers, for instance when important information is missing or is obviously outdated. Workflows can be routed back to direct predecessors or also to any other person who has worked earlier in the current workflow instance. Once predecessors have changed or added the requested information, workflow instances are continued at the place where the *route-back* operation was initiated.
- *Cancellation* of workflow instances can become necessary when the initial goal of a workflow has become obsolete. For example, a quotation workflow will be canceled if the respective customer is no longer interested in the product. It is reasonable that a workflow supervisor should decide on *cancellations* that are requested by users.
- *Roll-back* operations allow the activities of all or parts of the preceding workflow steps to be set back. This can be done by an *automated roll-back* as known from database transactions or a *user-performed roll-back*, where persons manually undo actions that they had previously carried out. *Roll-back and cancellation* means that all workflow steps that had already been executed are taken back and finally the execution is stopped. As distinct from this, *roll-back and resume* means to go back and compensate several or all previous workflow activities, but then re-execute the current workflow instance.

Depending on the terms of cooperation between organizations, the above-mentioned exceptions may also be permissible in *wide area workflows*. In some cases, it may be reasonable to check back with preceding users in other WFMSs, for example by *involvement*, *route-back* or *roll-back* operations. This will only be possible if other workflow parts are not only "black boxes", as is given within the coordination mechanism of *hierarchy* (*method A* and *B*). In these methods, all of the above-mentioned exceptions are possible in principle, but it may not be reasonable to permit them in all cases.

If other workflow parts are "black boxes", *involvement*, *partial* and *complete delegation*, *inclusion of new activity*, *pull-back*, and *route-back operations*, targeting users in other WFMSs are in most part impossible in practical application. Hence, they will not be further pursued in the following discussions. *Cancellation* of invoked workflow parts might be reasonable and is subject to the terms of the cooperation agreed upon among involved organizations. This is also true for *roll-back* operations.

When interfaces between workflow parts are fully defined and published in a *coordination directory*, as it is the case within the coordination mechanisms of *market* and *hierarchy (method C)*, run-time operation can be flexibly adapted by the following measures:

- *selection* from a pre-defined choice of external workflow connections;
- *change of pre-selection* by entitled users. For example, users in Case Study 2 might want to request a quotation from vendors other than the pre-defined PC supplier(s);
- *ad-hoc invocation* of subprocesses (*hierarchy, method C*) or subscribed workflows (*market*). In both cases, internal workflow information has to be mapped ad-hoc to the *interface specifications* in a process called *ad-hoc content management* (see Section 5.6.3, p. 162).

To allow for additional flexibility, internal workflow parts as well as external workflow connections can be widely altered by *instance-based variation* (also called *instance-based modeling*) of wide area workflows. Performers can make use of a modeling tool to completely change the structures of the underlying workflow models during run-time operation. Changes can only be made on the remaining steps of the workflow instance, including operations such as *change of performer*, *change of predefined activities*, *inclusion of new activities*, *change of preselection* of external connections and *inclusion of additional subprocesses* or *subscribed workflows*.

Instance-based modeling can also be used to develop routing paths within *milestones* where only goals have been set but no detailed activities have been defined during the planning phase.

5.6 Architectural concepts

In this section, fundamental architectural concepts for the realization of Wide Area Workflow Management (WAWM), based on the three coordination mechanisms introduced previously (Section 5.4, p. 125), are discussed.

To implement the coordination mechanisms of *hierarchy*, *method A* and *B* (see p. 126), the repository of one WFMS can be spread over several locations. This kind of information distribution is mostly achieved by applying the *Share Model*. The approach of using one WFMS at several locations will not be further discussed here. It can be achieved with technical measures already known, for instance replication technology, and is state of the art in various scientific prototypes and commercial WFMSs.

All other coordination mechanisms focus on the interaction of several WFMSs. On the following pages, concepts and solutions for cross-system interoperability architectures will be discussed based on the following assumptions:

- Owners of WFMSs want to stay as autonomous as possible while allowing their workflow systems to interact.
- In many cases, participants will not accept a central institution for the coordination of their activities. Coordination has to be achieved by mutual agreements.
- WFMSs involved are often heterogeneous.

These assumption are based on experiences gained in case studies on WAWM, as for example described in Chapter 2 (p. 9). Other approaches to WFMSs' interoperability rely on central brokers (Section 4.2.4.4, p. 91), hierarchical subordination or fail to discuss coordination aspects at all, only focusing on technical distribution.

The WfMC proposes different levels of WFMSs' integration, thereby assuming that it is desirable to connect WFMSs as tightly as possible (see Section 4.2.1.2, p. 78). This author does not subscribe to this notion, but wants to emphasize the necessity for autonomy, especially in interorganizational settings. Thus, the following fundamental architecture for the interaction of WFMSs is proposed (Figure 30).

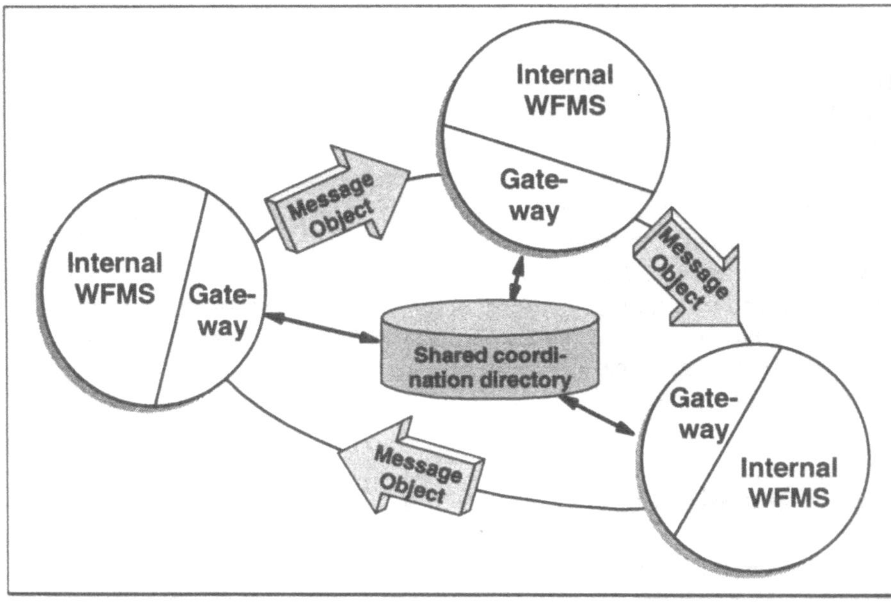

Figure 30: Fundamental architecture for Wide Area Workflow Management Systems

Internal workflow management systems (WFMSs) are connected by *message objects* used to transfer workflow information. The *interface specifications* needed for structuring and routing of *message objects* are shared among participants in *coordination directories*. The actual routing of *message objects* is performed by *gateways* that also allow for format conversion in order to bridge heterogeneous systems.

This architecture concept can be simplified in practical scenarios. If, for example, all involved WFMSs are homogeneous, *gateways* can become unnecessary because *message objects* may be directly exchanged between internal WFMSs with no need for format conversion. In other cases, a rather limited number of cross-system workflows with standardized structures might suffice (see for example 4.2.4.5, p. 92). Therefore specifications for interfaces and *message objects* can be directly stored in internal WFMSs, thereby avoiding the need for *coordination directories*.

However, to implement the different *coordination mechanisms* (see Figure 29, p. 137), *coordination directories*, *gateways* and *message objects* build a flexible platform of general applicability for the implementation Wide Area Workflow Management. The architecture concept presented in Figure 30 can be understood as a superset of possible WAWM implementations in practical scenarios. Its aim is to describe necessary components for WAWM, giving a general perspective. The different elements will be further introduced in the following sections.

5.6.1 Shared coordination directories

Widely dispersed organizational units or organizations can make use of a shared environment (*Share Model*) to exchange the information needed to coordinate the interaction of their workflow management systems. Shared environments used for the purpose of making structural information on organizations, persons or systems available to all participants are often called *directory services* [Chadwick 1994]. The ISO has released the international X.500 standard [ISO X.500 1993], recommending protocols for the definition, distribution and use of such *directory services*. The *Lightweight Directory Access Protocol (LDAP)* [Howes 95] eases the use of X.500 compliant *directory services* and has been implemented in many of today's software applications (e.g. Lotus Notes, MS Exchange etc.).

To make use of the three *coordination mechanisms* for WAWM introduced in Section 5.4 (p. 125), the building of a *coordination directory*, which can be accessed by multiple WFMSs, is very helpful. In this section, the structuring and distribution of such a *coordination directory* will be discussed. Also other authors recommend the use of *directory services* for the purpose of coordinating *office procedure* or *workflow management systems* [Prinz 1993], [Prinz 1994], [Adams/Dworkin 1997].

The method for connecting distinct process parts with the help of *directory services* is also included in the CORBA specifications (see Section 3.4.3, p. 64). The interfaces of objects are specified with an *Interface Definition Language (IDL)* and then published for the use by client programs with the help of directories called *shared repositories*. Designers of client programs can prepare the invocation of remote objects by adapting their programs to *interface definitions* of the respective objects. During run-time, requests are transferred to objects that in turn deliver the results that had been promised in the *interface definitions*. A similar approach has been taken in the *coordination mechanism* called *market* (see Section 5.4.2, p. 131).

5.6.1.1 Structure and contents of coordination directories

Coordination directories used in the context of WAWM serve to store *interface specifications* of workflow parts. The author and his team have found that a hierarchical approach to organizing the *interface specifications* is most appropriate, allowing users to navigate easily even within large *directories*. Other authors propose to store processes in hierarchical trees as well [Elgass/Krcmar 1994], [Malone et al. 1997] (see also Section 4.2.2.1, p. 83).

A fundamental question is then which categories should be used to build such a hierarchical tree within a *coordination directory*. Using the structure of departments, and thereby reflecting the organization chart, is a widely known method. This system is also very often used when implementing X.500 compliant *directory services*.

However for WAWM, this method is not helpful due to the fact that workflow designers from external organizations are usually not primarily interested in which department offers what workflows, but rather which services are offered by an organization in general. Looking at WWW sites of organizations, one rarely finds that structuring is done according to departments; the services a company can offer most often build the main focus and thus are the prime categories for a hierarchical arrangement of WWW pages. Therefore, the author recommends organizing interface definitions primarily according to service categories. Nevertheless, it must be stressed that a multiple categorization featuring services, departments, locations etc., which allows workflow designers to switch perspectives, can also be helpful in certain situations.

The hierarchical trees within *coordination directories* must have root elements, which can be used to describe the organizations involved in a general manner. Root elements will be called *headers* and can contain the following information:

- a descriptive name, which will most likely be the name of the organization;
- a unique identification number for worldwide use;
- the postal address of the organization;
- an electronic address for the delivery of *message objects*. In many cases, it is reasonable to provide the e-mail address of the main WAWM *gateway* of an organization; another possibility would be an IP-address of this *gateway*.
- optionally, a logo representing the organization, which can be used for recognition of different organizations when browsing a *coordination directory*.

Below the *headers*, *folders* can be inserted to categorize certain services. The services themselves are represented by *leaves*. An example of a hierarchy of services that a PC vendor in Case Study 2 (see p. 17) could offer to LLM is shown in Figure 31.

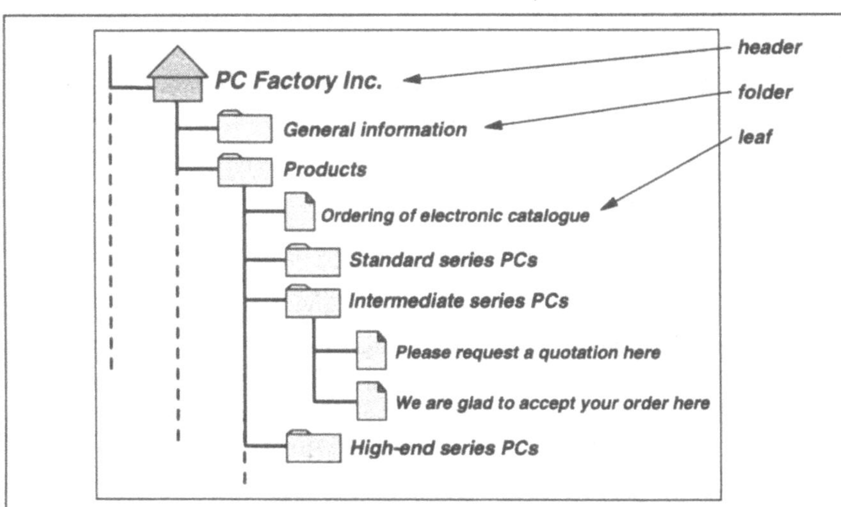

Figure 31: Example of contents of a coordination directory for Case Study 2

In the example of Figure 31, only the *leaves* of some *folders* are shown (for the sake of simplification). Further on, this example illustrates a scenario according to the *market mechanism* (see Section 5.4.2, p. 131).

The *leaves* for different elements of the *meta-model* for WAWM introduced in Section 5.4 (for a summary, see Figure 29, p. 137) have individually different *interface specifications.*

For the coordination mechanism of *hierarchy* (Section 5.4.1, p. 126), the following elements of interfaces can be specified in a *coordination directory* (Table 6).

Element of WAWM meta-model	*Interface specifications*
CLUSTER$_{CEN, WAW}$ 	▪ Name and unique identification number of cluster ▪ Identification (ID) of WFMS responsible for execution of workflow part
CLUSTER$_{PAR, WAW}$ 	▪ Name and unique identification number of cluster ▪ ID of WFMS responsible for execution of workflow part ▪ Description of workflow part's purpose ▪ Definition of incoming and outgoing information on field-level ▪ Status (values: *empty, completed, approved*) ▪ Dates of distribution and completion
SUBWORK-FLOW$_{DEC, WAW}$ 	▪ Name and unique identification number of subworkflow ▪ Description of subworkflow's purpose ▪ Definition of incoming and outgoing information on field-level ▪ Optionally, an identification number of a *message object type* assigned ▪ Format (e.g. XML, WfMC Internet e-mail/MIME-Binding, etc.) ▪ Version ▪ Maximum duration of execution ▪ Identifications and addresses of invoking and invoked WFMS ▪ Identifications of invoking and invoked workflow instances ▪ Status (values: *empty, completed, confirmed, denied*) ▪ Dates of distribution, completion, availability and expiration

Table 6: Hierarchical coordination – interface specifications for WAWM meta-model elements

With increasing autonomy of the subordinate workflow parts (downwards direction in Table 6), more information has to be specified in a *coordination directory* to assure a reliable interaction between the WFMSs of *initiators* and *addressees*. For CLUSTER$_{CEN,WAW}$ elements, only an identification of the cluster itself and the WFMS responsible for execution have to be indicated. The rest of the process definitions can be stored in a workflow repository shared among participants.

To make use of CLUSTER$_{PAR,WAW}$ elements, *master designers* additionally need to provide a description of the purpose of the cluster, define the information that will be transferred to *addressees* and those that will be given back, and set the values for the date and the status. Both cluster types will mainly be applied within homogeneous WFMS environments, for instance making use of a distributed, shared workflow repository (e.g. synchronized by selective replication) for run-time operation.

Since SUBWORKFLOW$_{DEC,WAW}$ nodes describe an interface between two distinct workflow parts, which can be executed by WFMSs with separate repositories, specifications must be rather extensive. The exchange of the definition of a common format to bridge heterogeneous system environments, a version number allowing for the handling of different interface states caused by updates, and identifications of involved WFMSs and workflow instances is of special importance. If participants have agreed to exchange definitions of *message object types* (see p. 155), an appropriate *message object* can be assigned to an *interface specification. Master designers* need to indicate a required maximum execution duration for the subordinate workflow part, allowing them to plan the further execution of the invoking workflow part in the sense of a *critical path* calculation known from project management. The indication of status and date values builds the basis for monitoring and tracking of activities.

Specifications of meta-model elements needed to make use of the coordination mechanism of *equal partnership* (see Section 5.4.3, p. 134) are described in Table 7.

Element of WAWM meta-model	***Interface specifications***
VSTART 	▪ Name and identification of virtual start node ▪ Identifications and addresses of WFMSs involved ▪ Identifications of the process definitions, from which instances should be derived and started ▪ Date & time of earliest and latest possible start of workflow instances ▪ Start parameters for respective workflow instances
S_ARROW 	▪ Name and identification of synchronization arrow ▪ Identifications of involved WFMSs and workflow instances to be synchronized ▪ Date & time of earliest and latest possible start of synchronization process ▪ Definition of possible initiators of synchronization (e.g. master instance, all instances) ▪ Information to be synchronized, specified on field level ▪ Conflict management mode (e.g. newer changes overwrite others, all changes are kept, etc.)

Table 7: Coordination mechanism of equal partnership – interface specifications for WAWM meta-model elements

In order for virtual start nodes (VSTART) to be set up, *coordination directories* would have to be implemented in the form of *active databases*, checking regularly on an automatic basis whether VSTART entries are due and thus respective WFMSs have to be triggered to start workflow instances. The start parameters defined in the VSTART specifications would then be handed over to workflow engines, for instance by sending an e-mail, using remote procedure calls (RPC) or implementing a

CORBA connection. By distributing *coordination directories* to all locations involved, it can be assured that the respective WFMSs, involved for instance in a *PWPS* or *CIWP* interaction (see Table 4, p. 119), will be informed in time to instantiate the respective workflows mentioned in the VSTART specifications.

For the synchronization of workflow parts executed in a parallel manner, specifications for synchronization arrows (S_ARROW) can be laid down in *coordination directories*. Apart from the identification of the WFMSs involved, information on the period of time in which synchronization is supposed to take place, the possible initiators of a joint operation and the contents concerned with synchronization must be determined. Further on, specifications must be made as to how conflicting changes to formerly identical information items in different workflow parts are to be resolved during synchronization. Conflict algorithms (e.g. prefer newer version, keep all changes etc.) are similar to those applied within replication technology, as found for instance in groupware platforms (see Section 3.4.4, p. 65).

Details of SYNC nodes, as discussed in conjunction with Figure 28 (p. 136), are specified only within the respective workflow part models and therefore do not have to be exchanged via *coordination directories*.

To enable an interaction of workflow parts according to the coordination mechanism of *market* (see Section 5.4.2, p. 131), interfaces for *subscribed workflows* can be specified as shown in Table 8.

Element of WAWM meta-model	***Interface specifications***
WORKFLOW$_{SUB,WAW}$ 	▪ Name and unique identification number of interface spec. ▪ General description of the results that can be expected ▪ Definition of required incoming information on field-level ▪ Definition of the delivered outgoing information on field-level ▪ Optionally, an identification number of a *message object type* assigned ▪ List of formats that the *addressee* (publisher) can deal with for incoming and outgoing information ▪ Version ▪ Date of expiration ▪ Recipients (e.g. selected partners, all partners, everyone) ▪ Optionally, a predicted maximum duration of execution

Table 8: Market-oriented coordination – interface specifications for WAWM meta-model elements

To allow subscribers of WORFKLOW$_{SUB,WAW}$ interfaces to plan their workflow parts, publishers have to provide a general description of the results that can be expected when invoking the workflow service offered. To assure a proper execution, they have to specify the incoming information necessary to invoke the respective workflow instance (*input*) as well as the outgoing information delivered in return (*output*) in a detailed manner. It is recommendable to describe the *input* and *output* on field level, containing *field name*, *field type* (e.g. text, number, date etc.) and a *field description* for each information item.

To facilitate the exchange of workflow information between heterogeneous WFMSs, a list of possible formats must be provided. The indication of a version number allows for updates to *interface specifications*. Older versions are kept within *coordination directories* to allow for the handling of incoming requests, which had been issued by senders before updates were broadcasted. If new versions of *interface specifications* contain significant changes, for instance concerning field definitions for *input* and *output*, then the workflow designers of subscribers must be informed so that they can adapt their workflow models accordingly. If offers of workflow services are time limited, this can be indicated by including an expiry date.

The organization making the offer has to decide who is going to receive the respective *interface specifications*, having for instance the following options:

- Only selected partners should receive the *interface specifications*.
- All partners with whom an organization cooperates by workflow means are chosen to be recipients.
- Potentially everyone on the anonymous market can read the *interface specifications*, for example by publication via catalogue or the WWW.

To facilitate planning for subscribers, publishers can indicate a predicted maximum duration after which they will return the specified *output* at the latest.

The *interface specifications* described in Table 6 - Table 8 do not necessarily have to be exchanged via *coordination directories*. For example, it might suffice to exchange the definition of $\text{CLUSTER}_{\text{CEN,WAW}}$ and $\text{CLUSTER}_{\text{PAR,WAW}}$ with the help of a shared workflow repository, which is also used to store process definitions of workflow models themselves. The more of the different elements of the *meta-model* for WAWM are used, and the more autonomous the participants are, the more useful the implementation of *coordination directories* is as a connecting element between different WFMSs.

The *interface specifications* in *coordination directories* have to be linked to the process definitions of workflow models stored in the internal workflow repositories of each of the involved WFMSs. For instance, if an *addressee* receives a *message object* containing a request to provide a workflow service specified in the *interface specification* XYZ123 of a $\text{WORKFLOW}_{\text{SUB,WAW}}$ offer, there must be an reference to the actual workflow engine and the process definition of which a workflow should be instantiated. These references can be made public in the *interface specifications* themselves or can be kept confidential, depending on the level of trust among participants.

In many cases, it is helpful to divide *coordination directories* into a *public part* shared with other participants in a WAWM scenario and a *private part*, which is only accessible to the respective owner of a WFMS, in order to preserve the autonomy of the participants. In the context of the Wide Area GroupFlow System introduced in Chapter 6 (p. 179), *interface specifications* published in the *public part* are called *global routing information (GRI)* while references to internal workflow engines in the *private part* are termed *internal routing information (IRI)*.

Further on, one can distinguish two *views* of *coordination directories*, seen from the perspective of each participant. A first *view* is what *interface specifications* a participant has put into a *coordination directory* for use by others, which will be called the *publisher's view*. These elements are seen by other participants in their *recipient's view* and vice versa.

Based on what has been introduced until here, the structure of *coordination directories* can be illustrated as shown in Figure 32.

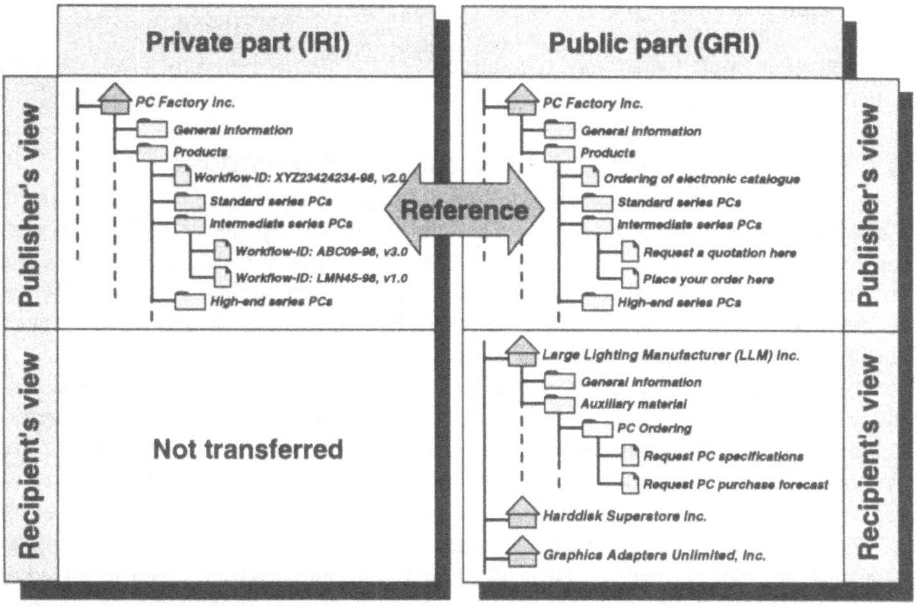

Figure 32: Structure of a coordination directory with examples from Case Study 2

In the public part of the *coordination directory* of "PC Factory Inc.", a fictitious supplier of LLM in Case Study 2 (p. 17), *interface specifications* offered are shown in a hierarchical tree (upper right segment of Figure 32). Customers of PC Factory can, for example, request a quotation for a PC of the intermediate series. Linked to this offer in the private part of the PC Factory's *coordination directory* (upper left segment), one can find the related workflow-ID of the process definition describing the procedure of providing such a quotation to customers.

In the lower right segment of Figure 32, offers from other organizations are displayed. Workflow designers of PC Factory can make use of these offers during the planning of workflow models. One example is that LLM provides the *interface specifications* of a workflow service, which allows PC suppliers to request the latest PC specifications issued by LLM. These can in turn adjust their offers – for instance in a recurrently used workflow for PC design – so that LLM can order PCs according to its latest specifications.

The references to the *internal routing information (IRI)* of LLM and other organizations, offering *interface specifications* to PC Factory, are not transferred to PC Factory's *coordination directory* for reasons of confidentiality.

Further elements of *coordination directories* can be:

- Templates for the fast definition and re-use of field-sets for the *input* and *output* specifications of WAWM elements such as $CLUSTER_{PAR,WAW}$, $SUBWORKFLOW_{DEC,WAW}$ and $WORKFLOW_{SUB,WAW}$.
- Definition of documents types used to exchange information on the structures of *message objects*. These document types can be based on standards like EDIFACT or may be defined individually. A further discussion of these options can be found in Section 5.6.2 (p. 153).

A practical example for an implementation of a *coordination directory* for WAWM, called *WAGS External Directory*, is described in Section 6.2.3 (p. 199).

5.6.1.2 Distribution and synchronization methods

Coordination directories must be accessible to all participants of a WAWM scenario. This can be achieved by placing them on central servers or by distributing (partial) copies to all locations involved. The latter possibility will be discussed further here, since a centrally available server is unlikely to be generally applicable, for instance in interorganizational scenarios.

The ISO standard for *directory services* describes details of distribution and synchronization in [ISO X.525 1993], speaking of *replication* technology. In this understanding, replication means to define a *master directory*, which can update *slave directories* distributed around the globe [Heinz 1997]. This kind of *master-slave* replication is different from the one applied in groupware platforms [Kawell et al. 1992], where all *replicas* have equal status. In this approach, called *equal* replication, changes can be made in all *replicas* and consequently transferred to all other related locations. Conflicts arising from concurrent changes to the same information item in different *replicas* are resolved by keeping all versions and informing users to join these manually.

In the scenario of WAWM, entries into *coordination directories* mostly have one owner responsible for changes (the *publisher*) and multiple users, who only perform read-operations (the *recipients*). Therefore, master-slave replication as described in X.525 is applicable in many cases. Still, there are situations where it reasonable to allow all participants to change entries in *coordination directories* regardless of their originator. This might for instance be given in the coordination mechanism of *equal partnership*, making use of VSTART and S_ARROW elements. These cases are better handled by replication technology as applied in groupware platforms.

The following scale of distribution and synchronization techniques reflects different degrees of independence among participants:

- If all involved organizational units or organizations make use of the same platform to support WAWM, e.g. a groupware system, then they can distribute multiple *replicas* of one *coordination directory*. This would allow them to synchronize their entries by built-in replication technology, which can be found in many products today. Both *master-slave* and *equal* replication can be realized this way. This scenario is limited to a closed group of participants who have simultaneously started to implement WAWM systems (for instance in intraorganizational settings).

- If participants are members in different groups of WAWM-use and have started to implement WAWM systems at different points in time, it is very unlikely that they will all be able to share a single, distributed *coordination directory* based on one set of homogeneous *replicas*. Participants will own different, basically non-connected *directories*. In this case, *publication* of new entries and changes to existing entries from *publishers* to *recipients* is an appropriate method. This *publication* can for example be achieved through the exchange of Internet e-mails between different *coordination directories*. Making use of messaging technology is a simple, but not always reliable solution, because e-mails might be lost during transfer. Another, more reliable possibility would be to connect different sites with the help of CORBA technology. One can also imagine allowing *all* participants (not only publishers) to change entries and, consequently, synchronizing these changes with the help of messaging systems. A conflict resolution method similar to the one applied in groupware-based replication would have to be implemented.
- A very open method of "broadcasting" entries in *coordination directories* is to publish them on the WWW. Recipients would have to mirror the relevant Web pages to their site to make them permanently available for their WFMS. This solution is only applicable in cases similar to the *master-slave* replication described in X.525, where only *publishers* have the right to change the entries they have originated.

5.6.2 Message objects – mobile workflow information carriers

To enable Wide Area Workflow Management, workflow-related information must be transferred between distinct WFMSs. Workflow management is basically *push-oriented*, meaning information is actively transferred from one performer to the next. Therefore in WAWM, there will mostly be an active sender bringing information carriers on their way and a recipient waiting for these to arrive in his workflow system. The related paradigm of information distribution is the *Send Model* (see Section 5.2.2.1, p. 113), which can for example be implemented with the help of messaging systems [Wilkens 1989].

It has already been mentioned that information handled in workflows is more than mere data (see Section 5.1, p. 104). Hence, carriers connecting distinct WFMSs have to be able to represent the richness of information found in today's office processes. An appropriate structure for this representation are *compound documents* as found in groupware platforms or the WWW, holding structured data as well contextual information. Making *compound documents* mobile for workflow purposes requires the embedding of further information apart from the actual contents to be transferred. For instance, routing and status information is needed to connect several WFMSs.

One can perceive mobile workflow information carriers as being specific types of *objects* having certain *properties*. Additionally, they may contain *methods* for handling these properties. This is similar to the approach of *object orientation* (see for example [Rumbaugh 1991]).

Since these workflow information carriers have similarities with *objects* in object orientation, and are meant to transport messages between systems and/or users, they are called *message objects*. Other authors have also used this term [Prinz/Pennelli 1992] or describe similar structures as *information carriers* [Barbara/Mehrota/Rusinkiewicz 1994], *active mail* [Goldberg/Safran/Shapiro 1992] or simply as *messages* [Malone et al. 1987], [Ishii/Ohkubo 1991], [Alonso et al. 1995].

Various specifications and prototypes have been devised that make use of messages to connect distinct WFMSs, for instance the *WfMC Interface 4 specification* for Internet e-mail MIME Binding, *Workonnector*, *Phanta Rhei*, *Exotica/FMQM* and more (see Section 4, p. 73). Additionally, some commercial WFMSs are also partially or fully message-oriented.

The majority of these approaches concentrate on transferring *structured data* with messages, not making use of the full potential of *message objects* to also represent *contextual information* handled in office procedures and to embed *methods* for the flexible handling of contents.

The author wants to emphasize the importance of *message objects* as *mobile compound documents*, allowing for a flexible connection of WFMSs by transferring "rich" information instead of mere data. *Message objects* can be used to support the paradigm of *automation & structure*, but also allow for the realization of systems designed to give room for *user support & flexibility* (see Section 5.1, p. 104). Thus, *message objects* help to widen the applicability of WAWM to the full scope of possible process types in office work– from highly structured and recurrent to unforeseeable and unique – found within and between organizations.

The possible structures of *message objects* will be discussed in more detail in the following section.

5.6.2.1 Structure of message objects

The main intention of *message objects* is to transfer *contents* between users in interacting WFMSs. Therefore, a fundamental requirement is that *message objects* be structured on field-level, making them capable of seamlessly taking over information from databases underlying the internal workflow management systems. Additionally, they should contain areas for the inclusion of contextual information such as drawings, spreadsheet calculations or speech annotations. These areas are often called *richtext fields* (see for example Section 3.4.4.2, p. 68) or fields for *binary large objects*.

Apart from the storage of data and contextual information, *message objects* should be able to include a *representation* to make them readable for users, following the paradigm of *user support & flexibility* (see Section 5.1, p. 104). In today's offices, enormous effort is being invested in designing information carriers (e.g. letters, faxes, brochures, etc.) in order to transport certain contextual information to outside recipients. For example, expensive stationery and impressive letterheads are meant to convey reliability and respectability as part of a corporate identity. Another example for the importance of representation features are found in the WWW, where organizations invest enormous amounts of time and money into the design of impressive home-pages in order to transport a certain corporate identity. Hence, also *message objects* should allow for the inclusion of representation-oriented elements.

A third component of *message objects* can be embedded *methods* that allow systems or users to manipulate the *contents* and *representation*. Figure 33 illustrates the proposed structure of *message objects*.

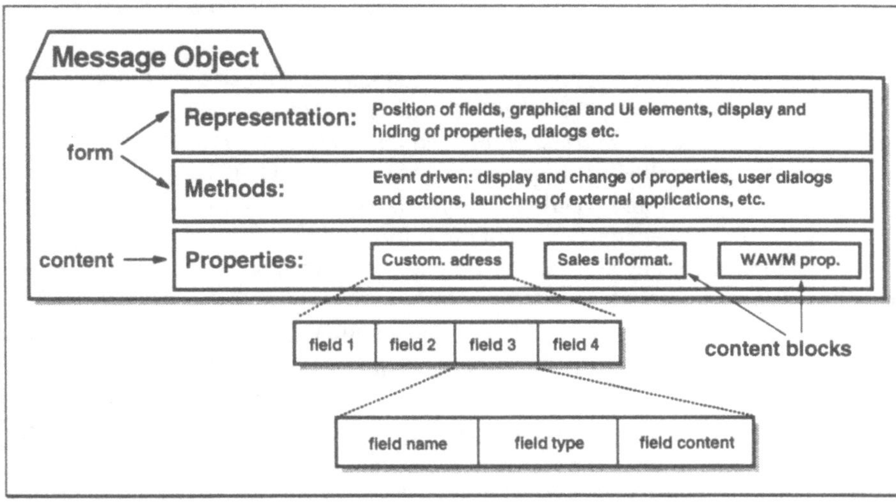

Figure 33: Structure of a message object

The *properties* of a *message object* contain the *content* that is to be exchanged between two workflow instances, for instance a customer's address as field-based data and sales information in the form of drawings and tables in *richtext fields* (Figure 33). The *content* can be divided into so-called *content blocks*, making it easier to identify information that belongs together and to re-use certain elements (such as a block for addresses) in various *message objects*. A special block contains the properties needed to enable *wide area workflow* functions, for example routing information such as the e-mail addresses of sender and recipient, priority, identification of sending and receiving workflow instance etc.

Representation and *methods* are presented to users in a so-called *form*, which can for example display the *contents* as a letter. Depending on the particular situation, it might be reasonable to offer *methods* to users through menus or buttons. These *methods* can be applied to change certain *contents*, invoke external applications or to route *message objects* to the next performers in the respective workflow instances.

To facilitate the definition of *message objects* and to allow for inheritance and reuse of *representation*, *methods* and *content blocks*, an *object hierarchy of message objects* as described in the following list can be set up:

- A *general message object* builds the root element of an hierarchical tree.

- It is followed in subsequent levels by *message object types* and *sub-types*. Examples of these *types* could be called letters, trade documents, marketing material etc. Letters could be further divided into *sub-types* termed internal memo, external letter, personnel information etc.; trade documents could be split up into *sub-types* labeled quotation, order, invoice and so on, and marketing material could be comprised of brochure, catalogue, handbook etc.
- The *message objects* themselves inherit *properties*, *methods* and *representation* from the elements placed above them in the hierarchical tree. One can also imagine the application of further object-oriented mechanisms such as multiple inheritance and polymorphism.
- The *properties* of *message objects* are structured into *content blocks*, allowing designers to aggregate fields in semantic groups. Content blocks can be assigned specific *representation* and *methods*, gathered in specific *sub-forms*. The total of all *sub-forms* included then builds the *form* of a *message object*. Apart from *specialized sub-forms* used to represent things like a letter head, address section etc., a *generic sub-form* in the form of a tabular list can be applied for any content, for instance if the recipient does not own a *specialized sub-form* for a certain *content block*.
- The elementary structure of *properties* within the *content blocks* is comprised of *fields*, built by 3 main elements: *field type*, *field name* and *field content*. Further on, a *field description* can facilitate the understanding of properties, for instance when presenting *message objects* to users for editing.

Such hierarchical trees for the definition of *message objects* can be stored in *coordination directories*, allowing participants in a WAWM scenario to exchange the respective specifications of *message objects* that they will subsequently send back and forth between their WFMSs.

5.6.2.2 Format and properties of message objects

If *message objects* are to be exchanged between heterogeneous WFMSs, the following questions have to be answered:

- What *format* is used to store and transfer *message objects*?
- How are the *properties* of *message objects* structured?

Many authors suggest using "standard formats" for the exchange of information carriers between WFMSs [Williams 1997]. The question is, what kind of information should be transferred with the help of these carriers, and hence, what "standard" format is appropriate? For the transfer of structured data, widespread standards are available [Patridge/Rose 1989]. It is of more interest here to find formats that can also be used to transport *contextual information* and *representation* between users in interacting workflow systems (see also [Casati et al. 1996]). These features can be found for instance in document description standards that would allow workflow designers to describe the *layout* of *message objects*.

Based on an idea presented in [Reich 1997], the following Figure 34 shows different possible formats for *message objects*. They are illustrated in a matrix, where one axis depicts the ability for structured storage and the other describes the relative strength of layout features. De facto standards for business documents, such as Microsoft Word, have far-reaching features for the generation and design of documents containing text and various embedded objects such as drawings etc. In addition, they offer limited capabilities for describing field-based structures. HTML documents are also well suited to the design of eye-catching *representations*, but structuring options are rather weak (see also Section 3.4.2, p. 62). In contrast to this, document standards such as SGML and HyTime are highly structured, but are not primarily designed for storing layout descriptions.

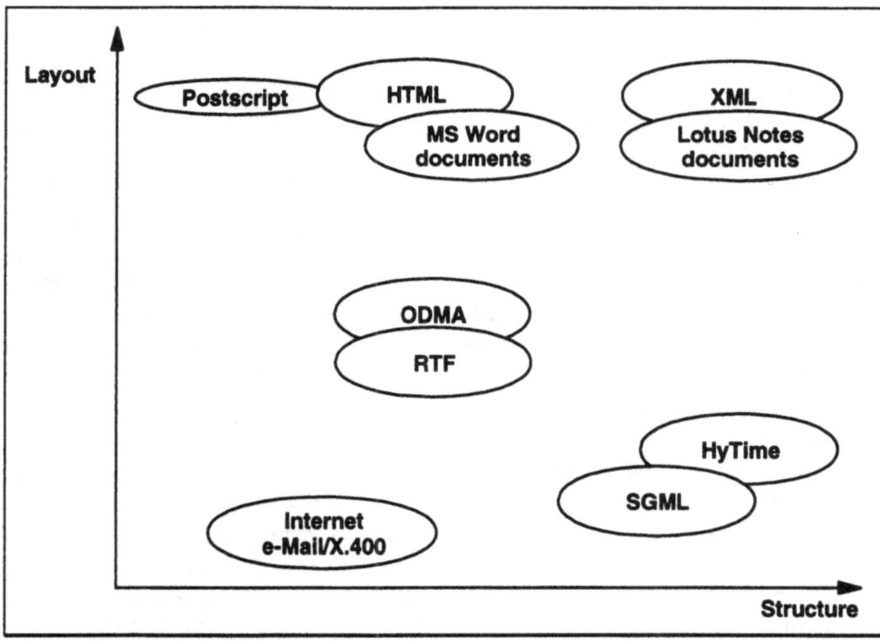

Figure 34: Structure versus layout of different possible formats for message objects

Proprietary systems such as Lotus Notes make use of documents that combine strong layout features with the ability for field-based structuring of information, but can only be used by a rather limited number of WFMSs currently available. An upcoming standard is the *extensible markup language (XML)*, which is derived from SGML and therefore offers the ability for highly structured document storage [Light 1997], [WWWJ 1997]. Basically, XML does not offer its own layout features, but provides the option to store layout descriptions of other document formats that can be decoded by the respective programs. Thereby, XML-based documents can carry for instance a *representation* based on Microsoft Word-documents, Lotus Notes-documents or HTML. Major companies have already announced support for XML, so that *document type definitions (DTDs)* describing the structure and layout of widespread document types should be available in the near future [Gross 1998].

Therefore, XML currently seems to be the most promising format for the exchange of *message objects* between interacting WFMSs, including the transfer of *structured data, contextual information, representation* and *methods.*

Regarding the structure of *message objects properties*, participants in a WAWM scenario have to find a compromise between the use of standardized document types and individually negotiated structures that allow for more flexibility.

Message object types and *sub-types* can be structured according to widespread standards for business documents, for instance using the ISO EDIFACT specifications (see Section 3.4.1, p. 59). This method has been chosen in the *Phanta Rhei* prototype (see Section 4.2.5.3, p. 96). It is certainly reasonable to do so as long as only *message objects* are needed that can be described using the respective specifications. Standards such as EDIFACT are limited to a specific set of document types and allow the transfer of mere data, based on the ASCII character set. They do not include the possibility of defining fully-featured *message objects* including *contextual information* and have no options to describe the *representation* of documents or to embed *methods.*

Therefore, flexible document descriptions based on XML are better suited for the definition of *message object* structures. XML can be used to re-build EDIFACT-based document types, but additionally allows for the specification of any field-based structure, including *richtext fields.* The fact that an XML-based document can always contain a *document type definition (DTD)* enables the recipient to first learn about the specific structure of an incoming *message object* and subsequently decode it, even though a *message object* of this type was unknown before.

Sharing XML-based DTDs with the help of *coordination directories* would allow for a very high degree of flexibility in WAWM. On one hand, often-used *message object* structures defined in XML can be based on international standards such as ISO EDIFACT and on the other hand, individually specified *message objects* can be handled as well. Partners in a WAWM scenario have thereby the choice to use widespread standards and additionally agree on further *message object types* and *sub-types.* A third option would be to make use of commercial services, for instance offering often used but non-standardized XML-based DTDs via the WWW.

5.6.2.3 Application of message objects

Within the context of the general architecture for WAWM presented in Figure 30 (p. 144), *message objects* play the role of an information carrier, connecting different workflow instances between distinct WFMSs. The definitions of the general structure of *message objects* can be defined in initial negotiations between participants in a WAWM scenario. Subsequently, these definitions can be distributed with the help of an *object hierarchy of message objects* stored in *coordination directories* (see p. 155). The actual *properties* (see Figure 33, p. 155) of a certain *message object* are derived from the field sets for *input* or *output* laid down in the related *interface specifications* (see for example Table 8, p. 149).

The procedure for the composition of *message objects* will be illustrated with the help of an example derived from Case Study 2: LLM and PC Factory want to cooperate by using WAWM. They define several *message object types* and *sub-types* and share the resulting definitions with the help of their shared *coordination directory*. One *message object sub-type* is called "quotation request" and is designed to invoke a workflow that delivers a quotation. This quotation is returned with another *message object sub-type* termed "quotation". In the following weeks, PC Factory offers an *interface specification* for a workflow service to LLM that delivers quotations for PCs produced by PC Factory. This *interface specification* requires a set of 14 fields to be sent as *input* for the workflow invoked, for example containing fields such as "order_quantity" (field type: *number*) or "order_description" (field type: *richtext*). The workflow designers of LLM subsequently design a model for a requisition workflow that allows staff members to request buying auxiliary material such as PCs. They include a $\text{WORKFLOW}_{\text{SUB,WAW}}$ element into their workflow model where LLM can request a quotation for PCs from PC Factory. Sending a *message object* during run-time operation is prepared during build-time by first selecting the *message object sub-type* "quotation request" and subsequently include the 14 fields of the *input* definition into the *message object* as empty "containers". Additionally, they make the appropriate settings for *content management* (see Section 5.6.3, p. 162) to make sure that the relevant contents from the internal workflow documents will be transferred into the respective fields in the *message object* during run-time phase.

On the side of PC Factory, workflow designers have prepared a *message object* returning the quotation to LLM and other customers in the same way: they have selected the *message object sub-type* "quotation" and have added the fields specified in the *output* definition of the *interface specification* they have published.

This example is supposed to illustrate that *message objects* consist of a general structure, for example derived from *message object types* or *sub-types*, and the actual *properties* needed to invoke a certain workflow service or to answer a request. These *properties* are derived from *interface specifications* laid down in *coordination directories*.

This system of combining general containers with actual properties needed for the invocation of certain workflow services allows for a high flexibility in the planning and execution of WAWM. However, this system is more complicated compared to completely predefined document structures. Therefore, in cases of a recurrent exchange of message objects with identical structures, *input* and *output properties* can be defined in *content blocks* with associated *subforms* in order to facilitate the composition of message objects. After these *content blocks* and *subforms* have been included in the *message object hierarchy* (p. 155), and subsequently been exchanged between WAWM participants with the help of *coordination directories*, completely predefined message objects for certain purposes are available. With the help of this two-stage method of first combining partially defined containers with individually negotiated *input* and *output properties*, and subsequently defining completely predefined *message objects* if necessary, both paradigms of *user support & flexibility* and *automation & structure* can be put to practice.

Furthermore, *message objects* need *routing information* in order to be exchanged correctly between several WFMSs. This information, which is necessary to navigate *message objects* between the workflow systems involved with the help of *gateways* (see Section 5.6.4, p. 166), can be stored and used in different ways (Table 9).

Related navigation	Mixed navigation	Self-navigation
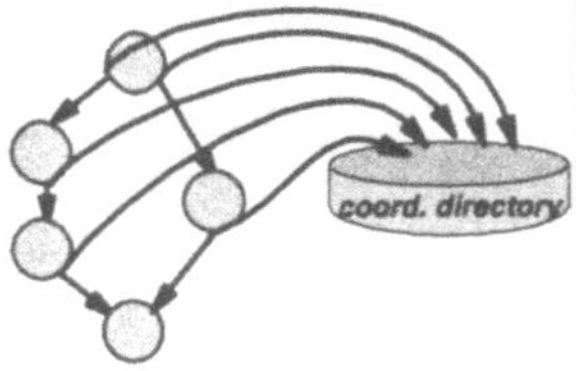	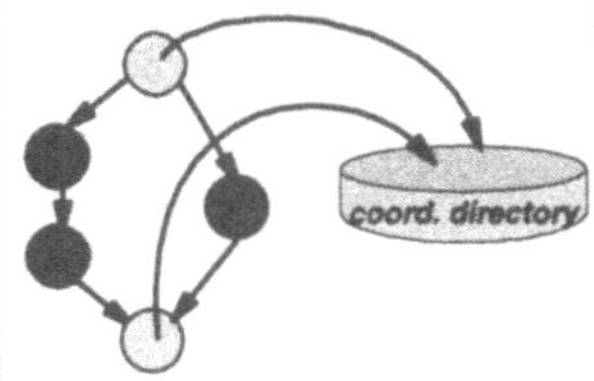	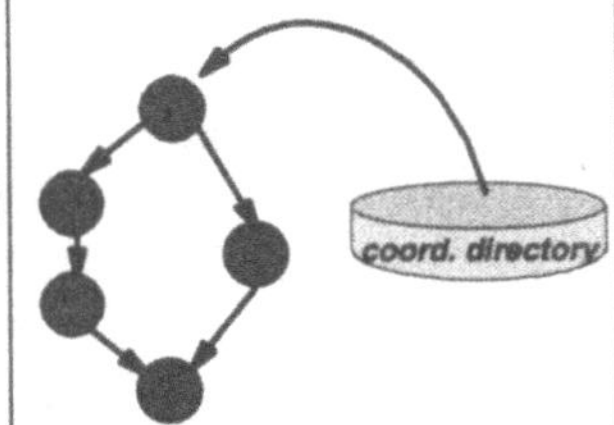
Look-up of routing information in coordination directory in each step	Embedded routing information with look-up in coordination directory at certain steps	One-time look-up in coordination directory to embed entire routing path

Table 9: Options for the navigation of message objects

On the left side of Table 9, *message objects* make use of routing information stored in *coordination directories* at each step on the way between the WFMSs involved, which is called *related navigation.* A typical arrangement of such steps for a *request & answer* scenario between two WFMSs A and B would be:

WFMS A → Gateway A → Gateway B → WFMS B
→ Gateway B → Gateway A → WFMS A.

On the right side of Table 9, the whole routing path described above would be embedded into a *message object* by WFMS A during an initial look-up in a *coordination directory* shared between WFMSs A and B. Thus, a *message object* would contain a list of addresses to work off with no further need for a connection to a *coordination directory*. This form of *self-navigation* is beneficial if a *message object* is supposed to be routed to different WFMSs as well as individual users' e-mail-boxes in a long chain of predefined activities. By embedding *methods* (e.g. making use of Java), individual e-mail users could participate in wide area workflows without possessing a workflow system themselves. In addition to the predefined routing path, individual detours can be allowed within certain limits in the form of *ad-hoc exceptions* (see also Section 5.5.2, p. 141). The handling of these exceptions could be supported by embedded *methods.*

Related navigation requires the availability of a *coordination directory* in each step of a wide area workflow, but allows for high flexibility concerning a conditional and flexible routing according to the newest routing information. In contrast to this, self-navigated *message objects* are highly independent of *coordination directories* but it is more difficult to adapt their routing path to short-term changes.

In between *related navigation* and *self-navigation,* compromises can be found in the form of *mixed navigation.* Allowing *message objects* to have routing information embedded but also to check back with *coordination directories* at certain steps can combine the advantages of both extremes.

If WFMSs exchange a limited set of well-defined *message objects* on a frequent basis, it is not efficient to embed the *form* (consisting of *representation* and *methods,* see Figure 33, p. 155) in each single *message object.* In these cases, it is reasonable to exchange *forms* in advance, e.g. making use of *coordination directories*, and subsequently to send *message objects* containing only *properties* and a reference to the respective *form*. Since *forms* are available to all participants in a WAWM scenario, they can be removed from *message objects* prior to sending and re-combined on the side of recipients. All features of *message objects* are thereby preserved while saving on bandwidth and thus costs. In other scenarios, the embedding of the *form* into *message objects* is a powerful method of realizing the paradigm of *user support & flexibility* (see Section 5.1, p. 104) for users working within occasionally connected WFMSs or making use of personal e-mail clients, who are working at home in the sense of *teleworking* [Dangelmaier/Kress/Wenski 1996].

Whether or not the embedding of *methods* into *message objects* is allowed is subject to the terms and conditions negotiated among the participants in a WAWM scenario. On one hand, the embedding of *methods* can enable powerful features for flexible WAWM, but on the other hand, this option can be abused to create so-called *e-mail viruses* or *Trojan horses*. The danger of receiving destructive program code embedded in *message objects* is high if the sender's identity cannot be completely clarified. Modern groupware platforms (see Section 3.4.4, p. 65) can authenticate the sender of a *message object* with the help of *digital signatures* based on trusted *certificates*. Each code is additionally signed by its originator and recipients can limit the execution of embedded *methods* to certain areas, thereby preventing for example destructive operations within the file system. Nevertheless, embedded *methods* in *message objects* are often rejected in practical scenarios for security reasons.

Another topic which participants in a WAWM cooperation have to clarify is the *tracking* of workflow instances and especially *message objects*. Hereby a fundamental question is whether the sender of a *message object* in WFMS A is allowed to track the processing of this *message object* in the recipient's WFMS B. If allowed by the recipient, the sender can control the processing of the invoking workflow instance in WFMS A as well as of the workflow instance invoked in WFMS B and all steps in-between the two systems. This is likely to be applicable in coordinative settings of *hierarchy* and *equal partnership* (see Section 5.4, p. 125), since one or several participants have overall process control. If such transparency is not welcome, tracking can be limited to local workflows only.

The following fundamental *tracking methods* can be applied within WAWM:

- *Send-tracking* describes a method in which a *tracking message* is sent to one or several *tracking databases* at the end of each step of a wide area workflow. An advantage of this method is its independence of system specifics and the current location of processing. It allows workflow administrators to check for the current status of local as well as remote processes at any time. One of the disadvantages of *send-tracking* is that tracking messages might get lost during transfer or may arrive in incorrect order due to delivery delays.
- In contrast, the application of *self-tracking* means that a tracking protocol is collected within workflow instances and *message objects*. This method is advantageous if for instance no messaging connection between *message objects* and tracking databases exists. Further on, originators can check the entire

routing path after the return of *message objects*. However, the location and current status of *message objects* being processed in remote locations cannot be easily monitored.

- The method of *mixed tracking* combines both tracking approaches mentioned above by collecting a tracking protocol, which can be sent to tracking databases either entirely or in segments at certain steps. It combines many of the advantages of *send-* and *self-tracking*, but requires more disk space and bandwidth, and might produce inconsistent tracking information due to redundancy.

Message objects as well as *tracking messages* can be transferred with the help of messaging systems (e-mail systems). Another possibility would be to make use of CORBA technology (see Section 3.4.3, p. 64) to connect several WFMSs and exchange messages, for instance with the help of the *Internet Inter-ORB Protocol (IIOP)*. Replication technology is also applicable to transfer *message objects* and *tracking protocols* as long as participants make use of shared databases.

5.6.3 Content management – filtering of information

Message objects are used to transfer certain information between WFMSs in intra- and interorganizational WAWM scenarios. But how is the information contained in the *message objects* selected from internal sources? This section deals with answers to this question, which is of high practical relevance.

It is unlikely that workflow designers or actual performers will want to send all of the information handled in internal workflow instances to external recipients. Before *message objects* can be posted, senders usually have to collect certain information from internal workflow instances and transfer them into these external information carriers. The process of actively filtering internal information to be included in *message objects* will be called *content management*.

The procedure of *content management* is well known from paper-based external communication. For instance: an engineer is responsible for the design of a machine part ordered by a customer. In order to clarify some specific issues, he wants to send a letter to this customer. In the course of writing, the engineer usually collects information from different sources (e.g. drawings, project plans, parts lists, price lists, former design studies, etc.). He transfers his findings into a letter that is intended to present certain contents in an appropriate way. The sources used by the engineer are often organized in files, containing folders and documents.

The engineer would certainly not package all related files and send them to the customer, leaving it up to him to find the information needed for a certain task. Much of the information the engineer needs in order to design the machine part is not intended for the customer. For instance, it might be a great disadvantage if the customer had knowledge of certain facts concerning pricing negotiations.

The same is true for Wide Area Workflow Management: as it is generally very important in workflow management systems to provide only the information needed by the performer of a certain task, this necessity for active filtering of information becomes even stronger if *WFMSs' interaction* is to be implemented, especially in interorganizational cooperation.

The main reasons for *content management* in WAWM are:

- filtering, assigning and providing the information needed to perform a certain task within an external workflow, including the access to related and the denial of access to restricted information;
- retaining confidential internal information;
- adjusting the workload according to the availability, transfer rates and costs of possible communication channels at different times, taking communication frequency into consideration.

In many WFMSs, information in internal workflow instances is presented to users in (compound) documents that are collected in folders. The underlying data structure can be based on records of (relational) databases or the WFMS might make use of shared document databases as found in groupware platforms.

Following the architecture model described at the beginning of Section 5.6 (p. 143), the structure and contents of *message objects* are derived from *message object types* and *sub-types* as well as *interface specifications* exchanged between participants of a WAWM scenario with the help of *coordination directories*.

Seen from a technical viewpoint, *content management* means to map certain fields of internal workflow documents to fields specified in *message objects* during build-time. Subsequently, the respective information (*content*) from internal sources must be transferred to external *message objects* during run-time operation at the point where a workflow instance of an *addressee* is invoked. This procedure is also called *outgoing content management*, because it is performed by the sender before information leaves his WFMS (Figure 35).

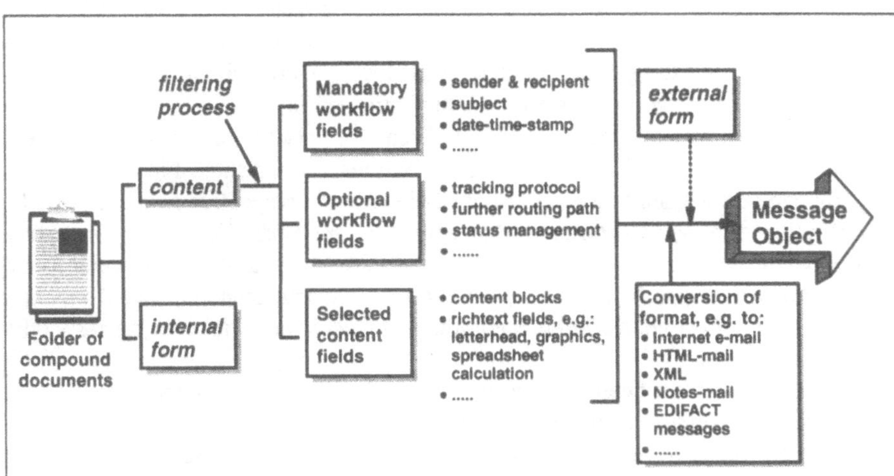

Figure 35: Outgoing content management - from internal compound documents to external message objects

In a first step, the internal *forms* (containing *representation* and *methods*) are disconnected from the compound documents of the respective workflow instance, which are stored in a folder in the internal WFMS (Figure 35). Subsequently, the content of these compound documents has to be filtered in an interactive or automated procedure to select the information that will be included in the *message object*. Depending on the underlying *coordination mechanism*, either the *initiator*, the *addressee* or both define the structure and contents of the *message objects* with the help of *message object types/sub-types* and *interface specifications*.

The actual mapping of internal fields to fields in *message objects*, aimed at transferring certain contents, can be achieved by the following methods:

- *1:1-mapping*: the content of one internal field is directly transferred into one field of a *message object*.
- *1:N-mapping*: the content of a single internal field (e.g. an address block) is split up into distinct fields in a *message object* (e.g. name, street, zip, city, etc.).
- *M:1-mapping*: the content of several internal fields is aggregated to fit into a single field of a *message object*.

It might be helpful to transfer only a fraction of certain information contained in an internal field into a related field of a *message object*, making use of either of the three methods. In many cases, this selection of relevant parts within internal fields can only be performed interactively by a user.

After selected content fields have been mapped to fields in *message objects*, additional information has to be set for WAWM purposes. *Mandatory workflow fields* like electronic addresses (e.g. e-mail addresses) of sender and recipient(s), a subject, a date-time-stamp, the unique identification of the *interface specification* referred to and for instance the indication of a priority are necessary to enable fundamental WAWM features. Additionally, *message objects* can contain *optional workflow fields* used to store things like a tracking protocol, a predefined routing path for several concatenated workflow steps or status information.

If the sender and the recipient use different formats for *message objects* (e.g. Lotus Notes versus XML), a format conversion must be executed. Finally, an *external form* can be assigned to a *message object* in case the respective format allows for the definition of a *representation* and/or embedded *methods*. *External forms* can be embedded in the *message object* itself. If participants in a WAWM scenario exchange *forms* with the help of a *coordination directory*, then the actual *message objects* would only contain a reference to the assigned *external form* in the respective *coordination directory*.

After contents have been filtered, mandatory and optional workflow fields been set, a format conversion been executed and an external *form* been assigned, a *message object* is ready to be transferred to the recipient's WFMS. Before it is actually sent, it can be presented to a user for a final check on content and representation (see Figure 17, p. 106).

Similarly, on the side of the recipient, an *incoming content management* must be executed. It can consist of the following steps:

- If the sender has provided the *message object* in a format that is not suited to comfortable handling by human actors (e.g. WfMC-compliant Internet e-mail MIME Binding), then a format conversion has to take place first.
- Subsequently, a user might want to check the incoming *message object* to see whether further processing is reasonable, following the paradigm of *user support & flexibility* (see Figure 17, p. 106). If the user decides to reject further steps (e.g. if important information in the *message object* is missing or the *addressee* is currently not capable of providing the requested service), the *message object* would be sent back to its originator, informing him that no processing took place.
- If accepted, optionally a predefined or interactive filtering of contents might follow in order to remove unnecessary or undesired information.
- Then, all or parts of the information stored in fields in the *message object* must be transferred into fields in internal workflow documents. Again, this must be achieved by a mapping of fields between the *message object* and the respective document.
- Additionally, the *message object* as whole can be included into the internal folder of workflow documents so that administrators and users can check incoming information from an external WFMS during the further processing of the respective workflow instance.

Figure 36 illustrates the steps of *incoming content management.*

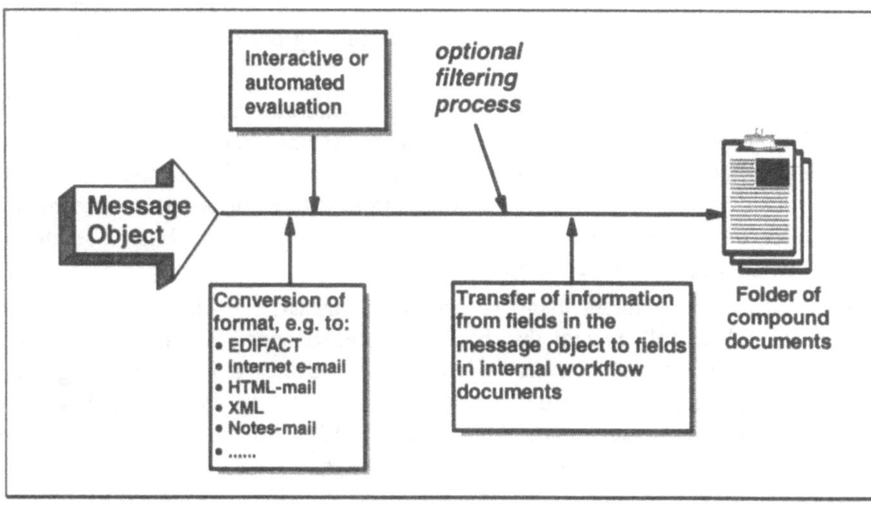

Figure 36: Incoming content management - inclusion of external information into folders of internal compound documents

Outgoing as well as *incoming content management* can be prepared during the build-time of workflow models, which is termed *predefined content management.* In cases of ad-hoc invocation of external workflow instances (see Section 5.5.2, p. 141), predefined settings for *content management* might not be available. Therefore, the following types of *content management (CM)* can be distinguished:

- *Predefined CM* means preparing the field mappings on the side of *initiators* or *addressees*, and optionally adjusting format settings so that conversion can take place during run-time operation.
- *Predefined CM with run-time control* is applied by predefining *content management* during build-time, but give users the opportunity to check the CM-settings during run-time operation before *content management* is actually performed. This type of CM follows the paradigm of *user support & flexibility* (see Figure 17, p. 106).
- *Ad-hoc CM* allows users to define CM-settings interactively during run-time operation if no predefined CM-settings are available. This kind of *content management* is necessary for instance in the case of an ad-hoc invocation of a workflow service offered according to the *coordination mechanism* of *market*, making use of an $\text{WORKFLOW}_{\text{SUB,WAW}}$ *interface specification.*

An example of the practical implementation of *content management* is described in Chapter 6, introducing the Wide Area GroupFlow System (WAGS).

5.6.4 Gateways – connection of heterogeneous WFMSs

There are several possible ways for autonomous WFMSs to interact. The Workflow Management Coalition (WfMC) has defined different levels of integration of WFMSs (see Section 4.2.1.2, p. 78), thereby discussing basic possibilities for interaction:

- WFMSs can provide *APIs* for other applications and thus other WFMSs. Using these *APIs*, workflow management systems can interact directly with each other. A prerequisite for this kind of interaction is that the WFMSs involved "know" each others' formats and structures in order for information to be exchanged. Further on, WFMSs must be able to establish a stable on-line-connection with each other.
- WFMSs can interact using *gateways* that translate exchanged information into a "neutral" *format* that both sides can decode. Within certain limits, *gateways* can also convert information into different *structures* (e.g. from WfMC-compliant Internet e-mail MIME Binding into WFMS-specific structures and vice versa), in case the WFMSs involved do not make use of the same structuring specifications. *Gateways* can make use of asynchronous transfer systems such as e-mail services, so WFMSs do not need a direct on-line-connection.

The author will concentrate on the *gateway* option because it is of general applicability in heterogeneous environments (see also [Fowler/Swatman/Swatman 1994]). The implementation of standardized *APIs* for WFMSs seems – at the moment – to be still in the distant future when looking at the rapidly evolving workflow systems' market. Since commercial WFMSs are still being improved at fast pace and new features are constantly being added, it is unlikely that APIs can be kept up-to-date in the near future. The *API* option will become more interesting once the workflow market has matured and a few large vendors will have the power to establish commonly accepted *APIs*, whether they are proprietary or standardized by an organization such as the WfMC.

In the context of the general WAWM architecture proposed in Figure 30 (p. 144), *gateways* can perform the following tasks:

Post office: *gateways* can build a single "post office" for multiple WFMSs of an organization, being responsible for all external connections to WFMSs in other organizations. Management questions such as "How many external workflow contacts did we have in the last week? What were the costs?" can thereby be answered promptly. Centralizing external WFMSs interaction to one place facilitates tracking, error handling, maintenance and controlling of WAWM.

For external organizations, a single entry point into the workflow domain of a partner organization is certainly more convenient than having to connect to various WFMSs of this organization with different settings, addresses, formats etc.

Routing: *gateways* route outgoing *message objects* to external organizations' *gateways* or to private users' e-mail-boxes. Incoming *message objects* are transferred to the internal WFMS responsible for execution. *Internal* and *external routing* are performed based on the information stored in the public and private parts of the respective *coordination directories*.

Request-and-answer tracking: Once the *gateway* of organization A has sent a *message object* to the *gateway* of organization B, requesting a certain workflow service offered by B (*"request"*), it will wait until the return of a related *"answer"*. If this *answer* does not arrive in time (see the predicted maximum duration in Table 8, p. 149), A's *gateway* can take certain actions, for example to inform the waiting workflow instance in organization A's WFMS that it should continue without the requested results.

Outgoing *message objects* can also be *"one-way"*. In this case, no *answer* is expected (see *SWP* interaction in Table 4, p. 119). Both *one-way* and completed *request-answer*-pairs can be transferred automatically into an archive. Apart from technical features, *request-and-answer tracking* in *gateways* allows for the provision of managerial information such as responses to the following questions: "How many unanswered workflow *requests* are currently pending? How many workflow connections do we have with organization X per week? Does the connection with organization X pay off? On average, how long does it take organization Y to send *answers* to our *requests*? What is the percentage of *requests* from organization Z that were successfully answered?".

Reminding: based on the method of *request-and-answer tracking*, *gateways* of *initiators* can remind *gateways* of *addressees* (and also – if allowed – *addressees'* workflow engines) that *requests* are due, based on the predicted maximum processing time published by the *addressees*. Likewise, *gateways* of *addressees* can remind performers in their internal WFMSs that *answers* to certain external *requests* will be due soon and should be immediately processed so that they can be delivered to *initiators* in time. Hence, *gateways* can prevent delays on the *initiator's* as well as the *addressee's* side.

Confidentiality and access protection: a *gateway* protects the WFMSs of an organization from direct access from outside, serving as a "buffer" or "workflow firewall". Making an *API* of a WFMS directly accessible to the outside may be an invitation for undesired activities. Therefore, using a *gateway* together with a *coordination directories'* function to disconnect internal and external routing (see Figure 32, p. 151) protects internal WFMSs from any direct access. An external organization B does not obtain information other than the electronic address of organization A's *gateway* (found in organization A's header document in the *coordination directory* shared between A and B) and the identification number of an *interface specification* offered by A (see Table 8, p. 149) to invoke a workflow instance in one of A's WFMSs. All that organization B must do is to drop a *message object* (e.g. in the form of an e-mail) in organization A's *gateway* containing the respective identification number and the required input fields in the format specified by A. Subsequently, A's *gateway* will check the private part of A's *coordination directory* to find the reference to the internal WFMS(s) responsible for the execution of the service offered. A's *gateway* will subsequently deliver the incoming *message object* to the WFMS responsible, where a workflow instance is invoked. Upon completion of this workflow instance, results are given back to A's *gateway*, which in turn sends an answering *message object* to organization B (in most cases to B's *gateway*). Organization B thus receives the desired results from organization A's *gateway*, not knowing who actually performed it within A.

Using this mechanism of disconnection of internal and external workflow routing with the help of *coordination directories* and *gateways* allows for workflow services to be offered while keeping the WFMSs involved completely autonomous. All internal information about the processing of workflow instances can be kept confidential, still allowing WFMSs to interoperate. If organizations involved agree on sharing more information about the processing of externally invoked workflow instances, they can achieve this by allowing for the exchange of status and tracking messages between workflow engines. However, there is no technically induced necessity to do so, which means that the choice to collaborate closely is left to the participants' free will. This is an essential difference to EDI technology, where information systems are directly linked.

The mechanism of complete disconnection of WFMSs allows workflow services to be offered to an anonymous market with the help of the WWW, not having to be afraid of undesired activities on the part of external persons or organizations.

Transparency: *gateways* – in conjunction with *coordination directories* – make WFMSs' interaction transparent. Neither the workflow designer of *initiators* needs to know details about the organization behind the offered service (e.g. addresses, responsible persons, details of communication, etc.), nor does a performer in a workflow instance need to be concerned about the correct routing of *message objects*. On the side of the *addressees*, *gateways* correctly deliver incoming *requests* to the WFMS responsible and in turn send back *answers* to the *initiators* of *requests*.

Format conversion: *gateways* should have the ability to convert outgoing *message objects* from the format used in the internal WFMS to a format that can be understood by the recipient. Likewise, incoming *message objects* may have to be converted so that the internal WFMS can handle the information included. Relevant formats for a "neutral" exchange of *message objects* between *gateways*, such as XML, have been discussed in Section 5.6.2.2 (p. 156).

Tracking: *gateways* can be designed so that they record *tracking protocols* or send *tracking messages* to *tracking databases* (see p. 161). Using *tracking databases*, a complete tracking history of all internal workflow steps as well as the steps between WFMSs can be collected in cases where all participants allow such an overall tracking. If an organization is not permitted to track activities in other organizations' WFMSs, *gateways* at least can inform the tracking database about details of *exits* from and *re-entries* into the organization's own workflow domain.

Group requests: *gateways* can send *requests* to groups of recipients (e.g. all PC suppliers in Case Study 2) and handle the incoming *answers*. For example, *answers* can be collected and sent to the internal workflow instance that has originated the *group request* as a bundle. Further on, *gateways* can remind recipients, enforce deadlines or execute rules such as "wait until 90% of the answers have returned or 14 days have gone by", before bundled *answers* are submitted to the requester.

Error prevention and handling: *gateways* can have options to avoid failures in WFMSs' interaction, such as *handshake* mechanisms with other *gateways*, *return receipts* or *re-send* functions. Additionally, in the case of failures, *gateways* can inform waiting workflow instances to proceed without *answers* or inform system administrators about non-deliverable *requests*, faults in incoming *message objects* or missing information in *coordination directories*.

Examples of the implementation and application of *gateways*, *coordination directories* and *message objects* will be presented in Chapter 6, introducing the Wide Area GroupFlow System, and Chapter 7 discussing results from case studies.

5.7 Models for implementation and continuous improvement of WAWM

The introduction of systems for (wide area) workflow management into organizations is a complex process. As with most IT-system implementations, the following basic phases can be distinguished:

- planning;
- implementation in a limited area;
- pilot use;
- analysis and improvement;
- spreading onto other areas of the organization;
- operative use;
- continuous improvement through analysis and redesign.

For the implementation of systems for local workflow management, various models reflecting similar phases have been devised. These models are sometimes called *lifecycles* (see also Figure 8, p. 49) because of the circular approach of continuous efforts at optimization [Hilpert 1994], [Deiters/Gruhn/Striemer 1995], [Derszteler 1996], [Heilmann 1996]. Other authors discuss *implementation models* for local WFMSs with a conceptual focus [Rathgeb 1994], [Striemer/Holten/Weske 1997] or based on practical experiences [Black Forest Group 1996], [Manhart 1996], [Rothenbacher 1996], [van Hoof/Altenhofen 1996]. Cathomen [1996] proposes a *lifecycle* concept for the use and optimization of interorganizational information systems (IOS, see also Section 3.2.4, p. 33).

The planning of systems for WAWM means to involve all participants in intra- and interorganizational scenarios. Thus, negotiations about the terms and conditions of a workflow-based collaboration – influenced by the respective power relationships – might be rather extensive. As the organizational units or organizations in a WAWM scenario involved might be largely autonomous – depending on the degree of organizational integration (see Section 5.2.2.3, p. 114) – *lifecycles* and *implementation models* for Wide Area Workflow Management differ from those for local workflow management in certain aspects.

In the following sections, such models for the structuring and support of the implementation and continuous improvement of systems for WAWM will be introduced.

5.7.1 Lifecycle for WAWM systems

The implementation of a workflow management system often requires fundamental organizational, technological and social changes within organizations. Process patterns long in use are examined, revised and changed, competencies of workers are shifted, social structures are altered. Moreover, privileges and status symbols are in danger of being removed.

Therefore, it is necessary that detailed planning, intensive communication and training during the start-up phase are initially implemented to prevent disappointment on the part of those making the decisions, doing the planning, installing the technical equipment and using the services. An important aspect hereby is the acceptance of changes on the part of the users in the initial phase of implementation. Without their conviction that the WFMS will definitely help them to enhance flexibility and quality of work while, at the same time, reducing processing time and costs, implementation is likely to fail. This conviction can only be achieved by presenting the workflow management system to the users involved at an early point in time, showing realistic scenarios to illustrate the benefits of the new system. Further on, an intensive training phase should be included to make users familiar with their new working environment.

Once a WFMS has been implemented, constant maintenance and optimization of the whole workflow environment is of high importance in order to really benefit from the investments made. The capability of workflow management systems to react in a flexible manner to changes occurring during the run-time phase helps to avoid inefficient performance caused by workflow model inadequacies which are almost always found. Deviations from predefined workflow models during the run-time operation provide important clues for workflow designers in their efforts at optimization. Just as real world scenarios are constantly changing, workflow models have to be actualized and adjusted in a continuous process of improvement.

What is true of local workflow management gains a new dimension with the step towards Wide Area Workflow Management: the coordination of more or less *autonomous* participants – in many cases across companies' boundaries – in this process of continuous improvement implies additional challenges. Therefore, a systematic approach to the opening of local WFMSs towards WAWM-based collaboration and the continuous optimization of the subsequent cross-WFMS interaction is suggested here.

The following Figure 37 shows a *lifecycle* for WAWM, describing necessary steps towards a systematic interoperation of WFMSs.

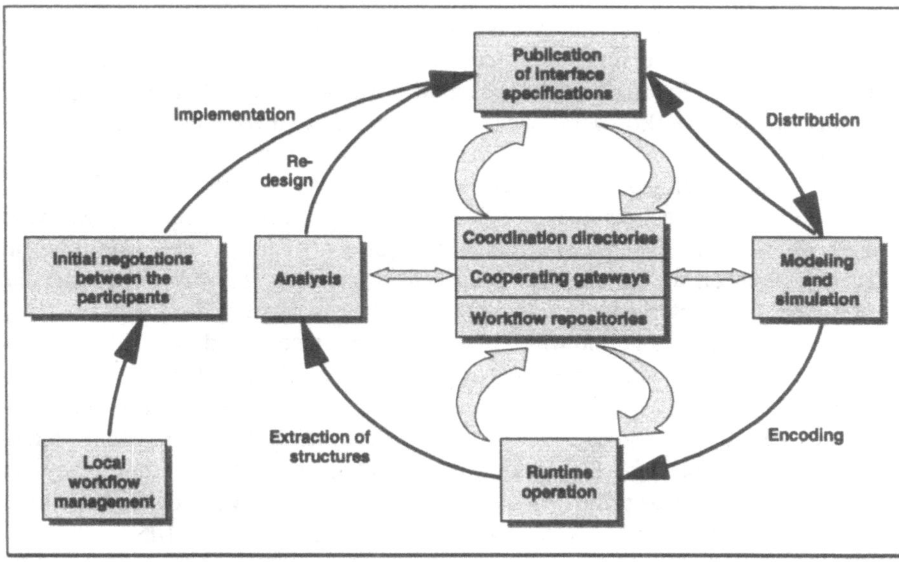

Figure 37: Lifecycle for Wide Area Workflow Management

Starting from existing local workflow applications within the participating organizations, the first step will most likely be *initial negotiations* about the aims and terms of collaboration. The topics that should be discussed within such negotiations are examined in the *implementation model* described in the following Section 5.7.2.

After the partner organizations have agreed on the terms and conditions of collaboration, they start to implement the technological and organizational infrastructure, which is also discussed in the *implementation model* (see Section 5.7.2). The next step in the *lifecycle* shown in Figure 37 is the publication of workflow *interface specifications* from each organization for the respective partners, using *coordination directories*. These *interface specifications* contain for instance information about services offered by an organization, the possible exchange formats, communication addresses and the structure of the information expected (see Section 5.6.1.1, p. 145). Services offered by an organization via *interface specifications* could be for example: "request quotation", "provide product information", "design machine part", "provide sales forecast" or many others. The *interface specifications* published initially are often a result of the preceding negotiations, allowing the planners to start with a limited "pilot use" of WAWM features for testing purposes.

Once *interface specifications* have been published and distributed, each of the partner organizations can start to design their own workflow models within the network of the planned cooperation. By including $\text{SUBWORKFLOW}_{\text{DEC,WAW}}$ or $\text{WORKFLOW}_{\text{SUB,WAW}}$ elements into workflow models (see Figure 29, p. 137), the exchange of *message objects* between the WFMSs involved during run-time operation is prepared. Through a simulation process, faults and inefficiencies are detected before workflow instances are actually started. If workflow designers experience problems with the use of *interface specifications*, they might have to go one step back and negotiate on changes to these specifications in order to allow for proper planning and execution of WAWM. Once workflow models have been tested, optimized and approved, they can be released for actual use.

During run-time operation, users create instances of the workflow models designed previously. External workflow connections are initiated at the respective positions in these workflow instances. Users can also invoke external workflow contacts in an ad-hoc manner in the form of exceptions (see Section 5.5.2, p. 141). As a first step, predefined or ad-hoc *content management* is performed to filter relevant information for the recipient (see Section 5.6.3, p. 162). Subsequently, *message objects* are sent to other WFMSs via *gateways*, connecting related workflow instances by transferring the contents described in *interface specifications*. After the results have been returned, the invoking workflow instances can continue. Thus, during run-time operation, one will find a mixture of internal and external workflow steps, based on the fundamental *interaction patterns* described in Table 4 (p. 119).

Users are informed via worklists about workflow folders, which have been supplied internally by colleagues and *message objects* coming in from external organizations. They can react by undertaking or neglecting the respective tasks they are supposed to perform; of prime importance is that they are ***aware*** of the difference between internal and external workflow steps (see also Figure 17, p. 106).

Run-time operation can be tracked in order to allow for a comparison between workflow models and the workflow instances actually performed. *Message objects* exchanged between organizations can also be tracked with the help of the *gateways* involved. If permission is granted by the partner organizations involved, entire cross-WFMSs workflows can be analyzed, allowing for an overall optimization. As Wide Area Workflow Management can create complex process structures, graphical analysis tools can support administrators and workflow designers in gaining an overview of internal and external workflow instances.

In many cases, the analysis of workflow instances actually performed will show partly inefficient or inadequate structures. These inefficiencies can often be found by looking at recurring exceptions performed by users whilst working on their respective tasks. Often, the reasons for these exceptions have to be clarified in communication with the respective performers. If the workflow-based interaction *between* organizations involved in a WAWM scenario is sub-optimal, strategies for the removal of obstacles must be negotiated.

After the clarification of inefficiencies and the subsequent definition of optimized procedures, a new cycle begins with the adaptation of published *interface specifications* and a reengineering of workflow models.

5.7.2 Implementation model for WAWM systems

The *lifecycle* for WAWM presented in the preceding section (Figure 37) is intended to support the whole process of planning, implementation and continuous improvement of systems for Wide Area Workflow Management. In order to refine a very important part of the *lifecycle*, the *implementation model* discussed in this section serves as a conceptual framework for the structuring of requirements for WAWM systems on the one hand, and a structured support for the realization of practical implementation of such systems on the other hand.

The following Figure 38 shows the structure of the *implementation model.* It is designed using discrete modules that help to reduce complexity and support a useful timely arrangement of consecutive steps during the implementation phase. By defining the interfaces between the modules, mainly on the *computing level* of the model, the development and adjustment of the modules can be partly carried out in parallel. Through the usage of defined interfaces, the replacement of certain modules is simplified and a re-use in similar cases is facilitated. With increasing experience in implementing systems for WAWM, reliable modules can be stored in module libraries.

Since the requirements for the use of Wide Area Workflow Management will constantly change, making it necessary to adapt systems continuously, the *implementation model* also has a circular approach that facilitates the entry into a new cycle of reengineering when adjustments become necessary.

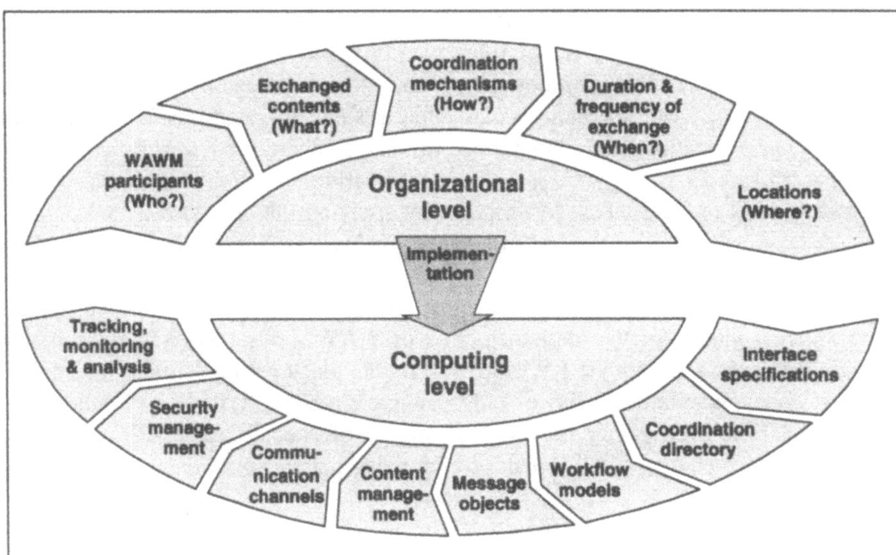

Figure 38: Implementation model for Wide Area Workflow Management Systems

Organizational level

The *organizational level* of the *implementation model* (see upper part of Figure 38) aims to support a clarification of the determinants of WAWM within and between the cooperating organizations. The topics indicated by the five questions should be discussed in the *initial negotiations* between the organizational units or organizations willing to cooperate by WAWM means.

The *WAWM participants* and their relationships with each other (*Who?*) have to be described in the form of a commonly shared information base (e.g. a shared *coordination directory*). The degree to which internal information is made available to partners will vary depending on the level of trust. While the description of such a network of organizations and their interdependencies is rather trivial for a small number of participants, it can become fairly complicated as the number of partners increases, especially in cases where the partner organizations consist of multiple subsidiaries at different locations.

The intention of the next step is to clarify the *contents* that should be exchanged within the WAWM scenario (*What?*). These contents are derived from the common goals of the participants and the actual projects that should be supported by means of WAWM. For instance, the participants of a *virtual organization* (see Section 3.2.6, p. 37) could agree on the common development, production and marketing of one or more products. Hence, they would agree to exchange information on product design, production plans and marketing strategies with the help of their interoperating WFMSs.

The *contents exchanged* can be described on different levels of granularity, ranging from qualitative textual lists to detailed definitions of *interface specifications* on field-level.

Appropriate *coordination mechanisms* (see Section 5.4, p. 125) for the respective WAWM scenario have to be found subsequently based on the power relationships among participants (*How?*). Options range from loose interorganizational communication, implemented with the help of messaging systems, to an intensive cooperation in intraorganizational settings, making use of shared, distributed workflow environments (see Figure 29, p. 137). Cooperating organizations can also choose approaches in-between these two extremes, for instance by applying the *market*-oriented coordination mechanism. This method allows for closer cooperation while keeping information systems separate.

The *duration and frequency of the exchange* (*When?*) determines which investments are reasonable for the implementation of WAWM systems. While a short or sporadic interaction between WFMSs may well take place with existing e-mail channels to exchange *message objects* of rather simple structure, extensive collaboration over a long time may justify the implementation of specialized WAWM servers, dedicated *gateways*, the establishment of high performance communication channels and other costly measures.

Finally, the geographical distribution (*Where?*) of the cooperating partners has to be described in a common structure such as *coordination directories*, allowing for the correct routing of *message objects* to subsidiaries responsible for certain workflow services in worldwide operating trusts.

The information gained from within the five modules of the *organizational level* can be shared between the participants of a WAWM scenario, for instance via *shared databases* or *directory services*, and build the basis for the practical implementation of WAWM systems on the *computing level*.

Computing level

The first task for the participants regarding the implementation of systems for WAWM is to define the *interface specifications* of the workflow services to be offered to partner organizations. Depending on the underlying *coordination mechanism*, *interface specifications* are defined by those who will later be *initiators* (*hierarchy*) or *addressees* (*market*) in the actual WFMSs' interoperation. In the mechanism of *equal partnership*, both sides have to agree on *interface specifications* in negotiations. The module *interface specifications* of the *computing level* is mainly influenced by the characteristics defined in the following modules of the *organizational level*: *WAWM participants*, *exchanged contents* and *coordination mechanisms*.

Once the *interface specifications* have been defined, *coordination directories* have to be set up for their publication. Depending on the proximity of organizational units or organizations, *coordination directories* can be realized with the help of shared databases and replication technology, or by exchanging messages between independent *directory services* (see Section 5.6.1.2, p. 152). Each of the participants has to announce the address of his *coordination directory* to the others, so that publication and synchronization can take place. The implementation of the module *coordination directory* depends largely on the decisions made in the modules *coordination mechanism*, *duration & frequency* and *locations* of the *organizational level*.

After *interface specifications* have been made available to the participants with the help of *coordination directories*, the workflow designers of each of the WFMSs can start to build *workflow models*, including WAWM-related elements such as $\text{SUBWORKFLOW}_{\text{DEC,WAW}}$ or $\text{WORKFLOW}_{\text{SUB,WAW}}$ to prepare for cross-WFMS interaction. Different *patterns of interaction* as described in Table 4 (p. 119) can be used to achieve the desired results in the networks of interoperating workflow instances. The design of *workflow models* mainly requires the clarification of relevant issues in the modules *WAWM participants*, *exchanged contents* and *coordination mechanisms* of the *organizational level*.

The procedures for defining *interface specifications*, publishing them in *coordination directories* and designing of *workflow models* are closely linked to each other, requiring an iterative process of several cycles throughout the three modules until final results can be achieved.

Now that the structures and contents of internal *workflow models* and their connection to workflows performed by other WFMSs have been clarified, the *properties* and *representation* of *message objects* have to be specified (see Section 5.6.2.1, p. 154). Workflow designers also have to decide whether *message objects* should contain embedded *methods* or not, depending on the security concerns of their partners.

The structure of *message objects* can be derived from *message object types* and *sub-types*, which can be stored in an *object hierarchy* in *coordination directories* (see p. 155). The actual *properties* of *message objects* are derived from the *interface specifications*. For instance, if organization A publishes certain *input* fields for a $\text{WORKFLOW}_{\text{SUB,WAW}}$ element in the *coordination directory* (see Table 8, p. 149), then organization B has to design *message objects*, which are supposed to use this service, so that they contain the required fields. Likewise, organization A has to design a *message object* that can transfer the promised results back to organization

B, based on the *output* fields published in the *coordination directory*. The definition of *message objects* is mainly influenced by the modules *exchanged contents* and *coordination mechanisms* of the *organizational level*.

Within the module *content management*, the contents carried in workflow folders of internal workflow instances have to be mapped to the content blocks and fields defined in the properties of the related *message objects* (see Section 5.6.3, p. 162). To enable this, workflow designers have to be aware of the fact that the necessary contents to be transferred into *message objects* during run-time operation are actually prepared in the preceding internal workflow steps. Thus, the modules *workflow models*, *message objects* and *content management* are closely linked to each other. Seen from the *organizational level* of the *implementation model*, *content management* is predominantly derived from the results of the initial negotiations in the module *exchanged contents*.

Achieving the connection of WFMSs on a technical level means that organizations have to establish one or more *communication channels* (e.g. connections via modem, ISDN, satellite etc.). All measures related to the provision of these channels in the context of WAWM are centralized in a module in order to facilitate the re-use of parameters etc. in similar situations. By publishing different *communication channels* to partner organizations via *header documents* in *coordination directories*, and assigning priorities and preferences to them, participants can make use of *least cost routing* of exchanged *message objects* depending on the respective time of day, channel costs, workload, urgency etc. The investments made for the implementation of *communication channels* are largely influenced by the characteristics of the respective WAWM scenario laid down in the modules *duration & frequency of exchange* and *locations* of the *organizational level*.

Information processed in workflow management systems is often highly confidential and therefore has to be protected with the best security mechanisms available. This is especially true for intra- and interorganizational WAWM, where *message objects* often have to be transferred using public networks. To achieve a reliable *security management*, WAWM participants have to implement systems for *access control*, *encryption* (e.g. public key encryption) and the exchange of *digital signatures* for authentication purposes. For example, WAWM participants can exchange trusted certificates as a foundation for the use of public key encryption and digital signatures. Today's information systems underlying WFMSs, for instance relational database management systems or groupware platforms, provide powerful mechanisms for securing the interoperation of WFMSs (see also Section 3.4.4, p. 65).

The respective measures and settings are realized in the module *security management* and are a crucial aspect of the functioning of WAWM systems. Discussions about security problems in the Internet/World Wide Web, tackled by systems such as firewalls or encryption standards (e.g. SSL, PGP), have shown the enormous sensitivity of organizations concerning the transfer of confidential information to outside recipients. Incoming information carriers are also subject to extensive checks aimed at protecting organizations' IT systems from the invasion of *viruses* or *Trojan horses*. The relevant modules in the *organizational level*, influencing the settings for *security management*, are: *WAWM participants*, *exchanged contents* and *locations*.

As a prerequisite for the implementation of the module *tracking, monitoring & analysis*, a unique *identification* of workflow instances and exchanged *message objects* is required. Since *message objects* often leave the domain of an organization, all answers and further requests referring to this *message object* have to be identified correctly in order to be routed to the internal WFMS responsible for further processing. Taking into account that large organizations have hundreds or even thousands of external contacts a day (see for example Case Studies 1 and 2, p. 9), it is necessary to have commonly accepted standards for the identification of *message objects* and the related workflow instances (see for example Table 8, p. 149). Today's methods used to tackle this challenge in paper-based office work are invoice numbers, customer numbers etc., which can be used and enriched for WAWM purposes.

On the basis of a correct identification, the module for *tracking, monitoring & analyzing* is aimed at helping administrators and workflow designers to keep control of the structure, use, failures, costs etc. of internal workflow instances as well as external workflow communication.

A detailed *tracking* of workflow steps provides the information needed for *monitoring* at a certain point in time or *analysis* of already completed workflow instances (see also p. 161). During the application of WAWM, *message objects* leave certain organizations and enter into others. Since the control over workflow information changes frequently, participants may want to gain an overview of the whole workflow network. For example, cooperating partners can agree on certain tracking measures in the *initial negotiations* which allow *gateways* to keep control of *message objects* exchanged between them (see Section 5.6.4, p. 166). The settings made in the module *tracking, monitoring & analysis* are mainly induced by decisions expressed in the modules *WAWM participants* and *coordination mechanisms*. The allowance to track workflows will probably differ depending on the underlying *coordination mechanism* of WAWM, such as *hierarchy, market* or *equal partnership*.

The modules of the *computing level* of the *implementation model* have different user groups within an organization and therefore have to fulfill different requirements. The following three views on the modules can be distinguished:

- Developer's view: developers are assigned to implement the functionality of the respective modules, based on the requirements stated in the *organizational level* of the *implementation model*, as far as given platforms and systems do not provide the relevant features as is.
- Administrator's view: administrators initially configure the different parameters of the modules and adjust settings when changes occur. They thereby allow for a sound run-time operation of WAWM systems.
- User's view: in order to make systems for Wide Area Workflow Management as easy to use as possible, most of the modules will need intuitive graphical user interfaces. Users should be enabled to handle the complexity inherent to WFMSs' interaction. A crucial aspect is providing users with extensive information about the differences between internal routing and external workflow interaction. This can be achieved by presenting *message objects* to users before sending – resembling the procedures involved in sending a letter to external recipients in paper-based offices. Presenting *message objects* to users makes them ***aware*** of the fact that information is now leaving their own workflow domain (see also Figure 17, p. 106).

By using these different perspectives, the structuring and handling of the modules can be simplified. Program sources, settings and other relevant information about modules of the *implementation model* can be stored in repositories for the purposes of structured archiving and re-use. Once a trustworthy relationship between participants in a WAWM scenario has been established, well-tried modules can also be exchanged between them.

This may make the implementation of new systems for WAWM as well as the adaptation of existing systems to new circumstances much easier.

The concepts and models presented in this 5th chapter build the basis for the prototypic Wide Area GroupFlow System, which will be introduced on the following pages.

A discussion of the concepts for Wide Area Workflow Management presented up until here can be found in Chapter 8 (p. 253).

6 Wide Area GroupFlow System (WAGS)

In this chapter, the *Wide Area GroupFlow System (WAGS)* will be introduced. It is a prototypic software framework, which was designed and implemented by the author and his team at the Groupware Competence Center at the University of Paderborn (http://gcc.uni-paderborn.de). The main purpose of WAGS is to illustrate the practical application of the concepts for WAWM described so far.

The core development team of WAGS was comprised of more than 20 persons, who have contributed to the various elements of WAGS during different phases of the 3 years' project which lasted until early 1998. Roughly the same number of people also helped the author to carry out case studies in the field of WAWM (see Chapter 7, p. 233), did extensive literature studies, tested and evaluated the WAGS environment, worked on publications and prepared practical demonstrations.

Despite this rather large project team, it was not intended to build or to prepare the building of a commercial workflow management system. WAGS was solely designed to be experimental software for demonstration purposes. Its aim is to contribute to the further development of scientific and commercial WFMSs regarding features for Wide Area Workflow Management.

The author would be glad if WAGS could help to transfer the results of the underlying research project on WAWM to researchers, WFMSs' designers as well as practitioners with the help of a hands-on system, ready to be evaluated and discussed.

In the following section, an introduction to the architecture of WAGS is given, the development environment is presented and fundamental terms used within the system are explained. Subsequently, the functionality of the different components of WAGS is examined in more detail. The sequence of presentation of these tools follows the *lifecycle* and *implementation model* introduced in Section 5.7 (p. 169).
The features of the different elements of WAGS are illustrated with the help of practical examples, which are derived from the case studies presented in Chapters 2 and 7. Nevertheless, describing software in written form, as in this chapter, can hardly replace practical experience with the respective system. Therefore, the author would like to invite the reader to try out WAGS in practical applications (for download see: http://gcc.uni-paderborn.de/wags or http://www.springer.co.uk/comp/support/index.html). The research and development team which implemented WAGS would be glad to receive feedback from explorative studies on the prototypic system and the underlying WAWM concepts.

6.1 Architecture

In this section, the architectural model underlying the Wide Area GroupFlow System is introduced. Subsequently, the technological basis on which WAGS was built will be described. Finally, important terms, which will be useful in understanding the tools presented in the following sections, are explained.

6.1.1 Design approach

The research project on Wide Area Workflow Management was implemented in 1995 at the Groupware Competence Center of the University of Paderborn, Germany (http://fb5www.uni-paderborn.de/winfo2). It is a follow-up project to an earlier task force, which had developed the *Workflow Continuum* and *GroupFlow* (see Section 4.2.3.1, p. 85). Therefore, the fundamental architecture of the Wide Area GroupFlow System is derived from *GroupFlow* in respect to techniques for internal workflow management such as the meta-model for the design of workflow models (see Figure 21, p. 117), routing of documents, flexible elements (e.g. *open team tasks*, see Figure 15, p. 85) or exception handling.

From a technical point of view, WAGS has been completely re-implemented on newer, more flexible development platforms to overcome several of the limitations inherent to *GroupFlow*. However, the layered architecture of WAGS, shown in Figure 39, is similar to the one devised for *GroupFlow*.

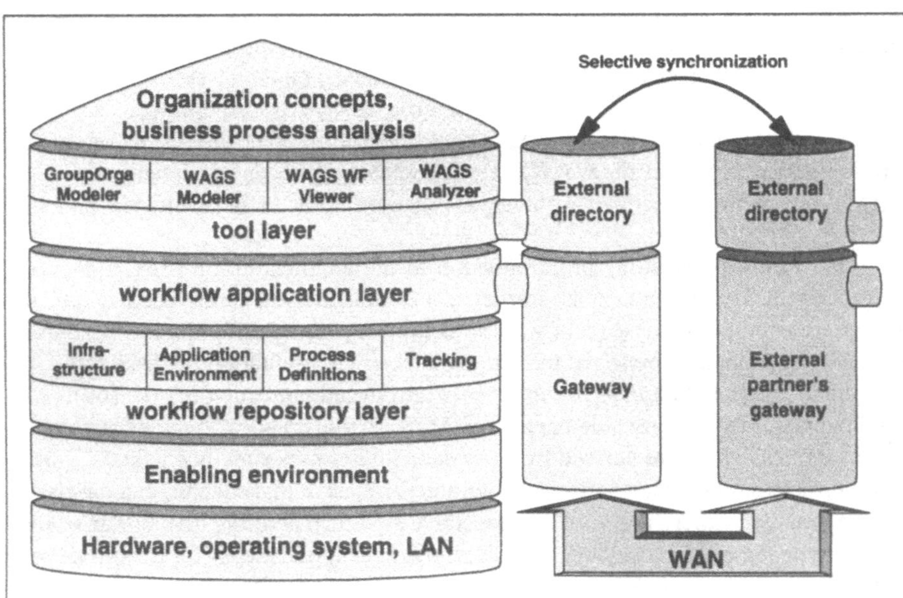

Figure 39: Architecture of the Wide Area GroupFlow System (WAGS)

WAGS has been built on a so-called *enabling environment*, which allows it to be independent of the specifics of hardware, operating systems as well as LAN/WAN standards (see lower left part of Figure 39). As with *GroupFlow*, the groupware platform Lotus Notes was chosen as this *enabling environment*, since it is available for all major operating system environments and provides a true cross-platform development basis. Further aspects of this decision will be discussed in Section 6.1.2 (p. 183).

The *workflow repository layer* of WAGS is implemented in the *enabling environment* in the form of four Lotus Notes applications, which are called *databases* in Lotus Notes terminology. The *WAGS Infrastructure* database describes the network of *persons*, *groups*, *departments* and *units* within the organization making use of WAGS. In the *WAGS Application Environment* database, the electronic forms presented to users during workflow execution are designed and the document folders routed in actual workflow instances are stored. Process definitions, which have been derived from workflow models, are stored in the *WAGS Process definitions* database. The *WAGS Tracking* database collects tracking protocols for monitoring and analysis of current and completed workflow instances.

The users interact with the workflow enactment service of WAGS – called *WAGS Engine* – in the *workflow application layer*, where they can for instance start and route workflow instances, handle exceptions or perform WAWM-related tasks, such as sending and receiving *message objects*. The functionality of WAGS is available to users with the help of a Lotus Notes-based client application as well as via a WWW-based front-end.

Several tools with a graphically oriented user interface have been added to WAGS in the *tool layer* to make the handling of the workflow system as simple and intuitive as possible. The *WAGS Modeler* is a process modeling tool that allows for the planning of local as well as *wide area workflows*, based on the *coordination mechanisms* introduced in Section 5.4 (p. 125). The *WAGS Modeler* stores workflow models in the *WAGS Process Definitions* database, where they are laid down in a structure that can be directly used by the *WAGS Engine* for the execution of workflow instances (see Figure 40, p. 182).

With the help of the *WAGS Workflow Viewer*, users can locate their current task graphically in the network of proceeding and succeeding workflow steps.

The analysis of workflow instances performed in local environments and between widely distributed WFMSs is supported by the *WAGS Analyzer*. The information on actual process structures evaluated by the *WAGS Analyzer* is collected in the *WAGS Tracking* database, where incoming tracking messages are aggregated in tracking protocols. This allows the evaluation of currently processed as well as completed workflow instances. The *WAGS Analyzer* can also read tracking protocols collected in the *WAGS Application Environment*, if no tracking messages are sent to the *WAGS Tracking* database for security reasons, for example.

In a further project at the Groupware Competence Center of the University of Paderborn, a graphical tool for the definition and maintenance of workflow-oriented organization structures has been implemented. This tool is called *GroupOrga Modeler* [Ott/Nastansky 1998] and can be used to manage the contents of the *WAGS Infrastructure* database, where the *WAGS Engine* retrieves information such as rights and roles of users in workflows.

On the right side of Figure 39 (p. 180), the elements specially developed to support WAWM features are shown. Interacting with the *WAGS Engine* in the *application layer*, the *WAGS Gateway* is responsible for the routing of *message objects*, which are used to connect different WFMSs. The *WAGS Gateway* sends for instance outgoing *message objects* to the *gateways* of other workflow systems with the help of wide area networks (WANs). The possible functionalities of *gateways* in WAWM environments have been described in more detail in Section 5.6.4 (p. 166).

The information needed to route the *message objects* between WFMSs is stored, together with other information needed to coordinate WAWM, in the *WAGS External Directory*. This is an implementation of a *coordination directory* in the WAGS framework, providing the services described in Section 5.6.1 (p. 145). The *WAGS External Directory* is displayed on the level of the *tool layer* in Figure 39 (p. 180), since it is used within the *WAGS Modeler* to coordinate different workflow parts. It is synchronized in whole or part with the corresponding *directory services* of other WFMSs.

Usually only one *WAGS Gateway* and *WAGS External Directory* exists in each organization because of the advantage of having a single interface with the WFMSs of other organizations in a WAWM scenario. These two elements of the WAGS framework can be connected to several internal workflow systems, comprised of the elements depicted on the left side of Figure 39 (p. 180).

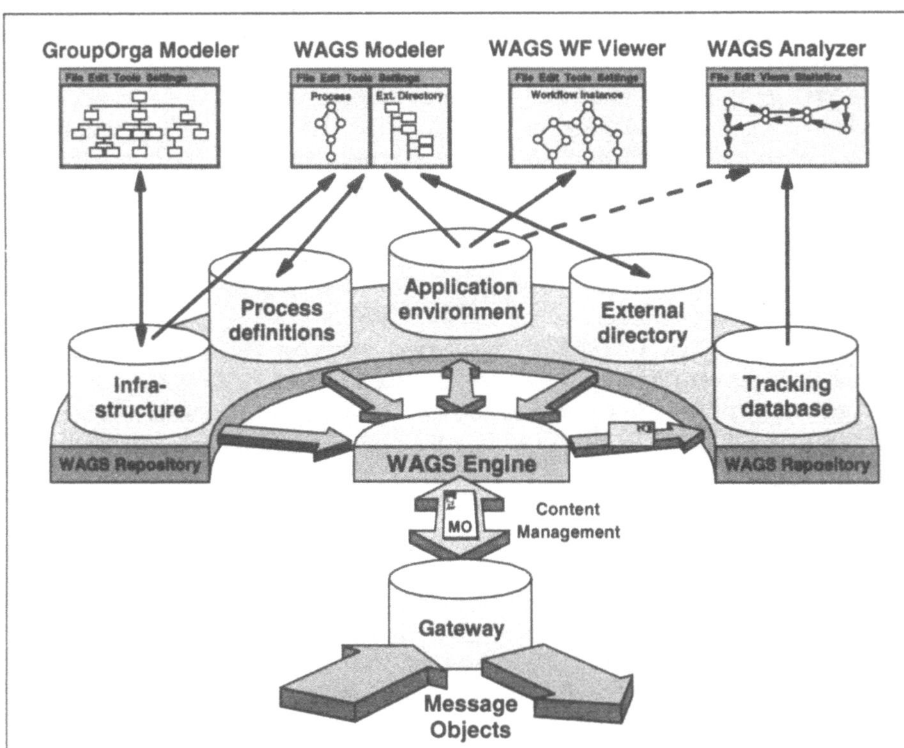

Figure 40: Tools, repository, engine and gateway of the WAGS prototype

Figure 40 shows the relations and interfaces between the different components of WAGS. The *WAGS Engine* reads and writes in the different databases of the *WAGS Repository*, sends *message objects* back and forth with the *WAGS Gateway* and delivers *tracking messages* to the *WAGS Tracking* database. The graphical tools of the *tool layer* perform *read* and *write operations* within the different elements of the *WAGS Repository*, as indicated by the arrows.

For the support of highly flexible as well as structured workflow management, the WAGS environment allows for the handling of workflow instances according to the different options of the *Workflow Continuum*, as shown in Figure 15 (p. 85). Workflows can be completely planned beforehand in the *WAGS Modeler*, as depicted in the right part of the *Workflow Continuum*, with allowance for the application of *exceptions* during the run-time phase in unforeseen situations, as described in Section 5.5.2 (p. 141). On the other hand, WAGS can be used to plan workflow models rather coarsely, only defining *milestones* with help of *open team tasks*. The patterns of workflow management in between *open team tasks* and *structured workflow*, as described in the *Workflow Continuum*, are also fully supported by WAGS. Additionally, the underlying groupware platform Lotus Notes allows for the handling of e-mail-based and shared database-oriented *ad-hoc workflow* in situations where no planning was possible beforehand.

Looking at WAWM features, WAGS was developed to allow for various ways of coordinating different workflow parts in *wide area workflows*, following the *continuum of coordination mechanisms for WAWM* shown in Figure 29 (p. 137). Different options of the *coordination mechanism* of *hierarchy* as well as the *market-oriented coordination* paradigm have been implemented in all elements of WAGS. An exception was the *coordination mechanism* labeled *equal partnership*, represented by the design technique of *joint modeling*, which could not be implemented within the first 3 years of the project. The implementation of the other mechanisms, which were given higher priority based on the experiences in the case studies, required extensive work on the part of the developers, making it necessary to postpone the realization of features for *joint modeling* to the second phase of the project.

Within the development of WAGS, both paradigms of *automation & structure* as well as *user support & flexibility* (see Section 5.1, p. 104) were equally considered and put into practice. WAGS therefore allows for the support of highly automated as well as individually controlled interaction within and between WFMSs. The respective features will be given special emphasis during the presentation of the different components of WAGS in Section 6.2 (p. 187).

6.1.2 Technological basis of WAGS

The *workflow repository*, the *application layer* as well as the *external directory* and the *gateway* of the Wide Area GroupFlow System were implemented on top of the groupware platform Lotus Notes (see also Section 3.4.4.2, p. 68). The WWW front-end – called *WAGS WebConnect* – was also implemented with the help of the Lotus Domino server and Lotus Notes databases for the generation of Web pages.

The decision to build WAGS on top of Lotus Notes was based on the following arguments:

- Lotus Notes is a true cross-platform development environment, available for all major operating systems and supporting all relevant network protocols for LANs as well as WANs.
- It is well integrated with the Internet and WWW, making applications available to users via the Notes client software as well as Web browsers. The Lotus Domino server used for Lotus Notes environments is also a fully featured Internet e-mail and Web server, supporting mostly all of the relevant standards such as HTML, POP 3, IMAP 4, LDAP, SMTP etc.
- The unique integration of the *messaging architecture* (Send Model) with the *replication technology* (Share Model) within Lotus Notes provides all necessary features for a flexible realization of different WAWM techniques as discussed in conjunction with the *continuum of coordination mechanisms for WAWM* (see Figure 29, p. 137).
- The Lotus Notes development environment allows for professional rapid prototyping and application development, providing all necessary elements to build flexible back-end and front-end components for workflow management systems. Examples of features of Lotus Notes, which can be directly used in systems supporting *local* and *wide area workflows*, are:
  - handling of *compound documents*, which are very well suited to represent "rich" information to be stored in workflow folders as well as to be transferred in *message objects*;
  - development of electronic forms with a comfortable GUI-based form builder;
  - a system-wide user authentication, on which security mechanisms, such as fine graduation of access rights to databases, folders and documents as well as reliable public key encryption and digital signatures, are based;
  - generation of worklists with *views*;
  - integration of documents from office applications with the help of object embedding technology;
  - integration of data from legacy systems with different possible interface software.
- Finally, the management of development projects is well supported within Lotus Notes by comfortable features for the implementation of complex applications in distributed teams, such as object-oriented program libraries, signing of code elements, sharing of code with replication technology etc.

For the building of a prototypic software framework designed to demonstrate WAWM technology, it is not a major limitation that the underlying Lotus Notes platform is a proprietary software system. Restrictions that come with the use of this platform are by far outweighed by the speed with which professional software applications can be built on top of Lotus Notes. Implementing a cross-platform workflow management system with WAWM features, which is fully integrated with the Internet and WWW, would require much more effort when making use of development techniques like native C++, CGI-script and HTML. In the estimation of the author, it would have taken more working hours using these techniques to implement the necessary messaging and replication architecture for WAWM alone, than it was to set up the entire WAGS environment on the basis of Lotus Notes.

The intention in developing WAGS was to illustrate the flexible use of WAWM technology. Therefore, it was reasonable to choose a platform which provides as much of the necessary technological foundations as possible rather having to re-implement technologies, which had earlier been realized by professional developers at high quality standards.

One limitation of the current version 4.6 of Lotus Notes is the absence of technical support for safe database transactions. Therefore, error recovery in case of system failures is limited to re-executing the steps between the state of the last document saved and the system crash manually. For the upcoming Lotus Domino 5.0 server release, Lotus has announced an integration of *transaction logs* with *roll back* and *roll forward* options, which is based on IBM database technology [Weber 1998]. Thereby, Lotus Domino becomes a server platform also for large-scale *transactional* workflow applications.

Figure 41 shows the Wide Area GroupFlow System on the Lotus Notes desktop. The three databases shown on the left side in the upper row – called *WAGS Application Environment*, *Process Definitions* and *Infrastructure* – have been derived from the *GroupFlow* system (see Section 4.2.3.1, p. 85). Since the program code in *GroupFlow* had been implemented in the very limited *formula language* of Lotus Notes 3.x, the new *WAGS Engine*, which is mainly implemented in these three databases, was re-coded in the new object oriented programming language *Lotus Script*, which has been available since Lotus Notes 4.x was issued.

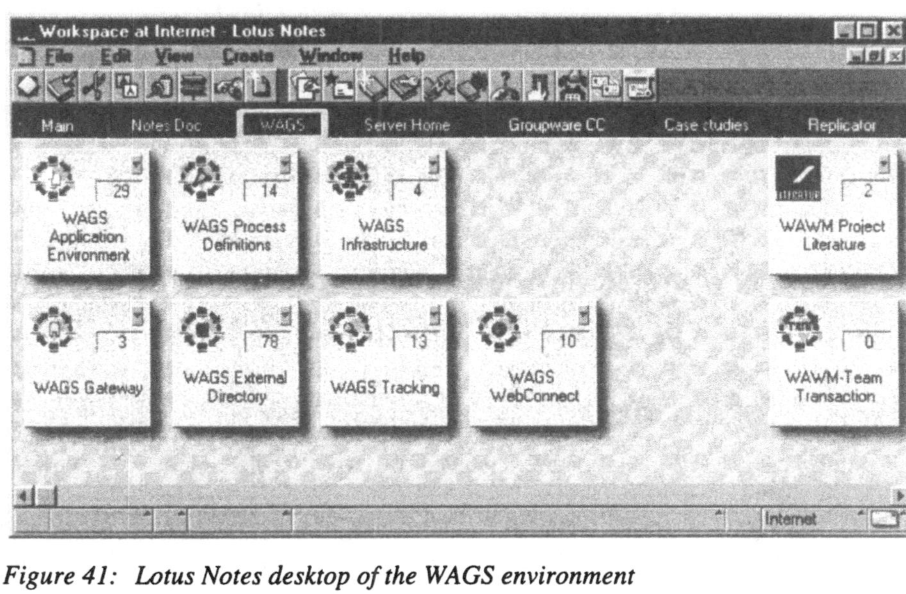

Figure 41: Lotus Notes desktop of the WAGS environment

On the left side of Figure 41 in the bottom corner, the new elements for Wide Area Workflow Management are shown, which have been already described above.

The developmental process of WAGS is itself an example of the successful application of flexible Wide Area Workflow Management: project members were working in widely distributed offices and did most of the communication, project management, exchange of program code, clarification of interfaces, preparation of practical demonstrations and much more with the help of the Lotus Notes database "WAWM-Team Transaction", shown on the right side of Figure 41. The literature found at the end of this book was collected, processed and routed with the help of the shared database "WAWM Project Literature", which is available to all project members with the help of replication technology [Sonnabend 1996], [Deleré 1998].

The programming environments of Microsoft Visual C++ 5.0, Microsoft Visual Basic 5.0 and Java 1.1 have been used for the object-oriented development of the graphical applications of the *tool layer* (see upper part of Figure 40, p. 182). The access to the workflow repository in Lotus Notes has been made possible with the help of Lotus Notes C++ API and the Lotus Notes C API. The latter was encapsulated in a dynamic linking library (called "Macroware-DLL"), which has also been developed at the Groupware Competence Center of the University of Paderborn, to allow Visual Basic programs to read and write in Lotus Notes databases.

The Java-based *WAGS Workflow Viewer* makes use of the RMI-technology ("remote method invocation") of Lotus Domino to access values in Notes databases.

6.1.3 Terms

In this section, fundamental terms will be explained briefly which will then be used to introduce the different components of WAGS in the following Section 6.2.

Definitions of ***workflow***, ***workflow management*** and ***workflow management system (WFMS)*** have already been introduced in Section 3.3.3 (p. 45)

Local workflow management describes the computer-based support of business processes within a single organization at one location. According to the definition of ***WAWM*** presented on p. 58, ***wide area workflows*** are executed across several distinct WFMSs, which interact in an intra- or interorganizational scenario.

A ***meta-model*** for *Wide Area Workflow Management* describes the different elements available for the description of business processes with a tool such as the *WAGS Modeler*. The *meta-model* for *local workflow management* used in the following sections has already been introduced in Figure 21 (p. 117). It contains elements such as ***nodes*** for ***workflow steps*** and ***arrows*** describing ***transitions*** between these *steps*. If two or more *arrows* leave a *node*, a ***split*** operation is performed depending on the ***conditions*** assigned to these *arrows*. Several *arrows* pointing at one *node* describe a ***join*** operation.

Extensions to this meta-model, intended to describe elements of *wide area workflows*, were presented in Figure 29 (p. 137).

Workflow parts describe segments of an overall *wide area workflow*, which are performed by a single WFMS. When *workflow parts* are invoked according to the *coordination mechanism* of *hierarchy (method C)* with $\text{SUBWORKFLOW}_{\text{DEC,WAW}}$

elements, the author will also use the term ***subworkflows*** in the following text. In contrast to this, *workflow parts* contacted according to the *coordination mechanism* of *market* with $\text{WORKFLOW}_{\text{SUB,WAW}}$ elements will be labeled ***external subscribed workflows***.

With the help of the extended *meta-model* for *wide area workflows*, ***workflow designers*** can develop ***workflow models*** (also called ***workflow types***) describing the intended structure of a business process that should be performed with the help of a WFMS in a local or widely distributed environment. In order to make *workflow models* ready to be executed by a WFMS, they are encoded in the form of ***process definitions***. Like many workflow modeling tools, the *WAGS Modeler* automatically generates executable *process definitions* out of *workflow models*, which are then stored in the *WAGS Process Definitions* database.

Workflow engines are the software services responsible for the execution of *workflows* within WFMSs. When starting a *workflow* based on a *workflow model*, the *workflow engine* generates a ***workflow instance*** derived from this model for a specific purpose. For instance, if customer X applies for credit in a bank, then the bank employee tells the *workflow engine* of the bank's WFMS to initiate a *workflow instance* called "credit application of customer X", which is executed according to the structure of the *process definition* of the *workflow model* "credit application".

Workflows consist of several consecutive or parallel *workflow steps*, which are called ***tasks*** in WAGS. Users can be asked or obliged to perform several ***activities*** within a ***task*** in form of a to-do-list which should be checked off.

WAGS uses ***workflow documents*** to store and transport information in *workflows*. Several *workflow documents* belonging to one *workflow instance* are stored in a ***folder***. The transfer of *folders* from one *task* to the next is called ***routing***.

The transfer of information between different WFMSs, which interact in the sense of WAWM, is achieved with the help of ***message objects*** (see Section 5.6.2, p. 153). Outgoing and incoming *message objects* are also stored in the *folder* of the respective *workflow instance*, together with internal *workflow documents*.

Workflow supervisors, which are responsible for the proper execution of certain business processes, control *workflow instances* currently being executed in a procedure called ***monitoring***. The ex post control of completed *workflow instances* by *workflow supervisors* or *workflow designers* is labeled workflow ***analysis***.

Persons who are responsible for the proper function of the hard- and software needed to perform workflow management, are called ***workflow administrators***. The ***users*** in workflow management systems are also called ***performers*** in the *tasks* where they are responsible for fulfilling certain *activities*.

6.2 Components

In this section, important features characterizing the different components of WAGS will be introduced. The examples shown in the screenshots are mostly taken from the solutions developed for the *wide area workflow* problems found in the case studies, which are more fully discussed in the Chapters 2 and 7.

6.2.1 Description of organizational structures with WAGS Infrastructure

One of the first tasks when implementing a workflow management system is to describe the structure of the persons, groups, departments and units involved. The information on this structure is stored in the *WAGS Infrastructure* database within the WAGS environment. It is used to describe the personnel infrastructure of the organization that owns an installation of WAGS, and is intended for internal use only. Thus, it is not accessible to partner organizations in a WAWM scenario.

If an organization wants to make all or part of this information available to partner organizations, it can use the *WAGS External Directory* for this purpose (see Section 6.2.3, p. 199).

Based on the methodology of *GroupFlow*, WAGS offers the following elements to describe the infrastructure of organizations:

- *Persons* are stored according to their hierarchical names used in the underlying groupware platform Lotus Notes. The hierarchical naming convention is based on the X.500 standard, for instance "Paula Andersen/Mobile/Sales/IB/DE" for a sales representative of IB.
- *Roles* can be used to describe positions, competencies, skills and rights of users in workflow management systems. For example, the *role* "SR" is owned by all sales representatives of IB, who have the right to start an auxiliary material requisition workflow. *Roles* are used to achieve more stability in the design of workflow models, since if there are changes in the staff structure, workflow models can be left untouched while role players change. In addition, roles can be used to assign several persons with similar skills and competencies to one task in a workflow, thereby providing flexibility about who takes over the job in an actual workflow instance.
- *Conditional roles* describe a feature of WAGS where the actual value of a role is the result of the evaluation of a function. A *conditional role* which is often used is "Manager (Initiator)". It can be applied for example by *workflow designers* to model a single travel application workflow for all the employees of an organization. After a workflow instance derived from this workflow model has been started, the name of the initiating employee is assigned to the variable "Initiator". Consequently, the workflow system can find the manager responsible for the approval of this travel application in the *WAGS Infrastructure* database.
- *Units* describe hierarchical elements in organizational structures such as groups and departments. A person usually belongs only to one *unit* (e.g. mobile sales force) in an organization, including all superior *units* (e.g. sales department) which contain the first one. The root element of the hierarchical tree of *units* is usually the organization itself. The *units* a person belongs to are expressed in its hierarchical name.
- *Workgroups* can be implemented to describe non-hierarchical groupings of persons, such as project teams and task forces. Users can belong to multiple *workgroups*, independently of the *unit* they belong to.

- *Resources* are used to handle equipment used in workflows such as printers, flip charts and also meeting rooms. By assigning *resources* to tasks in workflows, *workflow supervisors* can calculate for example the use of the respective equipment with the help of simulation technology.

Figure 42 shows the organizational structure of IB, as developed for the prototypic solution for WAWM at IB (see Section 7.1, p. 234).

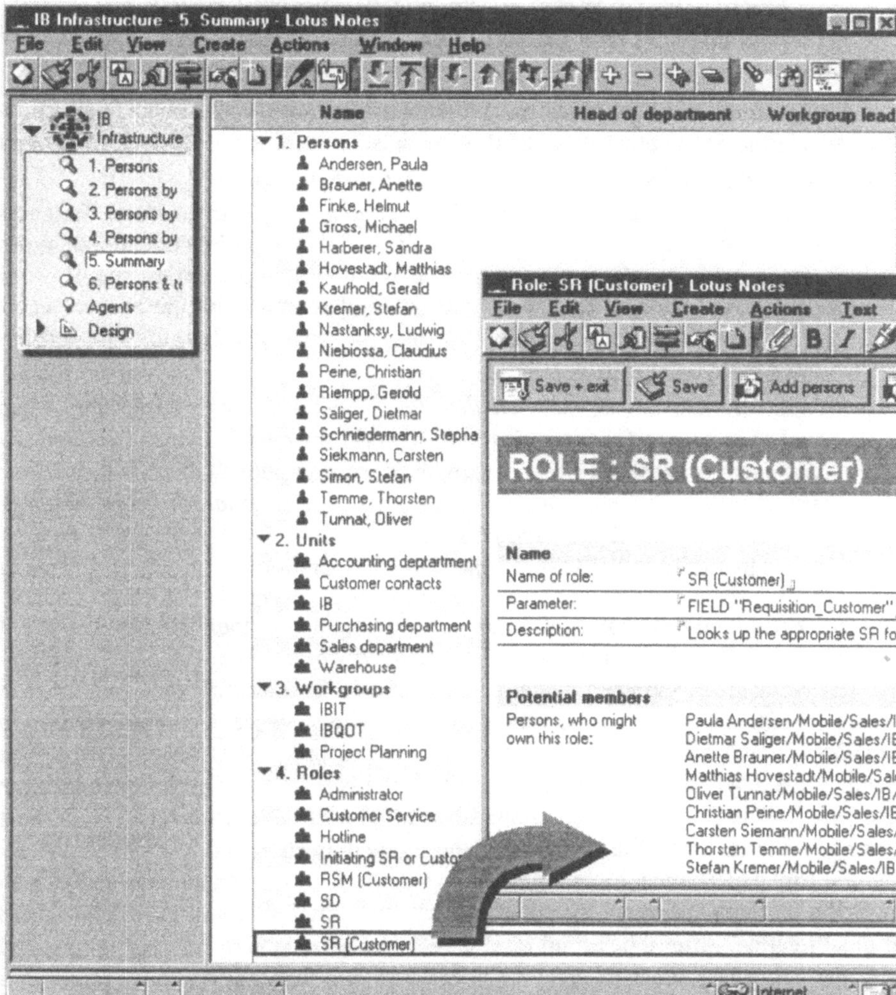

Figure 42: Example of a WAGS Infrastructure database for the IB case study

The definition and maintenance of the information stored in the *WAGS Infrastructure* database can also be handled with a graphical tool developed at the Groupware Competence Center of the University of Paderborn. It is called *GroupOrga Modeler* and allows *workflow designers* to visually assign persons to units or workgroups using simple drag-and-drop operations. Further on, a management tool for hierarchical trees helps planners to build and shift groups and departments when (re-)defining an organization's structure [Ott/Nastansky 1998].

The practical application of the *units*, *workgroups* and *roles* implemented for the IB case study (Figure 42) is illustrated in the workflow model for the auxiliary material support requisition procedure shown in Figure 66 (p. 237).

6.2.2 Planning of Wide Area Workflow Management with the WAGS Modeler

The *WAGS Modeler* is a graphical workflow planning tool, which supports workflow designers in the development of workflow models for *local* and *wide area workflows* [Touchard 1996], [Hovestadt/ Peine 1998]. It consists of two parts:

- The *process manager* provides a drawing area, on which workflow designers can develop graphical workflow models with the help of different node types and arrows for the connection of these nodes, representing the flow of workflow document folders. Workflow models built with the *process manager* are performed within the WFMS(s) the workflow designers are responsible for.
- With the help of the *external directory manager*, workflow designers can make use of *interface specifications* of workflow models owned by workflow designers of other WFMSs. In turn, they can also publish their own *interface specifications* for other workflow designers. The *external directory manager* thus supports the connection of several workflow parts, which will be executed by different WFMSs during run-time operation.

The *process manager* is comparable to workflow modeling tools already known. It can be used to describe workflow models for *local workflows* as a basic functionality. The elements of the meta-model needed for this have already been presented in Figure 21 (p. 117). The following Figure 43 shows these elements used in a workflow model for a simplified travel application procedure. An employee who wants to make a trip can initiate the workflow and is thereby identified with the role "Initiator". This first *task* is represented by an *internal node*, connected to the next *internal node* in which the manager of the initiator is supposed to approve the requested trip. The connection between the two nodes is illustrated by an *arrow*, which owns the property "*always*", meaning that the workflow folder will always be routed in this direction. After the second *task*, a *split* operation is performed. It is modeled with the help of "exclusive" arrows (XOR), meaning that the workflow folder will only be routed in the direction of one of the arrows. In the example, the further routing path depends on the decision of the manager to *approve* or *reject* the request, expressed by so-called *conditions* assigned to the *arrows*. *Arrows* of different types, such as "always", "multiple", "exclusive" and "conditional" can be mixed in one split operation in the *WAGS Modeler*, which is to an advantage compared to the specific AND-, OR- and XOR-nodes known from other workflow meta-models. So-called "mixed splits", which may consist of an exclusive choice between three arrows, two conditional arrows and two arrows which are always used, can be handled with only one split node in the *WAGS Modeler*, thereby preserving the clear structure of the workflow model.

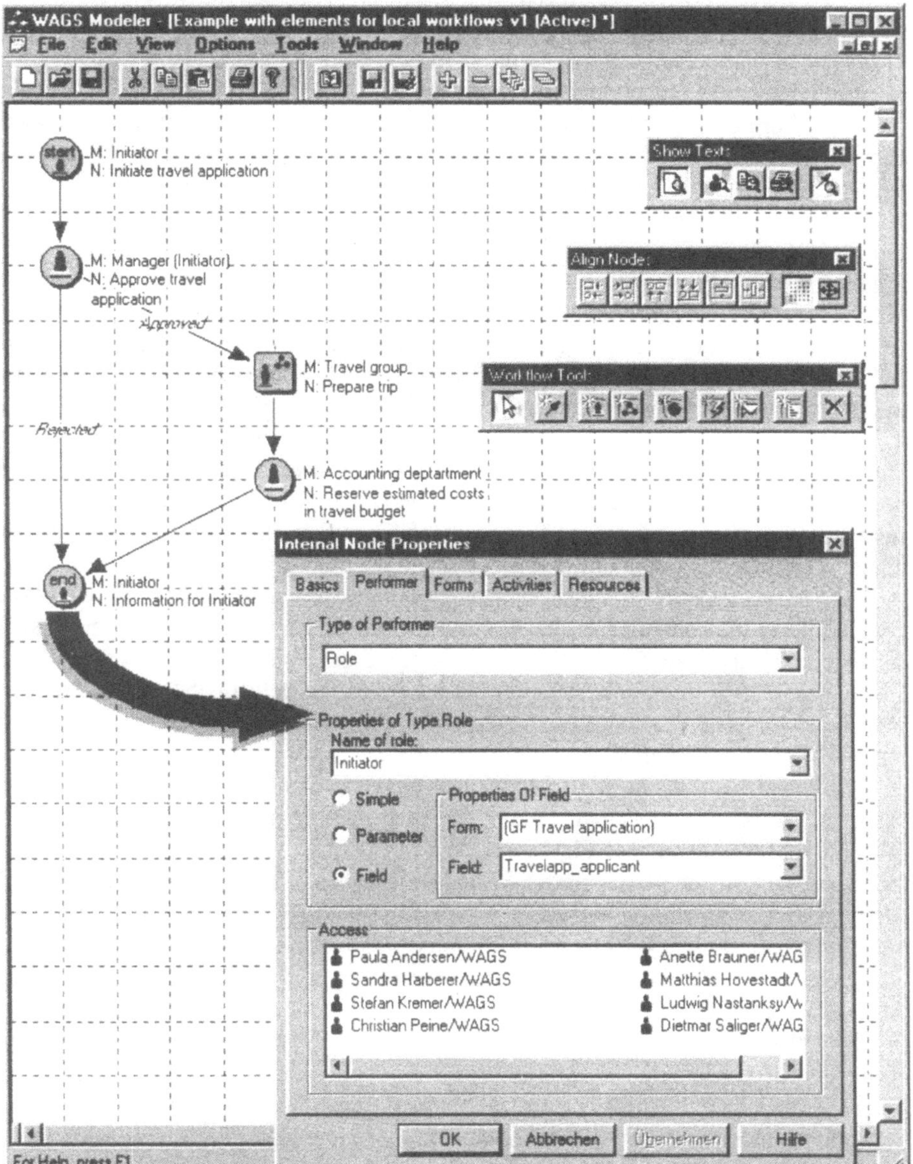

Figure 43: Example of a simplified travel application procedure, showing elements of the design of local workflows in the process manager of the WAGS Modeler

If the manager approves the travel application (Figure 43), the workflow folder is forwarded to the travel group, which performs several *tasks* to prepare the trip.

These tasks are aggregated in an *internal cluster*, represented by a rectangular icon (as distinct from circular icons of *internal nodes*). *Internal clusters* are only meant to make large workflow models easier to understand by hiding the details of certain workflow segments. By double-clicking *internal clusters*, the nodes within them are displayed in a separate window. *Internal clusters* do not influence the routing of workflow folders in actual workflow instances.

Apart from predefined tasks, *internal nodes* can also represent *open team tasks* and *controlled team tasks*, according to the *Workflow Continuum* (see Figure 15, p.85). This is achieved by choosing the respective settings for the *internal node*.

Each of the elements described up to this point can be placed in the drawing area by selecting the respective tool icon in the "*Workflow Tools*" palette of the *WAGS Modeler*. From left to right, the first four icons of this palette represent the *selection tool*, *arrows*, *internal nodes* and *internal clusters*. Once nodes, arrows and clusters have been placed on the drawing area, their individual *properties* can be displayed in a dialog box (see the lower right part of Figure 43). This dialog box is available with the help of a context menu, which can be accessed via the right mouse button.

The *properties'* window in the workflow example of Figure 43 shows that the value of the field "Travelapp_applicant", found in the electronic form "GF Travel application", determines the person in the role of the "Initiator" in a certain workflow instance. In the example, "Travelapp_applicant" is automatically set with the name of the user logged-in during the invocation of a workflow instance.

Further tool palettes facilitate the design of workflow models. The "Show Text" palette allows the name of the task or cluster ("N:" for *name*), the performers ("M:" for *members*), the main form ("O:" for *object*) and the resources ("R:" for *resource*) to be displayed or hidden besides the nodes. With the help of the "Align Nodes" palette, several selected nodes can be aligned in different to make the arrangement of the workflow model more clear.

What distinguishes the *WAGS Modeler* from other workflow modeling tools, are the meta-model elements, which can be used for the planning of Wide Area Workflow Management (see Figure 44).

These meta-model elements for WAWM have been implemented in the *WAGS Modeler* according to the *continuum of coordination mechanisms for WAWM*, which was introduced in Figure 29 (p. 137). On the left side of Figure 44, elements used for *hierarchical coordination* of workflow parts in different WFMSs are shown (see also Section 5.4.1, p. 126).

With the help of $\text{CLUSTER}_{\text{CEN,WAW}}$ elements (*hierarchy, method A*), workflow designers can prepare the execution of several workflow *tasks* in another location. In the WAGS architecture, this is achieved by distributing and synchronizing the *WAGS repository* databases between the relevant sites with the help of the replication technology of the underlying Lotus Notes platform. This way, *process definitions* as well as actual *workflow folders* are exchanged between the interacting WFMSs.

The use of $\text{CLUSTER}_{\text{PAR,WAW}}$ elements allows *master designers* of the main workflow to make use of the expertise of *part designers* (*hierarchy, method B*). The latter are responsible for the development of workflow models of those workflow parts, which are executed in their respective WFMS(s). *Master designers* place empty $\text{CLUSTER}_{\text{PAR,WAW}}$ elements in their workflow models. Subsequently, they transfer the specification of these elements (for further details, see Table 6, p. 147) to the *part designers* by selectively replicating the *WAGS Repository* with the workflow servers of the respective sites. There, *part designers* fill the empty clusters with workflow models according to the terms and goals specified by the *master designers.* Afterwards, these workflow models within the clusters are transferred to master designers by replicating the *WAGS Repository* again, which is (partially) shared by *master* and *part designers.* In the final phase, *master designers* have a complete workflow model, including filled-out *clusters.* The workflow models can now be saved in the *WAGS Process Definitions* database for execution by the *WAGS Engine.* During the run-time operation of workflow instances derived from these models, workflow folders are again transferred between the sites by replicating the *WAGS repository* – especially the *WAGS Application Environment* database.

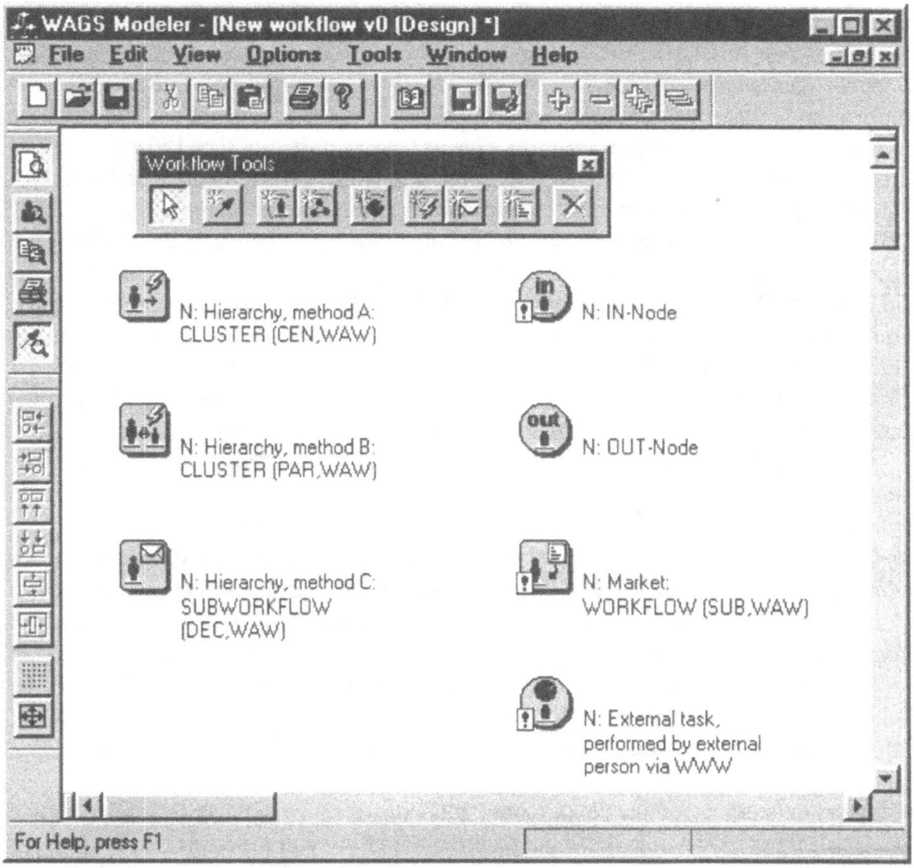

Figure 44: Elements of the meta-model for WAWM, shown in the WAGS Modeler

To make use of the *coordination mechanism* of *hierarchy, method C, master designers* can include $\mathrm{SUBWORKFLOW}_{\mathrm{DEC,WAW}}$ elements into their workflow models. They describe, amongst other things, the goal to be achieved by the *subworkflow*, specify *input* and *output* field sets and indicate the *format* in which information will be transferred, according to the *interface specifications* listed in Table 6 (p. 147).

These *interface specifications* are transferred to the WFMSs involved with the help of the *WAGS External Directory*, where entries for *subworkflows* with the initial status "specified" have been placed by *master designers.*

After the *external directories* of the participating WFMSs have been synchronized, the designers of the *subworkflows* have knowledge of the *interface specifications.* They start to design workflow models with the interfaces indicated by the *master designers.* After they have completed their task, they inform the *master designers* that *subworkflows* can be invoked by assigning the value "operational" to the status field of the respective entries in their *external directories.* After *external directories* have been synchronized again, the *master designers* can then release the workflow models of the *main workflows* for execution by their *WAGS Engine(s).*

Since *master designers* initiate the modeling of the subordinate workflow parts, these elements are also labeled *ordered subworkflows* in WAGS terminology.

In contrast to $\text{CLUSTER}_{\text{CEN,WAW}}$ and $\text{CLUSTER}_{\text{PAR,WAW}}$ elements, the information between *main workflows* and *ordered subworkflows* is not transferred using replication technology. To allow for more flexibility and independence, information is exchanged with the help of *message objects* (see Section 5.6.2, p. 153). Because of this, heterogeneous WFMSs can also cooperate using the method of *ordered subworkflows,* due to the fact that the workflow repositories remain separate during WAMW interaction. The *message objects* are transferred between the WFMSs involved with the help of messaging systems, such as the Lotus Domino server on the side of WAGS. With the inclusion of the *WAGS Gateway, message objects* can be converted into formats that can be understood by WFMSs involved. With regard to WFMSs other than WAGS, *gateways* with functionalities similar to the *WAGS Gateway* have to be implemented to allow for WAWM interaction according to the fundamental architectural concept introduced in Figure 30 (p. 144).

The workflow management systems executing the *ordered subworkflows* are waiting for *message objects* to come in from workflow instances of the *main workflows.* On arrival of the *message objects,* they invoke a workflow instance of the *ordered subworkflow* and send back a *message object* with an "answer" to the *main workflow* upon completion. This fact is illustrated by starting workflow models for *ordered subworkflows* with IN-nodes and terminating them with OUT-nodes (see upper right part of Figure 44, p. 193). These special node types are necessary to inform the *WAGS Engine* that *incoming* or *outgoing message objects* have to be handled, for example by performing a *content management* procedure to transfer information between *message objects* and *internal workflow folders* (see Section 5.6.3, p. 162).

Another element of the meta-model for *wide area workflows* is a node called "External Task", which is used to include workflow steps performed by persons outside of one's own organization (see lower right side of Figure 44, p. 193). Before *workflow designers* can make use of this feature, the respective external persons have to be registered in the *WAGS External Directory.* When a workflow instance reaches an "External Task" during run-time operation, the *WAGS Engine* automatically sends an e-mail to the external performer, informing him that a workflow task has been prepared for him. The e-mail contains a URL, leading the external performer to the respective Web page, where he can fulfill his task using the Web front-end of the *WAGS Engine.* Outside organizations can also register *roles, units* or *workgroups* apart from *persons* (see Section 6.2.1, p. 188) in the *WAGS External Directory*, thereby making them available to the respective organization. "External tasks" are a simple way of including external performers in workflows and can for example be used for teleworkers, freelancers, consultants and other persons, who normally do not maintain a WFMS of their own. From a technical point of view, "External Tasks" allow for the planning of a *remote access* to the *WAGS Engine* and are therefore not really WAWM elements, since they do not support the *interaction* of several autonomous WFMSs. Nevertheless, in discussions with workflow practitioners, "External Tasks" were considered to be highly practical.

To connect workflow parts in WAWM scenarios according to the *coordination mechanism* called *market*, *workflow designers* can make use of $\text{WORKFLOW}_{\text{SUB,WAW}}$ elements, which are also called *external subscribed workflows* in WAGS terminology (see lower right part of Figure 44, p. 193). After selecting the appropriate icon from the "Workflow Tools" palette and placing an *external subscribed workflow* element in the drawing area, workflow designers open the *external directory manager* of the *WAGS Modeler* and select an appropriate workflow service offered by a partner organization. The specifications necessary for *external subscribed workflows* were introduced in Table 8 (p. 149).

The assignment of a workflow service from the *external directory manager* to an *external subscribed workflow* element in the *process manager* is achieved with the help of a drag-and-drop operation (see middle part of Figure 45, p. 196).

Workflow designers can also publish *interface specifications* for workflow services that their own organization wants to offer. They design a workflow model, which starts with an IN-node preparing the initial receipt of a *message object* during run-time operation. Likewise, an OUT-node indicates that a resulting *message object* will be sent back at the end of the workflows. Publication is again achieved by a drag-and-drop operation, in which the *workflow designer* moves the IN-node (Ctrl-key pressed) from the *process manager* to the *external directory manager* (see upper part of Figure 45). The published *interface specification* first maintains the status "design", until it is fully specified with the help of its *properties'* window available in the context menu. After the settings for an *interface specification* have been completed, the value "operational" can be assigned to the status field. Thereby, the transfer of this *interface specification* to the partner organizations concerned is initiated and carried out by synchronizing the *external directories* involved.

The example in Figure 45 demonstrates a strongly simplified workflow model for handling auxiliary material support requisitions at IB (see case studies in Chapters 2 and 7). The workflow can be initiated from customers via the WWW, which is indicated by an initial IN-node in the workflow model. The *interface specifications* of this workflow service are made available to customers by publishing them via drag-and-drop in the public part of the *WAGS External directory* in the section called "Workflows published by Us".

After the regional sales manager responsible ("RSM (Customer)") has approved the requisition, dispensing equipment is ordered from an external supplier called "Dispensing Inc.". This company has offered a workflow service for ordering dispensing equipment, to which IB has subscribed via a drag-and-drop operation onto an *external subscribed workflow* element. After the order has been fulfilled and the equipment has been delivered to IB, the customer is informed by way of a *message object* in the final OUT-node of the workflow.

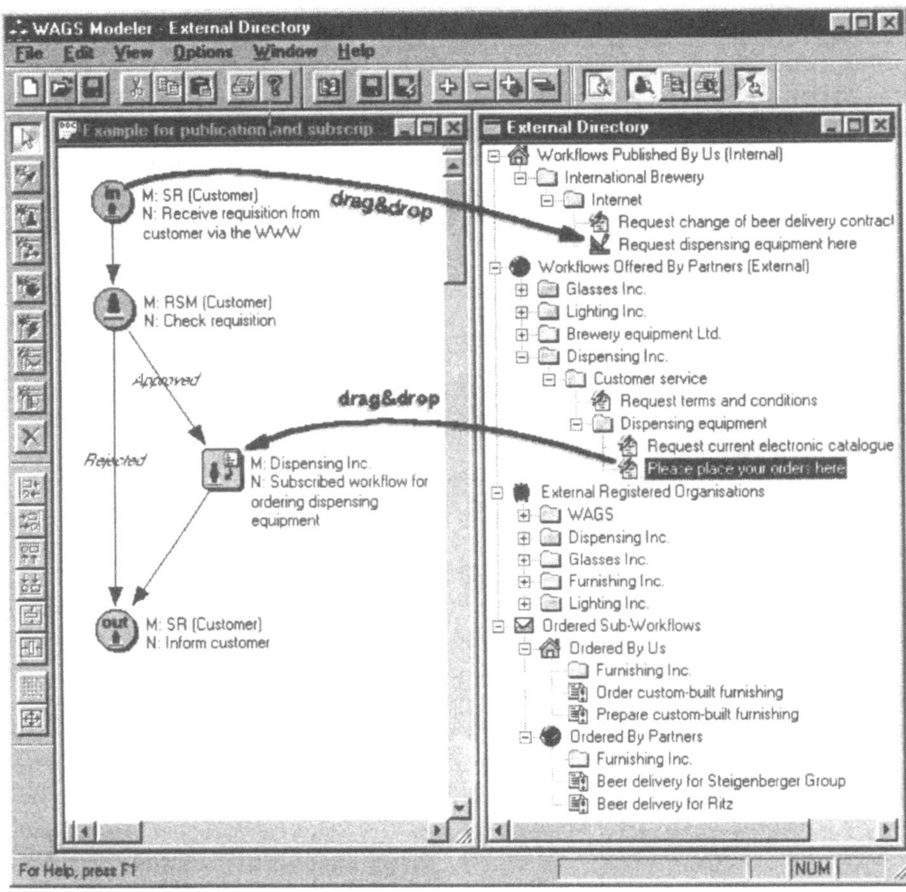

Figure 45: Publication and subscription of interface specifications for external subscribed workflows with the WAGS Modeler

A more detailed workflow model for the processing of auxiliary material support requisitions at IB is presented in Figure 66 (p. 237).

As long as IN-nodes have not been *published*, their icon displays an exclamation mark at the lower left edge. The same symbol is used to indicate that *external subscribed workflows* have not yet been connected with a workflow service (see the left part of Figure 46, p. 197). Icons of *interface specifications* in the *external directory manager* also have different symbols depending on their status, for instance "design" and "operational" for *interface specifications* of *external subscribed workflows* (see the upper right part of Figure 45). This feature makes it easier for workflow designers to keep control of the state of workflow models with WAWM elements included.

A further tool that supports workflow designers to build correct and consistent workflow models is the *Modeler Information Center*, which displays the results of a detailed *consistency check*. In the example of Figure 46, a consistency check has been performed on the workflow shown in Figure 45 before the IN-node has been published in the *external directory* and before a workflow service has been assigned to the *external subscribed workflow* element.

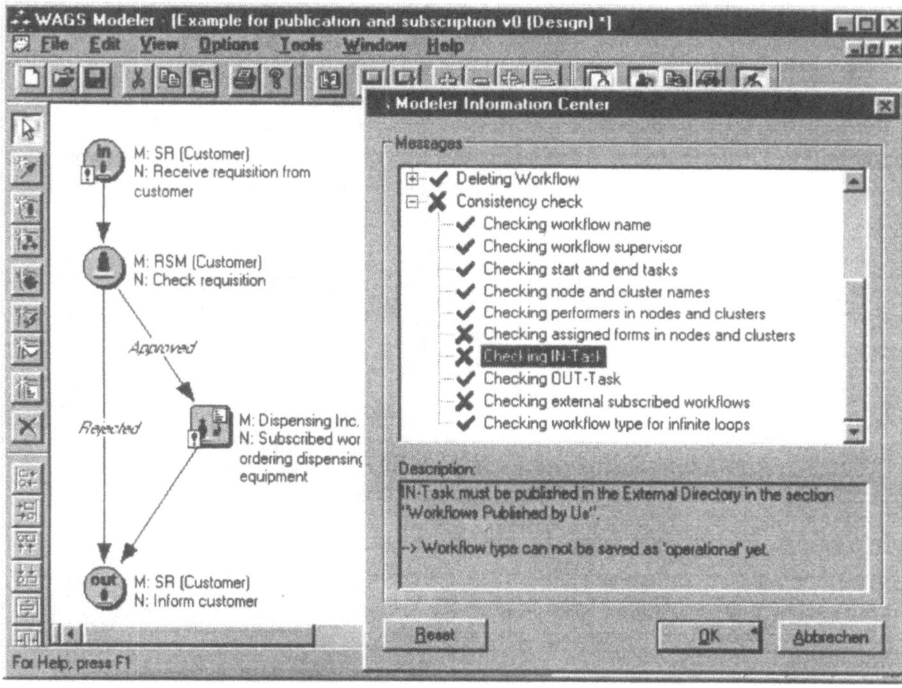

Figure 46: Modeler Information Center with results of a consistency check on the workflow in Figure 45 before publication and subscription operations

The *WAGS Modeler* has a versioning concept for workflow models, allowing different states of *process definitions* to be saved. As long as workflow models are in the process of development and have not successfully passed a *consistency check*, their status is "design". In this phase, no workflow instances can be derived from such workflow models and be started in the *WAGS Engine*.

After workflow designers have finished workflow models, they can save them in a preliminary version for testing purposes (see Figure 47, p. 198). *Process definitions* of workflow models with this status can be used by *workflow administrators* in order to initiate workflow instances, which are then processed by the *WAGS Engine* in a test mode. This feature can be used for a real-life trial of workflow models, including interaction with other WFMSs based on WAWM elements such as *ordered subworkflows* and *external subscribed workflows*.

Once workflow designers are sure that a workflow model will function properly, they can set it to the status "operational - active", allowing all entitled users to start workflow instances from *process definitions* of this workflow model. The first active workflow model that is saved has the version number "1" and all workflow instances derived also have this version number. After a period of use, workflow designers might want to update the workflow model. After changes have been made, the *WAGS Modeler* automatically increases the version number of the *process definition* to "2" during the save operation. At the same time, the status of the *process definition* with the former version number "1" is set to "freeze". Thereby, all workflow instances that are newly started are executed according to the new *process definition* (version "2"), while workflow instances already running are finished according to the version of the *process definition* with which they had been started (version "1"). With this feature, the *WAGS Modeler* prevents workflow designers from changes to *process definitions* of actively performed workflow instances, which might make the execution useless or destructive. After all workflow instances of an older version of a *process definition* have been completed, this *process definition* is set to the status "disabled", allowing it to be moved to an archive.

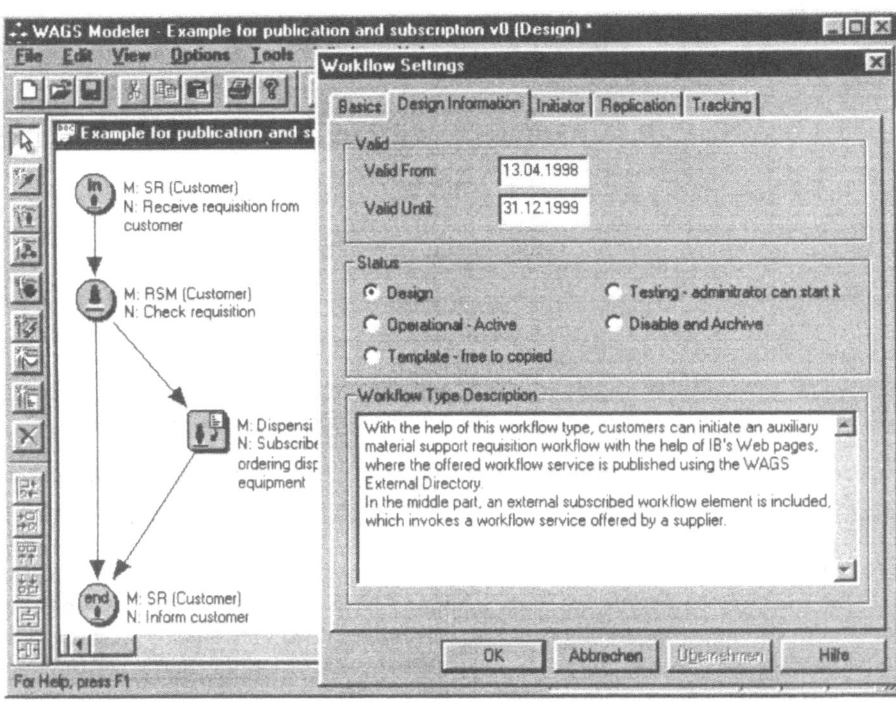

Figure 47: Versioning concept of the WAGS Modeler, shown in the dialog box for workflow settings

The *WAGS Modeler* has been implemented in a fully object-oriented manner, using the development framework of Microsoft Visual C++ 5.0. The read and write operations to the Lotus Notes databases of the *WAGS repository* are executed with the help of the Lotus Notes C++ API. The *WAGS Modeler* does not make use of the file system to store process definitions etc. All information about *workflow models* and *external directories* is stored in Lotus Notes databases, making them directly available to the *WAGS Engine*. For instance, *process definitions* of workflow models, saved with the status "operational – active", can be instantaneously used to start workflow instances, including the invocation of all WAWM-oriented connections to other WFMSs, which might be included. To ensure that workflow instances function properly, *process definitions* with this status can only be saved after a consistency check has been passed successfully.

As can be seen in the figures in this section, workflow designers do not see details of workflow parts other than their own when applying the WAWM elements of *ordered subworkflows* (*hierarchy, method C*) and *external subscribed workflows* (*market*). In these cases, they only see the *interface specifications* of the workflow parts they are connected to. Using these *coordination mechanisms*, the autonomy of the WFMSs involved can be preserved to a large part, while allowing for a flexible *planning* and *execution* of *wide area workflows* across several workflow systems.

If the organizations involved want to know more details of all the workflow parts, which are interacting in a *wide area workflow*, they can make use of the *coordination mechanisms* of *hierarchy*, *method A* and *B* ($CLUSTER_{CEN,WAW}$ and $CLUSTER_{PAR,WAW}$ elements). A further possibility would be to choose the *coordination mechanism* called *equal partnership*, which could make all workflow parts visible in the process of *joint modeling*. Due to limited time and resources, *joint modeling* was not implemented in the current version of the *WAGS Modeler*.

6.2.3 Exchange and use of workflow interface specifications with the WAGS External Directory

The *WAGS External Directory* is a practical implementation of a *coordination directory* (see Section 5.6.1, p. 145), which is primarily used within the WAGS architecture to exchange *interface specifications* between participants in a WAWM scenario [Kremer 1998]. These *interface specifications* have two main functions:

- They allow *workflow designers* to plan the interaction of workflow parts in the *WAGS Modeler* during the *build-time* of workflow models, as for example shown in Figure 45 (p. 196).
- During the *run-time* operation of workflow instances, *interface specifications* provide the information needed to define the properties of *message objects* and to route them between the WFMSs involved.

During the *build-time* of workflow models, the *WAGS External Directory* is accessible to workflow designers with the help of the *external directory manager* of the *WAGS Modeler* (see the right side of Figure 45, p. 196). Using the *external directory manager*, designers can include *interface specifications* of *external subscribed workflows* offered by other organizations or publish *interface specifications* of this type. Further on, *master designers* can exchange *interface specifications* for *ordered subworkflows* with *part designers* with the help of the *external directory manager*.

The fundamental approach to store processes in hierarchical trees was introduced in Section 5.6.1 (p. 145). Accordingly, the *interface specifications* of workflow services are displayed in a hierarchical manner in the *external directory manager* of the *WAGS Modeler* (see the left part of Figure 48, p. 200).

Figure 48 presents a prototypic *WAGS External Directory* for the case study of IB. As shown in the section "Workflows Published by US (Internal)", IB can make *interface specifications* of own workflow services available to partner organizations, such as customers and suppliers. Below, in the section "Workflows Offered by Partners (External)", the offers of the partner companies are listed. For example, the fictitious company "Dispensing Inc." offers a workflow service where dispensing equipment can be ordered.

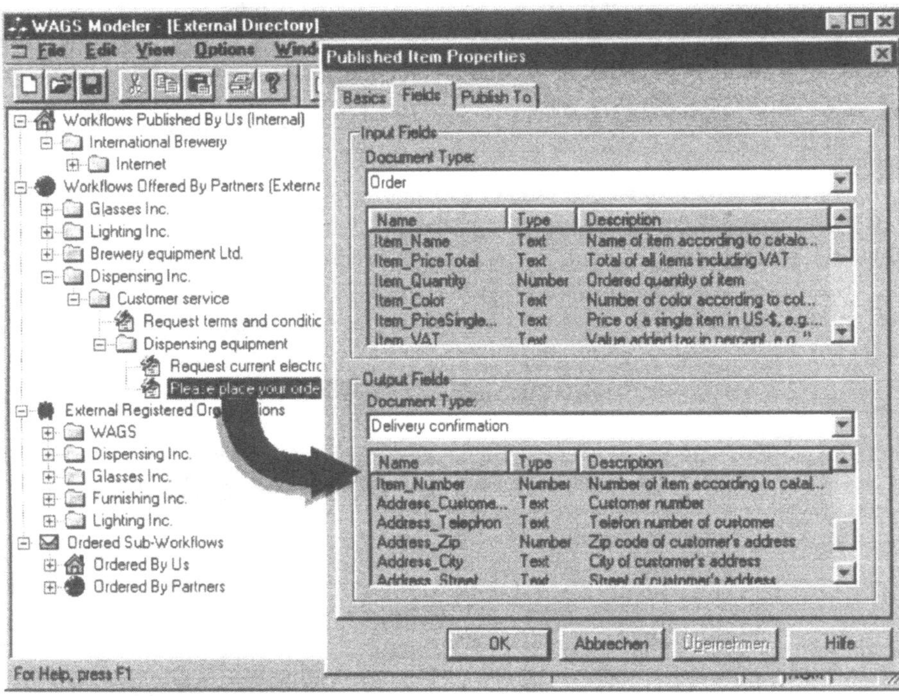

Figure 48: Properties' window of an interface specification of a workflow service offered according to the market-oriented coordination mechanism, shown in the external directory manager of the WAGS Modeler

Similar to the graphical elements of the *process manager*, such as *nodes* and *clusters*, the entries in the *external directory manager* also have *properties*, which can be displayed in a dialog box. The *properties'* window of the workflow service for ordering dispensing equipment is shown on the right side of Figure 48. It displays the required *input fields*, which have to be included in a *message object* that is supposed to invoke this workflow service (see also Table 8, p. 149). The *input fields* are derived from a *document type* called *order*, which is part of a *message object hierarchy*, as described in Section 5.6.2.1 on p. 155. In the example, a *message object hierarchy* including the document types "order" and "delivery confirmation" has been agreed upon between IB and its partner organizations, and is exchanged between them with the help of the *WAGS External Directory*.

After the company "Dispensing Inc." has processed the order, it will send a *message object* to IB confirming the delivery of the equipment. For this purpose, a *document type* called "Delivery confirmation" is applied, which contains a certain set of fields as shown in the lower right part of Figure 48.

By looking at the required *input* and *output fields* in the *interface specifications* of the workflow service of "Dispensing Inc.", IB's workflow designers establish which information they have to prepare in the internal workflow steps before this external workflow service can be invoked. Once they have prepared this information by placing certain *internal fields* in the appropriate electronic forms used in the preceding workflow steps, they can connect these *internal fields* with the required *input fields* of the *interface specification* in a procedure called *outgoing content management* (see also Figure 35, p. 163). Similarly, they have to include the information provided in the returning *message object* (described by the *output fields*) in the internal workflow folder by performing *incoming content management* (see also Figure 36, p. 165). In the *WAGS Modeler*, settings for *outgoing* and *incoming content management* can be made with the help of the *properties'* window of the *external subscribed workflow* symbol (Figure 49).

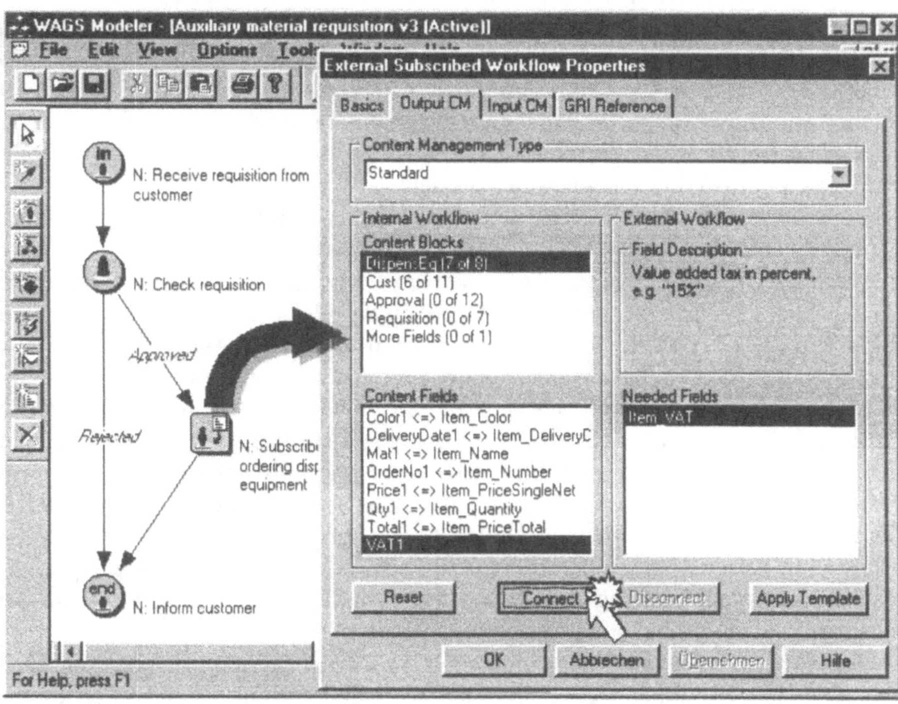

Figure 49: Settings for outgoing content management in the properties' window of an external subscribed workflow element in the WAGS Modeler

On the left side of the *properties'* window in Figure 49, the fields contained in the internal workflow documents are displayed. They are aggregated into *content blocks* for the purpose of showing fields that belong together and in order to make long lists easier to handle (see also Figure 33, p. 155). In Figure 49, fields of the *content block* "DispensEq" (for dispensing equipment) are mapped with fields required by the external workflow, which are listed on the right side of the *properties'* window. The mapping is achieved by selecting an *internal field* in the lower left list together with a field from the *interface specification* in the right list, and then clicking on the "Connect" button. As a result, the mapping is indicated by a notation such as "Price1 <=> Item_PriceSingleNet" to show that the content of the *internal field* "DispensEq_Price1" will transferred into the field "Item_PriceSingleNet" in the *message object*, which will be sent to invoke the workflow service for ordering dispensing equipment from "Dispensing Inc.". Often used field mappings for *content management* can be stored in so-called *CM templates*, which can be applied in order to speed up standard procedures, such as the mapping of fields between *content blocks* for addresses or orders and the related *document types*.

After all fields required by the *external subscribed workflow* have been mapped with *internal fields* in this procedure called *predefined* or *standard content management*, the workflow model can be set to the status "operational" and is thus ready for execution by the *WAGS Engine*. Another possibility would be *predefined content management with run-time control*, which would allow performers to control and change the field mappings during workflow processing. Finally, workflow designers can leave field mappings open for *ad-hoc content management* during workflow run-time (see Section 5.6.3, p. 162). This would be necessary for instance if contents in internal workflows cannot be exactly predicted during *build-time*, which can be the case when workflow designers make extensive use of *milestone modeling*, thereby only planning workflow models rather coarsely.

Another feature of the *WAGS External Directory* is the registration of external partner organizations. If workflow designers make use of "External Task" elements, they can assign *persons*, *roles*, *units* or *workgroups* of *external registered organizations*, which have previously been registered in the *WAGS External Directory*. The registration can be done by the *workflow administrator* of a WAGS-based WFMS at the request of the external organization. Alternatively, members of the external organization can register themselves with the help of the Web front-end of the *WAGS External Directory*. After this preliminary registration has been approved by the *workflow administrator* responsible, these persons are also available to workflow designers via the *external directory manager*. The assignment of external organizational elements, such as persons, roles or workgroups, to "External Tasks" is achieved by selecting the respective symbol in the *external directory manager* of the *WAGS Modeler* and moving it to the symbol of the "External Task" in the *process manager* with the help of a drag-and-drop operation.

Interface specifications stored in the *WAGS External Directory* can be exchanged with all registered partner organizations or only with parts of them. In both cases, the transfer of the *interface specifications* is achieved by selective synchronization of the *external directories* of the participants. If all participants make use of the Wide Area GroupFlow System, they can apply the replication technology of the underlying Lotus Notes platform for this purpose, as long as they all use replicas of the same *WAGS External Directory*. When organizations cooperate with many different partners through WAWM, it is unlikely that they will all use replicas of one *WAGS External Directory* database. In order to deal with cases like this, the *WAGS External*

Directory has been equipped with a set of *agents*, which synchronize *interface specifications* with other *external directories* by sending and receiving messages. This feature works with Lotus Notes-based *external directories*, where Lotus Notes e-mail can be applied. The *WAGS External Directory* can also exchange information with the help of structured ASCI-text in the body-field of Internet e-mails, thereby allowing for selective synchronization with many other platforms.

A further approach to distributing *interface specifications* is to publish them with the help of the Web front-end of the *WAGS External Directory*, thus making them (potentially) available to everyone using the World Wide Web.

Apart from the *external directory manager* in the *WAGS Modeler*, the *WAGS External Directory* is also accessible via a Lotus Notes front-end (Figure 50).

On the left side of Figure 50, the different elements of the *WAGS External Directory*, such as *interface specifications*, *message object hierarchy* or *external registered organizations*, are visible. To the right, one can see a *leaf* document, containing the *interface specification* of a workflow service for ordering dispensing equipment, which is offered by "Dispensing Inc." . This *interface specification* is the basis for the examples shown in the preceding Figures 48 and 49.

To facilitate the registration of external organizations and to allow for the storage of passwords for WWW access to the *WAGS Engine*, the *WAGS External Directory* has been based on the Lotus Notes 4.6 *name & address book (N&A)*. Thus, the *WAGS External Directory* can be used as a secondary *Notes N&A* for servers and clients, which for example builds the basis for handling groups of recipients or an LDAP access to the information in the *external directory* from outside.

Like *process definitions* (see Figure 47, p. 198), *interface specifications* also have a status and versioning system. During development, the status of the specifications is "design", meaning that they are not transferred to other *external directories*. Once they have been set to the status "active", they are automatically sent to the intended recipients in version "1". When updates have been made, version "1" is set to the status "freeze", while version "2" is now "active" and therefore will be distributed to all partners concerned. Thereby, incoming *message objects*, which had been issued before version "2" was available and for that reason refer to the *interface specifications* in version "1", can still be handled correctly. All newly issued *message objects* make use of version "2" of the *interface specifications*.

In all cases of transfer or publication of *interface specifications* using the *WAGS External Directory*, the fundamental approach to separating *public* and *private parts*, as introduced in Figure 32 (p. 151), is maintained. The *public part* – called *global routing information (GRI)* in WAGS terminology – contains all information necessary for external organizations to invoke the respective workflow service, but does not provide information on where and how the service is actually performed inside the offering organization. This information – called *internal routing information (IRI)* – is stored in the *private part* of the *WAGS External Directory* and is not available from outside.

With the help of this distinction between *public part* (GRI) and *private part* (IRI), incoming *message objects* can be dynamically mapped to actual workflows. Furthermore, the workload between several WFMSs can be balanced and it is easier to react on the spur of the moment by adapting workflow models prior to the fulfillment of the requested services.

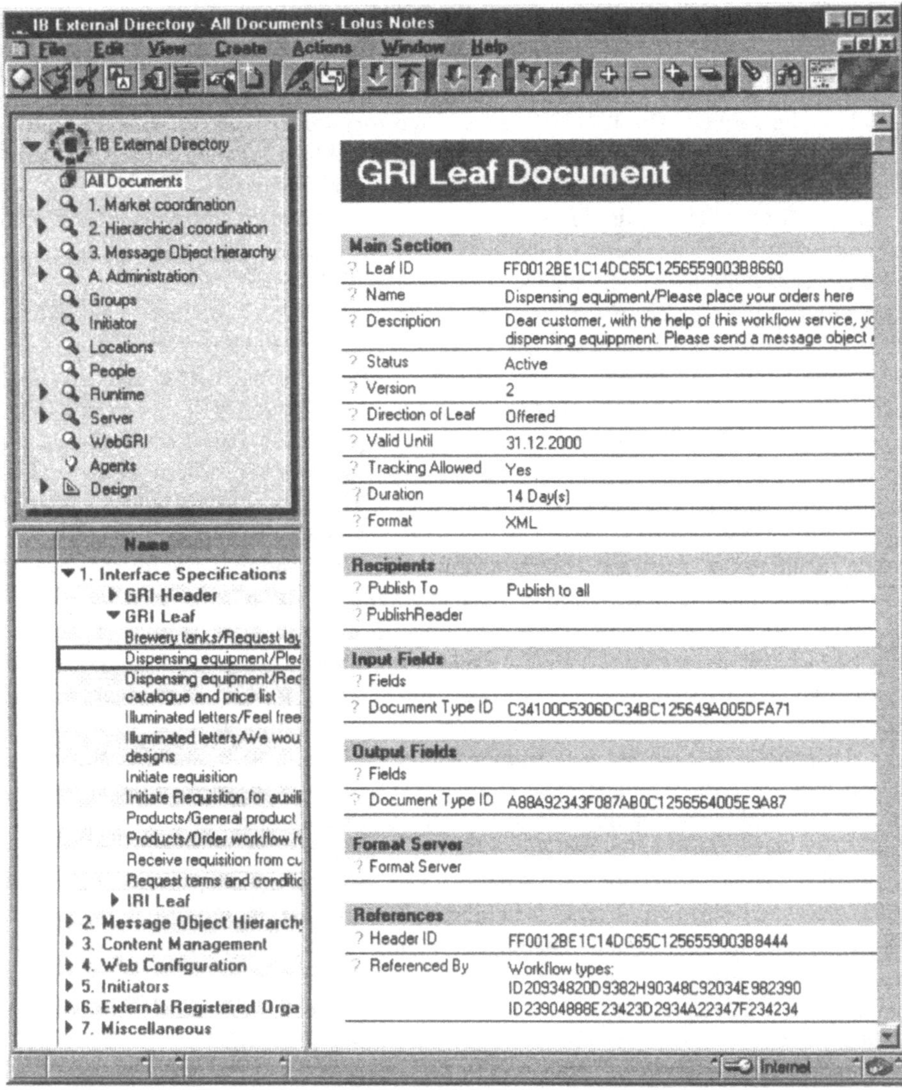

Figure 50: WAGS External Directory, showing the example of IB with the Lotus Notes front-end

Seen from an organizational point of view, the separation between a *public* and *private part* of *external directories* allows organizations to stay as autonomous as possible while still being able to cooperate flexibly and efficiently by WFMSs' interaction. This separation is therefore a fundamental prerequisite for the implementation of WAWM without forcing organizations into strong dependencies, such as has been observed in cases where information systems were directly connected using EDI technology (see Section 3.4.1, p. 59).

6.2.4 Workflow enactment service - WAGS Engine

In order to process *wide area workflows*, which had previously been planned with the help of *WAGS Modeler* and *WAGS External Directory*, a workflow enactment service was implemented in the WAGS environment. It is called *WAGS Engine* and has been realized on top of Lotus Notes 4.6 [Saliger 1997].

Apart from features of a workflow enactment service known from other scientific and commercial WFMSs, such as routing of workflow folders or handling of exceptions, the main focus during the development of the *WAGS Engine* was on the functionalities supporting WAWM in the sense of the *continuum of coordination mechanisms* (see Figure 29, p. 137). Similar to the *WAGS Modeler*, the *coordination mechanisms* of *hierarchy* and *market* have been implemented in the *WAGS Engine*, while the provision of technical support for WFMSs' interaction according to the paradigm of *equal partnership* has been postponed to a later project phase.

The *WAGS Engine* supports all options of the *Workflow Continuum* concerning flexible workflow management (Figure 15, p. 85). Users are thereby guided through completely predefined procedures as well as through workflows with rather open structures, which can be designed by *milestone modeling*. Since the *WAGS Engine* has been built on top of the groupware platform Lotus Notes, it also allows for ad-hoc workflows based on e-mail or shared databases, where no workflow models had been planned before.

In the following pages, selected features of the *WAGS Engine* will be presented on the basis of the workflow example of a simplified material support requisition procedure at IB, introduced in Figure 45 (p. 196).

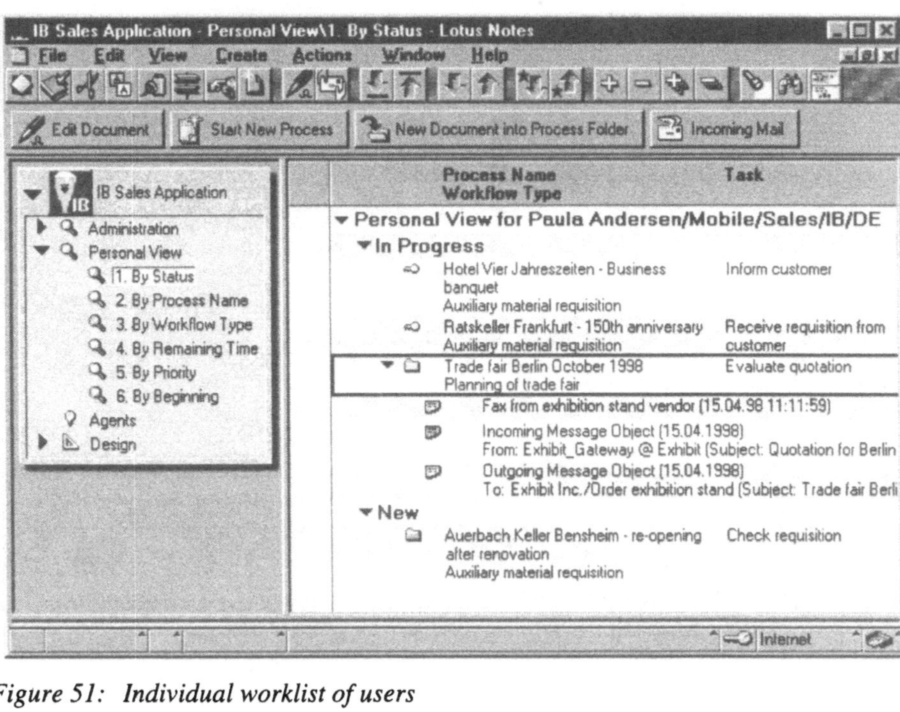

Figure 51: Individual worklist of users

The user interface of the *WAGS Engine* is found in the *WAGS Application Environment* database. There, users find their individual worklists (Figure 51) based on the authentication, which has to be performed when starting Lotus Notes.

Figure 51 shows *workflow folders* with different stati such as "New" and "In Progress". In the middle of Figure 51, an opened *workflow folder* is displayed with a *main document*, two *message objects* exchanged with a supplier, and a fax document, which has been added manually to the folder.

The *WAGS Engine* reads the *process definitions* for the routing of workflow instances in the *WAGS Process Definitions* database (Figure 52), where they had previously been stored by the *WAGS Modeler*. The *WAGS Process Definitions* database is normally located on a server and is not accessible to regular users in LAN environments. Mobile users, who also work in a disconnected mode, need a local replica of this database to perform local routing operations. Results are then transferred to the server during the next connection.

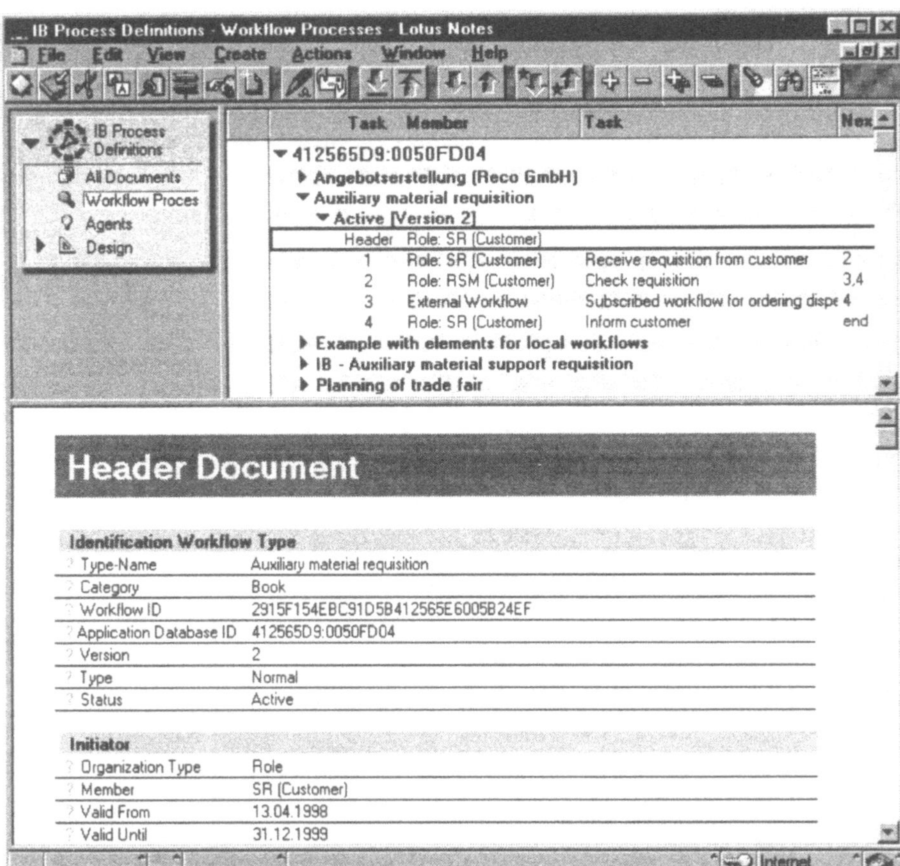

Figure 52: WAGS Process Definitions database, showing the process definition underlying the workflow model in Figure 45

For each node in a workflow model, a document describing its properties is laid down in the *WAGS Process Definitions* database. Additionally, a *header document* contains general information on the workflow (Figure 52).

Depending on the rights assigned by workflow designers, users can start workflow instances in the *WAGS Application Environment* database (Figure 53).

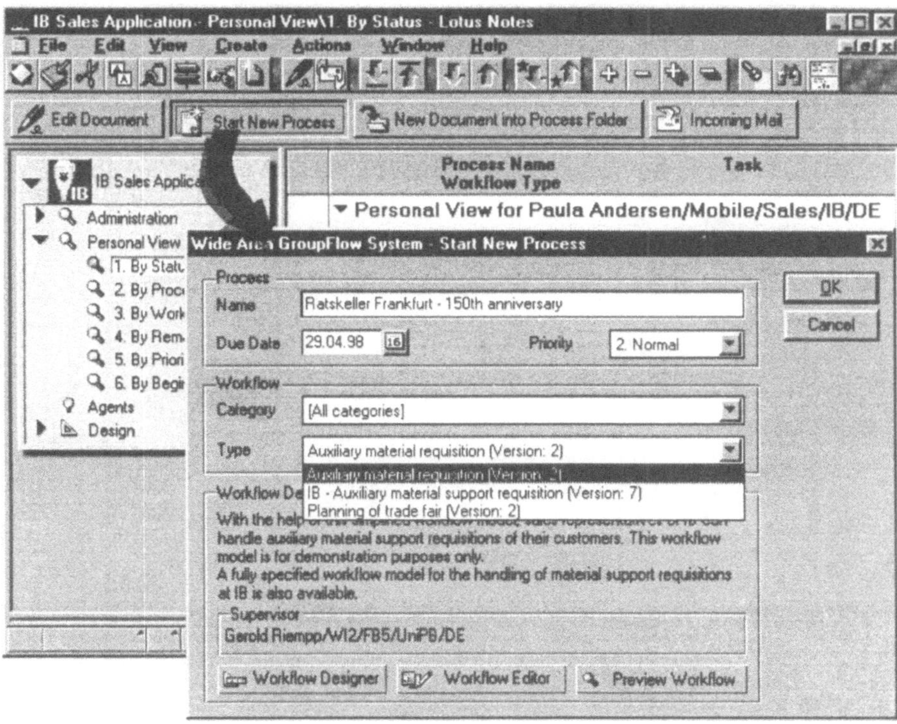

Figure 53: Start of a workflow instance in the WAGS Application Environment database

The *WAGS Engine* checks which workflow models are available for the current user and presents a start dialog, where an appropriate workflow type can be selected. After naming the new workflow instance and confirming the initiation, the *WAGS Engine* presents the *main form* of the first *task* to the current performer. Workflow designers can also specify *additional forms* for a *task*, for instance to display further relevant information, which the users may need during the processing of their *tasks*.

After a performer has finished his task and checked off the activities in the *activities list*, he can forward the workflow folder to the next workflow step with the help of the button "Next Task" (see Figure 54, p. 208). The *WAGS Engine* routes the workflow documents in the workflow folder to the next performer(s), depending on the *process definition* found in the *WAGS Process Definitions* database and the information in the *WAGS Infrastructure* database. In the case of ad-hoc workflows or within an open team task, the next performers are defined interactively.

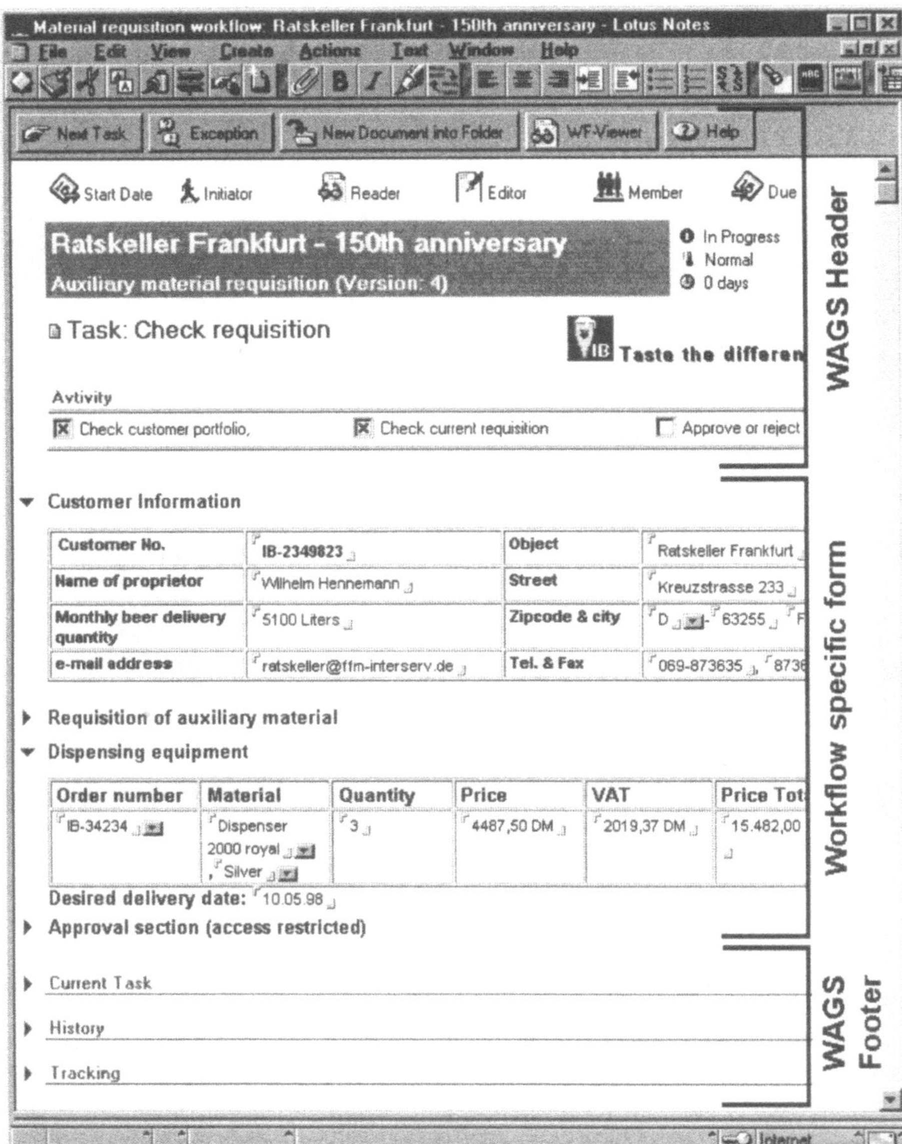

Figure 54: Structure of workflow documents in the WAGS Application Environment database

Figure 54 shows the structure of a workflow document in the *WAGS Application Environment* database. Workflow designers make use of two so-called *subforms* to build workflow documents, which can be routed by the *WAGS Engine*. In the *WAGS Header*, different functionalities are offered via buttons in the so-called "action bar". Further on, fundamental information on the workflow instance, such as name, status, performers, start date and due date, are displayed. The activities list is used to remind performers of single steps to be checked off during the processing of the respective *task*.

In the *WAGS Footer*, detailed information about the routing path (in the form of a history) as well as status information can be found. Regular users only need to make use of this information in exceptional situations, but it is needed for routing and tracking purposes.

From a technical point of view, *WAGS Header* and *WAGS Footer* have been implemented as *subforms* within Lotus Notes, so that they can be easily included during the design process. Between the *WAGS Header* and *Footer*, workflow designers include workflow specific forms, as shown in Figure 54 which illustrates the workflow of providing auxiliary material support to customers of IB. If organizations have already designed electronic forms based on Lotus Notes, they can simply add a *WAGS Header* and *Footer subform* in order to make these forms ready to be handled by the *WAGS Engine*.

Enabling Wide Area Workflow Management

The functionality of the *WAGS Engine* described so far can be used for *local* as well as *wide area workflows*. In the exemplary workflow model in Figure 45 (p. 196), the sales representative ("SR (Customer)") first receives and checks a requisition for auxiliary material from a customer. He forwards it to the regional sales manager ("RSM (Customer)"), who approves or rejects it. In the case of an approval, which will be assumed here, an *external subscribed workflow* is invoked. Here, the WAWM-related features of the *WAGS Engine* are needed, which will be described in the following pages.

After the regional sales manager has approved the requisition and pressed the "Next Task" button, a *message object* is generated. In the example of Figure 45, it must be sent to the supplier "Dispensing Inc." with an order for dispensing equipment.

The procedure of sending the *message object* now depends on the settings chosen by the workflow designers responsible. If a *wide area workflow* has become a routine procedure, which needs no further interaction by performers, a predefined *outgoing content management* will be performed automatically (see Section 5.6.3, p. 162). Afterwards, the *message object* will be sent directly to the *WAGS Gateway*. From there, it is forwarded to the *gateway* of "Dispensing Inc." and finally arrives in the workflow engine of this company, invoking a workflow instance of an order processing workflow. After this workflow instance has been successfully completed, the dispensing equipment is shipped to IB and a *message object* with a delivery confirmation returns to the workflow instance in IB's *WAGS Engine*. Information from this returning *message object* are included in the main document during an automated *incoming content management*, and the *message object* itself is added to the workflow folder. Now, the workflow instance at IB can be continued.

The procedure described so far follows the paradigm of *automation & structure* within WAWM, which was described in conjunction with Figure 16 (p. 106).

In many cases, the exchange of *message objects* between workflow systems cannot be completely predefined, for example if these WFMSs interact only sporadically. In other situations, the structure of the information carried in internal workflow folders is partially unknown during build-time, for instance when other organizations are supposed to deliver information earlier in the workflow and it is not yet clear exactly how this information will be structured. In cases like this, the application of the paradigm of *user support & flexibility* might be more appropriate (see Figure 17, p. 106) for handling exceptional situations interactively.

Workflow designers have different options for giving users more influence on WAWM-related functionalities. First, they can predefine the settings for *content management* as extensively as possible, but allow users to check these settings before *outgoing content management* is actually performed (see Figure 55 in comparison with Figure 49, p. 201).

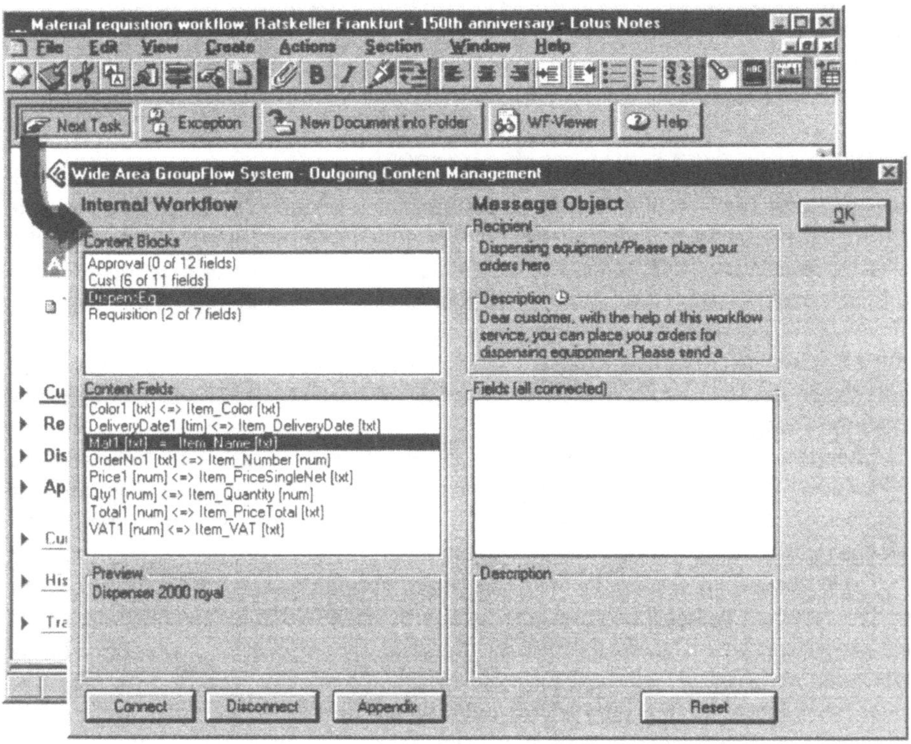

Figure 55: User-control of settings for outgoing content management according to the paradigm of user support & flexibility

After the actual performer has checked and approved the settings, the *outgoing content management* procedure is executed. As a result, the selected contents from internal workflow documents have been transferred into the newly generated *message object*. This *message object* can now be presented to the actual performer for checking purposes as a second option in *user support & flexibility* (Figure 56). This possibility to control the *message object* before sending is similar to the common habit of re-checking a letter for mistakes before putting it into an envelope and posting it.

The *message object* itself now contains the selected contents, which are also called *properties* (see Figure 33, p. 155). In addition, workflow designers can prepare *individual subforms* to influence the *representation* of a *message object*. In the example in Figure 56, the upper part is displayed with an *individual subform* called "IB letterhead", since it resembles the letterheads IB used formerly. Before an *individual subform* can be applied for the purpose of enhancing the *representation* of a *message object*, it must be exchanged between sender and recipient with the help of a *message object hierarchy*, which is stored in the *WAGS External Directory*, or similar techniques. The recipient can only restore the original *representation* of a *message object* if he possesses all *individual subforms* used by the sender.

To display information on the items ordered, a so-called *generic subform* was applied. It can be used to show any field-structured *properties* in a list, consisting of four columns: *field description* (found in a pop-up window at the "?"), *field name*, *field value* and *field type* (hidden to users in the example in Figure 56). *Generic subforms* can be applied in cases where no *document types* or whole *message object hierarchies* has been exchanged between participants.

If senders have applied *individual subforms*, but recipients do not possess these *individual subforms* for some reason, they can still display the *properties* of a *message object* through the application of the *generic subform*. Thus, the formatting is lost, but users in the recipients' WFMSs nevertheless can check the contents of the incoming *message object*.

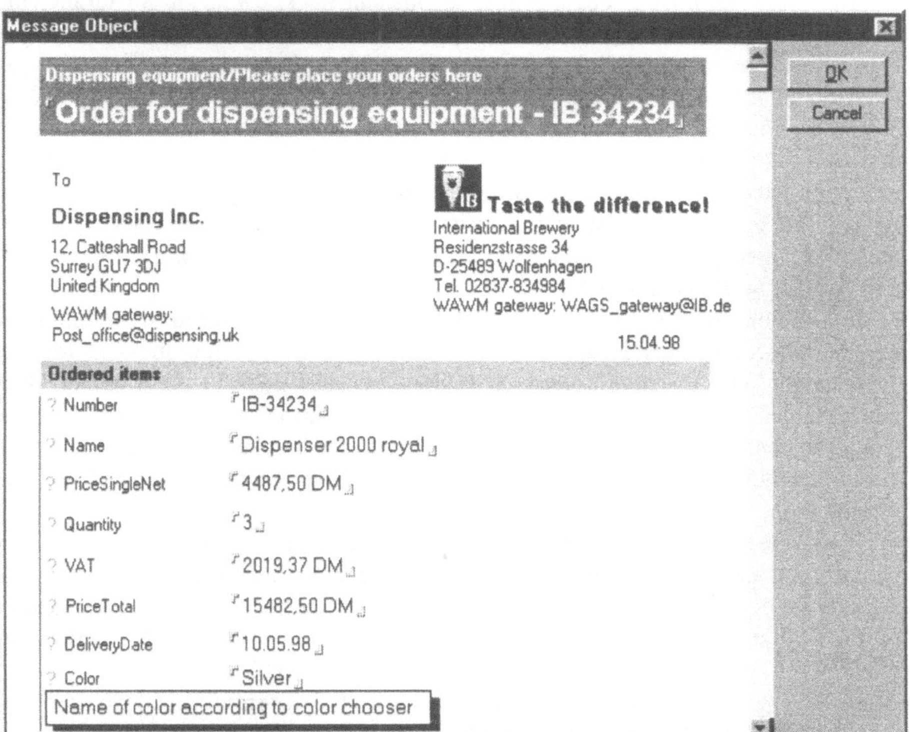

Figure 56: Control of a message object by the actual performer before sending

When sending *message objects* with the help of Internet e-mails, *generic subforms* are automatically transformed into tabular lists, so that the structure of the properties is maintained and can be read by the recipient(s). However, *individual subforms* cannot be used this way. They can only be applied if the format of the *message object* allows for the embedding of a *representation*, as is the case with HTML-mail, XML, MS Exchange e-mail or Lotus Notes e-mail.

On the part of *message object* recipients, the paradigm of *user support & flexibility* can be put into practice by presenting the requests for workflow services, coming in from other organizations, to the respective performers responsible. Being in possession of the *individual subforms* applied by the sender, they will see the respective *message objects* in a readable form, as shown in Figure 54. These persons can now decide whether they want to process the request and thereby invoke a related workflow instance, or whether they reject further handling and send back a rejection note. In real life business, many requests from outside organizations are rejected. For example, companies selling complicated machinery equipment usually only provide quotations to customers whom they assume to be potential buyers. Since the provision of a quotation costs considerable amounts of time and money, to do the layout and calculation, these companies try to concentrate on a few promising bids.

The notion that WFMSs can be invoked from outside without preceding human control can be very dangerous in reality. Publishing workflow services with the help of the WWW, which can be done with the *WAGS External Directory*, makes companies vulnerable to "attacks" from outside. Even when there is no bad intention, an overflow of incoming *message objects* might bring a WFMS to a complete halt. If *message objects* are sent with a deceitful purpose, senders can for example modify the *properties* slightly, so that the receiving WFMS is forced to perform ongoing exception handling, thereby suppressing the proper functioning of the other services. As with all software systems with an interface to the outside world, workflow systems with interoperability features must also be protected from "workflow viruses" and "workflow Trojan horses".

In addition, technical problems might cause useless overload in WFMSs, which may be induced by outside sources. For instance, a malfunctioning message transfer agent might send *message objects* repeatedly, because delivery confirmation does not come through. Thereby, multiple workflow instances with the same purpose would be generated. Further on, if workflow instances invoked are specified in such a way that they invoke further workflow systems themselves, they might end up in an infinite loop.

There are many other examples that emphasize the need for *technical* and particularly *human* control of incoming *message objects* before workflow instances are actually invoked. The automatic invocation of workflow services will be reasonable in practical application only in cases of comparably high trust between participants in a WAWM scenario, and a closed group of interacting WFMSs.

In the example discussed so far, an employee of "Dispensing Inc." would check the incoming *message object* and decide whether the order can be fulfilled or not. Since in the example, the company is happy to deliver the equipment, the actual performer initiates a workflow instance of an order processing workflow with a start dialog similar to Figure 53 (p. 207). After this workflow instance has been completed, a *message object* with a delivery confirmation is sent back, according to the *interface specifications* shown in Figure 48 (p. 200). Again, options for the inclusion of human actors in the process of generating the delivery confirmation are to let them check the settings for the *outgoing content management* and to present the *message object* for a final check before sending.

Using WAGS, workflow instances can be concatenated on the side of recipients (see also Figure 23, p.124), following the interaction pattern called *complete integration of workflow parts (CIWP)*, which was introduced in Table 4 (p. 119).

To illustrate the technical implementation of this concatenation feature, the example described so far will be extended. Now, IB first invokes a workflow service providing a quotation for certain dispensing equipment with "Dispensing Inc.". After the resulting *message object* has transferred the quotation from "Dispensing Inc." to IB, the purchasing department of IB decides on the buying of the equipment.

If the terms and prices offered are accepted by IB, a second workflow service for order processing is invoked, as has been described in the preceding pages. The *message object* now sent to "Dispensing Inc." contains a *reference* to the preceding interaction between the WFMSs. In technical terms, this reference consists of the unique identification number of the earlier *message object*, which IB had sent to "Dispensing Inc." to request a quotation.

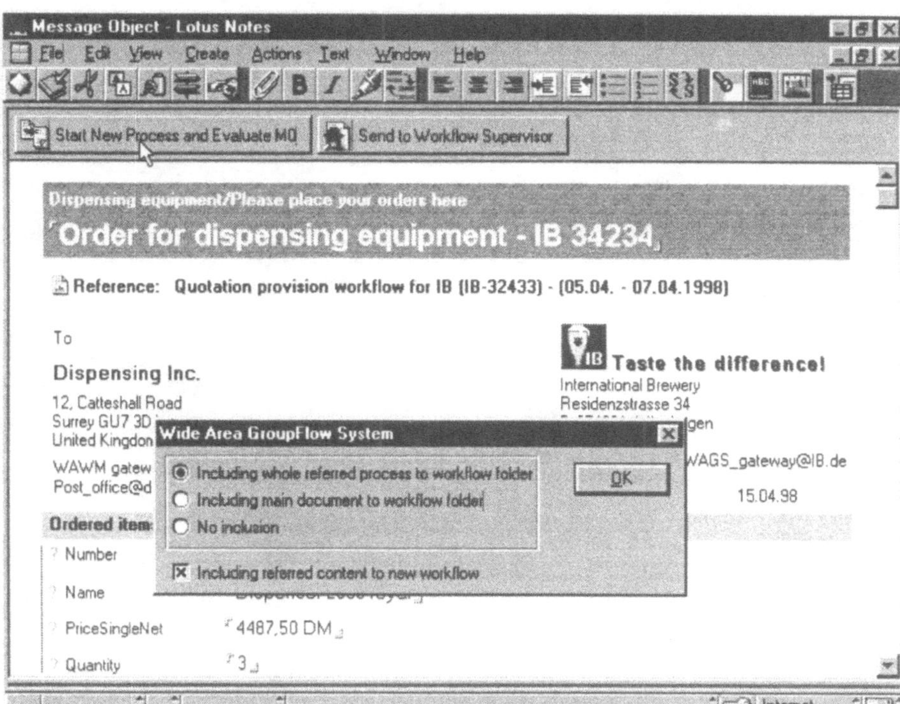

Figure 57: Options for the inclusion of information from an earlier, referenced workflow instance

The receiving WFMS of "Dispensing Inc." can now locate the workflow folder of the preceding *workflow instance*, in which the quotation had been generated. When the *WAGS Engine* has found the respective workflow folder, it displays a hyperlink together with a reference text in the incoming *message object*, so that the user can take a quick look at the documents in the preceding *workflow instance* to inform himself (Figure 57).

As a result, the user is given several options prior to the invocation of the new workflow instance. He can choose to include the documents from the referenced workflow instance into the new workflow folder and also import the contents of the former process into the main document of the new workflow instance.

Up to this point, examples of *structured workflow management* have been presented, where workflow models build the basis for the execution of workflow instances. The *WAGS Engine* additionally supports a wide range of exceptions to allow users to modify the predefined routing paths.

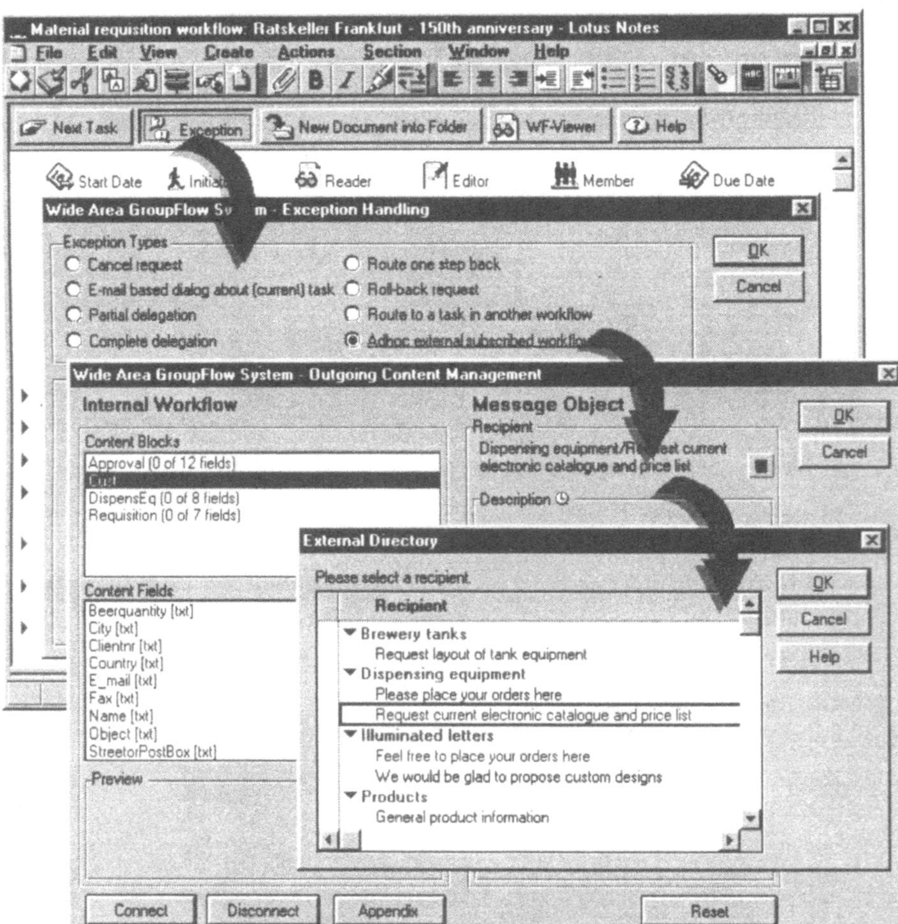

Figure 58: Ad-hoc invocation of an external subscribed workflow

The example in Figure 58 shows an ad-hoc invocation of an *external subscribed workflow* as a WAWM-related feature of exception handling. Within the exemplary workflow described so far, the regional sales manager might want to take a look at the current catalogue and price list of "Dispensing Inc." before deciding on whether or not to order the equipment. He selects the appropriate option in the "Exception Handling" dialog and is presented with the dialog for *ad-hoc content management.* There, he selects the appropriate workflow service (GRI) from the *WAGS External Directory*, which is the provision of an electronic catalogue and price list in the example in Figure 58. Further on, he maps parts of the internal fields with the fields described in the *interface specifications* of the workflow service, which are displayed after the selection of the GRI has been made.

Consequently, he sends a *message object* to "Dispensing Inc." and receives an up-to-date electronic catalogue and price list, which he includes into the workflow folder.

Other options for exception handling, such as roll-back requests or delegation features, are also visible in Figure 58. They are based on the concepts for the flexible execution of WAWM described in Section 5.5.2 (p. 141).

An important element in the support of users during the handling of *local* and *wide area workflows* is to give them an overview of the process they are currently participating in.

One important feature of this focus on *user awareness* has been demonstrated in the last few pages where *content management* settings and *message objects* are presented to users prior to invoking external workflows. Similarly, the users in workflow systems can be made aware of the existence and the consequences of *wide area workflows* by presenting incoming *message objects* to them.

A further option for improving users' *awareness* of the processes they are dealing with has been implemented with the *WAGS Workflow Viewer* [Siekmann 1998]. It can be used for workflow *monitoring* by graphically showing the position of the current performer. Users can thereby locate their current task in the network of preceding and succeeding workflow steps. In addition, they can see the results of exception handling, which might have been executed in workflow steps before the current *task*.

The *WAGS Workflow Viewer* has been implemented with the help of Java 1.1. Thereby, this tool is available to users within the Lotus Notes-based client application of the *WAGS Engine* as well as within the WWW front-end.

It is intended to develop the *WAGS Workflow Viewer* further into a tool for *instance-based variation* and *modeling* of workflows. Thus, users will have the option to influence the routing path of the future steps of a workflow instance with the help of an interactive graphical modeling tool. They can apply all the options for exception handling, which are now available in standard dialog boxes (see Figure 58), depending on their individual rights. In addition, they can include further workflow steps, add or change performers of tasks and include *external subscribed workflows* based on the *interface specifications* in the *WAGS External Directory*.

These options allow for an even higher degree of flexibility within the planning and execution of Wide Area Workflow Management, compared to the options currently available within the *WAGS Modeler* and the *WAGS Engine*.

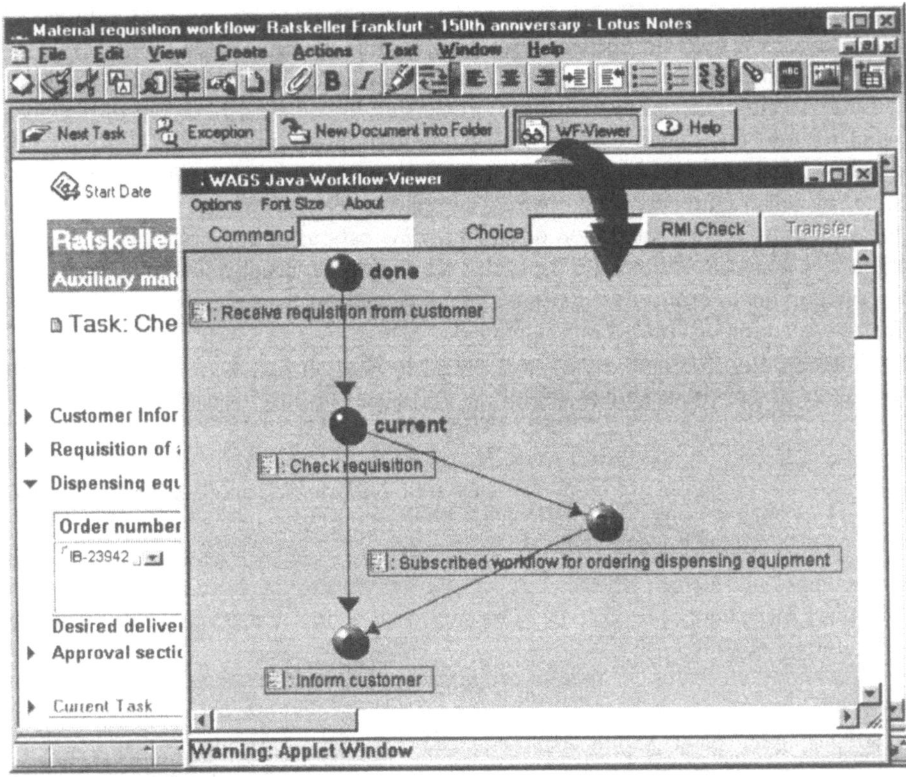

Figure 59: Workflow monitoring with the WAGS Workflow Viewer

The structure of the workflow instance shown in Figure 59 reflects the underlying *process definition*, from which this workflow instance was derived. This structure can also be seen in the *WAGS Modeler* in Figure 45 (p. 196), where the workflow model for the simplified material support requisition procedure was designed.

The *WAGS Engine* was implemented with the help of the object-oriented programming language *Lotus Script* in the version available since Lotus Notes 4.6. The main functionalities of the *WAGS Engine* have been split up into several *script libraries*, for example performing the *routing* of workflow folders, *content management*, *exception handling* and *user interaction*. The different functions of these libraries are partially used by the *front-end components* of the *WAGS Engine*, such as buttons (called "actions" in Lotus Notes terminology) and dialog boxes. Other functions are applied in the so-called *back-end components*, which are mostly performed on the Lotus Domino server in the background.

One of the main design goals for the implementation of the Wide Area GroupFlow System was to equally support mobile workers and workflow performers in local networks. Therefore, the workflow client software performs as many of the necessary functions of the *WAGS Engine* as possible. Mobile users can store local replicas of the different databases of the *WAGS Repository* on their notebooks. After an initial replication, they can work in disconnected mode and process the tasks they are responsible for in the different workflow instances. The *WAGS Engine* prepares the workflow documents as far as possible via the client software. This includes the sending of *message objects*, which are stored in the local *outgoing mailbox* of the Lotus Notes client software, ready to be transferred during the next online connection. When the mobile workers are connected to their workflow server again, the final steps of the routing procedure, such as the joining of parallel branches and sending of tracking messages, are executed.

Other functionalities of the *WAGS Engine*, which are performed by the *back-end components* on the server, are the receipt of incoming *message objects*, workflow roll-back, workflow cancellation and reminders to performers when tasks are due.

Despite being only a prototype, the *WAGS Engine* has proven to be working so well, that it is currently implemented by a large private educational institution as an operative workflow system. There, over 400 office workers in more than 60 subsidiaries will be doing their everyday *wide area workflows* with the head office and external contractors with the help of this software service [Niebiossa 1998]. The operative use of this installation of WAGS was (at the time of writing) due to begin in mid 1998.

6.2.5 Connection of widely distributed WFMSs with WAGS Gateways

Within the architectural concept for WAWM introduced in conjunction with Figure 30 (p. 144), *gateways* have the role of routing *message objects*, which contain information that connect several workflow parts, between autonomous WFMSs. Further features of *gateways* are to convert *message objects* to different formats in order to bridge heterogeneous workflow systems and to perform *request-answer tracking* (see also Section 5.6.4, p. 166).

In this sense, the *WAGS Gateway* was developed to build a "post office" for the *WAGS Engine*, where all functionalities regarding the stable and safe interaction of heterogeneous WFMSs have been aggregated in a single software service [Kuethe 1996], [Haasper/Hovestadt/Peine 1997], [Tunnat 1998].

Regular users of WAGS do not see or work in the *WAGS Gateway*, since it is located on a Lotus Domino server and operates in the background. It is equipped with a set of routines, called *agents* in Lotus Notes terminology, that react on the event of newly arriving *message objects* in the sense of an *active database*. Upon the arrival of such a new workflow carrier, an *agent* first detects whether this item was posted by an internal *WAGS Engine* (and is thus "outgoing") or originates from an external source (thus labeled "incoming"). This detection is achieved with the help of the addresses in the field describing the sender and an additional flag called "message_source", which is set by an internal *WAGS Engine* to the value "internal". In *outgoing message objects*, this flag is removed before the *WAGS Gateway* forwards the final version in order to prevent confusion in the *gateways* of other WFMSs.

Outgoing message objects contain the identification number of a workflow service offered by an external organization (called *Leaf ID*, see Figure 60, p. 218). The *WAGS Gateway* searches for the respective *GRI leaf document* in the *WAGS External Directory* to verify whether the address of the *message object* is correct. With the help of the *GRI leaf document*, the *WAGS Gateway* finds the affiliated *header document* of the organization with the help of the *Header ID* (see lower part of Figure 50, p. 204). There, the *WAGS Gateway* looks up the (e-mail) address of the receiving *gateway* and transfers it into the field for the recipient of the *message object*.

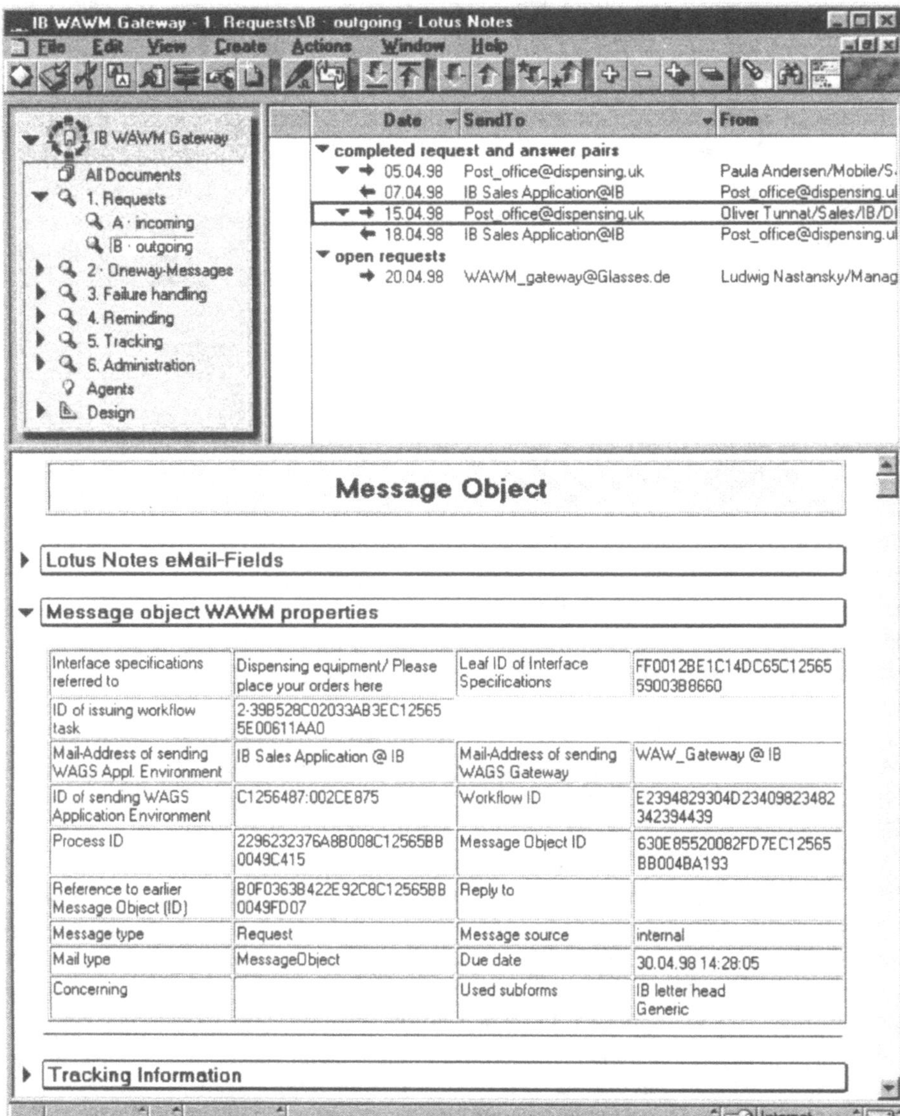

Figure 60: Administration view of the WAGS Gateway database

After establishing that the *outgoing message object* has been specified correctly by its internal sender, and setting the address of the receiving *gateway*, the *WAGS Gateway* generates a new copy of the *message object*. This copy will actually be sent to the receiving organization. Only those *contents* and *WAWM properties* which the recipient actually needs and is allowed to see are transferred into this copy. A large set of fields of *WAWM properties* is needed for internal purposes only and is therefore kept in the original, which is shown in the lower part of Figure 60 (p. 218). The original is stored in the *WAGS Gateway* for the purposes of *reminding*, *request-answer-tracking* and *error prevention and handling* (see Section 5.6.4, p. 166).

After the new copy has been generated, the *format* specified by the recipient is checked in the *GRI leaf document* in the *WAGS External Directory* (see the middle right part of Figure 50, p. 204). In the example of the auxiliary material requisition procedure discussed so far, this *format* is XML. Therefore, the *WAGS Gateway* converts the *message object*, which is shown in Figure 60 in the Lotus Notes environment, into the XML format (Figure 61).


```
<?XML Version="1.0"?>
<!DOCTYPE messageobject SYSTEM "mo.dtd">
<messageobject>
<moaddressname>Dispensing equipment/Please place your orders
here</moaddressname>
<mocode>2-39B528C02033AB3EC125655E00611AA0</mocode>
<moconcerning></moconcerning>
<modbapplid>C1256487:002CE875</modbapplid>
<modbapplmail>IB Sales Application @ IB</modbapplmail>
<modbgatewaymail>WAWM_Gateway @ IB</modbgatewaymail>
<moleafid>FF0012BE1C14DC65C1256559003B8660</moleafid>
<momailtype>MessageObject</momailtype>
<momessageobjectid>630E85520082FD7EC12565BB004BA193</momessageobjectid>
<momessagereferenceid>0F0363B422E92C8C12565BB0049FD07
</momessagereferenceid>
<momessagereplyto></momessagereplyto>
<momessagetype>Request</momessagetype>
<mosubforms>IB letter head; Generic</mosubforms>
<moworkflowid>E2394829304D23409823482342394439</moworkflowid>
<motrackmail>WAWM_Tracking @ IB</motrackmail>
<motrackcode>*!*wfCodell2-39B528C02033AB3EC125655E00611AA0:1*!*wfTaskllSending
Message*!*</motrackcode>
<motrackheader>*!*wfProcessIDll2296232376A8B008C12565BB0049C415*!*wfTypellAuxili
ary material requisition*!*wfJobllRatskeller Frankfurt – 150th anniversary*!* wfStartDatell
15.04.98 14:25:43*!*wfFinishDatell*!*</motrackheader>
<motrackprev>*!*wfTrackPrevCodell1-39B528C02033AB3EC125655E00611AA0:0*!*
wfTrackPrevTaskllCheck requisition*!*</motrackprev>
<contentblock name="address">
<variable name="Name">
<vartype>[txt]</vartype>
<varhelp>First and last name of recipient</varhelp>
<varbody>Dispensing Inc.</varbody>
</variable>
...
</variable>
</contentblock>
</messageobject>
```


Figure 61: Example of a message object in XML format

In the example in Figure 61, the *WAWM properties* in the *outgoing message object* are listed in XML. Additionally, tracking protocols are transferred, since IB and "Dispensing Inc." have agreed to exchange this information for an overall control of WAWM procedures by each participant.

The XML code can now for example be embedded in the body field of an Internet e-mail for the purpose of transferring the *message object* to the recipient's *gateway*, where it will be decoded into a format that the receiving WFMS can handle.

Additional prototypic converters for the generation of *message objects* in the form of WfMC-compliant Internet e-mail, HTML-mail and EDIFACT messages have been successfully tested in the *WAGS Gateway*.

After an *incoming message object* has been detected, the *WAGS Gateway* first converts it into the format used by the internal WFMS, which is Lotus Notes in the case of WAGS. Afterwards, it checks whether all *properties* needed for a WAWM interaction can be found in this workflow carrier. Subsequently, the *WAGS Gateway* uses the *Leaf ID* provided in the *incoming message object* to check if this workflow service has really been published in the *WAGS External Directory* by its own organization. In addition, an *agent* performs a consistency check on the information found in the *message object* against that specified in the *GRI leaf document*.

After all checks have been passed successfully, the *WAGS Gateway* searches for the affiliated *IRI leaf document* in the private part of the *WAGS External Directory*. This document contains information on the actual *WAGS Engine* inside the receiving organization, which is supposed to process the incoming *request*. Further on, the *IRI leaf document* contains the ID of the *process definition*, from which a workflow instance should be derived. The *WAGS Gateway* forwards the *incoming message object* to the *WAGS Engine* responsible. There, a workflow instance is initiated, starting with the respective IN-node. Again, the *WAGS Gateway* keeps a copy of the *incoming message object* for purposes of *request-answer-tracking* and *reminding*.

When the *WAGS Engine* invoked delivers the *answer* in the form of an *outgoing message object* to the *WAGS Gateway*, it is processed in the same way as described above, so that the workflow instance in the invoking WFMS finally receives the *answer* to the *request* issued earlier.

Periodical *agents* in the *WAGS Gateway* database, performed in the background on the Lotus Domino server, check for open *requests* and can thus remind performers via the *WAGS Engine* to process pending tasks. Once an *answer* for a "waiting" *request* has arrived in the *WAGS Gateway*, this completed *request-answer-pair* is moved to an archive for tracking purposes.

For each *message object* processed, the *WAGS Gateway* sends a *tracking message* to the *WAGS Tracking* database, so that all external WFMSs' interaction can be monitored and analyzed.

If failures occur during the different checks performed on *outgoing* and *incoming message objects*, the *WAGS Gateway* reacts by informing the *workflow administrator* responsible. He can now fix minor inconsistencies or send the *message objects* concerned back to their originators. If certain errors occur recurrently, the administrator can automate the return with the help of agents. Additionally, he might have to contact the internal or external source of faulty *message objects*, so that the causes of these errors can be tackled.

6.2.6 Control of workflows with WAGS Tracking and the WAGS Analyzer

In order to control, analyze and improve *wide area workflows* in the sense of the *lifecycle for WAWM* (see Figure 37, p. 171), the *WAGS Tracking* database and the *WAGS Analyzer* have been developed [Hein 1997], [Tunnat 1998].

Based on the fundamental tracking methods for WAWM introduced in Section 5.6.2.3 (p. 158), the WAGS framework supports *self-tracking, send-tracking* as well as mixed forms of both.

Within the *WAGS Engine, tracking protocols* are recorded including each single workflow step within internal workflow instances. In addition, workflow designers can adjust the settings for tracking so that in each single *task*, or alternatively in every second, third, fourth etc. workflow step, *tracking messages* are sent to the *WAGS Tracking* database. These *tracking messages* include information on the *task* currently finished and all preceding workflow steps, for which no *tracking messages* had been sent yet.

The tracking feature of the *WAGS Engine* records the current performer(s), the organizational type (e.g. *role, workgroup*), the workflow instance, the underlying workflow model, the times of arrival of a workflow folder, start of processing, end of processing and delivery to the next workflow step. Additionally, an identification of the preceding workflow steps and an incremental number are included in the tracking protocol for each workflow step, so that parallel execution and route-back operations can be detected (see the lower part of Figure 62, p. 222).

Optionally, some of these elements can be excluded from tracking, if employees or works councils object to such a detailed control of activities within the workflow system.

External organizations can be included in the list of recipients of *tracking messages* as a special feature of WAGS. This way, not only one's own organization, but also other participants in a WAWM scenario can be informed about the current status of processing workflow instances that have been invoked from outside. Optionally, tracking messages to external recipients can only include organizational units (e.g. departments) instead of single persons, so that control of workflow instances cannot be executed in full detail from outside.

As well as the *WAGS Engine*, the *WAGS Gateway* also sends *tracking messages* on *outgoing* and *incoming message objects* to the *WAGS Tracking* database. In this way, all the stations of *wide area workflows* can be traced, if allowed by the respective participants in a WAWM scenario.

If organizations do not allow external workflow systems to track workflow instances within them, the *tracking protocol* only contains information about sending *requests* in form of *message objects* to such "black box" organizations, and the reentry of the related *answers*.

The *WAGS Tracking* database reacts to incoming *tracking messages* with the help of event-triggered *agents*. The routines of these *agents* first check which workflow instance a *tracking message* belongs to. If entries for this workflow instance can already be found in the *WAGS Tracking* database, then the information on preceding workflow steps and the incremental number in the *tracking message* are checked. Thereby, incoming tracking information can be sorted into the correct order of workflow steps, as they have actually been performed. This is very important, since *tracking messages* from remote locations or mobile workers might arrive later than those of subsequent workflow steps in local environments, thereby possibly corrupting the correct order of tracking.

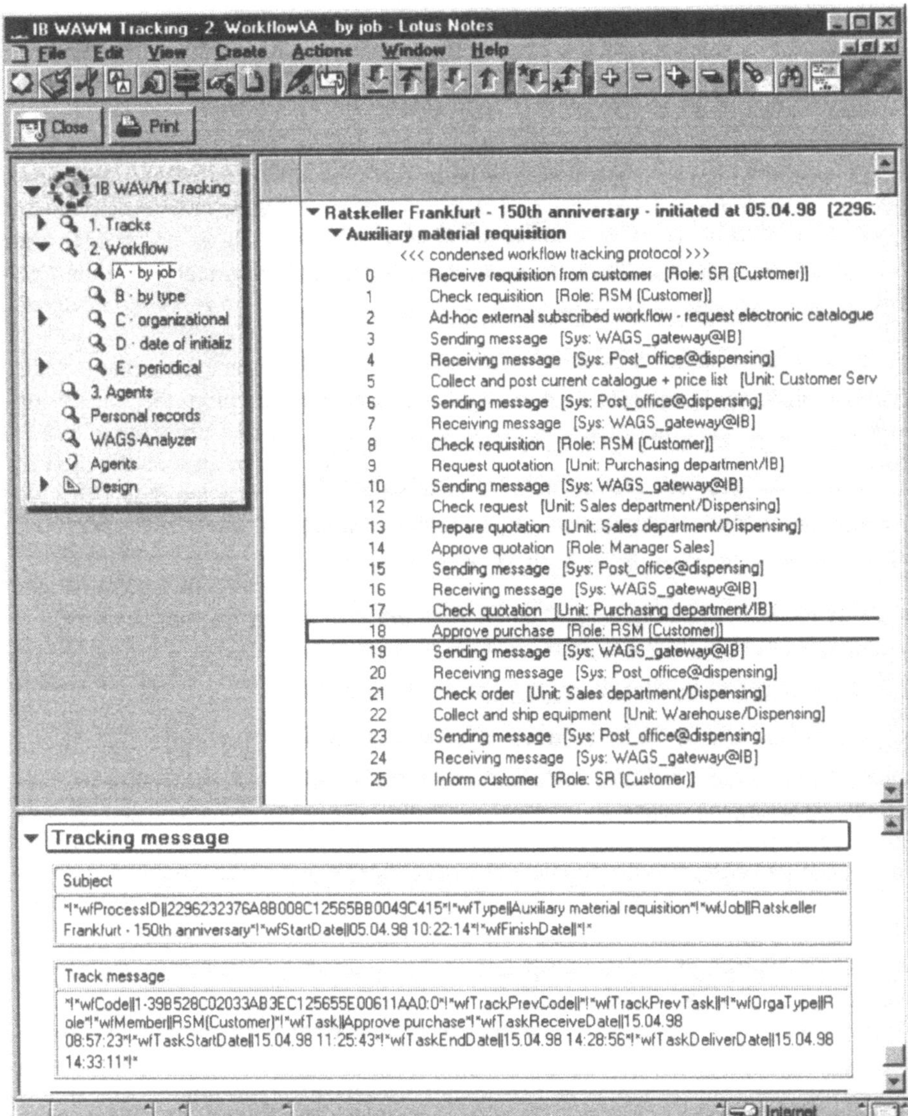

Figure 62: Administration view of the WAGS Tracking database

Subsequently, incoming *tracking messages* are evaluated in a process called *condensing*, in which one complete tracking history of a workflow instance is collected up to the present point of execution. This *condensed workflow tracking protocol* (see the upper right part of Figure 62) can be used by workflow administrators, supervisors and designers to gain a quick overview of current and completed workflow instances. In addition, it is evaluated by the *WAGS Analyzer* in order to graphically illustrate the workflow structures.

Figure 62 shows an example of the tracking history of the exemplary *wide area workflow* of auxiliary material requisition between IB and "Dispensing Inc.", which has also been described earlier in this section. The tracking history shows an ad-hoc *external subscribed workflow* for the provision of a catalogue and price list, the provision of a quotation and the ordering and delivery of dispensing equipment. Hence, three concatenated *external subscribed workflows* have been processed by "Dispensing Inc." for IB, building a *wide area workflow* network according to the interaction pattern labeled *complete integration of workflow parts (CIWP)*, as introduced in Table 4 (p. 119).

After workflow instances have been completely worked through in the *WAGS Engine* and eventually other workflow systems, and therefore *condensed workflow tracking protocols* are complete, the single *tracking messages* can be deleted in order to save on disk space.

Further features of the *WAGS Tracking* database are found in different *views* (as report lists are called in Lotus Notes terminology), where different evaluations, such as total time of processing, number of open and completed workflow instances of one workflow model etc., can be found for the purpose of giving *workflow supervisors* and *developers* as much information as possible for the improvement of workflow planning and execution.

The *WAGS Analyzer* is a graphical tool, which can be used to illustrate the actual routing paths and other details of current or completed workflow instances.

With the help of import filters, the *WAGS Analyzer* can be adjusted to any Lotus Notes database for the purpose of reading and displaying workflow structures. Since Lotus Notes automatically records all persons who have edited and saved documents in internal fields called "$UpdatedBy", the *WAGS Analyzer* can be used as a general analysis tool for workflows which are performed on the basis of this groupware platform.

Figure 63 (p. 224) shows an example of workflow structures within a documentation database for Lotus Notes 4.5, which have been evaluated with the *WAGS Analyzer* by reading the "$UpdatedBy" field. The *view* applied in the *WAGS Analyzer* is called "interaction of agents", due to the fact that the role of persons in workflows is given special emphasis. The arrows indicate the routing path of workflow documents among the performers in the different workflows.

In addition to Lotus Notes databases, the *WAGS Analyzer* can read regular files which have been structured in a certain way. This way, the tool can also be used to evaluate workflow structures of WFMSs which were built on other platforms.

Apart from the view "interaction of agents", the *WAGS Analyzer* can arrange workflow steps according to their actual sequence in workflow instances, thereby rebuilding the perspective which workflow designers have in workflow modeling tools such as the *WAGS Modeler*.

Depending on the richness of the tracking information, the *WAGS Analyzer* automatically adjusts the different possible options for displaying workflow structures in nine *views* altogether. Each of these views emphasizes a different element of the workflow instances, such as interaction of persons, sequence of workflow tasks or the role of single activities in workflow networks, thereby allowing *workflow supervisors* and *designers* to find bottlenecks.

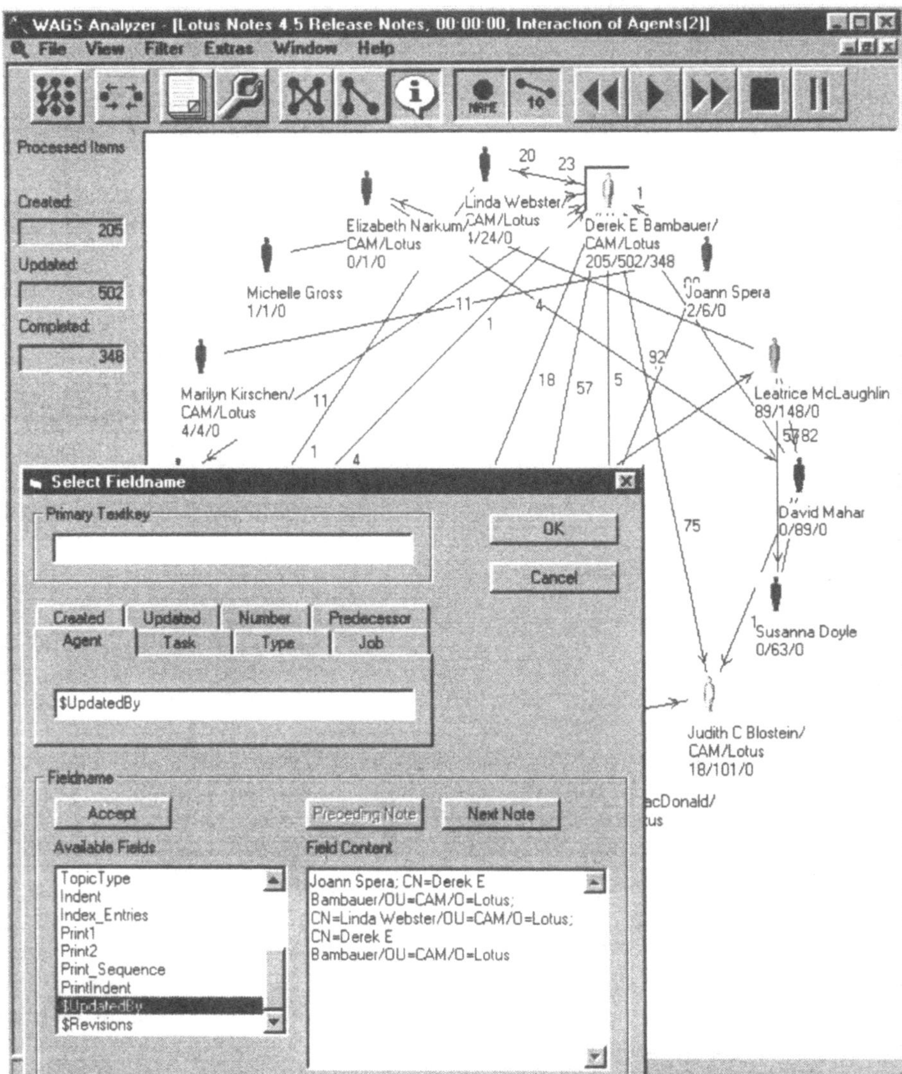

Figure 63: Analysis of the workflows in a Lotus Notes documentation database with the WAGS Analyzer

The following Figure 64 shows the results of the tracking feature of the *WAGS Engine* and *WAGS Gateway*, which have sent *tracking messages* to the *WAGS Tracking* database during the processing of the exemplary workflow of auxiliary material requisition at IB, which has been repeatedly discussed in the course of this section.

To display the structure of the actual workflow, the *condensed workflow tracking protocol* shown in Figure 62 (p. 222) has been evaluated by the *WAGS Analyzer*.

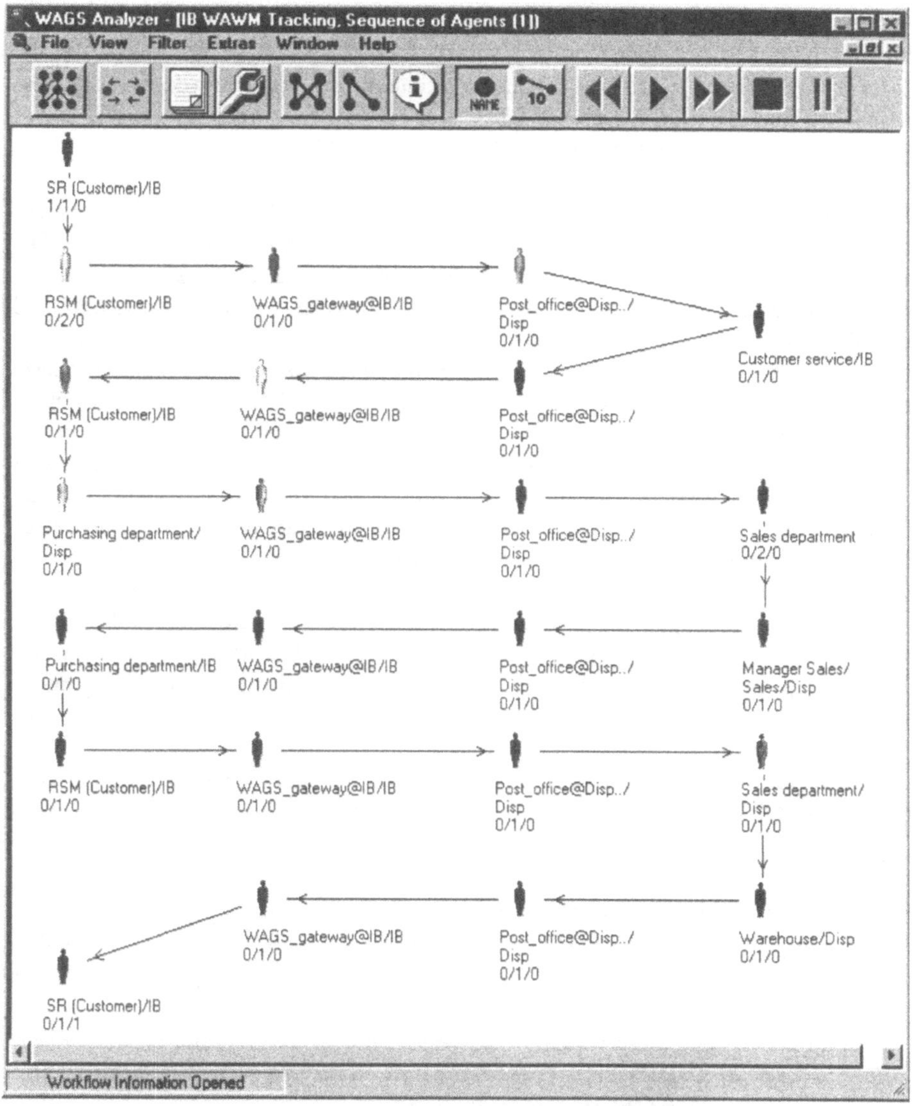

Figure 64: WAGS Analyzer with exemplary workflow of auxiliary material requisition at IB, based on the tracking history shown in Figure 62

In Figure 64, the sequence of performers in the workflow of auxiliary material requisition, including an ad-hoc invocation of an external subscribed workflow, is illustrated. The icons have been arranged so that performers within IB are shown in the left column, while persons working at "Dispensing Inc." are found in the outermost right column. In between these two companies, the respective *gateways* are displayed in the two middle columns. This way, the structure of the *wide area workflow* connecting the two organizations can be analyzed, including all stages between the core workflow systems involved.

The structure of the *wide area workflow* shown in Figure 64 resembles the fundamental pattern of *complete integration of workflow parts (CIWP)*, shown in the lower part of Table 4 (p. 119). This complete integration was achieved by a concatenation of three *external subscribed workflows* on the part of "Dispensing Inc.", as has been discussed in conjunction with Figure 27 (p. 133).

Workflow structures, which have been read in from the *WAGS Tracking* database or other sources, can be stored by the *WAGS Analyzer* in separate files. *Workflow supervisors* and *designers* can thereby analyze the structures of workflow instances, which have been derived from a certain workflow model, at one point in time and save these structures in a file. They will most likely try to improve the workflow model in order to overcome the inefficiencies they have found in the actual processing of workflows. After a certain time, they use the *WAGS Analyzer* again to check the newly processed workflow instances and see whether their changes have actually improved the handling of the processes. To support their work, the *WAGS Analyzer* has the capacity to also load the former structures, which have been stored in the file, and compare the two states. The older version can be "subtracted" from the newer one, so that only the differences between them remain visible. Thus, *workflow supervisors* and *designers* can judge the effects of the measures they have taken.

Another feature supporting the analysis of workflow structures is called *dynamic animation*. It is used to demonstrate the actual flow of workflow documents by showing the routing paths with the help of moving objects. With this option, *workflow supervisors* and *designers* can visually detect recurrent process patterns and bottlenecks.

The *WAGS Analyzer* allows the data on structures of workflows to be exported to spreadsheet tables in Microsoft Excel. There, the data are automatically evaluated and displayed in different chart categories with the help of the so-called *OLE automation* feature. Using this feature, the *WAGS Analyzer* can induce actions to be taken by Microsoft Excel to achieve certain results.

By exporting the data on workflow structures to this spreadsheet software, statistical evaluations and other mathematical operations for the further analysis of workflows can be carried out.

6.2.7 Integration with the Internet and World Wide Web using WAGS WebConnect

With the enormous growth of the Internet and World Wide Web (WWW), a common platform has become available that provides important fundamental building blocks for a facilitated definition of techniques for the implementation and use of workflow systems. Especially in the field of WAWM, where certain formats and specifications for the exchange of workflow related information items are needed, the highly dynamic development of the Internet and WWW has induced a welcome "push" towards WFMSs' interoperability.

To reflect this important development, *WAGS WebConnect* offers several options for accessing and using different parts of the Wide Area GroupFlow System with the help of the Internet and WWW [Kremer 1998], [Temme 1998]. The main functionalities of this integration of WAGS with Internet technologies are:

- publication of *interface specifications* of workflow services using the Web front-end of the *WAGS External Directory*;
- invocation of workflow instances from the WWW;
- exchange of *message objects* with the help of Internet e-mail, HTML-mail or XML;
- participation of internal employees in workflow instances with a Web front-end instead of a "regular" client application;
- registration of organizational elements of external organizations, such as *persons*, *roles*, *workgroups* and *units*;
- inclusion of these external organizational elements in workflow models with the help of so-called "External Tasks".

In the following paragraphs, these points will be further discussed.

Interface specifications of workflow services can be published with the help of the WWW interface of the *WAGS External Directory* for the anonymous market. The option to offer services via the WWW is already used by many organizations. The Web front-end of the *WAGS External Directory* additionally links these offers directly to the respective workflow models, which can be used to instantiate concrete processes for the fulfillment of the incoming requests or orders. As an alternative to the general publication of *interface specifications*, closed user-groups requiring explicit authentication can be set up to limit the number of recipients in the WWW.

Once *interface specifications* have been published, organizations interested in certain offers have two options:

- They can mirror the respective Web pages to their own site in order to have them locally available. Workflow designers can thus make use of *interface specifications* for the building of workflow models in the way described for instance in Figure 45 (p. 196). The interaction of the workflow systems involved is achieved by sending *message objects* during run-time operation. The method of mirroring Web pages from the *WAGS External Directory* to other locations is similar to *master-slave* replication discussed in Section 5.6.1.2 (p. 152).
- Workflow users within an organization can start their Web browser at certain workflow steps to view the workflow services offered in the *WAGS External Directory* or similar structures of other organizations. When they have found an appropriate offer to help them in fulfilling their current task, they directly invoke a workflow instance in the WFMS of another organization. Consequently, they receive an e-mail containing the promised results which they can include in their current workflow folder. This way, users "manually" connect workflow instances in different workflow systems.

The application of the second option does not require major changes to existing systems and allows for a simple interaction of workflow systems.

The exchange of Internet e-mails between workflow systems has already been discussed by many authors (see Sections 4.2.1.2 (p. 78), 4.2.4 (p. 89) and 4.2.5 (p. 95)). Enriching these e-mails with *representation* features and eventually *methods* in the sense of *message objects* has not yet been discussed in these approaches. With the help of the prototypic converters of the *WAGS Gateway*, HTML-mail can be generated instead of Internet e-mail, allowing the sender to embed a *representation* for the recipient. The most powerful method for the encoding of *message objects* within the *WAGS Gateway* is the conversion to XML. *Message objects* in XML can then be transferred with the help of Internet e-mail again.

Employees of an organization can participate in workflow instances with the help of *WAGS WebConnect* (see Figure 65 in comparison with Figure 54, p. 208).

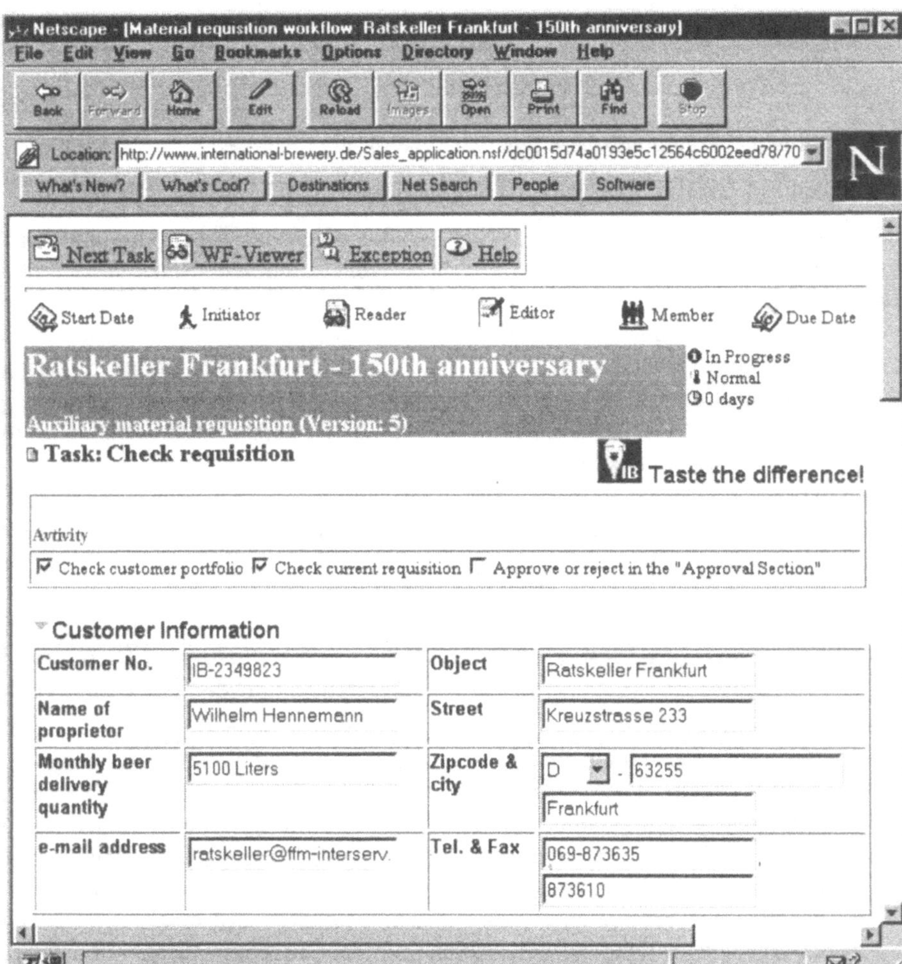

Figure 65: WAGS WebConnect – WWW front-end of the WAGS Engine

Offering a WWW-based front-end to the *WAGS Engine*, users can also work in remote subsidiaries or at home, while still being able to access their workflow system (Figure 65). *WAGS WebConnect* requires users to authenticate and can make use of *SSL (secure socket layer)* to protect the data transferred from undesired access. After users have logged in successfully, they see their individual worklist and can open documents in workflow folders. While processing workflow tasks, performers can locate their current position in the workflow instance by starting the *WAGS Workflow Viewer*. Since this tool has been implemented in Java, it is available in both the Lotus Notes and the WWW front-end.

A further feature is the registration of organizational elements of external companies with the help of *WAGS WebConnect*. After *workflow administrators* have approved registrations and have assigned HTML passwords, *workflow designers* can include *persons*, *roles*, *workgroups* or *units* in other organizations into their workflow models. The element of the workflow meta-model, which is used for the inclusion, is called "External Task" (see Figure 44, p. 193). During run-time operation, the external performers are informed by the *WAGS Engine* with the help of an Internet e-mail that they are asked to process a workflow step in the sender's workflow management system. The e-mail contains a URL address, leading the external performer to the respective Web page, where he can work through the predefined activities and finally complete his task by forwarding the workflow folder to the next workflow step.

"External Tasks" allow for a *remote access* to workflow systems for persons outside of one's own organization. However, this is not really a WAWM feature, since workflow instances are solely executed by one workflow system.

6.3 Further developments

Prototypic software frameworks such as the Wide Area GroupFlow System are never complete. Therefore, the author would like to mention some of the plans and ideas for the further development of the system.

An important part of the concepts for WAWM, which has not yet been implemented in WAGS, are the different elements of the coordination mechanism of *equal partnership* (see Section 5.4.3, p. 134). A major challenge lies in the further refinement of the concepts for *joint modeling* and the subsequent development of software, which would allow *workflow designers* to share drawing areas for the interactive design of workflow models for interoperating workflow systems. To allow the storage of the *interface specifications* needed for this purpose, for instance for elements such as *virtual start nodes* and *synchronization nodes*, the *WAGS External Directory* would have to be extended. Finally, major steps would have to be taken to implement the synchronization of workflow instances during the run-time operation within the *WAGS Engine*.

In the estimation of the author, developing the different features of the coordination mechanism labeled *equal partnership* will require approximately the same amount of time that has been spent to build the WAGS environment up until now.

An interesting project would be to develop *external directories* and *gateways* for other scientific and in particular commercial WFMSs, in order to test the concepts for WAWM described in this book in practical application between heterogeneous workflow management systems.

In addition, the practical application of WAGS itself will help to gain important insights into the advantages and disadvantages of the approach taken. A first step in this direction has been taken by introducing WAGS in a private educational institution, where more than 400 office workers will be included in *wide area workflows*. There is certainly very much to be learned from the feedback of practitioners, who plan models for *wide area workflows* and participate in the actual execution of the derived workflow instances.

An important feature missing in the current version of WAGS is feedback from subscribers of workflow services during the planning of workflow models and the preparation of their execution. At the moment, organizations that have included *external subscribed workflow* elements in their workflow models cannot tell the organizations that have offered the respective *interface specifications* when and at what frequency they plan to make use of the services offered. Therefore, organizations offering workflow services cannot predict the upcoming workflow load, but a reliable forecast would definitely be useful in practical WAWM applications. A feedback cycle informing publishers about the plans of subscribers could be implemented with the help of the *WAGS External Directory*.

Further on, a more detailed coordination of organizations within the *coordination mechanism* called *market* can be achieved by including an optional "workflow preview" into the *interface specifications* offered for external subscribed workflows. Thereby, the subscribing workflow designers could for instance double-click on the icon of the *external subscribed workflow* element and see the structure and other details of the workflow they will invoke during the run-time operation. This would allow for a better adjustment of the two interacting workflow parts in case of closer collaboration. However, the autonomy of the organizations and confidentiality of the internal processing of workflow services would decrease.

Another feature for a closer integration of the invoking and the invoked workflow system would be to make parameters of workflow instances, such as the values of the roles *workflow supervisor* or *initiator*, available to be set from outside. Similar to the invocation of sub-programs, invoking workflow systems could set these parameters during invocation, thereby gaining more influence on the processing of invoked workflow instances in other systems. This feature would for example facilitate the interaction of several WFMSs within a single organization, where the exchange of parameter specifications would not be objected to by participants, seen from the viewpoint of confidentiality. At the moment, *message objects* generated in WAGS only transfer *contents*, not such parameters.

The provision of features for dynamic simulation of workflow models within the *WAGS Modeler* would allow *workflow designers* to detect inefficient structures, such as branches never used, bottlenecks or long queues at certain workflow steps, before actual execution. A dynamic simulation component had already been implemented in the modeling tool of *GroupFlow*. It could be taken as a basis for the development of software simulating *wide area workflows*.

The further development of the *WAGS Workflow Viewer* in the direction of *instance-based variation* of workflow instances in execution would allow for an increased degree of flexibility in WAWM (see also Section 5.5.2, p. 141 and Figure 59, p. 216). Performers can thereby define routing paths within *open team tasks* (see Figure 15, p. 85), where no structures have been predefined by workflow designers. In addition, the further execution of predefined workflows could be influenced with an interactive graphical tool by users who are entitled to do so.

Within the modules for *content management* in the *WAGS Modeler* and the *WAGS Engine*, the mapping patterns of 1:N and M:1 could be implemented in addition to the currently existing 1:1-mapping. Flexibility of *content management* could thus be improved by allowing *workflow designers* and actual *performers* to split or aggregate contents, which will subsequently be transferred from internal workflow documents to *message objects*.

The converters for changing the format of *message objects* in the *WAGS Gateway* can be improved. While the XML converter is of general use and works reliably, the other converters for WfMC-compliant Internet e-mail, HTML-mail and EDIFACT can only be used for very limited purposes of demonstration. Much work will have to be done to make these converters stable and applicable in practical scenarios.

Finally, defining a *message object hierarchy* (see p. 155) for general use would be very important for the practical application of WAWM. For example, it would be beneficial to use XML to specify the document types of the EDIFACT standard in such a hierarchy, thereby making them available to future workflow systems. In addition, other document types with general applicability could in this way be made available to the public. The authors sees the availability of a commonly accepted set of document definitions in a modern format, such as XML, as a major prerequisite for the widespread use of WFMSs' interoperability. This would be an interesting field for standardization by organizations such as the Workflow Management Coalition.

7 Wide Area Workflow Management in practical application

In mid 1996 the author and his research team started doing the case studies, which are described in Chapter 2 and in the following sections. At that time, the management of both companies surveyed was strongly of the opinion that the processes dealt with here should be improved. The wave of *business process reengineering (BPR)* was about at its peak. Project teams had been formed and there was much hope that new information technology would help to remove major inefficiencies soon. In initial meetings, the time frames needed for the implementation of improved procedures was estimated to be around 18 months. It is astonishing that this estimated time frame was the same for both the brewery (IB) and the lighting manufacturer (LLM), since the areas of optimization are of a very different nature.

Now in early 1998 at the time of writing this book, neither of the projects has been finished. Smaller steps have been taken, but major breakthroughs leading to a sound operation of systems for Wide Area Workflow Management have not been achieved. The author would certainly have preferred to present the results of a long–term case study about the use of WAWM systems. What can be done at this stage is to look at the reasons why the implementations took longer than expected and to present the results currently available. In addition, plans for future operation of systems supporting WAWM, as proposed by the author and his team, will be presented to give the reader an impression of how the concepts and practical solutions for Wide Area Workflow Management, as discussed so far, can be applied in practical scenarios.

It is very important to realize that, in both cases, project members, IT managers and top management were only partially aware of the possibilities offered by new information technology that was already available in 1996. Workflow management systems and groupware platforms, such as Lotus Notes, were known to a certain degree, but their potential for redesigning business processes was widely underestimated. On the other hand, the efforts necessary to exploit this potential were even more underestimated. In both cases, the initial attempts to optimize processes were directed at enhancing existing systems to allow for workflow management, thereby trying to avoid costs. These attempts failed in both projects.

The largest part of the work of the author's team was to provide information about the possibilities of workflow management systems on the one hand and groupware platforms on the other. It could be observed that the IT managers in particular listened to the good news, but took a long time to persuade. They often made the point that switching the fundamental platform to achieve improvements would pose enormous problems and incur high costs, which is certainly true. In the course of the projects, they realized that trying to tackle the problems by taking only small steps, based on the existing systems, was also enormously costly but did not lead to the results desired. Additionally, precious time was wasted.

The problems encountered in the projects were mainly caused by a lack of ***awareness*** of the extent of the challenges involved in exchanging paper-based office work for IT-enabled process orientation in and between distributed organizations. In addition, the options that come with technologies such as Wide Area Workflow Management Systems and groupware platforms were not sufficiently recognized.

Now, in 1998, the awareness of the possibilities and limitations of WAWM has been improved by some trends, which have become obvious in recent times:

- Workflow management systems are seen as key enablers for process orientation in offices. Products on the market are more mature than in 1996 and there is more expertise available on the part of users, vendors and consultants.
- Groupware platforms have become a mainstream technology, used by a large percentage of major companies.
- The rapid spread of the Internet and WWW – among other things – has brought the enormous opportunities of interorganizational interaction of information systems to our attention.

As has already been mentioned earlier in this book, these technologies are closely linked to each other. For example, behind interesting offers on WWW pages, there might be WFMSs to take over the job of routing the orders or service requests through an organization. Groupware platforms might form the basis of such workflow systems as well as being used for the generation of the WWW pages.

Now that these technologies have spread, making important platforms for WAWM widely known, one can assume that further projects aimed at the implementation of WAWM systems will proceed faster and will be completed within more cautiously planned project schedules.

In the following sections, results from the case studies introduced in Chapter 2 will be presented together with proposed measures for the implementation of WAWM systems.

7.1 Case study 1: sales activities in an international brewery

An important point in the discussions with members of IB was to convince them that the solutions tested so far, as described in Section 2.1 (p. 10), would not lead to significantly improved procedures. The first attempt at optimization using Penbooks to print out the forms had obviously failed, so there was no need for further explanations here. However, the second approach, using new notebooks and updated software, was persistently defended by IB's IT managers. As they were already under pressure due to the enormous costs of the first attempt, which led to no improvements, it was very difficult for them to admit that the second attempt might also have been sub-optimal in many respects.

In addition, there was an ongoing conflict between the IT department and the sales department concerning the best way to optimize the procedure for auxiliary material support. Proposals from either side were mostly rejected – more for political than for objective reasons. The sales department submitted the following main arguments for a completely new solution:

- The current software was not user friendly enough.
- Sales persons should be able to present auxiliary material via a multimedia-based catalogue, to give them a competitive advantage over other breweries.
- Processing times should be reduced drastically; this had not been achieved with the current software in the pilot phase. The main reason for this was that there was no integration of the incoming e-mails from sales representatives (SRs) with the existing software systems in the head office.

The IT department basically agreed, but made the following critical points:

- Integration of incoming data from SRs with the existing midrange-based warehouse and accounting system was given top priority. IT managers wanted to develop their own solution for a batch-oriented import of incoming e-mails from SRs.
- IT managers were concerned about high costs and level of effort needed for the implementation of completely new software, such as a workflow management system.

A critical point in the discussions was the question of whether the SRs, who were still skeptical about the use of notebooks and software systems in general, would accept innovation. The managers of both departments agreed that convincing the SRs would be a main prerequisite for the success of the entire project.

For these reasons, the first measure that members of the author's team undertook was to implement a prototypic sales information system based on Lotus Notes [Ising 1997]. It included a prototypic database of available material as well as a small workflow application with two forms for the requisition of auxiliary material support. Special attention was given to the user interface, for instance by making the selection of material from the database as simple as possible. The prototype was demonstrated to managers and members of the IT as well as the sales department, including SRs and RSMs.

With this prototype, the following points could be proved:

- SRs and RSMs were impressed by how easy the electronic forms in the groupware platform could be used. The vision of getting rid of extensive paperwork by using a flexible, easy to handle new tool for sales optimization suddenly seemed close at hand. This perspective made SRs optimistic about the use of notebooks for the first time.

- The numerous paper-based forms could be replaced by one single, flexible electronic form.
- The enormous potential of replication technology could be demonstrated by showing that the material database as well as the requisitions could be updated by SRs at any time, at least in the mornings before leaving home and in the evenings after coming home.
- Transparency of the whole procedure was also easy to achieve with replication technology. For instance, information for the initiating SR on the status of requisitions was easily available. Each SR would have a complete record with all of his requisitions currently being processed, including information on acceptance or rejection, delivery status etc.
- A solution for integrating Lotus Notes databases with the midrange warehouse and accounting system (based on AS/400) was available and would not cause major costs and problems. IT managers were especially positive about the fact that the existing material data could be exported to Lotus Notes databases and that data from requisitions could be imported.

This demonstration caused a long phase of discussion which finally led to the decision on the part of IB's management to drop the proprietary software in pilot use. Further plans for the implementation of sales information software were postponed until the installation of a new warehouse and accounting system, which is supposed to replace the current solution, is completed. The plans are to re-launch the project to streamline the material support requisition processing in early 1999.

The author and his team have proposed a solution for Wide Area Workflow Management in the field of auxiliary material support at IB, based on the WAGS environment, which will be introduced briefly in the following pages [Schniedermann 1998].

The former process for auxiliary material support requisition, as described in Figure 2 (p. 13), was completely revised as a first measure. The new process is shown in Figure 66 (p. 237) in form of a workflow model designed with the *WAGS Modeler*. Workflow steps are illustrated by different icons in Figure 66, while performers are indicated at the right side, beginning with an "M:", standing for *member*. The description of the task to be performed starts with an "N:" for *name*.

The initiating SR begins the workflow by filling out an electronic requisition form (see Figure 67, p. 238, showing a fictitious workflow instance of an auxiliary material support requisition for "Ratskeller Frankfurt"). The SR is given as much support as possible to provide a variety of information by a database containing existing data about the respective customer. For example, when the customer number is typed in, all the available information on this customer is automatically filled out. The relevant fields can still be edited to include changes about the customer's address for example. Changes in these fields are marked as such and can thus be automatically updated in the head office's database.

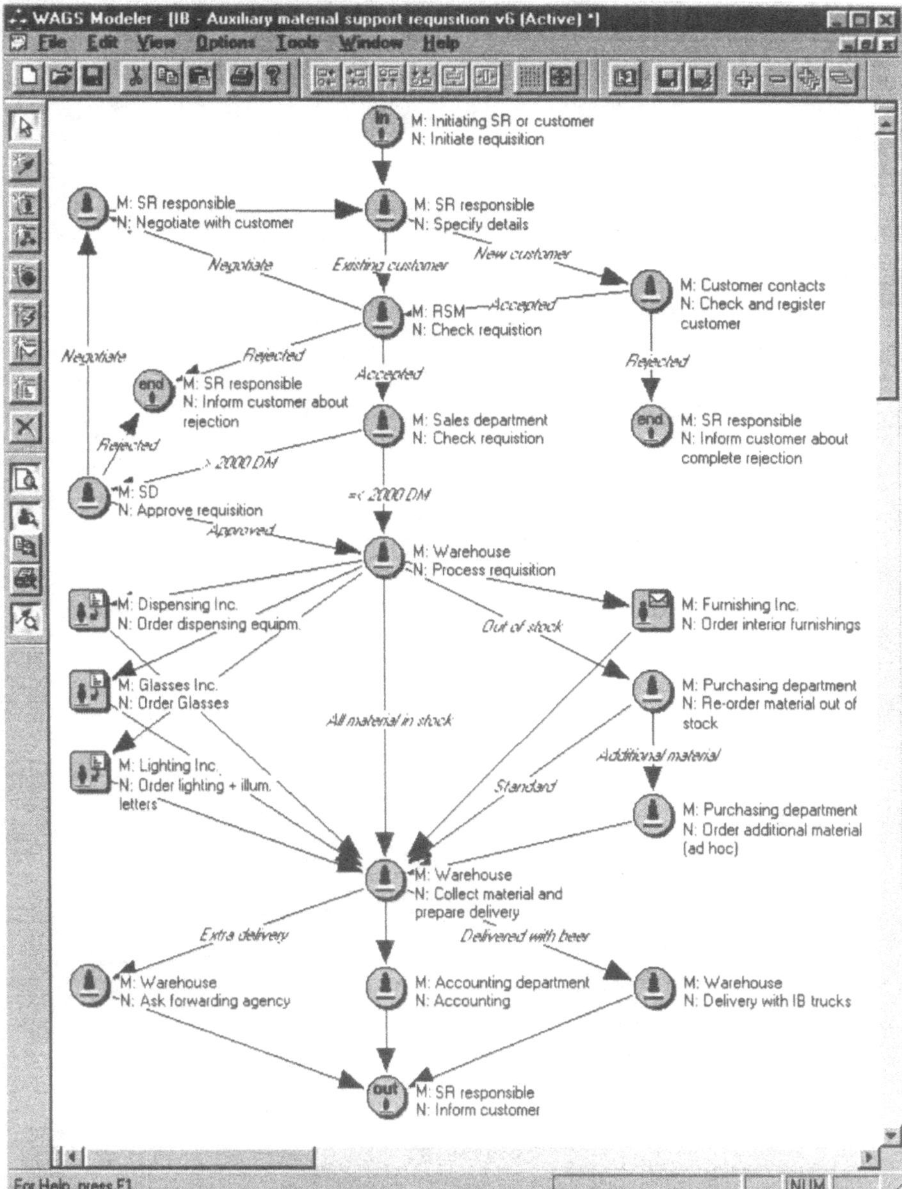

Figure 66: Process of auxiliary material support requisition at IB, developed in WAGS Modeler. Different WAWM elements are included.

An important step towards optimization is to check and register new customers at the beginning of the process (upper right branch in Figure 66). The ensuing processing of customers' requisitions which can later be rejected by the sales department, due for instance to a low beer consumption or lack of trustworthiness on the part of the customer, is therefore avoided. If customers are rejected, the workflow ends after informing the initiating SR about the complete rejection, who then passes this information on to the respective customer.

Figure 67: Initiation of a workflow instance for a fictitious material support requisition for the "Ratskeller Frankfurt", as shown in the WAGS Engine. Material is selected from a material database.

The RSM responsible next checks the requisition for newly accepted and existing customers. He can see all information about the requisition such as total amount of the current request, material support granted in the last 12 months etc. (see Figure 68).

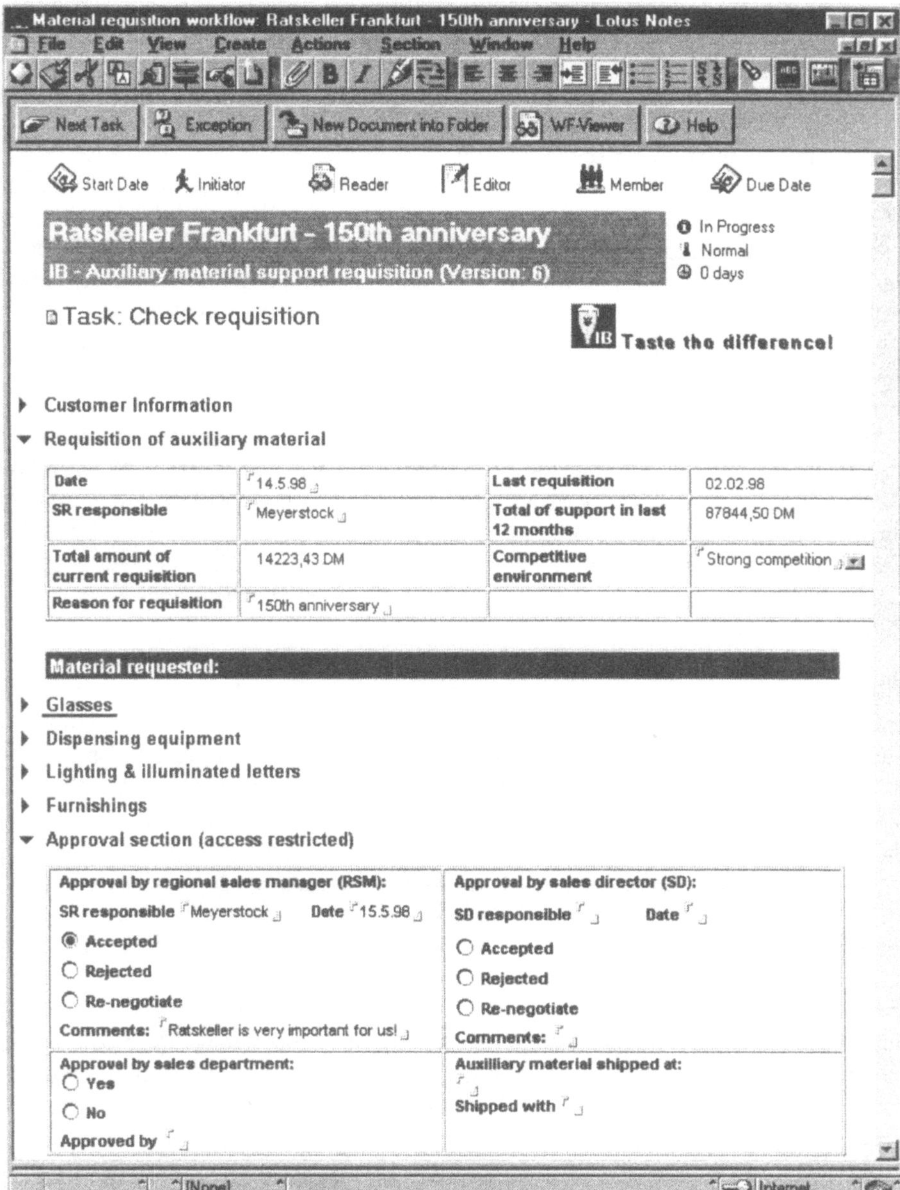

Figure 68: Approval of material support requisition by regional sales manager (RSM) shown in the WAGS Engine (fictitious example)

Based on the information provided, the RSM can then decide to accept or reject the requisition or to give it back to the initiating SR in order to re-negotiate with the customer about the amount of material requested, for example (see the lower part of Figure 68, p. 239). In the case of re-negotiation, the workflow enters a loop shown in the upper left side of Figure 66 (p. 237).

If the RSM accepts the requisition, it is passed on to the sales department of the head office for a further check. If the amount of the requisition is above 2,000 German marks, then the sales director responsible (SD) is included into the workflow. As for the RSM, he has the option to reject the requisition, to accept it or to give it back to the initiating SR for re-negotiation.

If the RSM or the SD reject the requisition, it is also given back to the initiating SR so he can inform the customer.

If the requisition is approved by the RSM and, if necessary, by the SD, it is passed on to the warehouse in order to collect the material requested. In many cases, not all the material is in stock. The warehouse clerk than can select one or more of the parallel branches offered, for instance to let the purchasing department re-order material which is out of stock or to invoke *external subscribed workflows* with external suppliers (middle part of Figure 66, p. 237).

Different types of external processes have been included in the workflow model for IB. In the middle of Figure 66 to the left, three *external subscribed workflow* ($WORKFLOW_{SUB,WAW}$) elements have been included to make orders with suppliers for dispensing equipment, glasses and lighting. The names of these suppliers have been disguised. These *external subscribed workflows* correspond with services offered by these suppliers listed in the *external directory* of IB, which is shown in Figure 69 (p. 241).

In the middle of Figure 66 to the right, an *ordered subworkflow* ($SUBWORKFLOW_{DEC,WAW}$) element has been included to order custom-built furnishings from one of IB's contractors. Since this contractor works solely for IB, it is preferable to include his services in the form of a *subworkflow* in contrast to independently published workflow offers of other suppliers. The workflow interaction with the furnishing contractor is also coordinated with the help of IB's *external directory* (see the lower part of the following Figure 69).

After all material has been taken from stock or has arrived from external suppliers, it is collected and packaged in the warehouse. A dispatcher now decides whether the material is delivered by IB trucks or if a forwarding agency is to be included. In some cases, both options might be reasonable, so this is not an exclusive *split* operation. The folder of electronic documents collected so far is sent to the accounting department, and after a short routine check there, the customer is informed that the material he requested is underway. The information to the customer can be sent as a paper-based letter or via e-mail. Both messages are prepared by the workflow system.

In the workflow model in Figure 66 (p. 237) the standard procedure is represented by the straight line of arrows in the middle. Alternatives and exceptions are located on the left and right, so that managers, workflow designers and workflow users have as few problems as possible in understanding the model.

Documents in the workflow internal to IB are forwarded by replicating the underlying Lotus Notes databases. Interaction with the external suppliers is realized with the help of *message objects* exchanged between the workflow engines using *gateways*.

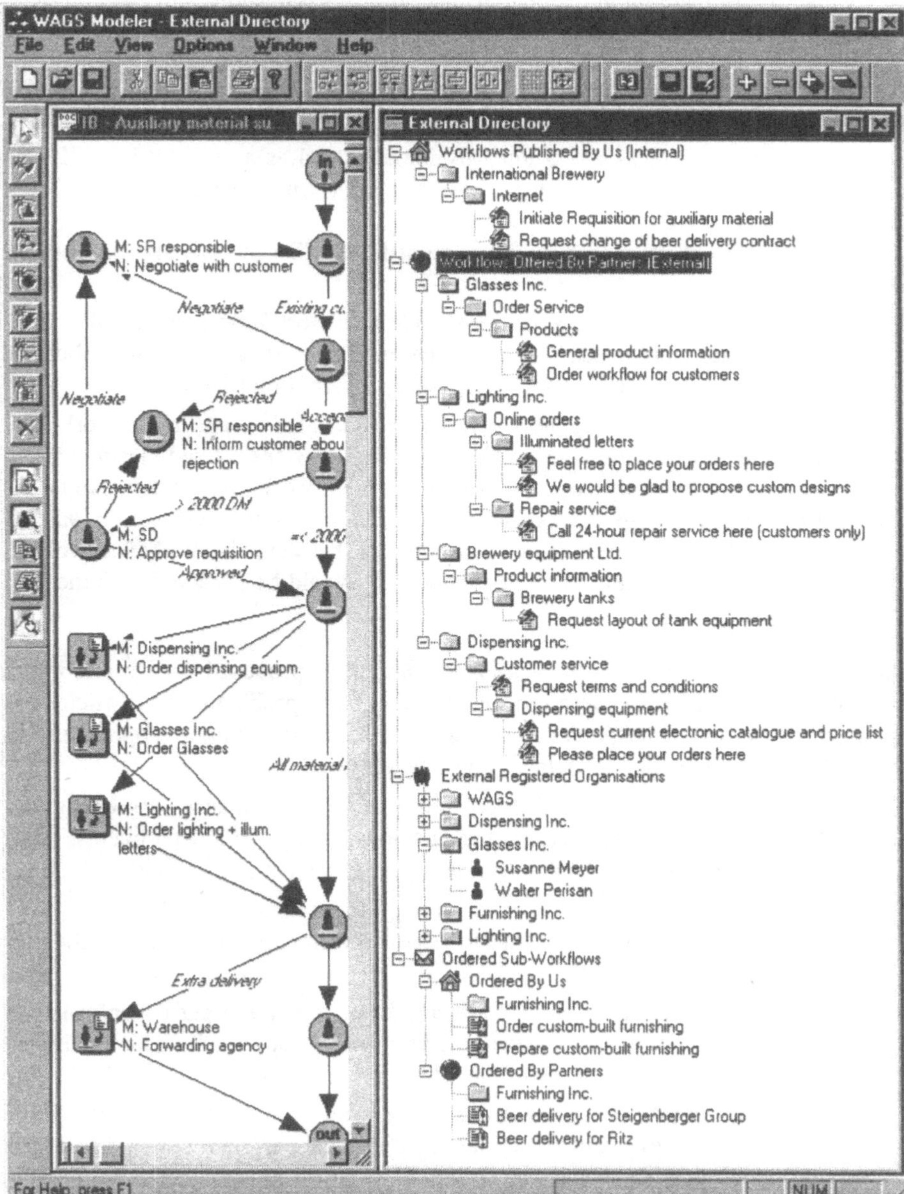

Figure 69: External directory of IB, showing published workflows by IB and suppliers

Internal workflow information, which is stored in Lotus Notes documents, can be exchanged with IB's old and new warehouse and accounting systems with the help of commercial interface software, so that media breaks in the workflow are minimized. Warehouse and accounting data can thus be kept up-to-date, allowing SRs to check the availability of material in the central warehouse by replicating the material database onto the hard disk of their notebooks.

Suppliers can also make use of workflow engines other than WAGS. Since they are included in IB's workflow models with the help of *external subscribed workflow* and *ordered subworkflow* elements, *message objects* are used for interaction purposes. With the help of a *WAGS gateway* implemented as a prototype for IB, the suppliers could receive and send these *message objects* in formats other than Lotus Notes.

Based on the workflow architecture proposed here, IB can make use of WAWM in two phases:

- In a first phase, intraorganizational wide area workflows between SRs, local subsidiaries and the head office can be implemented based on the replication technology of the underlying groupware platform Lotus Notes.
- In a second phase, suppliers can also be included in electronic workflows with the help of externally invoked workflow services offered via an *external directory*. The *interface specifications* for these workflow services can be defined according to *market-oriented* or *hierarchical coordination mechanisms*. The actual exchange of information between the WFMSs involved, which are most likely to be heterogeneous, would be achieved with the help of *message objects*.

The implementation of a WAWM-oriented solution as proposed by the author and his team would help IB to overcome many of the major problems and inefficiencies encountered in the former procedure of handling auxiliary material support requisitions. The following major advantages could be achieved:

- Significant acceleration of processing by abolishing unnecessary transportation times, optimized routing of requisitions through IB's departments, faster decision-making due to the availability of complete information and the removal of media breaks.
- Transparency of processes through status information and confirmations for all parties involved in the workflow.
- Introduction of user-friendly software, fewer forms and current information on auxiliary material and prices, leading to less paperwork and a significant increase in the productivity of the sales representatives.
- Reduction of processing times due to the inclusion of suppliers in electronic workflows. By evaluating material ordered in the past, more precise forecasts of upcoming demand for material could be given to suppliers. Additionally, by evaluating all initiated requisitions on a daily basis, suppliers could be informed about anticipated ordering volumes for the near future. Orders could also be bundled to reduce unnecessary transactions.

Interface specifications for the workflow model shown in Figure 66 (p. 237) have been published in the *WAGS External Directory* implemented as a prototype for IB.

This publication can be recognized with the help of the IN- and OUT-nodes in Figure 66 (p. 237) and the related entry in the *external directory manager* of the *WAGS Modeler* (see the upper right part of Figure 69, p. 241).

The publication of *interface specifications* – connected to a customer-oriented start form on the WWW – would allow IB's customers to initiate auxiliary material support requisitions themselves via the WWW, so that they can provide initial information to their SR. The SR can then complete the form in the next step, clarify open points with the customer and forward the workflow folder to the RSM responsible, according to the underlying workflow model.

7.2 Case study 2: collaboration between a large lighting manufacturer and suppliers

At LLM, an important strategic decision regarding *additional goods* supply was to decentralize the ordering process for the majority of their products, which were ordered centrally until then. Now, the individual production sites are fully responsible for ordering, taking control of goods received, warehousing, accounting and payment for most of the *additional goods.* Documents no longer need to be sent back and forth to the head office. In addition, the majority of the low-cost *additional goods* (e.g. erasers, pencils etc.) no longer need to be added to the inventory, neither in the head office nor in the production sites. These low-cost goods are now bought and used by the individual profit centers at their own discretion and are paid for from their own budgets. Through these measures, ordering costs have been reduced drastically, outweighing by far the loss of previous bulk order discounts.

Central ordering was maintained in all production sites in Germany for more important and expensive additional goods, such as drills or milling heads for the manufacturing sector, but the number of suppliers was drastically reduced. One company, which offers all of the necessary tools and has already implemented electronic ordering based on electronic catalogues, was chosen as the main supplier. The electronic ordering system offered by this company was linked to the new integrated business software system allowing the supply management in this field to be significantly streamlined. Only those tools that cannot be ordered via this channel are still treated manually with paper-based orders sent by mail. The new integrated business software system improved the internal management of both mail-based and electronically transmitted orders. Major inefficiencies in the former process, such as the need for printing lists and re-typing of values for data transfer between systems etc., have been removed (see Section 2.2, p. 17) by integrating warehouse, ordering and accounting transactions.

In the field of the PC acquisition procedure, which serves as a reference workflow for this case study, a strategic decision by the top management of LLM's IT department changed the situation fundamentally. Previously, numerous suppliers had delivered PCs to LLM's head office and different production sites. Now one supplier – which will be called *PC Factory* - was chosen to take over the entire PC delivery business with LLM in Germany. Various other functions such as PC maintenance, software installation and initial training of users were also outsourced to PC Factory.

Compared to the former situation, where numerous vendors with different systems were supposed to be integrated in an interorganizational workflow network, the implementation of a WAWM system was made much easier by the decision to include only one supplier.

The author and his team had been involved in the project up to this point. Based on the decision of LLM's top management to choose Lotus Notes as a strategic platform in early 1997, the author and his team had developed a prototypic Notes-based application to illustrate different possibilities for streamlining the process of PC ordering with external suppliers [Marr 1997]. Now that only one supplier was left, the development of such a workflow application was made much easier.

By early 1998, a task force at LLM had implemented a Lotus Notes-based application to handle maintenance requests for PCs and orders for additional equipment. With this application, called *PC service*, users in the head office and production sites in Germany can:

- request repair services for PCs, monitors, printers etc.;
- order new hardware parts, such as CD-ROM drives etc.;
- request installation of new standard software such as wordprocessor and spreadsheet applications;
- book software training courses.

All orders and requests issued this way are directly taken over by PC Factory and are mostly fulfilled on the same or the next day. Several employees of PC Factory are present at each of LLM's sites to be directly available for users during working hours. The transfer of requests and orders in the *PC service* database between the different locations of LLM and PC Factory is achieved through replication between the Lotus Domino servers involved. Employees of PC Factory can also access the *PC service* database at the LLM location they are currently working at, for example to check for new jobs or to set the status orders and requests that they have processed to "completed".

To order PCs, a paper-based form that helps users to find the appropriate configuration for a PC is still used. The IT department regularly provides an updated file for downloading, which can be used to print out this form. After users have manually filled out the form, the responsible group or department manager has to approve the purchase. The form is then forwarded via fax from all German locations to the purchasing department of the head office, where orders are collected in paper-based lists and then handed over to PC Factory.

In the following paragraphs, a solution for the handling of PC orders with WAWM technology – as proposed by the author and his team – is presented based on the Wide Area GroupFlow System.

Figure 70 (p. 245) shows the workflow model of the revised ordering process. All employees at LLM, who want to order a PC, can start a workflow instance derived from this model via the Lotus Notes database "PC ordering and support", which is based on the *WAGS Application* database. The initiator will see the first form where he enters information about his person and position as well as details of the PC he wants to order (Figure 71, p. 246).

As a result of discussions with members of LLM about the inefficiencies of the previous PC ordering procedure, a "PC coordinator" was introduced for each department. This person in most cases will be a member of the IT department who is specially assigned to coordinate the purchase, installation, upgrading and maintenance of the PC equipment within a certain area of LLM. This new function is based on the experience that neither the employees nor the management of a department is usually capable of selecting the appropriate PC equipment for a certain job. Furthermore, through this coordination function the re-use of PCs and other hardware is facilitated.

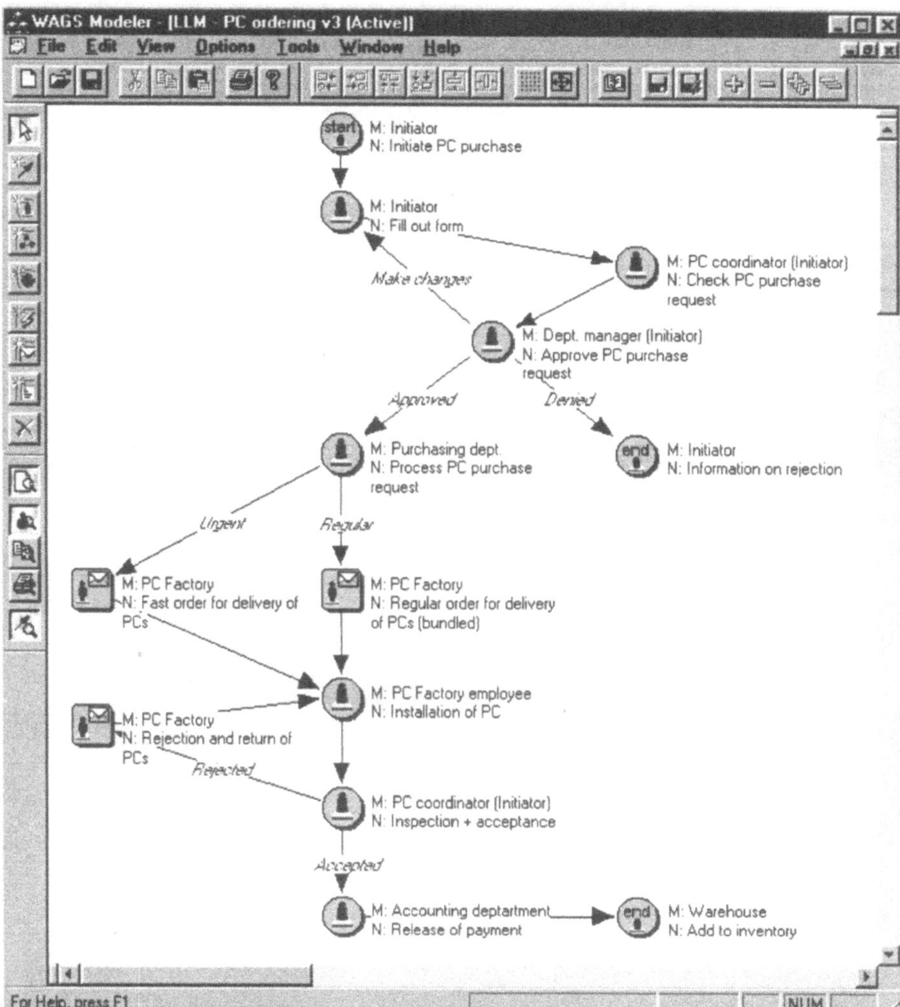

Figure 70: Process of PC ordering at LLM, developed in WAGS Modeler. Subworkflows at PC Factory are included for interorganizational WAWM

After the initiator of a PC ordering process has filled out the initial form, the PC coordinator responsible checks the purchase request, to see whether the equipment requested is suitable or whether existing hardware can be re-used. The PC coordinator can propose changes to the request, recommend the buying of further equipment such as printers to complete the equipment and render it suitable for the job, or discuss with the initiator taking a smaller version of the proposed PC configurations to save on costs.

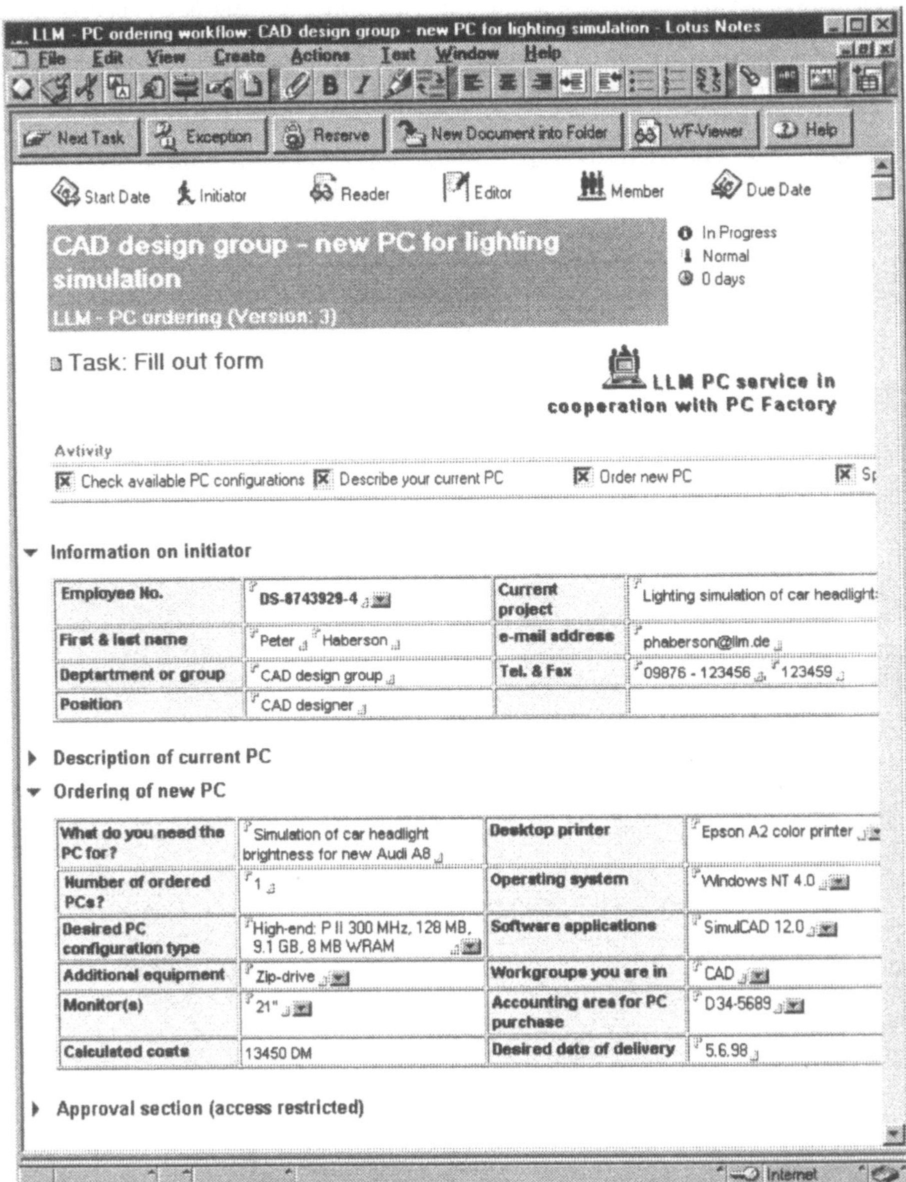

Figure 71: Form for ordering of PCs at LLM - shown in WAGS Engine

After the PC coordinator has finished his work, the workflow folder is routed to the head of the department in which the initiator works.

Both the PC coordinator and the head of department responsible for checking the PC purchase request are determined with the help of so-called *conditional roles*. The notation for this kind of role is "PC coordinator (Initiator)" or "Dept. manager (Initiator)", indicating that the actual persons assigned to these roles are found depending on the value of the variable "Initiator". When starting a workflow instance to order a PC, the variable "Initiator" is set by the workflow system based on the identification of the person who has logged in.

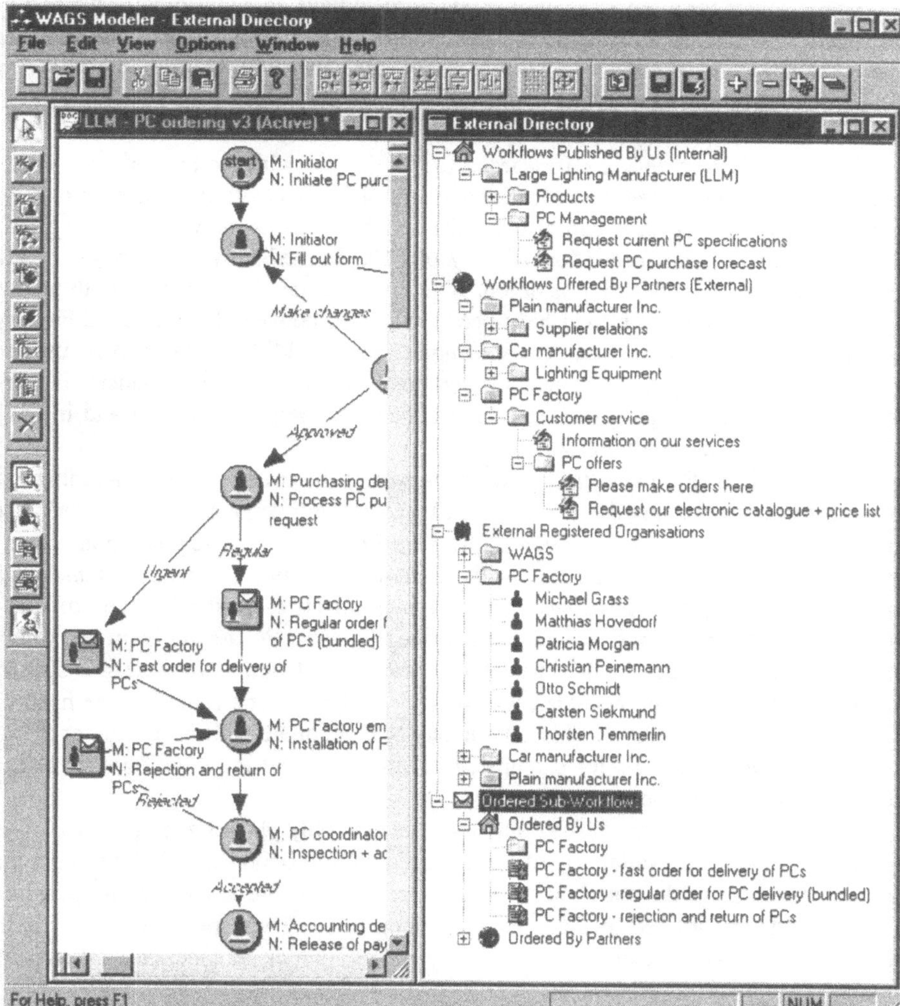

Figure 72: External directory of LLM – showing examples of subworkflows ordered by LLM from PC Factory

The head of department now has the opportunity to accept the request, to reject it or to give it back to the initiator with the provision to change the equipment proposed by the initiator.

If the head of department has approved the PC ordering request, it is then forwarded to the purchasing department. All employees of the group responsible for ordering the PCs see the workflow task in their worklist until one of them claims the workflow folder and assumes the job of processing the respective order.

The employee in the purchasing department, who is now responsible for the job, first checks whether it is an urgent or a regular order. The latter are collected in an electronic folder for a few days until enough orders have come in to be forwarded to PC Factory. Members PC Factory's sales group can look at this electronic folder at the purchasing department of LLM to see how many PCs will be ordered in the near future. This is achieved by LLM publishing a workflow *interface specification* to PC Factory (see the upper right part of Figure 72, p. 247).

Regular orders of PCs are forwarded to PC Factory with the help of an *ordered subworkflow* termed "Regular order for delivery of PCs (bundled)". The employee in the purchasing department can also invoke a different *ordered subworkflow* at PC Factory – called "Fast order for delivery of PCs" immediately after arrival of the ordering request, if processing is urgent. The *interface specifications* for both urgent and regular PC order workflows have been exchanged between LLM and PC Factory using a *WAGS External Directory* (Figure 72, p. 247). LLM makes use of $\text{SUBWORKFLOW}_{\text{DEC,WAW}}$ elements based on the coordination mechanism of *hierarchy*. This is appropriate since LLM is PC Factory's largest customer and in turn, PC Factory is LLM's only PC supplier.

On the side of PC Factory, incoming *message objects* from LLM containing PC ordering information invoke workflow instances of the respective order workflow models. Figure 73 shows an example of a workflow model for regular (non-urgent) PC orders at PC Factory, starting with an *IN*-node, where the incoming *message object* is checked by an employee of the sales group. If the order is based on standard prices and conditions, it is forwarded directly to the PC assembly group, which includes the new order in the current PC assembly planning. If there are special prices and conditions in the order, the workflow folder is first routed to the head of the sales group for approval. This person may also negotiate with the customer (here: LLM), via telephone calls for example, to change some of the conditions or prices sent in the *message object*.

After the assembly group has completed the assembly planning, employees in the warehouse check the availability of the parts required to build the PCs. They take the parts in stock from the warehouse and forward them to the assembly group, while missing parts are ordered by the purchasing department. They are shipped directly to the assembly group so that production can begin as soon as all necessary parts are in place.

Parallel to the collection of the necessary parts, the PC assembly group calculates the costs in close cooperation with the purchasing department and the warehouse, supported by the integrated business software making all necessary data available. Cost calculation can only be finalized after all missing parts have been ordered and prices of these parts are thus known.

For the predefined PC configurations offered by PC Factory to LLM, which are built according to LLM's specifications, cost calculation is done in advance. PC Factory endeavors to have all necessary parts for these PCs in stock, based on the PC purchase forecast that can be requested from LLM. In this case, the step of cost calculation in the workflow of PC ordering only serves to check for exceptions that would require actions to be taken by the head of the sales group, who is informed about the results of the cost calculation in the next step. Since prices for standard models for LLM have been negotiated in advance, it is his responsibility to keep costs within range in order to achieve profit.

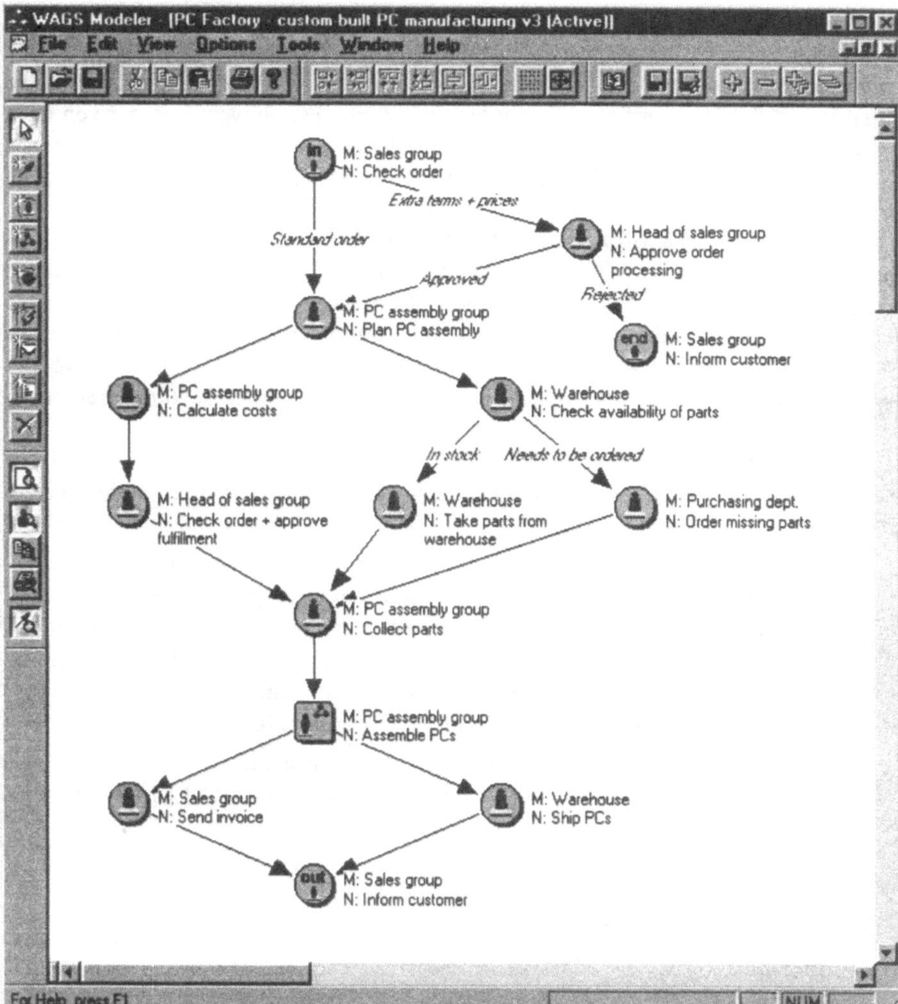

Figure 73: Workflow model of subworkflow ordered by LLM: fulfillment of regular orders for PC delivery at PC Factory, shown in WAGS Modeler

After all parts are available and the head of the sales group has approved the fulfillment of the order, the PC assembly group starts production. The relevant workflow steps have been aggregated in an *internal cluster* in Figure 73 (p. 249) to provide a clear arrangement.

Upon completion of the PC assembly, the sales group prepares and sends off an invoice while the warehouse ships the PCs to the customer. Finally, a *message object* is sent back to LLM's purchasing department confirming the delivery of the PCs ordered and at the same time transmitting the invoice prepared by the sales group.

Now the workflow instance for ordering PCs at LLM (see Figure 70, p. 245) can continue. An employee of PC Factory, who is present at the respective site of LLM, installs the PC at the workplace of the employee who had initiated the order. In the next step, LLM's PC coordinator checks the PC delivered – sometimes supported by the initiator – and checks to see if the related order and invoice are in line with the actual PC. If the PC coordinator is not happy with the PC delivered, it is given back to PC Factory and a "rejection and return" subworkflow is invoked at PC Factory. As a result, a new or updated PC is delivered to LLM and installed by an employee of PC Factory.

After the PC coordinator has checked the PC and approved it to be correct and working properly, the workflow folder is forwarded to the accounting department to release payment of the invoice. There, results from the workflow are also transferred to the integrated business software via a defined interface in order to keep workflow system and business software synchronized. The last step of the workflow is to add the new PC to the inventory, after which the workflow folder is transferred to an archive.

With the help of the proposed WAWM solution for PC ordering between LLM and PC Factory, the following inefficiencies could be removed from the current procedure:

- The extensive handling of exceptions – due to deviations between order, invoice and PC delivered – would be minimized through better specification of orders, quality control of goods received by an expert and the simplification of overseeing the process of ordering, issuing an invoice and checking the actual equipment. The exceptions which remain could be handled by the exception features of the underlying workflow system (here: WAGS).
- Processing time would be drastically reduced through the removal of media breaks and an optimized interaction of workflows between LLM and its supplier.
- Initiators can check the status of their order at any time with the help of the monitoring features of the workflow system.
- The supplier would receive order forecasts at the earliest point in time possible.

Since all employees of LLM and PC Factory make use of the same groupware platform, the workflow management system for internal and wide area workflows could be easily integrated into their everyday working environment. Additional costs for WAWM would be low compared to separate systems.

The handling of PC orders does not differ between employees in the head office and those in the production sites. Workflow folders initiated in the production sites would be replicated to the head office's purchasing department after approval by the relevant head of department. After delivery of the PC to the initiator, the workflow would proceed at the site where it was initiated.

The sending of *message objects* between LLM and PC Factory would be handled by *gateways*, so that internal distribution to the relevant locations would be transparent for both parties.

In the next chapter, the author will draw conclusions from the concepts and solutions for WAWM described up until here and the experiences made in the case studies.

8 Conclusions and outlook

Conclusions

It has already been mentioned in the introduction to this book that the concepts and solutions for WAWM presented must be positioned in a rather early stage of the general lifecycle, which all technologies run through. The thoughts expressed in this book are the outcome of a 3 year research and development project on possible concepts and solutions for a flexible interaction of workflow management systems in order to efficiently support business processes in widely distributed environments. As such, these thoughts are a contribution to a discussion on possible ways to network widely dispersed offices in an increasingly information-driven world. The author would appreciate feedback and criticism on the findings and propositions expressed in this book.

In order to distinguish the various challenges that arise when moving from *local workflow management* to *WAWM*, the author and his team have found it helpful to look at the topic from different *perspectives* (see Section 1.3, p. 5) and to identify different *levels* of WAWM (see Figure 10, p. 56). Awareness of the importance of the 4th level, describing *strategic* and *organizational* settings and decisions, leads to recognition of the necessity of having multiple options for planning and executing *wide area workflows*. This recognition has encouraged the author and his team to be innovative in finding largely new approaches and thus going beyond what is offered in existing literature on WAWM and currently available commercial WFMSs.

The author adheres to the principal notion that solutions for the real world need to be balanced at different positions between the extremes, which can be traced back to Aristotle or the Eastern Asian philosophy of Ying and Yang. This has kept him from looking for the panacea solution. On the contrary, it was the author's initial approach to define a *toolbox* of different possible options for the realization of WAWM, which can be applied in adaptation to the organizational circumstances of concrete scenarios. This *toolbox* is described in the form of the *continuum of coordination mechanisms for WAWM*, which is shown in Figure 29 (p. 137).

An important step hereby was to realize that fundamental *interaction patterns* for distributed workflow parts, as described in Table 4 (p. 119), are *neutral* with regard to the organizational settings that accompany WAWM. Only in combination with coordination strategies, such as *hierarchy*, *equal partnership* and *market*, do they become applicable in real-world settings.

All concepts and solutions described in this book are based on the following empirical observations, which also reflect the principal idea of *multiple* balanced positions:

- In the reality of intra- and interorganizational cooperation, one finds a variety of *power relationships* between the participants, ranging from strong dependencies to far-reaching autonomy (see Figure 20, p. 115), all of which have to be reflected by appropriate technical measures for Wide Area Workflow Management.
- A second scale that largely influences the actual implementation of systems for WAWM spans the different requirements for *automation & structure* and *user support & flexibility* (see Section 5.1, p. 104). In order to make both local workflow management and WAWM applicable to the wide range of different *forms of office work* (see Table 2, p. 54), both paradigms and especially the forms in-between them have to be respected and put to practice.

It can be observed that the majority of scientific authors tend to propose concepts and prototypic systems for the support of *local* and *wide area workflows,* which are based on the paradigms of *centralized, hierarchical coordination* and *automation & structure*. The same is largely true of commercial WFMSs. Further on, none of the scientific or commercial approaches known to the author explicitly reflects the requirements of different *strategic* and *organizational* settings, as described in the 4th level of Figure 10 (p. 56).

Since the author assumes that this might be part of the reason why the use of workflow systems, especially those for WAWM, has not yet become wide-spread in organizations, he has also discussed and partly emphasized concepts and solutions on the other side of the two scales mentioned above – more oriented towards *autonomy* of the participants and *user support & flexibility*. However, only those systems for Wide Area Workflow Management which fully support a wide range of options on both of these scales can be considered adequate for the realization of *process orientation* in globally networked offices.

It is reasonable that the first and second generations of WFMSs (see Figure 11, p. 57) have concentrated on *local* workflows and mainly support the paradigm of *automation & structure*, since these are the areas where the largest initial gains in efficiency can be expected. Nevertheless, the third generation will have to provide convincing solutions to the challenges of *flexible WAWM supporting different degrees of autonomy* of the participants in order to keep up with the trends of *globalization* as well as intra- and interorganizational *process orientation*. In addition, it must be recognized that predefined as well as ad-hoc procedures need to be equally supported.

In this respect, the specifications for WFMSs' interoperability issued by the Workflow Management Coalition (WfMC, see Section 4.2.1.2, p. 78) cannot yet be considered sufficient to achieve this goal. They are only aimed at the definition of structured workflow management with predefined workflow models and adhere to the paradigm of *main processes*, calling and controlling *sub-processes* in a strictly hierarchical manner. Prior to the invocation of remote workflow systems, detailed *process definitions* have to be exchanged between the participants, thereby forcing them to reveal details of internal office procedures, which might be highly sensitive. In the judgement of the author, this approach is only applicable in strictly hierarchical settings, which are mainly found in *intra*organizational scenarios. Based on the empirical studies of the author, it cannot be assumed that this style of WFMSs' interoperation would be accepted by a large percentage of legally independent organizations for the interaction of their office workers.

The WfMC Interface 4 specifications have been available since 1996 and have since then been implemented in several commercial WFMSs for demonstration purposes. Despite this availability, there are no reports of serious practical applications of the related interoperability features.

To overemphasize things, the WfMC has re-implemented EDI technology for workflow systems and therefore users of Interface 4 specifications might experience the same effects as can be observed with many EDI applications (see Section 3.4.1, p. 59). Research has shown that EDI is often used in cases where large companies can force their suppliers to implement such systems. Furthermore, it causes considerable dependencies between the participants. This leads to high transition costs when suppliers or customers are changed and therefore hinders the fluctuation needed for the optimal functioning of market-oriented systems.

To avoid these effects, the author proposes the use of *coordination directories* for the purpose of connecting distributed workflow parts (see Section 5.6.1, p. 145). By making a strict division between externally available *interface specifications*, which allow for reliable interaction between workflow systems, and the internal information about the actual processing, the *autonomy* and *flexibility* of the participants can be preserved. This fundamental principle is also used within the CORBA specification of the OMG (see Section 3.4.3, p. 64) to make the interaction of objects *transparent*, meaning that the sender of a request does not need to know where the actual service that he calls up will be performed. Similarly, companies can let their workflow systems interact without needing to know – and maybe not even being allowed to know – details about the internal processing of anything more than their own office procedures.

Basically, this is not new: when companies send paper-based orders to their suppliers, it is not common for these suppliers to first send detailed specifications of how they will handle the orders. Why should this be necessary within WFMSs-based cooperation?

Further elements missing in the WfMC specifications are concepts for the distributed planning of *wide area workflows*. Since it is one of the essential paradigms of workflow management to plan office procedures as thoroughly possible and to the extent that is reasonable from the perspective of coordination costs (see Table 5, p. 139), this approach should also be feasible for WAWM. Some of the scientific prototypes (*Workonnector, Phanta Rhei, FUNSOFT Nets*) and commercial WFMSs provide methods for the hierarchical modeling of *wide area workflows* according to the paradigm of *main processes* and *sub-processes* (see Sections 4.2.4, 4.2.5 and 4.3, starting from p. 89).

In order to reflect the different possible *power relationships* between the participants in a WAWM scenario, the author has proposed mechanisms for *centralized*, *participative, joint* and *de-centralized* modeling of *wide area workflows* (see Section 5.4, p. 125). Organizations can therefore choose which mechanism is most appropriate for each particular situation. By integrating the *interface specifications* of all of these modeling approaches in the structure of one *coordination directory*, organizations can apply different *planning mechanisms* within a single workflow system for WAWM. This allows them to switch flexibly between different cooperative modes according to actual needs.

In addition to considering the possibility of completely predefining *wide area workflows* during the build-time, the author discusses various methods of making and keeping the planning and the execution of WAWM as flexible as possible in order to adapt to unforeseeable and unforeseen situations as well (see Section 5.5, p. 139). This way, both the paradigms of *automation & structure* and *user support & flexibility* can be applied in WAWM.

A further building block which allows for high *flexibility* and adequate *user support* in WAWM are *message objects*, which can transfer structured *data*, *contextual information*, *representation* features and *methods* (see Section 5.6.2, p. 153). With the help of *document types* that are exchanged using *coordination directories*, these *message objects* can be specified according to international standards such as EDIFACT as well as on the basis of individually negotiated structures and representations. Hence, *message objects* are an essential enabler of the flexible exchange of *information* and *knowledge* as distinct from mere *data*.

With the help of *gateways*, *message objects* can be converted to different formats, which allow heterogeneous WFMSs to interoperate. An upcoming standard, which promises to become widely accepted, is the *extensible markup language (XML)*, which would be ideally suited to the definition of *message objects* connecting WFMSs.

The Wide Area GroupFlow System (WAGS) has been implemented in order to demonstrate the conceptual approaches discussed in this book. Its aim is to help both workflow practitioners and system designers to gain a more precise impression of possible ways to realize WAWM. During the development of WAGS, attempts were made to find appropriate solutions for all four *levels* of WAWM (see Figure 10, p. 56), providing the *tools* needed in a practical system, which were previously described in a conceptual manner in the *toolbox* of Figure 29 (p. 137).

To reflect the wide range of *ex ante structured* to *ex ante unstructured* office procedures, WAGS offers options for the realization of both the paradigms of *automation & structure* and *user support & flexibility*.

WAGS differs from other prototypes for WAWM primarily in providing various options for the *flexible modeling* of *wide area workflows*, which help to prepare an efficient run-time operation. Efficient in this sense means that workflow designers are not forced to predefine workflow models in areas where the actual structures of processes cannot be predicted. On the other hand, they *can* determine *internal* and *external* workflow interaction, if all necessary information is available. In addition, the modeling mechanisms in WAGS reflect different degrees of autonomy of the participants. For instance, with the use of *external subscribed workflow* elements, workflow designers can connect workflow parts between companies without having to know any information other than the *interface specifications* published by the respective organizations. The author sees a fundamental difference between this method and other approaches to WAWM, since the autonomy of the participants is preserved as far as possible, while fully featured workflow systems' interoperation is enabled.

Furthermore, WAGS features a *coordination directory*, *message objects* and a *gateway*, all of which demonstrate the synergetic combination of *structured* as well as *flexible WAWM* within a single workflow system. These building blocks additionally show that with current technology, the handling of *information* and *knowledge* can be implemented in workflow systems, thus overcoming the limitation to mere *data*. Systems for WAWM can thereby come much closer to re-building the manifold structures of *information* exchange, which are actually used between organizations today.

By implementing WAGS, it could be proved that groupware platforms with their highly efficient integration of *messaging* and *replication* technology are suitable *enabling environments* for building workflow systems for WAWM.

In order to base both the concepts as well as WAGS on empirical observations, the author and his team have carried out two case studies (see Chapters 2 (p. 9) and 7 (p. 233)). The emphasis on systems for WAWM which also provide concepts for the *highly flexible* interaction of *autonomous* organizations in this book is based on findings from these empirical surveys. The inflexibility of the former interorganizational procedures caused severe problems and high costs, especially in the case of LLM.

Some more insights that can be derived from the case studies are:

- In organizations where no workflows systems or groupware platforms have previously been in use, it is a long process to implement systems for WAWM and apply them in everyday business. It seems reasonable in many cases to start with the *internal use* of WFMSs and groupware platforms, despite the remaining inefficiencies at the boundaries of organizations.
- Implementing workflow systems – especially those supporting WAWM – means initiating a fundamental paradigm shift in the handling of office processes. The use of such systems has considerable effects on the social structures within and between organizations, which have to be anticipated correctly to avoid disappointments on the part of planners and users.
- Organizations have to develop a new culture of internal and external cooperation, which can only be achieved in long-term projects. Quick gains in efficiency cannot be expected.
- The fundamental decisions to re-structure the way business is done, for example by concentrating on fewer suppliers or abolishing the control of goods received in the warehouse (Case Study 2), lead to measurable improvements in efficiency. These decisions – which can be located in the 4th level of the level model for WAWM – seem to be more important for significant enhancements of office processes than the actual choice of a certain product for workflow management.

- For the most part, the provision of prototypic systems to envision future options for improved processes lead to the necessary *awareness* of the possibilities of formerly unknown systems such as WFMSs and groupware platforms. The important decisions of the 4th level, which are mentioned in the point above, were only made after the top management was informed about and aware of these new possibilities.

Due to the long duration of both projects, which was caused by indecision as to whether new technologies would be adopted or old systems improved, the author could only propose solutions for Wide Area Workflow Management between the companies in the case studies instead of reporting on implementation. This is unfortunate, since an evaluation of the concepts for WAWM and the Wide Area GroupFlow System would have helped to judge their applicability better.

Further limitations of the approaches described in this book should be mentioned:

- No technical concepts for transactional workflow management were discussed here. Despite the importance of the paradigm of *user support & flexibility*, a relevant percentage of workflow applications need transaction concepts for the handling of large data volumes. Therefore, concepts for *transactional WAWM* are certainly also needed in intra- and interorganizational cooperation. The author wants to refer to other researchers who concentrate on this topic, for example in the projects *Exotica/FMQM*, *ORBWork* or *WorldFlow* (see Sections 4.2.4 and 4.2.5, starting from p. 89).
- The Wide Area GroupFlow System must be considered as an early version of a prototype, which definitely needs extensive improvements (see for instance Section 6.3, p. 229) in order to better demonstrate the concepts for WAWM.
- Only a thorough practical application of the different coordination mechanisms for WAWM described in this book (*hierarchy, equal partnership, and market*) will lead to a profound judgement on their individual strengths and weaknesses. This experience cannot be gained with prototypes but rather with commercial WFMSs, applied in real-world settings on a long-term basis.
- The author has critically discussed the attempts of the WfMC to standardize specifications for WFMSs' interoperability. This is rather simple so long as one is not in the position of having to define such standards. The author is at least partially aware of the problems that come with standardization and wants to express his appreciation to the authors of the WfMC. It is not his intention to reduce the importance of their efforts. The author would be glad if the propositions in this book could help the WfMC to further improve its specifications, even if this only can be achieved by *not* using the concepts proposed here.

Outlook

Some trends in technology have become visible in recent times, which are important for the building of systems for WAWM. A first development is the blending of groupware platforms and the WWW, which will be completed for instance with the release of Lotus Notes / Lotus Domino 5.0 [Weber 1998]. Similar observations can be made about other groupware products such as Microsoft Exchange or Novell GroupWise. The development and maintenance of two alternative front-ends for groupware-based workflow management systems will thereby become obsolete, which especially facilitates the handling of *intra*organizational WAWM.

Furthermore, the increasing use of object management standards such as the *Internet Inter-ORB Protocol (IIOP)* (see Section 3.4.3, p. 64) will make the Internet a powerful platform for the safe exchange of *(message) objects* between widely distributed workflow systems.

The upcoming standard XML offers a flexible architecture, which promises to be widely accepted by major software vendors. It can be applied to define the structures of *message objects* as well as to embed representation features. Hence, XML can be very valuable in WAWM for exchanging *contextual information*, not only *data*, between users in distinct WFMSs based on a commonly agreed standard. Finally, the development of workflow systems in platform-independent languages such as *Java* will facilitate the interaction of workflow instances across heterogeneous operating system platforms.

All of these technological developments will help to build future WAWM-enabled workflow systems, which can interoperate with fewer obstacles than must be overcome today.

A further technological challenge will be to find flexible solutions for the exchange of information between integrated business software systems (e.g. SAP R/3, Baan IV) and WAWM-enabled WFMSs. This is of high practical importance to avoid duplicated handling of similar or identical information, which is needed in both worlds. A seamless transfer of business information between these systems will definitely help to improve the efficiency of office work further.

The concepts and prototypic solutions for WAWM proposed in this book will have to be further developed on the basis of extensive practical application. A major aspect of WAWM, which could not be covered here due to the rather early phase of discussions, is the empirical cost-benefit-comparison of current approaches for the interaction of widely dispersed office workers and the concepts for Wide Area Workflow Management introduced in this book. This would be an interesting starting point for further empirical research.

The author hopes to have formulated concepts and possible solutions for a world where *global business* can be supported better based on the paradigms of *process orientation*. The aim of Wide Area Workflow Management is to help widely dispersed clerical workers to handle *information* and perhaps even *knowledge* efficiently in their everyday communication within and between organizations in a humane and flexible manner. At the same time, this should reduce pollution and waste, thereby contributing to *environmental protection*. The propositions found in this book are certainly only a small mosaic piece in the big picture of work cultures in the future. What has been proposed here should be further assessed through practical application in order to (im-)prove its relevance.

9 Summary

In this book, concepts and possible solutions for Wide Area Workflow Management (WAWM) are presented. In the first chapter, an introduction is given to the general scenario accompanying the development of systems for WAWM, followed by a short definition of the term WAWM itself. Furthermore, principal perspectives regarding the topic and the structure of this book are illustrated.

In Chapter 2 (p. 9), the author describes the cases of two companies, which were planning to implement systems for the support of *wide area workflows*, and invited the author and his team to participate in these projects starting in mid 1996. The general circumstances of these companies, their suppliers and customers as well as the business processes selected for optimization are presented as an empirical basis for the subsequent description of concepts and practical solutions for WAWM.

Conceptual and technological foundations of systems supporting *wide area workflows* are briefly introduced in the third chapter (p. 23). Starting with a look at general developments in the application of computer systems in business (see Figure 4, p. 24), the author subsequently examines scientific and practical approaches to facilitate the collaboration of office workers in decentralized scenarios (see Section 3.2, p. 26). Examples of such approaches are research in *CSCW*, *coordination science*, *transaction cost theory*, *interorganizational information systems* and *electronic commerce*. Furthermore, concepts for cooperation among companies, such as *virtual organizations*, are described.

This is followed by a discussion of the main characteristics of *process orientation* in office work, highlighted by the Business Process Reengineering approach, and the description of the accompanying tools – workflow management systems (see Section 3.3, p. 41). Starting with *structured workflow management* in local environments, the author subsequently introduces other ways to handle office procedures, such as *flexible* and *ad-hoc workflow management* (see Figure 9, p. 52). Based on this recapitulation, the new characteristics and challenges of Wide Area Workflow Management are described. An important element of this is the recognition of *four levels of WAWM* (see Figure 10, p. 56), which help to outline the different requirements for systems supporting *wide area workflows*. This level model is referred to throughout the remaining chapters of this book. In addition, three generations of workflow systems are differentiated; the goal of the third generation is to facilitate WAWM (see Figure 11, p. 57).

In Section 3.4 (p. 59), technologies that can be used for building systems for WAWM, such as *EDIFACT*, the *Internet* and *World Wide Web*, *object management standards* and *groupware* are introduced. A more detailed description of Lotus Notes concludes this review of technologies, since this groupware product provides the basis for the prototypic implementations by the author and his team. All of the systems presented in this section are referred to during the introduction of concepts for WAWM and the presentation of the Wide Area GroupFlow System.

In Chapter 4 (p. 73), the author attempts to provide an overview of the state-of-the-art of WAWM-related approaches of other authors. Initially, a classification scheme is derived from the literature and the author's own research in order to better describe and distinguish the systems presented in the following sections (see Figure 12, p. 76). Subsequently, the *Interface 4* specifications of the Workflow Management Coalition (WfMC), which aim at WAWM, are described and evaluated (see Section 4.2.1, p. 77).

Further sections introduce conceptual and practical approaches to *flexible* workflow management (Section 4.2.3, p. 85), *widely distributed* workflow management (Section 4.2.4, p. 89) and *WWW-oriented* WFMSs (Section 4.2.5, p. 95). In the judgement of the author, the systems *Workflow Continuum* and *GroupFlow* (p. 85), *FUNSOFT Nets* (p. 91), *Workonnector* (p. 92) and *Phanta Rhei* (p. 96) make the most valuable contributions to the topic of this book.

Section 4.3 (p. 98) provides a short overview of the WAWM-related features of commercial WFMSs, to the extent that these are described in the literature available or in addition are known in more detail to the author. The chapter ends with a conclusive summary of the approaches presented and several questions about WAWM, which have not been answered so far (Section 4.4, p. 100).

In Chapter 5 (p. 103), the author starts to introduce his own concepts for WAWM. In order to reflect the full scale of office work and find appropriate balanced positions for various practical requirements, the chapter begins by comparing the paradigm of *automation & structure* with that of *user support & flexibility* (Section 5.1, p. 104). The fundamental thoughts expressed regarding this topic are referred to throughout the rest the book.

The aim of Section 5.2 (p. 109) is to describe the new challenges of *WAWM* in contrast to *local* workflow management. They are aggregated in *three dimensions of WAWM* (see Figure 18, p. 111), which are explained in further detail in the following sections.

Based on these more general observations on the topic, Section 5.3 (p. 117) now introduces concrete measures for connecting distributed workflow parts. For this purpose, four fundamental *interaction patterns* are described in Table 4 (p. 119), based on the description of a *meta-model* for models of *local workflows* (Figure 21, p. 117). In order to describe *wide area workflows* as well, this meta-model is extended as shown in Figure 22 (p. 122) and subsequently simplified in order to make large workflow models easier for workflow designers to understand (see Figure 23, p. 124).

The fundamental *interaction patterns* described in this section are neutral regarding the *power relationships* between the participants in WAWM scenarios. Since Wide Area Workflow Management does not occur in an "organizational vacuum", but rather must be implemented in real-world settings, the following Section 5.4 (p. 125) presents *three coordination mechanisms for WAWM*. These mechanisms make use of the fundamental coordination strategies of *hierarchy*, *equal partnership* and *market*, thereby reflecting different degrees of *autonomy* between organizations collaborating via WAWM. For these *three coordination mechanisms*, the author attempts to describe solutions for all of the four *levels of WAWM* (see Figure 10 (p. 56). Possible combinations of the *coordination mechanisms* and *levels* are depicted in the *continuum of coordination mechanisms for WAWM* (Figure 29, p. 137), which forms the conceptual heart of this book.

Since the *coordination mechanisms* have been explained for *structured workflow management* in first place, Section 5.5 (p. 139) proposes measures to make the planning and execution of *wide area workflows* more flexible. Both workflow designers and actual performers can thereby adapt to unforeseeable and unforeseen situations.

Concrete recommendations for the design of workflow systems supporting WAWM are given in Section 5.6 (p. 143). It starts with the introduction of *shared coordination directories*, which help to plan and execute *wide area workflows* in an efficient manner, while preventing participants from having to reveal confidential information about the internal processing of office procedures. To enable the exchange of *information* (as opposed to mere *data*) between users in distinct WFMSs, the structure and use of flexible *message objects* is subsequently explained. Finally, the possible functionalities of *gateways*, which can be used to bridge heterogeneous workflow systems, are described.

The chapter on concepts concludes with the introduction of a *lifecycle* and an *implementation model* for WAWM systems, which propose a methodology for planning, building, using and continuously improving the components needed to support *wide area workflows* efficiently (Section 5.7, p. 169).

Based on the concepts described so far, Chapter 6 (p. 179) presents the Wide Area GroupFlow System (WAGS) as a prototypic software framework for the planning and execution of WAWM. Firstly, the architecture of WAGS and the underlying technologies are described (p. 180). Secondly, the components of WAGS are explained in further detail on the basis of examples derived from the case studies (p. 187). Thirdly, an outlook on possible further developments of the framework is given (p. 229).

Now that concepts and possible solutions for WAWM have been described, the author comes back to the two case studies in Chapter 7 (p. 233) and presents the results which were available in the spring of 1998. In addition, solutions for the WAWM-related business processes described in Chapter 2 are proposed on the basis of the prototypic Wide Area GroupFlow System. To the regret of the author, no reports on the actual implementation and use of these propositions can be provided, since the projects have not proceeded far enough at the time of writing this book. Nevertheless, the reader can get a more precise impression of how the different *coordination mechanisms for WAWM* can be applied in practical scenarios.

In Chapter 8 (p. 253), the author attempts to draw conclusions from his work on WAWM, which had been described in the preceding chapters. Furthermore, an overview of possible future developments in this field is given.

Following this summary, an extensive collection of references and indices is provided by the author to help the reader locate sources (both within this book and elsewhere) relating to workflow management and WAWM in particular.

10 References

10.1 Literature references

[Abbott/Sarin 1994]
Abbott, Kenneth R.; Sarin, Sunil K.: Experiences with workflow management – issues for the next generation, in: Proc. of CSCW'94, ACM, New York, 1994, pp. 113-120.

[Adam/Yesha 1996]
Adam, N. R.; Yesha, Y. (Eds.): Electronic commerce, Springer Verlag, Berlin etc., 1996.

[Adams/Dworkin 1997]
Adams, Thomas; Dworkin, Steve: Workflow interoperability between businesses, in: Lawrence, P. (Ed.): Workflow Handbook 1997, Wiley, Chichester etc., 1997, pp. 211-221.

[Alonso et al. 1995]
Alonso, G.; Agrawal, D.; Abbadi A.; Mohan, C.; Günthör, R.; Kamath, M.: Exotica/FMQM: A persistent message-based architecture for distributed workflow management, IBM Research Report, San Jose, CA, 1994; also in: Proceedings of IFIP WG 8.1 Workgroup Conference on Information Systems, Development for Decentralized Organizations (ISDO 95), Trondheim, Norway, 1995.

[Alonso/Reinwald/Mohan 1997]
Alonso, Gustavo; Reinwald, Berthold; Mohan, C.: Distributed data management in workflow environments, in: 7th Int. Workshop on Research Issues in Data Engineering (RIDE'97), Birmingham, England, 1997.

[Alpar 1996]
Alpar, Pavle: Kommerzielle Nutzung des Internet – Unterstützung von Marketing, Produktion, Logistik und Querschnittsfunktionen durch Internet und kommerzielle Online-Dienste, Springer Verlag, Berlin etc., 1996.

[Alt 1997]
Alt, Rainer: Interorganisationssysteme in der Logistik – Interaktionsorientierte Gestaltung von Koordinationsinstrumenten, DUV - Gabler Edition Wissenschaft, Wiesbaden, 1997.

[Amberg 1996]
Amberg, Michael: Modeling adaptive workflows in distributed environments, in: Proc. of first intl. conf. on practical aspects of knowledge management, Basel, Switzerland, 1996. See also: http://www.seda.sowi.uni-bamberg.de/workflow/document/vmod02/vmod-e.htm.

[American Heritage Dict. 1994]
The American Heritage Dictionary of the English Language, CD-ROM edition, Vers. 3.6a, Softkey International, 1994.

[Andrews 1991]
Andrews, G.: Paradigms for process interaction in distributed programs, in: ACM Computing Surveys, Vol. 23, No. 1, 1991, pp. 49-90.

[Andrews/Stalick 1994]
Andrews, Dorine C.; Stalick, Susan K.: Business reengineering – the survival guide, Yourdon Press, Englewood Cliffs, NJ, 1994.

[Backhaus/Meyer 1993]
Backhaus, Klaus; Meyer, Margit: Strategische Allianzen und strategische Netzwerke, in: Wirtschaftswissenschaftliches Studium (WiSt), Vol. 22, No. 7, 1993, pp. 330-334.

[Barbara/Mehrota/Rusinkiewicz 1994]
Barbara, D.; Mehrota, S.; Rusinkiewicz, M.: INCAS – A computation model for dynamic workflows in autonomous distributed environments, technical report, Matsushita Information Technology Laboratory, 1994.

[Barbara/Mehrota/Rusinkiewicz 1996]
Barbara, D.; Mehrota, S.; Rusinkiewicz, M.: INCAS – managing dynamic workflows in distributed environments, in: Journal of Database Management, Vol. 7, No. 1, 1996, pp. 5-15.

[Bauknecht/Holbein 1996]
Bauknecht, Kurt; Holbein, Ralph: Workflow-management-systems – source and solution of privacy problems in organisations, in: Österle, H.; Vogler, P. (Eds.): Praxis des Workflow Managements, Vieweg, Braunschweig, Wiesbaden, 1996, pp. 271-300.

[Becker 1996]
Becker, Matthias: Workflow-Management - Szenarien und Potentiale, in: Österle, H.; Vogler, P. (Eds.): Praxis des Workflow Managements, Vieweg, Braunschweig, Wiesbaden, 1996, pp. 319-341.

[Benjamin/DeLong/Scott Morton 1990]
Benjamin, R. I.; DeLong, D. W.; Scott Morton, M. S.: Electronic data interchange – how much competitive advantage?, in: Long Range Planning, 23 (1), 1990, pp. 29-40.

[Benjamin/Wigand 1995]
Benjamin, R. I.; Wigand, R.: Electronic markets and virtual value-chains on the information superhighway, in: Sloan Management Review, 36 (2), 1995, pp. 62-72.

[Berglund 1997]
Berglund, Hakan: Das Internet verknüpft die Zulieferkette einfacher und preiswerter als bisher – für die Nutzung im weltweiten Netz fehlt zur Zeit die Software zur Integration, in: Computer Zeitung, No. 37, 11.9., 1997, p. 12.

[Beuthner 1997]
Beuthner, Andreas: Workflow-Anbieter surfen auf der Internet-Welle, in: Computer Zeitung, No. 33, 14.8., 1997, p. 9.

[Beyer 1997]
Beyer, Thomas: Kosten und Nutzen von elektronisch unterstützter in Abgrenzung zu papierbasierter Büroarbeit – Modellbildung und empirische Untersuchung in einem Unternehmen des Computerhandels, Master thesis, Dept. of Business Computing, University of Paderborn, 1997.

[BIFOA 1993]
BIFOA, (Ed.): Vorgangsmanagementsysteme, BIFOA-Marktstudie, BIFOA-Selbstverlag, Köln, 1993.

[Black Forest Group 1996]
Black Forest Group: Workflow requirements of the Black Forest Group, in: Österle, H.; Vogler, P. (Eds.): Praxis des Workflow Managements, Vieweg, Braunschweig, Wiesbaden, 1996, pp. 83-105.

[Borghoff/Schlichter 1995]
Borghoff, Uwe M.; Schlichter, Johann H.: Rechnergestützte Gruppenarbeit – eine Einführung in verteilte Anwendungen, Springer Verlag, Berlin etc., 1995.

[Bowers/Benford 1991]
Bowers, J.M.; Benford, S.D.: Study in computer supported cooperative work – theory, practice and design, Elsevier, North Holland, 1991.

[Bowers/Button/Sharrock 1995]
Bowers, John; Button, Graham; Sharrock, Wes: Workflow from within and without, in: Proc. of ECSCW '95, Kluwer Academic Publishers, Dordrecht etc., 1995.

[Bracchi/Pernici 1984]
Bracchi, G.; Pernici, B.: The design requirements of office systems, in: ACM Transactions on Office Information Systems, Vol.2, No. 2, 1984, pp. 151-170.

[Bragen 1994]
Bragen, Michael A.: Go with the flow – workflow automation software, in: PC Magazine, Ziff-Davis Publishing Company, New York, June 14, 1994, pp. 253-302.

[Brousseau 1994]
Brousseau, E.: EDI and inter-firm relationships – toward a standardization of coordination processes?, in: Information Economics and Policy, 6, 1994, pp. 319-347.

[Byrne/Brand/Port 1993]
Byrne, J.; Brand, R.; Port, O.: The virtual corporation, in: Business Week, Feb. 08, 1993, pp. 36-40.

[Calabria/Plumley 1997]
Calabria, Jane; Plumley, Sue: Lotus Notes 4.5 and the Internet – 6 in 1, QUE, Indianapolis, 1997.

[Carlsen 1995]
Carlsen, Steinar: Organizational perspectives of workflow technology, research paper, Information Systems Group SINTEF Informatics, University of Trondheim, Oslo, 1995, pp. 1-78.

[Carlsen et al. 1997]
Carlsen, Steinar; Krogstie, John; Solvberg, Arne; Lindland, Odd Ivar: Evaluating flexible workflow systems, in: Proc. of Hawaii International Conference on System Sciences (HICSS-30), Maui, Hawaii, 1997.

[Carr/Johansson 1995]
Carr, David K.; Johansson, Henry J.: Best practices in reengineering – what works and what doesn't in the reengineering process, McGraw-Hill, New York, 1995.

[Casati et al. 1996]
Casati, F.; Ceri, S.; Pernici, B.; Pozzi, G.: Semantic workflow interoperability, in: Proc. of the 5th International Conference on Extending Database Technology, Lectures Notes in Computer Science, Springer Verlag, Berlin etc., 1996, pp. 443-462.

[Cash/Konsynski 1985]
Cash, James I.; Konsynski, Benn R.: IS redraws competitive boundaries, in: Harvard Business Review, Vol. 62, No. 1, 1985, pp. 134-142.

[Cathomen 1996]
Cathomen, I.: Der Lebenszyklus von Interorganisationssystemen, Verlag Josef Eul, Lohmar, 1996.

[Chadwick 1994]
Chadwick, David: Understanding directories, Chapman Hall, London, 1994.

[Chatfield/Murray 1997]
Chatfield, Akemi T.; Murray, Alston: Small and medium-sized enterprises in electronic commerce – a case study of barriers to financial EDI adoption, in: Galliers, R. et al. (Eds.): Proceedings of the 5th European Conference on Information Systems, Cork, Vol. III, 1997, pp. 1219-1233.

[Chen 1976]
Chen, P.P.-S.: The entity relationship model – toward a unified view of data, in: ACM Transactions on Database Systems, ACM, Vol. 1, No. 1, 1976, pp. 9-36.

[Chroust/Benczúr 1994]
Chroust, G.; Benczúr, A.: Workflow management – challenges, paradigms and products, R. Oldenbourg, Vienna, Munich, 1994.

[Clark/Schiano 1996]
Clark, Theodore H.; Schiano, William T.: Seven levels of interorganizational connectivity – an examination of the u.s. grocery distribution channel, in: Nunamaker jr., J. F. et al. (Eds.): Proceedings of the 29th Annual Hawaii International Conference on System Science, IEEE Computer Society Press, Los Alamitos, 1996, pp. 281-289.

[Clark/Stoddard 1996]
Clark, Theodore H.; Stoddard, Donna B.: Interorganizational business process redesign – merging technological and process innovation, in: Nunamaker jr., J. F. et al. (Eds.): Proceedings of the 29th Annual Hawaii International Conference on System Science, IEEE Computer Society Press, Los Alamitos, 1996, pp. 349-358.

[CSCW 1988]
Proceedings of the conference on Computer Supported Cooperative Work, Portland, OR, Sept. 26-28, ACM, 1988.

[CSCW 1990]
Proceedings of the conference on Computer Supported Cooperative Work, Los Angeles, CA, Oct. 7-10, ACM, 1990.

[CSCW 1992]
Proceedings of the conference on Computer Supported Cooperative Work, Toronto, Canada, Oct. 31. - Nov. 4., ACM, 1992.

[CSCW 1994]
Proceedings of the conference on Computer Supported Cooperative Work, Chapel Hill, NC, Oct. 22-26, ACM, 1994.

[CSCW 1996]
Proceedings of the conference on Computer Supported Cooperative Work, Boston, MA, Nov. 16-20, ACM, 1996.

[CZ 1997a]
OMG wird ISO-Gruppe, in: Computer Zeitung, No. 48, 1997, p. 1.

[CZ 1997b]
Norm für Workflow, in: Computer Zeitung, No. 28, 1997, p. 4.

[Dangelmaier/Kress/Wenski 1996]
Dangelmaier, W.; Kress, S.; Wenski, R.: Workflow management in telematics – a new approach to increase productivity by the use of a flexible time management of teleworkers, in: Proc. of Euromedia 96, London, 1996. See also: http://hni.uni-paderborn.de/cim/mitarb/ruediger/TelCow.html.

[Das et al. 1997]
Das, S.; Kochut, K.; Miller, J.; Sheth, Amit; Worah, D.: ORBWork – a reliable distributed CORBA-based workflow enactment system for METEOR_2, technical report #UGA-CS-TR-97-001, Department of Computer Science, University of Georgia, February, 1997, pp. 1-24.

[Date 1990]
Date, C. J.: An introduction to database systems, Addison-Wesley, 5th edition, New York etc., Vol. 1, 1990.

[Davenport 1993]
Davenport, Thomas H.: Process innovation – reengineering work through information technology, Harvard Business School Press, Boston, 1993.

[Davidow/Malone 1992]
Davidow, William H.; Malone, Michael S.: The virtual corporation – structuring and revitalizing the corporation for the 21st century, Harper Business, New York, 1992.

[Deiters et al. 1996]
Deiters, Wolfgang; Herrmann, Thomas; Löffeler, Thorsten; Striemer, Rüdiger: Identifikation, Klassifikation und Unterstützung semi-strukturierter Prozesse in prozeßorientierten Telekooperationssystemn, in: Krcmar, H., Lewe, H., Schwabe, G. (Eds.): Herausforderung Telekooperation - Proceedings of the 2nd German Computer Supported Cooperative Work Conference '96, Springer Verlag, Berlin etc., 1996, pp. 261-274.

[Deiters/Gruhn/Striemer 1995]
Deiters, Wolfgang; Gruhn, Volker; Striemer, Rüdiger: Der FUNSOFT-Ansatz zum integrierten Geschäftsprozeßmanagement, in: Wirtschaftsinformatik, Vol. 37, No. 5, 1995, pp. 459-466.

[Deiters/Lindert 1996]
Deiters, Wolfgang; Lindert, Frank: Konzepte für verteiltes Workflow Management am Beispiel VORTEL, in: Softwaretechnik für Kommunikationssysteme, VDI Verlag, Düsseldorf, Fortschrittsbericht VDI-Reihe 10, No. 439, 1996, pp. 131-145.

[Deiters/Lindert et al. 1996]
Deiters, Wolfgang; Lindert, F.; Böhm, Markus; Friedrich, W.: Workflow management as teleservice, in: Computer Networks and ISDN Systems, Vol. 28, No. 4, 1996, pp. 1961-1969.

[Deiters/Lindert/Friedrich 1996]
Deiters, Wolfgang; Lindert, Frank; Friedrich, Manuel: Der Vorgangsbearbeitungs-Teledienst zur Integration von Vorgangssteuerungssystemen, in: Sandkuhl, K.; Weber, H. (Hrsg.): Tagungsband des Workshops "Telekooperations-Systeme in dezentralen Organisationen", Fraunhofer ISST 31/96, Berlin, 1996, pp. 33-51.

[Deleré 1998]
Deleré, Dirk: Von lokalem zu weit-verteiltem Workflow Management - Stand der Entwicklung in Forschung und Praxis, Master thesis, Business Computing 2, University of Paderborn, 1998.

[Derszteler 1996]
Derszteler, Gérard: Workflow Management Cycle – ein Ansatz zur Integration von Modellierung, Ausführung und Bewertung workflowgestützter Geschäftsprozesse, in: Wirtschaftsinformatik, Vol. 38, No. 6, 1996, pp. 591-600.

[Derungs/Vogler/Oesterle 1997]
Derungs, Marc; Vogler, Petra; Österle, Hubert: From BPR models to workflow applications, in: Lawrence, P. (Ed.): Workflow Handbook 1997, Wiley, Chichester etc., 1997, pp. 49-59.

[Dibb et al. 1991]
Dibb, S.; Simkin, L.; Pride, W. M.; Ferrell, O. C.: Marketing – concepts and strategies, Houghton Mifflin, Boston etc., 1991.

[Dierker/Sander 1997]
Dierker, Markus; Sander, Martin: Lotus Notes 4.5 und Domino – Integration von Groupware und Internet, Addison-Wesley, Bonn etc., 1997.

[Dinkhoff et al. 1994]
Dinkhoff, Guido; Gruhn, Volker; Saalmann, Armin; Zielonka, Michael: Business process modeling in the workflow management environment LEU, in: Loucopolous, P. (Ed.): Proc. of 13th Int. Conf. on the Entity Relationship Approach, Manchester, UK, 1994, pp. 46-63.

[Dourish et al. 1996]
Dourish, Paul; Holmes, Jim; MacLean, Allan; Marqvardsen, Pernille; Zbyslaw, Alex: FreeFlow – mediating between representation and action in workflow systems, in: Proc. of CSCW'96, Boston, MA, ACM, 1996, pp. 190-198.

[Dutton 1993]
Dutton, James E.: Commonsense approach to process modeling, in: IEEE Software, Vol. 4, No. 10, 1993, pp. 56-64.

[ECSCW 1991]
Proceedings of the Second European Conference on Computer Supported Cooperative Work, Amsterdam, Netherlands. Eds.: Bannon, L., Robinson, M., Schmidt, K., Kluwer Academic Publishers, Dordrecht etc., 1991.

[ECSCW 1993]
Proceedings of the Third European Conference on Computer-Supported Cooperative Work, Mailand, Italy. Eds.: DeMichelis, G.; Simone, C.; Schmidt, K., Kluwer Academic Publishers, Dordrecht etc., 1993.

[ECSCW 1995]
Proceedings of the Fourth European Conference on Computer-Supported Cooperative Work, Stockholm, Sweden. Eds.: Marmolin, H.; Sundblad, Y.; Schmidt, K., Kluwer Academic Publishers, Dordrecht etc., 1995.

[ECSCW 1997]
Proceedings of the Fifth European Conference on Computer Supported Cooperative Work, Lancaster, UK. Eds.: Prinz, W.; Rodden, T.; Hughes, H.; Schmidt, K., Kluwer Academic Publishers, Dordrecht etc., 1997.

[Ehlers 1997]
Ehlers, Peter: Integriertes Projekt- und Prozeßmanagement auf Basis innovativer Informations- und Kommunikationstechnologien – das GroupProject-System, Dissertation thesis, University of Paderborn, 1997.

[Eistert 1996]
Eistert, Thorsten: EDI adoption and diffusion – international comparative analysis of the automotive and retail industries, DUV - Gabler Edition Wissenschaft, Wiesbaden, 1996.

[Elgass/Krcmar 1994]
Elgass, Petra; Krcmar, Helmut: Computergestützung für die Planung von Geschäftsprozessen, in: Hasenkamp, U.; Kirn, S.; Syring, M. (Eds.): CSCW - Computer Supported Cooperative Work, Addison-Wesley, Bonn, 1994, pp. 67-83.

[Ellis 1979]
Ellis, Clarence A.: Information control nets – a mathematical model of office information flow, in: Proc. of the Conf. on Simulation, Modeling and Measurement of Computer Systems, ACM, 1979.

[Ellis 1983]
Ellis, Clarence A.: Formal and informal models of office activity, in: Mason, R.E.A. (Ed.): Information Processing, North-Holland Publishing Co., 1983, pp. 11-22.

[Ellis/Gibbs/Rein 1991]
Ellis, C. A.; Gibbs, S. J.; Rein, G. L.: Groupware – some issues and experiences, in: Communications of the ACM, 34 (1), 1991, pp. 38-58.

[Ellis/Keddara/Rozenberg 1995]
Ellis, Clarence A.; Keddara, Karim; Rozenberg, Gzregorz: Dynamic change within workflow systems, in: Comstock, N. et al. (Eds.): Conference on Organizational Computing Systems, ACM Press, Milpitas, 1995, pp. 10-21.

[Ellis/Nutt 1980]
Ellis, Clarence A.; Nutt, G.J.: Office information systems and computer science, in: Computing Surveys, Vol.12, No.1, 1980, pp. 27-60.

[Ellis/Nutt 1993]
Ellis, Clarence A.; Nutt, G.J.: Modeling and enactment of workflow systems, in: Marsan, M.A. (Ed.): Proceedings of the 14th international conference on application theory of petri nets, Springer Verlag, Chicago, 1993, pp. 1-16.

[Emmelhainz 1993]
Emmelhainz, M. A.: EDI – a total management guide, Van Nostrand Reinhold, New York, 1993.

[Engelbart/English 1968]
Engelbart, D. C.; English, W. K.: A research center for augmenting human intellect, in: Proceedings of the Fall Joint Computer Conference, San Francisco, Calif., Dec. 9-11, AFIPS, Reston, VA, 1968, pp. 395-410.

[Erdl/Schoenecker 1993]
Erdl, Günther; Schönecker, Horst G.: Vorgangssteuerungssysteme im Überblick – Herkunft, Vorausssetzungen, Einsatzschwerpunkte, Ausblick, in: Office Management, FBO Fachverlag für Büro- und Organisationstechnik, Baden-Baden, No. 3, 1993.

[Erdl/Schoenecker 1995]
Erdl, Günther; Schönecker, Horst G.: Geschäftsprozeßmanagement, Vorgangssteuerungssysteme und integrierte Vorgangsbearbeitung, B.BIT CONSULT GmbH (Ed.), FBO Verlag, 2. Auflage, Baden-Baden, 1995.

[Faisst 1997]
Faisst, Wolfgang: Information technology as an enabler of virtual enterprises – a life-cycle-oriented description, Working Paper, University of Erlangen, Business Computing, 1997.

[Finnegan/Galliers/Powell 1997]
Finnegan, Pat; Galliers, Robert; Powell, Philip: Investigating inter-organisational information systems planning practices in Ireland and the UK, in: Galliers, R. et al. (Eds.): Proceedings of the 5th European Conference on Information Systems, Cork, Vol. I, 1997, pp. 281-294.

[Fischer 1993]
Fischer, J.: Unternehmensübergreifende Datenmodellierung - der nächste folgerichtige Schritt der zwischenbetrieblichen Datenverarbeitung!, in: Wirtschaftsinformatik, Vol. 35, No. 3, 1993, pp. 241-254.

[Fischer 1995]
Fischer, Layna: New tools for new times – the workflow paradigm: the impact of information technology on business process reengineering, Future Strategies, 2nd edition, Lighthouse Point, Florida, 1995.

[Fowler/Swatman/Swatman 1994]
Fowler, Danielle C.; Swatman, Paula M.C.; Swatman, Paul A.: Corporate EDI gateways – a centralised approach to integrating EDI, in: 5th Australian Conference on Information Systems, Melbourne, September, 1994.

[Frappaolo 1997]
Frappaolo, Carl: Webflow - document management systems get a new life as they get tied to the Internet, in: Computerworld, Aug-25., 1997, see also: http://www.computerworld.com/guide/970825guide_1.html.

[Gagne 1997]
Gagne, Cathleen A.: Five years from now, groupware may be a memory, in: Hayes, Garrett M.; MacLeish, Kenneth I.: Group(where), Computerworld, Nov., 24., 1997, pp. 87-96.

[Gaitanides 1983]
Gaitanides, Michael: Prozeßorganisation – Entwicklung, Ansätze und Programme prozeßorientierter Organisationsgestaltung, Vahlen, München, 1983.

[Galler 1995]
Galler, Jürgen: Metamodelle des Workflow Managements, in: Scheer, A.W. (Ed.): Veröffentlichungen des Instituts für Wirtschaftsinformatik, Heft 121, 1995.

[Galler/Hagemeyer/Scheer 1995]
Galler, Jürgen; Hagemeyer, Jens; Scheer, August-Wilhelm: The coordination of interdisciplinary teams in workflow projects, in: Proceedings of the 3rd Interdisciplinary Information Management Talks - IDIMT-95, Kubova Hut, Czech Republic, also: http://www.iwi.uni-sb.de/forschungsprojekte/contact/cont_2in.html, 1995.

[Galler/Hagemeyer/Scheer 1996]
Galler, Jürgen; Hagemeyer, Jens; Scheer, August-Wilhelm: Asynchronous cooperation support for distributed collaborative information modeling, in: Sandkuhl, K.; Weber, H. (Eds.): Proc. of Workshops "Telekooperations-Systeme in dezentralen Organisationen", Fraunhofer ISST, Berlin, 1996, pp. 67-79.

[Galler/Scheer/Peter 1995]
Galler, Jürgen; Scheer, August W.; Peter, S.: Workflow-Projekte – Erfahrungen aus Fallstudien und Vorgehensmodell, in: Veröffentlichungen des Instituts für Wirtschaftsinformatik an der Universität des Saarlandes, 1995.

[Gemmill/Wilemon 1980]
Gemmill, G. R.; Wilemon, D. L.: The product manager as an influence agent, in: Dune, P.; Obenhouse, S. (Eds.): Product Management – A Reader, American Marketing Association, Chicago, 1980.

[Georgakopoulos/Hornick/Sheth 1995]
Georgakopoulos, Diimitrios; Hornick, Mark; Sheth, Amit: An overview of workflow management – from process modeling to workflow automation infrastructure, in: Journal on Distributed and Parallel Database Systems, Kluwer Academic Publishers, Boston, 3 (2), April, 1995, pp. 119-153.

[Goesmann et al. 1997]
Goesmann, Thomas; Hagemeyer, Jens; Löffeler, Thorsten; Rolles, Roland; Striemer, Rüdiger: Einführung von Workflow-Management in die Praxis aus Sicht verschiedener Perspektiven – das Projekt MOVE, in: Becker, J.; Rosemann, M. (Eds.): Proc. of Workshop "Organisatorische und technische Aspekte beim Einsatz von Workflowmanagementsystemen", Universität Münster, Institut für Wirtschaftsinformatik, Arbeitsbericht No. 54, 1997, pp. 51-68.

[Goetzer 1997]
Götzer, Klaus: Workflow – Unternehmenserfolg durch effizientere Arbeitsabläufe, Computerwoche Verlag EDITION, 2 Aufl., München, 1997.

[Goldberg/Safran/Shapiro 1992]
Goldberg, Y.; Safran, M.; Shapiro, E.: Active Mail – a framework for implementing groupware, in: Proc. of CSCW'92, ACM Press, Toronto, Canada, 1992, pp. 75-83.

[Golden/Powell 1996]
Golden, William; Powell, Philip: The effects of inter-organisational systems on flexibility, in: Krcmar, H. et al (Eds.): Proceedings of the 4th European Conference on Information Systems, Lisbon, 1996, pp. 1133-1140.

[Golden/Powell 1997]
Golden, William; Powell, Philip: Inter-organisational information systems and the gains from organisational flexibility, in: Galliers, R. et al. (Eds.): Proceedings of the 5th European Conference on Information Systems, Cork, Vol. I, 1997, pp. 266-280.

[Greenberg 1991]
Greenberg, Saul: Computer-supported cooperative work and groupware, 1991.

[Greif 1988]
Greif, Irene: Computer-supported work – a book of readings, Morgan Kaufmann Publishers, San Mateo, California, 1988.

[Groiss/Eder 1996]
Groiss, Herbert; Eder, Johann: Kooperation von Workflowsystemen im World Wide Web, in: Proc. of EMISA Jahrestagung, Aachen, 1996.

[Groiss/Eder 1997]
Groiss, Herbert; Eder, Johann: Bringing workflow systems to the web, URL: http://www.ifi.uni-klu.ac.at/~herb/Overview.html, Klagenfurt, 1997.

[Gross 1998]
Gross, Michael: Austauschformate für die Interoperabilität heterogener, weitverteilter Workflow Management Systeme – Auswahl, Bewertung und prototypische Implementierung von Formatstandards für Message Objekte im Rahmen des Wide Area GroupFlow Systems, Master thesis, Business Computing 2, University of Paderborn, 1998.

[Grote/Malley 1997]
Grote, A.; Malley, J.: Schwergewicht – Der PC hinterläßt enorme Spuren in der Umwelt, in: c't: Magazin für Computer Technik, Verlag Heinz Heise, Hannover, No. 5, 1997, pp. 170-173.

[Grudin 1994]
Grudin, Jonathan: Groupware and social dynamics – eight challenges for developers, in: Communications of the ACM, Vol. 37, No. 1, January, 1994, pp. 92-105.

[Gruhn 1997]
Gruhn, Volker: Elektronischer Datenaustausch in zwischenbetrieblichen Geschäftsprozessen, in: Wirtschaftsinformatik, Vol. 39, No. 3, 1997, pp. 225-230.

[Gruhn/Kampmann 1996]
Gruhn, Volker; Kampmann, Martin: Modellierung unternehmensübergreifender Geschäftsprozesse mit FUNSOFT-Netzen, in: Wirtschaftsinformatik, Vol. 38, No. 4, 1996, pp. 383-390.

[Grund-Ludwig 1997]
Grund-Ludwig, Pia: Diebold erwartet 1998 fast zehn Milliarden Mark Online-Umsatz, in: Computer Zeitung, No. 28, 10.7., 1997, p. 29.

[Gulledge/Hirschmann/Scheer 1997]
Gulledge, Thomas; Hirschmann, Petra; Scheer, August-Wilhelm: Value-based management of inter-organizational business process, in: Krallmann, H. (Ed.): Proc. of Wirtschaftsinformatik '97, Physica-Verlag, 1997, pp. 73-98.

[Haasper/Hovestadt/Peine 1997]
Haasper, Alexander; Hovestadt, Matthias; Peine, Christian: Weiterentwicklung einer Gateway-Anwendung zur Unterstützung weitverteilter Vorgangsbearbeitung im Rahmen des Wide Area GroupFlow Systems, Project thesis, Business Computing 2, University of Paderborn, 1998.

[Hagemeyer et al. 1997]
Hagemeyer, Jens; Herrmann, Thomas; Just-Hahn, Katharina; Striemer, Rüdiger: Flexibilität bei Workflow-Management Systemen, in: Tagungsband "Software Ergonomie 97", Dresden, 3.3.-6.3., 1997, pp. 179-190.

[Hagemeyer/Galler/Scheer 1996]
Hagemeyer, Jens; Galler, Jürgen; Scheer, August-Wilhelm: Koordination verteilter Workflowmodellierung mit ContAct, in: Rosemann, M., Becker, J. (Eds.): Workflowmanagement - State-of-the-Art aus Sicht von Theorie und Praxis, Arbeitsbericht No. 47, Universität Münster, Institut für Wirtschaftsinformatik, 1997, pp. 22-27

[Hales 1997]
Hales, Keith: Workflow management products, Sodan, see also: http://www.sodan.co.uk/wfmgmt.htm, 1997.

[Hales/Lavery 1991]
Hales, K.; Lavery, M.: Workflow management software – the business opportunity, Ovum Report, Ovum, London, 1991.

[Hammer 1990]
Hammer, Michael: Reengineering work – don't automate, obliterate: managers can release the real power of computers by challenging centuries-old notions about work, Harvard Business Review, July/August, 1990, pp. 104-112.

[Hammer/Champy 1993]
Hammer, Michael; Champy, James: Reengineering the corporation – a manifesto for business revolution, Harper Business, New York, 1993.

[Hammer/Stanton 1995]
Hammer, Michael; Stanton, S.: The reengineering revolution, Harper Collins, New York, 1995.

[Hammond 1993]
Hammond, J. H.: Quick response in retail/manufacturing channels, in: Bradley, S. P.; Hausman, J. A.; Nolan, R. L. (Eds.): Globalization, Technology and Competition – The Fusion of Computer and Telecommunications in the 1990s, Boston, 1993, pp. 185-214.

[Handy 1997]
Handy, C.: Trust and the virtual corporation, in: Harvard Business Review, 73 (3), 1997, pp. 40-50.

[Hansen 1992]
Hansen, Hans R.: Wirtschaftsinformatik I - Einführung in die betriebliche Datenverarbeitung, Gustav Fischer Verlag, 6. Auflage, Stuttgart, Jena, 1992.

[Hansen 1996]
Hansen, Hans R.: Klare Sicht am Info-Highway – Geschäfte via Internet & Co., Orac, Wien, 1996.

[Harrington 1991]
Harrington, H. James: Business process improvement – the breaktrough strategy for total quality, productivity, and competitiveness, McGraw-Hill, New York, 1991.

[Hart/Estrin 1990]
Hart, Paul; Estrin, Deborah: Computer integration – a co-requirement for effective organization of computer network implementation, in: Proc. of CSCW '90, ACM, 1990, pp. 131-142.

[Hasenkamp 1987]
Hasenkamp, Ulrich: Konzipierung eines Bürovorgangssystems - Informations- und Kommunikationstechnik zur aktiven Steuerung von Bürovorgängen, Habilitationsschrift, Wirtschafts- und Sozialwissenschaftliche Fakultät, Universität Köln, 1987.

[Hasenkamp/Kirn/Syring 1994]
Hasenkamp, Ulrich; Kirn, Stefan; Syring, Michael (Eds.): CSCW - Computer Supported Cooperative Work – Informationssysteme für dezentralisierte Unternehmensstrukturen, Addison-Wesley, Bonn, 1994.

[Hasenkamp/Syring 1993]
Hasenkamp, Ulrich; Syring, Michael: Konzepte und Einsatzmöglichkeiten von Workflow-Management-Systemen, in: Kurbel, K. (Ed.): Proc. of Wirtschaftsinformatik '93, Physica, Heidelberg, 1993, pp. 105-121.

[Hawker et al. 1996]
Hawker, Marion; Arteaga, Joe; Krause, Gerald; Morrison, Dave; Nakamura, Hiroki; Strobl, Reinhold: Lotus Notes Release 4.5 – a developer's handbook, International Technical Support Organization, IBM, First Edition, NC, 1996.

[Hayes/MacLeish 1997]
Hayes, Garrett M.; MacLeish, Kenneth I.: Group(where), in: ComputerWorld, 24.11., 1997, pp. 87-96.

[Heilmann 1996]
Heilmann, Heidi: Die Integration der Aufbauorganisation in Workflow-Management-Systeme, in: Heilmann, H.; Heinrich, L.; Roithmayer, F. (Eds.): Information Engineering, Oldenbourg, München, Wien, 1996, pp. 147-165.

[Hein 1997]
Hein, Olaf: Graphische Visualisierung und Analyse verteilten Workflow Managements – Konzeption und prototypische Implementierung des Wide Area GroupFlow Analyzers, Master thesis, Business Computing 2, University of Paderborn, 1997.

[Heinrich 1997]
Heinrich, Wilfried: Im Workflow-Warenkorb liegen auch faule Eier, in: Computer Zeitung, No. 31 / 31.07., 1997, p. 17.

[Heinz 1997]
Heinz, Oliver: Standards for groupware-based organizational subsystems within information systems - the impact on workflow-supporting office platforms, Masters Thesis, Business Computing 2, University of Paderborn, 1997.

[Herget 1994]
Herget, Josef: Schwer zu beweisen - Wirtschaftlichkeit der Bürokommunikation, in: Business Computing, No. 1, 1994, pp. 42-46.

[Herrmann/Pernul 1997]
Herrmann, Gaby; Pernul, Günther: Zur Bedeutung von Sicherheit in interorganisationellen Workflows, in: Wirtschaftsinformatik, Vol. 39, No. 3, 1997, pp. 217-224.

[Herrmann/Scheer/Weber 1998]
Herrmann, T.; Scheer, A.-W.; Weber, H.: Verbesserung von Geschäftsprozessen mit flexiblen Workflow-Management-Systemen – von der Erhebung zum Sollkonzept, Physica Verlag, Heidelberg, 1998.

[Herrmann/Walter 1997]
Herrmann, Thomas; Walter, Thomas: Participatory design and cyclic improvement of business processes with workflow management systems, in: Jatinder N.D. (Ed.): Proc. of Americas Conference on Information Systems (AIS), August 15 -17, Gupta Ball State University, Muncie, IN, 1997, pp. 925-928.

[Hilpert 1993a]
Hilpert, Wolfgang: GroupFlow – groupware-based workflow management, White paper, University of Paderborn, Business Computing, 1993.

[Hilpert 1993b]
Hilpert, Wolfgang: Workflow Management im Office-Bereich mit verteilten Dokumentendatenbanken, in: Workgroup Computing, S+W Steuer und Wirtschaftsverlag, Hamburg, 1993, pp. 127-140.

[Hilpert 1994]
Hilpert, Wolfgang: Effiziente und wirtschaftliche Einsatzplanung von Workflow Management-Systemen auf Groupware-Basis - vom Pilotprojekt zur unternehmensweiten Lösung, White paper, University of Paderborn, Business Computing, 1994.

[Hilpert/Riempp/Nastansky 1994]
Hilpert, Wolfgang; Riempp, Gerold; Nastansky, Ludwig: The GroupFlow system – workflow management in distributed organizations, White Paper, University of Paderborn, Business Computing, 1994.

[Hirschheim 1985]
Hirschheim, Rudy A.: Office automation – a social and organizational perspective, Wiley, Chichester, 1985.

[Hirschheim 1986]
Hirschheim, Rudy A.: Understanding the office – a social-analytic perspective, ACM Transactions on Office Information Systems, Vol. 4, 1986, p. 331-334.

[Hirschmann 1996]
Hirschmann, Petra: Wertorientiertes Management unternehmensübergreifender Geschäftsprozesse, in: Berkau, C., Hirschmann, P. (Eds.): Kostenorientiertes Geschäftsprozeßmanagement, Vahlen, München, 1996, pp. 229-254.

[Hirschmann/Scheer 1997]
Hirschmann, Petra; Scheer, August-Wilhelm: Architecture of a co-operation exchange for the continuous design of virtual enterprises, in: Galliers, R. et al. (Eds.): Proc. of the 5th European Conference on Information Systems, Cork, Vol. III, 1997, pp. 1191-1198.

[Hofland/Utsler 1997]
Hofland, Peter; Utsler, Jim: Reorganize your business – web-smart, business-process-aware applications are jump-starting a new era of workflow proficiency, in: Byte, No. 5, 1997, see also:
http://www.byte.com/art/9705/sec17/art1.htm.

[Hohberger 1995]
Hohberger, Peter: Was bewirkt die Reorganistion?, in: Business Computing, No. 12, 1995, pp. 24-27.

[Holland 1997]
Holland, Christopher P.: The evolution of electronic hierarchies in business markets, in: Wirtschaftsinformatik, Vol. 39, No. 3, 1997, pp. 245-251.

[Hovestadt/Peine 1998]
Hovestadt, Matthias; Peine, Christian: Grafische Modellierung von weitverteiltem Workflow Management - Konzeption und prototypische Implementierung eines Planungswerkzeuges für das Wide Area GroupFlow System, Master thesis, Business Computing 2, University of Paderborn, 1998.

[Howes 95]
Howes Timothy A.: The lightweight directory access protocol – X.500 lite, CITI Technical Report 95-8, University of Michigan, 1995.

[Hummel/Schoder/Strauss 1996]
Hummel, Thomas; Schoder, Detlef; Strauss, R.E.: Why CSCW applications fail – problems in the support of lateral cooperation and the appropriateness of CSCW applications, in: Proc. of the Annual Meeting of the Northeast Decision Sciences Institute (NEDSI), St. Croix, USA, 17-19 April, 1996.

[Hundehege 1997]
Hundehege, Frank: Neuordnung von intra- und interorganisationalen Geschäftsprozessen – Konzepte und Modelle zur Integration der Ansätze des Business Process Reengineering und des Wide Area Workflow Managements, Master thesis, Business Computing 2, University of Paderborn, 1997.

[Introna/Tiow 1997]
Introna, Lucas D.; Tiow, Bee L.: Thinking about virtual organisations and the future, in: Galliers, R. et al. (Eds.): Proc. of the 5th European Conference on Information Systems, Cork, Vol. II, 1997, pp. 996-1009.

[Ishii/Ohkubo 1991]
Ishii, Hiroshi; Ohkubo, M.: Message-driven groupware design based on an office procedure model – OM-1, in: Journal of Information Processing, Japan, Vol. 14, No. 2, 1991, pp. 184-191.

[Ising 1997]
Ising, Barbara: Groupware-Unterstützung für den mobilen Außendienstes – Analyse und Konzeption eines Vertriebsinformationssystems mit Anbindung an zentrale Backendstrukturen für ein Unternehmen der Lebensmittelbranche, Master thesis, Business Computing, University of Paderborn, 1997.

[ISO X.500 1993]
ISO: The Directory – overview of concepts, models and services, X.500, ISO 9594-1, 1993.

[ISO X.501 1993]
ISO: The Directory – models, recommendation X.501, ISO 9594-2, 1993.

[ISO X.525 1993]
ISO: The Directory – replication, X.525, ISO 9594-9, 1993.

[Iten 1996]
Iten, Anton: Workflow-Management bei Landis & Gyr, in: Österle, H., Vogler, P. (Eds.): Praxis des Workflow Managements, Vieweg, Braunschweig, Wiesbaden, 1996, pp. 253-270.

[Jablonski 1995]
Jablonski, Stefan: Workflow-Management-Systeme – Motivation, Modellierung, Architektur, in: Informatik Spektrum, Springer Verlag, 18, 1995, pp. 13-24.

[Jablonski 1996]
Jablonski, Stefan: Anforderungen an die Modellierung von Workflows, in: Österle, H.; Vogler, P. (Eds.): Praxis des Workflow Managements, Vieweg, Braunschweig, Wiesbaden, 1996, pp. 65-81.

[Jablonski 1997]
Jablonski, Stefan: Architektur von Workflow Management Systemen, in: Informatik, Forschung und Entwicklung, Vol. 12, No. 2, 1997.

[Jablonski/Böhm/Schulze 1997]
Jablonski, Stefan; Böhm, Markus; Schulze, Wolfgang: Workflow-Management – Entwicklung von Anwendungen und Systemen: Facetten einer neuen Technologie, dpunkt Verlag, 1997.

[Jablonski/Bussler 1996]
Jablonski, Stefan; Bussler, Christoph: Workflow management – modeling concepts, architecture and implementation, International Thomson Computer Press, London etc., 1996.

[JCSCW 1996]
CSCW – computer supported cooperative work – the journal of collaborative computing, Schmidt, K. et al. (Eds.), Kluwer Academic Publishers Group, Dordrecht, 1996.

[Johansen 1991]
Johansen, Robert: Leading business teams – how teams can use technology and group process tools to enhance performance, Addison-Wesley, New York, 1991.

[Johanson/Mattsson 1987]
Johanson, J.; Mattsson, L.-G.: Interorganizational relations in industrial systems – a network approach compared with the transaction-cost concept, in: International Studies of Management & Organization, Vol. 17, No. 1, 1987, pp. 34-48.

[Johansson et al. 1994]
Johansson, Henry J.; McHugh, Patrick; Pendlebury, A. John; Wheeler III, William A.: Business process reengineering – breakpoint strategies for market dominance, Wiley, Chichester, 1994.

[Johnston/Lawrence 1988]
Johnston, Russell; Lawrence, Paul R.: Beyond vertical integration – the rise of the value-adding partnership, in: Harvard Business Review, Vol. 66, No. 4, 1988, pp. 94-101.

[Joosten 1995]
Joosten, Stef: A method for analysing workflows, white paper, Center for Telematics and Information Technology, University of Twente, 1995, pp. 1-32.

[Joosten et al. 1994]
Joosten, Stef; Aussems, Gaston; Duitshof, Matthijs; Huffmeier, Richard; Mulder, Erik: WA-12: An empirical study about the practice of workflow management, University of Twente, 2nd edition, Twente, 1994.

[Joosten/Brinkkemper 1995]
Joosten, Stef; Brinkkemper, Sjaak: Fundamental concepts for workflow automation in practice, white paper, Center for Telematics and Information Technology, University of Twente, 1995, pp. 1-18.

[Joosten/Ploeger/Brinkkemper 1995]
Joosten, Stef; Ploeger, Eelco; Brinkkemper, Sjaak: The contribution of groupware to corporate communication – towards the horizontal organization, white paper, Center for Telematics and Information Technology, University of Twente, 1995, pp. 1-14.

[Kamath et al. 1997]
Kamath, Mohan; Ramamritham, Krithi; Gehani, Narain; Lieuwen, Daniel: WorldFlow – a system for building global transactional workflows, Proc. of 7th International Workshop on High Performance Transaction Systems, Asilomar, California, 1997.

[Kaneshige 1995]
Kaneshige, Thomas: Messaging wird mit Workflow verknüpft, in: Computer Zeitung, No. 39, 28.9., 1995, p. 9.

[Kanter/Myers 1991]
Kanter, R. M.; Myers, P. S.: Interorganizational bonds and intraorganizational behavior – how alliances and partnerships change the organizations forming them, in: Etzioni, A.; Lawrence, P. (Eds.): Socio-Economics – Towards a New Synthesis, Studies in Socio-Economics Series, Sharpe Publishing, London, 1991, pp. 329-344.

[Karl 1997/1998]
Karl, Renate: Workflow Management - Einordnung und Marktsichtung (Teil 1), Produkteinordnung (Teil 2), in: IS report, No. 12, 1997, pp. 6-9 and No. 1, 1998, pp. 32-34.

[Karl/Deiters 1994]
Karl, Renate; Deiters, Wolfgang: Studie Workflow Management – Groupware Computing, Eigenverlag dsk Beratungs-GmbH, Pfaffenhofen, 1994.

[Karszt 1996]
Karszt, Jakob: EDI goes Internet, in: Computer Zeitung, No. 27, 4.7., 1996, p. 15.

[Kaufman 1966]
Kaufman, Felix: Data systems that cross company boundaries, in: Harvard Business Review, 44/1, 2, 1966, pp. 141-155.

[Kawell et al. 1992]
Kawell, Leonard; Beckhardt, Steven; Halvorsen, Timothy; Ozzie, Raymond; Greif, Irene: Replicated document management in a group communication system, in: Marca, D., Bock, G. (eds.): Groupware – Software for Computer Supported Cooperative Work, IEEE Computer Society Press, 1992, pp. 226-235.

[Khoshafian/Buckiewicz 1995]
Khoshafian, Setrag; Buckiewicz, Marek: Groupware, workflow and workgroup computing, Wiley, New York, 1995.

[Kilian et al.1994]
Kilian, Wolfgang; Picot, Arnold; Neuburger, Rahild; Niggl, Johann; Scholtes, Kay-Larsen; Seiler, Wolfgang: EDI – aus ökonomischer und juristischer Sicht, Nomos Verlagsgesellschaft, Baden-Baden, 1994.

[Killer 1997]
Killer, Achim: R/3 greift nach Daten von Lieferanten und Kunden , in: Computer Zeitung, No. 37, 9.11., 1997, p. 9.

[Kingsbury 1997]
Kingsbury, Nick: Workflow in insurance, in: Lawrence, P. (Ed.): Workflow Handbook 1997, Wiley, Chichester etc., 1997, pp. 91-100.

[Klein 1996]
Klein, Stefan: Interorganisationssysteme und Unternehmensnetzwerke – Wechselwirkungen zwischen organisatorischer und informationstechnischer Entwicklung, DUV - Gabler Edition Wissenschaft, Wiesbaden, 1996.

[Klöckner et al. 1995]
Klöckner, K.; Mambrey, P.; Solenkamp, M.; Prinz, W.; Fuchs, L.; Kolvenbach, S.; Pankoke-Babatz, U.; Syri, A.: POLITeam – bridging the gap between Bonn and Berlin for and with the users, in: Proc. of ECSCW '95, Kluwer Academic Publishers, Dordrecht, 1995, pp. 17-32.

[Kobielus 1997]
Kobielus, James G.: Workflow strategies, IDG Books Worldwide, Foster City, CA etc., 1997.

[Koepke/Kettler 1997]
Koepke, Irene; Kettler, Hermann: Der Außendienst benötigt Notebooks mit einer Anbindung an das Firmennetz – die Aachener und Münchener Versicherung stellte in einer Woche auf mobile PCs um, in: Computer Zeitung, No. 43, 23.10., 1997, p. 22.

[Koulopoulos 1995]
Koulopoulos, Thomas: The workflow imperative – building real world business solutions, van Nostrand Reinhold, 2nd edition, New York etc., 1995.

[Kozlowski 1997a]
Kozlowski, Mary Ann: Delphi presents wide area workflow seminar at BPR conference, press release, Delphi Consulting Group, http://www.delphigroup.com/pressreleases/1997-PR/02131997DelphiGigaSeminar.html, 1997.

[Kozlowski 1997b]
Kozlowski, Mary Ann: Delphi research shows workflow market continues modest growth as technology proliferates, press release, Delphi Consulting Group, http://www.delphigroup.com/pressreleases/1997-PR/08281997WFMkt.html, 1997.

[Krallmann/Derszteler 1996]
Krallmann, Herrmann; Derszteler, Gérard: Workflow management cycle – an integrated approach to the modelling, execution, and monitoring of workflow-based processes, in: Scholz-Reiter, B.; Stickel, E. (Eds.): Business Process Modelling, Springer Verlag, Berlin etc., 1996, pp. 23-42.

[Krcmar 1993]
Krcmar, Helmut: EDI in Europe – empirical analysis of a multi-industry study, in: institute publication, No. 49, University of Hohenheim, 1993, pp. 1-18.

[Krcmar et al. 1996]
Krcmar, Helmut; Lewe, Henrik; Schwabe, Gerhard (Eds.): Herausforderung Telekooperation – Einsatzerfahrung und Lösungsansätze für ökonomische und ökologische, technische und soziale Fragen unserer Gesellschaft, Proc. of the 2nd German CSCW Conference, Springer Verlag, Berlin etc., 1996.

[Krcmar/Zerbe 1996]
Krcmar, Helmut; Zerbe, Stefan: Negotiation enabled workflow (NEW) – Workflowsysteme zur Unterstützung flexibler Geschäftsprozesse, in: Rosemann, M., Becker, J. (Eds.): Workflowmanagement - State-of-the-Art aus Sicht von Theorie und Praxis, Arbeitsbericht No. 47, Universität Münster, Institut für Wirtschaftsinformatik, 1996, pp. 28-36.

[Kreifelts et al. 1984]
Kreifelts, Thomas; Licht, U.; Seuffert, P.; Woetzel, G.: DOMINO – a system for the specification and automation of cooperative office processes, in: Myhrhaug, Wilson (Eds.): Proc. of EUROMICRO 1984, North-Holland, 1984.

[Kreifelts et al. 1991]
Kreifelts, Thomas; Hinrichs, E.; Klein, K.-H.; Seuffert, P.; Woetzel, G.: Experiences with the DOMINO office procedure system, in: Bannon, L., Robinson, M., Schmidt, K. (eds.): Proc. of ECSCW '91, Kluwer, Dordrecht, 1991, pp. 117-130.

[Kremer 1998]
Kremer, Stefan: Verteiltes Workflow Management mit Hilfe des WWW – Konzeption und prototypische Implementierung von Web-basierten Directory Services für das Wide Area GroupFlow System, Project thesis, Business Computing 2, University of Paderborn, 1998.

[Kuethe 1996]
Kuethe, Michael: Message object routing – Prototyp einer Gateway Datenbank für Vorgangsbearbeitung in weitverteilten Netzen, Master thesis, Business Computing 2, University of Paderborn, 1996.

[Kurbel 1997]
Kurbel, Karl: Internet-Nutzung im Business-to-Business-Bereich – Stand der Entwicklung, Typologie und Anwendungsbeispiele, in: Proc. of the 3rd International Conference "Wirtschaftsinformatik '97", Physica-Verlag, Berlin, 1997, pp. 23-34.

[Laudon/Laudon 1996]
Laudon, Kenneth C.; Laudon, Jane P.: Management information systems – organization and technology, Prentice Hall International, 4th edition, New Jersey, 1996.

[Law 1974]
Law, P.: Product management, Harper & Row, Boston etc., 1974.

[Lawrence 1997]
Lawrence, Peter: Directory of workflow products – workflow on the Web, Concordium Ltd., 1997, see: http://www.concordium.co.uk/.

[Lee et al. 1996]
Lee, Jintae; Gruninger, Michael; Jin, Yan; Malone, Thomas; Tate, Austin; Yost, Gregg: The PIF process interchange format and framework, in: Center for Coordination Science, MIT, working paper No. 194, Cambridge, MA, 1996.

[Leymann 1995]
Leymann, Frank: Supporting business transactions via partial backward recovery in workflow management systems, in: Lausen, G. (Ed.): Datenbanksysteme in Büro, Technik und Wissenschaft, Proc. of BTW '95, Springer Verlag, Berlin etc., 1995, pp. 51-70.

[Leymann 1996]
Leymann, Frank: Transaktionskonzepte für Workflow-Management-Systeme, in: Vossen, G.; Becker, J. (Eds.): Geschäftsprozeßmodellierung und Workflow Management – Modelle, Methoden, Werkzeuge, International Thomson Publishing, Bonn etc., 1996, pp. 335-352.

[Leymann 1997]
Leymann, Frank: Transaktionsunterstützung für Workflow, in: Informatik, Forschung und Entwicklung, Springer Verlag, No. 12, 1997, pp. 82-90.

[Leymann/Altenhuber 1994]
Leymann, Frank; Altenhuber, W.: Managing business processes as an information resource, in: IBM Systems Journal, Vol. 33, No. 2, 1994, pp. 326-348.

[Light 1997]
Light, Richard: Presenting XML, Samsnet, First edition, 1997.

[Lindemann/Klein 1997]
Lindemann, Markus; Klein, Stefan: Die Nutzung von Internet-Diensten im Rahmen des Elektronischen Datenaustauschs – Architekturvarianten und ein Anwendungsszenario , in: Krallmann, H. (Ed.): Proc. of the 3rd International Conference "Wirtschaftsinformatik '97", Physica-Verlag, 1997, pp. 513-531.

[Lloyd/Whitehead 1996]
Lloyd, Peter; Whitehead, Roger: Transforming organisations through groupware – Lotus Notes in Action, Springer Verlag, Berlin etc., 1996.

[Lyons 1996]
Lyons, Daniel: Lotus leads in groupware, in: Computer Reseller News, Issue 701, 16.9., 1996.

[Malone et al. 1987]
Malone, Thomas W.; Grant, K.; Lai, K.; Rao, R.; Rosenblitt, D.: Semistructured messages are surprisingly useful for computer-supported coordination, in: ACM Transactions on Office Information Systems, Vol. 5, No. 2, 1987, pp. 115-131.

[Malone et al. 1993]
Malone, Thomas W.; Crowston, Kevin; Lee, Jintae; Pentland, Brian: Tools for inventing organizations – toward a handbook of organizational processes, in: In Proceedings of the 2nd IEEE Workshop on Enabling Technologies Infrastructure for Collaborative Enterprises, Morgantown, WV, April 20-22, 1993.

[Malone et al. 1997]
Malone, Thomas W.; Crowston, Kevin; Lee, Jintae; Pentland, Brian; Dellarocas, Chrysanthos; Wyner, George; Quimby, John; Osborne, Charley; Bernstein, Abraham: Tools for inventing organizations – toward a handbook of organizational processes, working paper No. 198, Center of Coordination Science, MIT, Cambridge, MA, 1997. See also: http://ccs.mit.edu/ccswp198/.

[Malone/Crowston 1990]
Malone, Thomas W.; Crowston, Kevin: What is coordination theory and how can it help design cooperative systems?, in: Proc. of CSCW '90, ACM, New York, 1990, pp. 357-370.

[Malone/Crowston 1994]
Malone, Thomas W.; Crowston, Kevin: The interdisciplinary study of coordination, in: ACM Computing Surveys, 26, 1994, pp. 185-201.

[Malone/Rockart 1993]
Malone, Thomas W.; Rockart, John F.: How will information technology reshape organizations? – computers as coordination technology, in: Bradley et al. (Eds.): Globalization, Technology and Competition – the Fusion of Computer and Telecommunications in the 1990s, Harvard Business School Press, Boston, MA, 1993, pp. 36-56.

[Malone/Yates/Benjamin 1987]
Malone, Thomas W.; Yates, J.; Benjamin, R. I.: Electronic markets and electronic hierarchies, in: Communications of the ACM, Vol. 30, No. 6, 1987, pp. 297-304.

[Manganelli/Klein 1994]
Manganelli, Raymond L.; Klein, Mark M.: The reengineering handbook – a step-by-step guide to business transformation, AMACON, New York, 1994.

[Manhart 1996]
Manhart, Markus: Evaluation eines Workflow-Systems, in: Österle, H.; Vogler, P. (Eds.): Praxis des Workflow Managements, Vieweg, Braunschweig, Wiesbaden, 1996, pp. 107-122.

[Marr 1997]
Marr, Michael: Redesign von organisatorischen Abläufen im Bereich der Bestellabwicklung von Gemeinkostenkomponenten am Beispiel eines weltweiten agierenden Beleuchtungsherstellers, Master thesis, Business Computing 2, University of Paderborn, 1997.

[Marshak 1992]
Marshak, Ronni T.: Requirements for workflow, in: Office Computing Report, Seybold, Boston, Vol. 15, No. 3, 1992, pp. 3-16.

[Marshak 1993]
Marshak, Ronni T.: Action Technologies' workflow products – coordinating the activities of people as they work together, in: Workgroup Computing Report, Seybold, Boston, Vol. 16, No. 5, 1993, pp. 4-11.

[Marshak 1995]
Marshak, Ronni T.: Pavone GroupFlow – providing a workflow suite for Lotus Notes environments, in: Workgroup Computing Report, Vol. 18, No. 11, Seybold, Boston, 1995, pp. 3 - 23.

[McCready et al. 1994]
McCready, Scott C.; Palermo, Ann M.; Murray, Gerry; Johnson, Darby: Lotus Notes – agent of change, the financial impact of Lotus Notes on business, International Data Corporation (IDC), Nov., 1994.

[McMellan 1996]
McMellan, Mark: Workflow metrics - one of the great benefits of workflow, in: Österle, H.; Vogler, P. (Eds.): Praxis des Workflow Managements, Vieweg, Braunschweig, Wiesbaden, 1996, pp. 301-318.

[McMichael/Mackay/Altmann 1997]
McMichael, H.; Mackay, D. R.; Altmann, G. L.: Quick response in the Australian textile clothing and footwear industry, in: Galliers, R. et al. (Eds.): Proc. of the 5th European Conference on Information Systems, Cork, Vol. I, 1997, pp. 295-312.

[Mertens 1966]
Mertens, Peter: Die zwischenbetriebliche Kooperation und Integration bei der automatisierten Datenverarbeitung, Verlag Anton Hain, Meisenheim am Glan, 1966.

[Mertens 1985]
Mertens, Peter: Zwischenbetriebliche Integration der EDV, in: Informatik-Spektrum, Vol. 8, No. 2, 1985, pp. 81-90.

[Mertens 1994]
Mertens, Peter: Virtuelle Unternehmen, in: Wirtschaftsinformatik, Vol. 36, No. 2, 1994, pp. 169-172.

[Mertens 1995]
Mertens, Peter: Supply Chain Management (SCM), in: Wirtschaftsinformatik, Vol. 37, No. 2, 1995, pp. 177-179.

[Mertens/Faisst 1995]
Mertens, Peter; Faisst, Wolfgang: Virtuelle Unternehmen - eine Organisationsstruktur für die Zukunft?, in: technologie & management, Vol. 44, No. 2, 1995, pp. 61-68.

[Microsoft WF MAPI 1996]
Microsoft Corporation: Microsoft MAPI workflow framework – overview and reference, Version 2.0, Microsoft Corporation, Redmond, WA, May-1., 1996, pp. 1-88.

[Miller et al. 1996]
Miller, John A.; Sheth, Amit; Kochut, Krys J.; Wang, Xuzhong: CORBA-based run-time architectures for workflow management systems, in: Journal of Database Management, Special Issue on Multidatabases, Vol. 7, No. 1, 1996, pp. 16-27.

[Miller et al. 1997a]
Miller, John; Palaniswami, Devanand; Sheth, Amit; Kochut, Krys; Singh, Harvinder: WebWork – METEOR's Web-based workflow management system, technical report #UGA-CS-TR-97-002, Department of Computer Science, University of Georgia, 1997.

[Miller et al. 1997b]
Miller, J.; Sheth, A.; Kochut, K.; Palaniswami, D.: The future of Web-based workflows, in: Proc. of the International Workshop on Research Directions in Process Technology, Nancy, France, July, 1997.

[Miller/Clemons/Row 1993]
Miller, David B.; Clemons, Eric K.; Row, Michael C.: Information technology and the global virtual corporation, in: Bradley et al. (Eds.): Globalization, Technology and Competition – the Fusion of Computer and Telecommunications in the 1990s, Harvard Business School Press, Boston, 1993, pp. 283-307.

[Mohan et al. 1995]
Mohan, C.; Alonso, G.; Günthör, R.; Kamath, M.: Exotica – a research perspective on workflow management systems, in: Bulletin of the Technical Committee on Data Engineering, IEEE Computer Society, Vol. 18, No. 1, 1995, pp. 19-26.

[Morris/Brandon 1994]
Morris, Daniel C.; Brandon, Joel S.: Re-engineering your business, McGraw-Hill, New York, 1994.

[Morschheuser 1997]
Morschheuser, Stefan: Integrierte Informationsverarbeitung durch Dokumenten- und Workflow-Management, dargestellt am Angebotsprozeß von Maschinenbauunternehmen, Dissertation, DUV - Gabler Edition Wissenschaft, Wiesbaden, 1997.

[Morschheuser/Raufer/Wargitsch 1996]
Morschheuser, Stefan; Raufer, H.; Wargitsch, Christoph: Challenges and solutions of document and workflow management in a manufacturing enterprise – a case study, in: Nunamaker jr., J. F. et al. (Eds.): Proc. of the 29th Annual Hawaii International Conference on System Science, IEEE Computer Society Press, Los Alamitos, Vol. V, 1996, pp. 4-13.

[Mummert 1996]
Mummert + Partner Unternehmensberatungs GmbH: Marktübersicht Vorgangssteuerungssysteme, Frankfurt, 1996.

[Mummert 1997]
Mummert + Partner Unternehmensberatungs GmbH: Marktübersicht Vorgangssteuerungssysteme, Frankfurt, 1997.

[Munkvold 1997]
Munkvold, Bjoern Erik: Challenges of IT implementation for supporting collaboration in distributed organisations – experiences from four implementation teams, in: Galliers, R. et al. (Eds.): Proc. of the 5th European Conference on Information Systems, Cork, Vol. I, 1997, pp. 497-510.

[Nastansky 1993]
Nastansky, Ludwig: Nach 20 Jahren CSCW-Forschung – Durchbruch in der Praxis bei Groupware-Anwendungen in Client-Server Architekturen, in: Nastansky, L. (Ed.): Workgroup Computing, S+W Steuer und Wirtschaftsverlag, Hamburg, 1993, pp. 1-20.

[Nastansky/Hilpert 1994]
Nastansky, Ludwig; Hilpert, Wolfgang: The GroupFlow System – a scalable approach to workflow management between cooperation and automation, in: Wolfinger, B. (Ed.): Innovationen bei Rechen- und Kommunikationssystemen - Eine Herausforderung an die Informatik, Proc. of 24th Annual Conference of the German Computer Society during 13th World Computer Congress, IFIP '94, Springer Verlag, Berlin etc., 1994, pp. 473 - 479.

[Nastansky/Hilpert 1995]
Nastansky, Ludwig; Hilpert, Wolfgang: Das GroupFlow System für Workflow-Management – Balance zwischen Struktur und Flexibilität, in: Business Computing, No. 7, 1995, pp. 30 - 31.

[Nastansky/Hilpert 1996]
Nastansky, Ludwig; Hilpert, Wolfgang: The GroupFlow framework – enterprise model and architecture of the workflow system, in: Koenig, W., Kurbel, K., Mertens, P., Pressmar, D. (Eds.): Distributed Information Systems in Business, Springer Verlag, Berlin etc., 1996, pp. 201-212.

[Niebiossa 1998]
Niebiossa, Claudius: Weitverteiltes Workflow Management im Office eines Bildungsträgers – Konzeption und prototypische Realisierung auf Basis des Wide Area GroupFlow Systems, Master thesis, Business Computing 2, University of Paderborn, 1998.

[Norman/Ramirez 1993]
Norman, Richard; Ramirez, Rafael: From value chain to value constellation – designing interactive strategy, in: Harvard Business Review, July/August, 1993, pp. 65-77.

[Oberweis et al. 1997]
Oberweis, Andreas; Schätzle, Roland; Stucky, Wolffried; Weitz, Wolfgang; Zimmermann, Gabriele: INCOME/WF – a petri net based approach to workflow management, in: Krallmann, H. (Ed.): Proc. of 3rd International Conference "Wirtschaftsinformatik '97", Physica-Verlag, Heidelberg, 1997, pp. 557-580.

[Oesterle 1996]
Österle, Hubert: Business Engineering: Von intuitiver Organisation zu rationalen Workflows, in: Österle, H.; Vogler, P. (Eds.): Praxis des Workflow Managements, Vieweg, Braunschweig, Wiesbaden, 1996, pp. 1-18.

[Oesterle/Vogler 1996]
Österle, Hubert; Vogler, Petra (Eds.): Praxis des Workflow Managements – Grundlagen, Vorgehen, Beispiele, Vieweg, Braunschweig, Wiesbaden, 1996.

[Oesterwind/Rohloff 1996]
Oesterwind, Christian; Rohloff, Michael: An order management & provisioning system based on workgroup computing with Lotus Notes for an international joint venture in the field of telecommunications, in: Uellner, St. (Ed.): Proc. of the Workshop "CSCW in large enterprises", Deutsche Telekom AG, Darmstadt, 1996, pp. 99-105.

[Oliver/Webber 1992]
Oliver, R. K.; Webber, M. D.: Supply chain management – logistics catches up with strategy, in: Christopher, M. (Ed.): Logistics - the strategic issue, Chapman & Hall, London, 1992, pp. 63-75.

[Orlikowski 1992]
Orlikowski, Wanda J.: Learning from Notes – organisational issues in groupware implementation, in: Proc. of CSCW '92, ACM Press, New York, 1992, pp. 362-369.

[Orlikowski 1995]
Orlikowski, Wanda J.: Evolving with Notes – organizational change around groupware technology, White Paper, Center for Coordination Science, MIT, Boston, 1995.

[Orlikowski/Hofman 1996]
Orlikowski, Wanda J.; Hofman, Debra J.: An improvisational model of change management – the case of groupware technologies, working paper No. 191, Center for Coordination Science, MIT, Cambridge, MA, 1996.

[Ott/Nastansky 1998]
Ott, Marcus; Nastansky, Ludwig: Groupware technology for a new approach to organization design systems, in: Watson, H. J.; Nunamaker jr., F.; Sprague, R.H. (Eds.): Proc. of the 31st Hawaii International Conference On System Sciences, Vol. VI, IEEE Computer Society Press, Los Alamitos CA, Washington etc., 1998, pp. 562-571.

[Ottomeier 1996]
Ottomeier, Martin: EDI im Internet benötigt mehr Sicherheit – für Datenaustausch fehlen Standards, in: Computer Zeitung, No. 42, 17.10., 1996, p. 22.

[Ottomeier 1997]
Ottomeier, Martin: Schlechte Noten für Objekt-Middleware – Ovum zerreißt DCOM ebenso wie CORBA, in: Computer Zeitung, No. 33, 14.8., 1997, p. 1.

[Palermo/McCready 1992]
Palermo, Ann M.; McCready, Scott C.: Workflow software – a primer, in: Proc. of the Conference Groupware '92, San Jose, California, 1992, pp. 155-159.

[Pankoke-Babatz/Syri 1996]
Pankoke-Babatz, Uta; Syri, Anja: Gemeinsame Arbeitsbereiche – eine neue Form der Telekooperation?, in: Krcmar, H., Lewe, H., Schwabe, G. (Eds.): Herausforderung Telekooperation – Proc. of German CSCW Conference '96, Springer Verlag, Berlin etc., 1996, pp. 51-68.

[Patridge/Rose 1989]
Patridge, Craig; Rose, Marshall T.: A comparison of external data formats, in: Stefferud E. et al. (Eds.): Message Handling Systems and Distributed Applications, Elsevier, Amsterdam, 1989, pp. 233-280.

[Peters 1995]
Peters, Joachim: Bei INA Wälzlager nimmt man BPR ernst, in: Business Computing, No. 12, 1995, pp. 42-44.

[Peters 1997]
Peters, Hanno: Elektronische Teamarbeit, in: IT-Services, No. 8-9, 1997, pp. 42-44.

[Petri 1974]
Petri, C.: Introduction to general net theory of processes and systems, Hamburg, 1974.

[Petrovic/Kopperger 1997]
Petrovic, Mirjana; Kopperger, Dietmar: POLIFlow treibt Amtsschimmel zwischen Berlin und Bonn an – Öffentliche Verwaltung lernt verteiltes elektronisches Arbeiten, in: Computer Zeitung, No. 42, 16.10., 1997, pp. 32.

[Pfeiffer 1996]
Pfeiffer, Stefan: Keine Lösung für die Ewigkeit suchen – kurzfristige Produktivitätssteigerungen durch Dokumentenmanagement-Systeme nutzen, in: Computerwoche Focus: Workflow - die Geschäftsprozesse beschleunigen, 15.3., 1996, pp. 16-19.

[Picot/Neuburger/Niggl 1991]
Picot, Arnold; Neuburger, Rahild; Niggl, Johann: Ökonomische Perspektiven eines Electronic Data Interchange, in: Information Management, No. 2, 1991, pp. 22-29.

[Picot/Rohrbach 1995]
Picot, Arnold; Rohrbach, Peter: Organisatorische Aspekte von Workflow-Management-Systemen, in: Information Management, No. 1, 1995, pp. 28-35.

[Powell 1990]
Powell, W. W.: Neither market nor hierarchy – network forms of organization, in: Staw, B. M.; Cummings, L. L. (Eds.): Research in Organizational Behaviour, Greenwich, Conn., Vol. 12, 1990, pp. 295-336.

[Power 1993]
Power, Richard J.D.: Cooperation among organizations – the potential of computer supported cooperative work, Springer Verlag, Berlin etc., 1993.

[Premkumar/Ramamurthy 1995]
Premkumar, G.; Ramamurthy, K.: The role of inter-organisational and organisational factors on the decision mode for adoption of inter-organisational systems, in: Decision Sciences, Vol. 26, No. 3, 1995, pp. 305-327.

[Prinz 1993]
Prinz, Wolfgang: TOSCA: Providing to organisational information CSCW applications, in: Michelis, G., Schmidt, K., Simone, C. (Eds.) Proc. of ECSCW'93, Kluwer, Dordrecht, 1993, pp. 139-154.

[Prinz 1994]
Prinz, Wolfgang: TOSCA – Organisationswissen für CSCW-Anwendungen, in: Hasenkamp, U., Kirn, S., Syring, M. (Eds.): CSCW - Computer Supported Cooperative Work – Informationssysteme für dezentralisierte Unternehmensstrukturen, 2. Auflage, Addison Wesley, Bonn etc., 1994, pp. 161-177.

[Prinz/Kolvenbach 1996]
Prinz, Wolfgang; Kolvenbach, Sabine: Support for workflows in a ministerial environment, in: Proc. of CSCW'96, ACM, Boston, MA, 1996, pp. 199-208.

[Prinz/Pennelli 1992]
Prinz, Wolfgang; Pennelli, Paola: Relevance of the X.500 directory to CSCW applications, in: Marca, D., Bock, G. (Eds.): Groupware – software for computer supported cooperative work, IEEE Computer Society Press, 1992, pp. 209-225.

[Rathgeb 1994]
Rathgeb, Michael: Einführung von Workflow-Management-Systemen, in: Hasenkamp, U.; Kirn, S,; Syring, M. (Eds.): CSCW – Computer Supported Cooperative Work – Informationssysteme für dezentralisierte Unternehmensstrukturen, 2. Auflage, Addison Wesley, Bonn etc., 1994, pp. 45-66.

[Rathgeb 1996]
Rathgeb, Michael: Verfahren zur Gestaltung rechnergestützter Büroprozesse, Springer Verlag, Berlin etc., 1996.

[Reekers/Smithson 1994]
Reekers, Norbert; Smithson, Steve: EDI and interorganizational coordination in the european automotive industry, Proc. of Second SISnet Conference, Barcelona, 26-28 September, 1994, see also: publications of London School of Economics and Political Science, Information Systems Department.

[Reekers/Smithson 1995]
Reekers, Norbert; Smithson, Steve: The impact of electronic data interchange on interorganizational relationships – integrating theoretical perspectives, in: Watson, H. J.; Nunamaker jr., F.; Sprague, R.H. (Eds.): Proc. of the 28th Hawaii International Conference On System Sciences, Minitrack: Measuring the Effectiveness/Impact of Emerging Technologies, Maui, Hawaii, January 3-6, 1995.

[Reich 1997]
Reich, Siegfried: De modo operandi – towards the interoperability of workflow information, doctoral thesis at the University of Vienna, WUV - Universitätsverlag, Band 34, Wien, 1997.

[Reichwald 1984]
Reichwald, Ralf: Cooperation in the office – office communication systems as management tool, in: Proc. of the 2nd ACM SIGOA Conference on Office Information Systems, ACM, New York, June, 1984, pp. 212-218.

[Reichwald et al. 1998]
Reichwald, R.; Moeslein, K.; Sachenbacher, H.; Englberger, H.; Oldenburg, S.: Telekooperation – Verteilte Arbeits- und Organisationsformen, Springer Verlag, Berlin etc., 1998.

[Reinwald 1995]
Reinwald, Berthold: Workflow-Management in verteilten Systemen, Dissertation, University of Nuernberg-Erlangen, Teubner, 2nd edition, Stuttgart, 1995.

[Reinwald/Wedekind 1992]
Reinwald, Berthold; Wedekind, Helmut: Automation of control and data flow in distributed application systems, in:, Proc. of the International Conference on Database and Expert System Applications, Valencia, Spain, Springer Verlag, Berlin etc., 1992, pp. 475-481.

[Reiter 1997a]
Reiter, Michael: Die professionelle Revolution im Web heißt Extensible Markup Language (XML) – strukturierte Daten behalten mit der neuen Internet-Sprache XML ihre Gliederung, in: Computer Zeitung, No. 32, 07.08., 1997, p. 16.

[Reiter 1997b]
Reiter, Michael: Java ist gerettet - und gefordert, in: Computer Zeitung, No. 48, 1997, p. 11.

[Reiter 1997c]
Reiter, Michael: Microsoft stellt mit COM+ den Nachfolger von COM vor – Gates beerdigt Active X und hebt Win-DNA aus der Taufe, in: Computer Zeitung, No. 41, 9.10., 1997, p. 19.

[Reiter 1997d]
Reiter, Michael: Der PC besitzt zu unrecht den Mythos einer umweltgerechten Technologie – ein Computer verschlingt während seines gesamten Lebens 19 Tonnen Ressourcen, in: Computer Zeitung, No. 34, 21.8, 1997, p. 6.

[Richards 1997]
Richards, Cate: Using Lotus Notes 4.5, QUE, Indianapolis, 1997.

[Riempp 1994]
Riempp, Gerold: Modellentwurf für Workflow Management mit verteilten Dokumenten-Datenbanken im WAN-Verbund, master thesis, Technical University of Darmstadt and University of Paderborn, 1994.

[Riempp/Nastansky 1996a]
Riempp, Gerold; Nastansky, Ludwig: Workflow management between distributed organizations - the Wide Area GroupFlow approach, in: Krcmar, H. et al. (Eds.): Herausforderung Telekooperation – Proc. of German CSCW 1996, Springer Verlag, Berlin etc., 1996, pp. 275-292.

[Riempp/Nastansky 1996b]
Riempp, Gerold; Nastansky, Ludwig: Workflow Management zwischen verteilten Groupware-basierten Büros (Wide Area OfficeFlow) – die WideOffice-Infrastruktur zur Interaktion vernetzter Teams, in: Uellner, St. (Eds.): Proc. of Workshop "CSCW in großen Unternehmungen", Telekom AG, Darmstadt, 1996, pp. 193-207.

[Riempp/Nastansky 1997a]
Riempp, Gerold; Nastansky, Ludwig: From islands to flexible business process networks - enabling the interaction of distributed workflow management systems, in: Galliers, R. et al. (Eds.): Proc. of the 5th European Conference on Information Systems, Cork, Vol. I, 1997, pp. 481-496.

[Riempp/Nastansky 1997b]
Riempp, Gerold; Nastansky, Ludwig: Workflow management between distributed organizations - the Wide Area GroupFlow System, in: Lehner, F.; Dustar, S. (Eds.): Telekooperation in Unternehmen, Deutscher Universitäts Verlag, Gabler Edition Wissenschaft, Wiesbaden, 1997, pp. 265-282.

[Riempp/Nastansky 1997c]
Riempp, Gerold; Nastansky, Ludwig: Conceptions and solutions for the interaction of distributed workflow management systems, in: Abramowicz, W. (Ed.): Proc. of Business Information Systems '97 (BIS'97), Poznań, Poland, 1997, pp. 583-599.

[Riempp/Nastansky 1997d]
Riempp, Gerold; Nastansky, Ludwig: Managing business processes in virtual enterprises – interaction of distributed workflow management systems, in: Proc. of IT-Vision – Virtual Enterprises & Networked Solutions – new Perspectives on Management, Communication and Information Technology, ESTIEM, VISION Week, 1997.

[Roberts 1996]
Roberts, Bill: Groupwar strategies, in: Byte, July, 1996, pp. 68-78.

[Robson 1991]
Robson, George D.: Continuous process improvement – simplifying workflow systems, Free Press, New York, 1991.

[Roller 1996]
Roller, Dieter: Verifikation von Workflows in IBM FlowMark, in: Vossen, G.; Becker, J. (Eds.): Geschäftsprozeßmodellierung und Workflow Management – Modelle, Methoden, Werkzeuge, International Thomson Publishing, Bonn, Albany, 1996, pp. 353-368.

[Rothenbacher 1996]
Rothenbacher, Christine: Prozeßorientiertes Vorgehen – Praxiserfahrung umsetzen, in: Business Computing, No. 8, 1996, pp. 37-39.

[Rumbaugh 1991]
Rumbaugh, James: Object-oriented modelling and design, Prentice-Hall, Englewood Cliffs, New Jersey, 1991.

[Rupprecht-Daeullary 1994]
Rupprecht-Däullary, Marita: Zwischenbetriebliche Kooperation – Möglichkeiten und Grenzen durch neue Informations- und Kommunikationstechnologien, DUV - Gabler Edition Wissenschaft, Wiesbaden, 1994.

[Saliger 1997]
Saliger, Dietmar: Laufzeitumgebung für Groupware-basiertes, weitverteiltes Workflow Management – Konzeption und prototypische Implementierung einer Runtime-Engine für die Wide Area GroupFlow Umgebung, Master thesis, Business Computing 2, University of Paderborn, 1997.

[Scheer 1987]
Scheer, August-Wilhelm: Betriebsübergreifende Vorgangsketten durch Vernetzung der Informationsverarbeitung, Information Management, 2/3, 1987, pp. 56-63.

[Scheer 1992]
Scheer, August-Wilhelm: Architektur integrierter Informationssysteme - Grundlagen der Unternehmensmodellierung, 2. Auflage, Springer Verlag, Berlin etc., 1992.

[Scheer 1994]
Scheer, August-Wilhelm: Business process reengineering – reference models for industrial enterprises, 2nd edition, Springer Verlag, Berlin etc., 1994.

[Scheller et al. 1994]
Scheller, M; Boden, K.-P.; Geenen, A.; Kampermann, J.: Internet – Werkzeuge und Dienste von Archie bis World Wide Web, Springer Verlag, Berlin etc., 1994.

[Schmider 1995]
Schmider, Ekkehard: Einsparungspotentiale nutzen – Workflow-Systeme sollen im Verwaltungsbereich leisten, was PPS-Systeme in der Produktion vollbringen: Wirtschaftlichkeit durch bessere und kostengünstigere Arbeitsorganisation., in: Business Computing, No. 7, 1995, pp. 40-43.

[Schniedermann 1998]
Schniedermann, Stephan: Modellierung weitverteilten Workflow Managements mit Hilfe des Wide Area GroupFlow Systems – Analyse und Vorgangsdesign von praktischen Szenarien, Master thesis, Business Computing 2, University of Paderborn, 1998.

[Schugt/Wolf 1997]
Schugt, Gaby; Wolf, Gritta: Ein Workflow-System macht Papier überflüssig und verkürzt die Abwicklungszeit – bei Quelle sprudeln die Küchenideen aus dem Laptop des Beraters vor Ort, in: Computer Zeitung, No. 24, 12.7., 1997, pp. 23.

[Schulze/Boehm 1996]
Schulze, Wolfgang; Böhm, Markus: Klassifikation von Vorgangsverwaltungssystemen, in: Vossen, G.; Becker, J. (Eds.): Geschäftsprozeßmodellierung und Workflow Management – Modelle, Methoden, Werkzeuge, International Thomson Publishing, Bonn etc., 1996, pp. 279-293.

[Schumann 1992]
Schumann, Matthias: Betriebliche Nutzeffekte und Strategiebeiträge der großintegrierten Informationsverarbeitung, Springer Verlag, Berlin etc., 1992.

[Schwab 1996]
Schwab, Klaus: Koordinationsmodelle und Softwarearchitekturen als Basis für die Auswahl und Spezialisierung von Workflow-Management-Systemen, in: Vossen, G.; Becker, J. (Eds.): Geschäftsprozeßmodellierung und Workflow Management – Modelle, Methoden, Werkzeuge, International Thomson Publishing, Bonn etc., 1996, pp. 295-317.

[Schwarz 1997]
Schwarz, Martin: 'Moment, ich verbinde ...': COM, SOM und CORBA – oder die Suche nach dem Software-Esperanto, in: c't - Magazin für Computer Technik, Verlag Heinz Heise, Hannover, No. 3, 1997, pp. 256-273.

[Schwarzer/Zerbe/Krcmar 1997]
Schwarzer, Bettina; Zerbe, Stefan; Krcmar, Helmut: A material perspective towards IT-enabled co-operation, in: Galliers, R. et al. (Eds.): Proc. of the 5th European Conference on Information Systems, Cork, Vol. II, 1997, pp. 928-942.

[Searle 1969]
Searle, John R.: Speech acts – an essay in the philosophy of language, Cambridge University Press, London, 1969.

[Semich 1994]
Semich, J. W.: Information replaces inventory at the virtual corporation, in: Datamation, Vol. 15, No. 7, 1994, pp. 37-42.

[Senge 1990]
Senge, P. M.: The fifth discipline – the art and practice of the learning organization, Doubleday, New York, 1990.

[Senge 1997]
Senge, Peter: Keynote speech at the international conference "Wirtschaftsinformatik '97", Berlin, February, 1997.

[Sieber 1997]
Sieber, Pascal: Virtuality in the IT industry – some examples, in: Galliers, R. et al. (Eds.): Proc. of the 5th European Conference on Information Systems, Cork, Vol. III, 1997, pp. 1343-1356.

[Siebert/Kindler/Soyez 1997]
Siebert, Reiner; Kindler, Thomas; Soyez, Tobias: Integrated workflow and telecooperation support for the German government, in: Symposium on Applied Computing (SAC'97), Stuttgart, 1997. see also: http://www.informatik.uni-stuttgart.de/ipvr/vs/Publications/1997-siebert-01.ps.gz.

[Siekmann 1998]
Siekmann, Carsten: Flexibilität durch fallbasiertes Wide Area Workflow Management – Visualisierung und Variation von Workflow-Instanzen auf Basis von Java-basierten Prototypen am Beispiel des Wide Area GroupFlow Systems, Master thesis, Business Computing 2, University of Paderborn, 1998.

[Simon 1998]
Simon, Stefan: Zwischenbetriebliche Integration – Stand der Forschung und Praxis bei der Verbindung operativer Informationssysteme über Organisationsgrenzen hinweg, Master thesis, Business Computing 2, University of Paderborn, 1998.

[Sodan 1994]
Sodan (Ed.): Workflow management products, Uxbridge, 1994.

[Sonnabend 1996]
Sonnabend, Marc: Workflow Management zwischen verteilten Organisationen – Stand der Entwicklung in Forschung und Praxis, Master thesis, Business Computing 2, University of Paderborn, 1996.

[Stark 1997]
Stark, Heather: Understanding workflow, in: Lawrence, P. (Ed.): Workflow Handbook 1997, Wiley, Chichester etc., 1997, pp. 5-25.

[Striemer/Holten/Weske 1997]
Striemer, Rüdiger; Holten, Roland; Weske, Mathias: Darstellung und Vergleich von Vorgehensmodellen zur Entwicklung von Workflow - Anwendungen, in: ISST - Berichte, Berlin, Dortmund, No. 34, 1997.

[Stubner 1997]
Stubner, Stephan: Laptop löst im Außendienst zentimeterhohe Listen ab, in: Computer Zeitung, No. 46, 13.11., 1997, p. 20.

[Swatman/Swatman 1991]
Swatman, P. M. C.; Swatman, P. A.: Electronic data interchange – organisational opportunity, not technical problem, in: Srinivasan, B.; Zeleznikow, J. (Eds.): Databases in the 1990's, World Scientific Press, Singapore, 1991, pp. 354-374.

[Swatman/Swatman 1993]
Swatman, Paula; Swatman, Paul A.: Business process redesign using EDI – an Australian success story, in: J. Griclar (Ed.): EDI & IOS – Strategic Systems in the Global Economy of the '90s - Proc. of the 5th International Electronic Data Interchange Conference, Bled, Slovenia, June, 1993.

[Temme 1998]
Temme, Thorsten: Weitverteiltes Workflow Management im World Wide Web – Konzeption und prototypische Umsetzung einer Integration des Wide Area GroupFlow Systems mit dem WWW, Master thesis, Business Computing 2, University of Paderborn, 1998.

[Teufel et al. 1995]
Teufel, S.; Sauter, C.; Mühlherr, T.; Bauknecht, K.: Computerunterstützung für die Gruppenarbeit, Addison Wesley, Bonn etc., 1995.

[Thompson/Chapman-Pincher 1994]
Thompson, Debra; Chapman-Pincher, Michael: Perspectives on Lotus Notes – survey on 120 IT- and business managers, in: Lotus Notes and Groupware User Group Report, Lotus Notes Users Europe, April, 1994.

[Touchard 1996]
Touchard, Jörg: Modellierung verteilter Vorgangsbearbeitung – Konzeption und prototypische Implementierung eines graphischen Vorgangseditors für verteiltes, Groupware-basiertes Workflow Management, Master thesis, Business Computing 2, University of Paderborn, 1996.

[Tunnat 1998]
Tunnat, Oliver: Methoden der Weiterleitung und des Vorgangscontrolling für weit-verteiltes Workflow Management – Konzeption und prototypische Implementierung einer Gateway- und Tracking-Anwendung für das Wide Area GroupFlow System unter besonderer Berücksichtigung rechtlicher Aspekte, Master thesis, Business Computing 2, University of Paderborn, 1998.

[Turrell 1995]
Turrell, Mark: Supporting the multicultural multinational – Lotus Notes at Asea Brown Boveri, research report, City University Business School, London, 1995.

[Tuunainen/Saarinen 1997]
Tuunainen, Virpi Kristiina; Saarinen, Timo: EDI and Internet-EDI – opportunities of effective integration for small businesses, in: Galliers, R. et al. (Eds.): Proc. of the 5th European Conference on Information Systems, Cork, Vol. I, 1997, pp. 164-177.

[Ueberhorst 1996]
Überhorst, Stefan: Gremium feiert Erfolg – Workflow-Systeme nutzen einheitliche Schnittstelle, in: Computerwoche No. 30, 26.07., 1996, p. 16.

[van Hoof/Altenhofen 1996]
van Hoof, Antonius; Altenhofen, Christoph: Ein System hat viele Komponenten – Herstellermix bei Dokumentenmanagement schafft Stolpersteine, in: Computerwoche Focus: Workflow – die Geschäftsprozesse beschleunigen, 15.3., 1996, pp. 13-15.

[van Koenig/Wijk 1991]
van Koenig, C.; Wijk, G.: Inter-firm alliances – the role of trust, in: Thepot, J.; Thierart, R. (Eds.): Microeconomic Contributions to Strategic Management, Advanced Series in Management, Elsevier Science, New York, Vol. 16, 1991, pp. 169-183.

[van Leuwen 1997]
van Leuwen, Fred: Relating groupware and workflow, in: Lawrence, P. (Ed.): Workflow Handbook 1997, Wiley, Chichester etc., 1997, pp. 75-88.

[VDP 1997]
Verband Deutscher Papierfabriken VDP (Ed.): Papier `97 – ein Leistungsbericht, Selbstverlag, Bonn, 1997.

[Vinoski 1997]
Vinoski, Steve: CORBA – integrating diverse applications within distributed heterogeneous environments, in: IEEE Communications Magazine, Vol. 14, No. 2, 1997.

[Vogedes 1997]
Vogedes, Thorsten: Kosten und Nutzen papierbasierter in Abgrenzung zu elektronisch unterstützter Büroarbeit – Modellbildung und empirische Untersuchung in einem Unternehmen der Telekommunikationsbranche, Master thesis, Business Computing 2, University of Paderborn, 1997.

[Vogler 1996]
Vogler, Petra: Chancen und Risiken von Workflow-Management, in: Österle, H.; Vogler, P. (Eds.): Praxis des Workflow Managements, Vieweg, Braunschweig, Wiesbaden, 1996, pp. 343-362.

[Wallace 1988]
Wallace, B.: Suppliers slow to profit from EDI, in: Network World, 36, Feb. 8, 1988, pp. 1-8.

[Wargitsch/Wewers 1997]
Wargitsch, Christoph; Wewers, Thorsten: FLEXWARE – fallorientiertes Konfigurieren von komplexen Workflows, Konzepte und Implementierung, in: Müller, M. et al. (Eds.), Proc of 11. Workshop 'Planen und Konfigurieren' im Rahmen der 4. Deutschen Tagung “Wissensbasierte Systeme” (XPS-97), Erlangen, 1997, pp. 45-55.

[Wargitsch/Wewers/Theisinger 1998]
Wargitsch, Christoph; Wewers, Thorsten; Theisinger, F.: An organizational-memory-based approach for an evolutionary workflow management system - concepts and implementation, in: Proc. of 31st Hawaii International Conference on System Sciences, Hawaii, 1998.

[Wargitsch/Wewers/Wirthmüller 1997]
Wargitsch, Christoph; Wewers, Thorsten; Wirthmüller, Andreas: WWW front-ends for document and workflow management systems, in: Proc. of IT-Vision – Virtual Enterprises & Networked Solutions – new Perspectives on Management, Communication and Information Technology, ESTIEM, VISION Week, 1997.

[Weber 1997a]
Weber, Volker: Stellwerk – Workflow mit Lotus Notes und ONEstone proZessware, in: c't - Magazin für Computer Technik, Heise Verlag, Hannover, No. 1, 1997, pp. 104-106.

[Weber 1997b]
Weber, Volker: Notizen, standardisiert – Lotus Domino 4.6 Server und Notes 4.6 Client, in: c't - Magazin für Computer Technik, Heise Verlag, Hannover, No. 12, 1997, pp. 138-142.

[Weber 1997c]
Weber, Volker: Workflow von Mainframe bis Browser – ONEstone stellt proZessware 1.5 vor, in: c't - Magazin für Computer Technik, Heise Verlag, Hannover, No. 16, 1997, p. 36.

[Weber 1998]
Weber, Volker: Rien ne va plus – Domino 5, Intranet und Java im Mittelpunkt der Lotusphere 98, in: c't - Magazin für Computer Technik, Heise Verlag, Hannover, No. 4, 1998, pp. 50-53.

[Weick 1979]
Weick, K. E.: The social psychology of organizing, 2nd edition, Addison Wesley, Reading, MA, 1979.

[Weiss 1994]
Weiss, Dietmar: Workflow-Systeme sollten eher Assistenten als Polizisten sein – wenige Systeme werden den Anforderungen gerecht, in: Computerwoche, Vol. 22, No. 22, 1994, pp. 15-18.

[Weiss/Krcmar 1996]
Weiss, Dietmar; Krcmar, Helmut: Workflow management – Herkunft und Klassifikation, in: Wirtschaftsinformatik, Vol. 38, No. 5, 1996, pp. 503-513.

[Wesseler 1993]
Wesseler, Berthold: Nutzen der Bürosysteme bleibt umstritten, in: Online, No. 1, 1993, pp. 26-29.

[Wewers 1996]
Wewers, Thorsten: Zwischenbetrieblich integrierte Informationsverarbeitung für die Abfallwirtschaft – dargestellt am Beispiel eines Workflow-Management-Systems für die Entsorgung von Sonderabfällen, Arbeitspapier No. 4/96 des Bereichs Wirtschaftsinformatik 1, Universität Nürnberg-Erlangen, 1996.

[Wewers/Faisst 1996]
Wewers, Thorsten; Faisst, Wolfgang: Kooperierende Workflow-Management-Systeme für Virtuelle Unternehmen, in: Uellner, St. (Ed.): Proc. of Workshop "CSCW in großen Unternehmen", Deutsche Telekom AG, Darmstadt, 1996, pp. 167-175.

[Wewers/Wargitsch 1997]
Wewers, Thorsten; Wargitsch, Christoph: Zwischenbetrieblich integriertes Workflow-Management – dargestellt am Beispiel der Sonderabfallentsorgung, in: Mambrey, P. et al. (Eds.): Proc. of Workshop "Rechnergestützte Kooperation in Verwaltungen und großen Unternehmen", Aachen, 1997, pp. 64-85.

[Wewers/Wargitsch 1998]
Wewers, Thorsten; Wargitsch, Christoph: Four dimensions of interorganizational, document-oriented workflow – a case study of the approval of hazardous-waste disposal, in: Proc. of 31st Hawaii International Conference on System Sciences, Hawaii, 1998.

[WfMC 1997]
WfMC, Workflow Management Coalition: The workflow reference model, in: Lawrence, P. (Ed.): Workflow Handbook 1997, Wiley, Chichester etc., 1997, pp. 243-293.

[WfMC IF1 1995]
WfMC, Workflow Management Coalition: Interface 1 – workflow process definition read/write interface: request for comment, document number WFMC-WG01-1000, 17-Feb, 1995.

[WfMC IF4 Abstr. 1996]
Workflow Management Coalition: Workflow standard – interoperability abstract specification, document number WFMC-TC-1012, Version 1.0, 20-Oct, 1996.

[WfMC IF4 MIME 1996]
WfMC, Workflow Management Coalition: Workflow standard – interoperability internet e-mail mime binding, document number WFMC-TC-1018, Version 1.0, 20-Oct, 1996.

[WfMC Ref. Mod. 1994]
WfMC, Workflow Management Coalition: The workflow reference model, document number TC00-1003, Issue 1.1, by David Hollingworth, 29-Nov, 1994.

[Whitehead 1996]
Whitehead, Roger: Lotus Notes - an introduction, in: Lloyd, P.; Whitehead, R. (Eds.): Transforming organisations through groupware - Lotus Notes in action, Springer Verlag, Berlin etc., 1996, pp. 1-10.

[Wilkens 1989]
Wilkens, Maria Janilce A..: Message systems as communications media among computer processes, in: Stefferud, E. et al. (Eds.): Message Handling Systems and Distributed Applications, Elsevier, Amsterdam, 1989, pp. 281-286.

[Willcocks/Currie/Jackson 1997]
Willcocks, Leslie; Currie, Wendy; Jackson, Sylvie: Radical re-engineering and information systems – evidence from UK public services, in: Galliers, R. et al. (Eds.): Proc. of the 5th European Conference on Information Systems, Cork, Vol. I, 1997, pp. 460-480.

[Williams 1997]
Williams, John: Planning for the clustered corporation, in: Lawrence, P. (Ed.): Workflow Handbook 1997, Wiley, Chichester etc., 1997, pp. 205-209.

[Williamson 1981]
Williamson, O. E.: The modern corporation – origin, evolution, attributes, in: Journal of Economic Literature, XIX, 1981, pp. 1537-1568.

[Williamson 1985]
Williamson, O. E.: The economic institutions of capitalism – firms, markets, relational contracting, Free Press, New York, 1985.

[Willis 1997]
Willis, David: Kampf der Giganten – Lotus Notes 4.1 und Microsoft Exchange im Vergleich, in: Client Server Computing, No. 1, 1997, pp. 20-27.

[Winograd/Flores 1986]
Winograd, Terry; Flores, Fernando: Understanding computers and cognition - a new foundation for design, Ablex Publishing Corporation, Norwood, NJ, 1986.

[WWWJ 1997]
World Wide Web Journal: XML – principles, tools and techniques, O'Reilly & Associates, Sebastopol, CA , Vol. 2, Issue 4 (Fall), 1997.

[Zicari 1995]
Zicari, Roberto: Interoperabilität – Broker für Objekte, in: Business Computing, No.10, 1995, pp. 114-117.

[Zisman 1977]
Zisman, M. D.: Representation, specification and automation of office procedures, Ph.D. dissertation, Wharton School, Univ. of Pennsylvania, Philadelphia, 1977.

[Zumbach 1996]
Zumbach, Peter: Fingerspitzengefühl und umdenken erforderlich – "Notes für alle" ist weltweite Strategie bei Babcock, in: Computerwoche Focus: Workflow – die Geschäftsprozesse beschleunigen, 15.3., 1996, pp. 32-34.

[zur Muehlen/Rosemann 1997]
zur Mühlen, Michael; Rosemann, Michael: Der Lösungsbeitrag von Metadatenmodellen beim Vergleich von Workflowmanagementsystemen, in: Rosemann, M., Becker, J. (Eds.): Workflowmanagement - State-of-the-Art aus Sicht von Theorie und Praxis, Arbeitsbericht No. 42, Universität Münster, Institut für Wirtschaftsinformatik, 1997, pp. 12-21.

10.2 Online references

Workflow management (general):

- Workflow Management Coalition (WfMC):
  http://www.aiim.org/wfmc/
- WARIA, the Workflow And Reengineering International Association:
  http://www.waria.com/

Workflow products and vendors:

- Linkpage of the WfMC:
  http://www.aiim.org/wfmc/members.html
- Linkpage of the Fraunhofer Institute:
  http://www.do.isst.fhg.de/workflow/pages/Produkte_Englisch.html

Workflow management-related research at scientific institutions:

- Fraunhofer Institute:
  http://www.do.isst.fhg.de/workflow/pages/index.html
- German Computer Society – workflow activities:
  http://wwwdb.inf.tu-dresden.de/~www/AK-Workflow/
- *MOVE* project (see also p. 88):
  http://www.do.isst.fhg.de/move
- Politecnico de Milano:
  http://www.elet.polimi.it:80/section/compeng/db/wf/index.html
- University of Bamberg:
  http://www.seda.sowi.uni-bamberg.de/~workflow/index.htm
- University of Dresden:
  http://wwwdb.inf.tu-dresden.de/~www/LS-Dokumente/index_wf.html
- University of Erlangen:
  http://www6.informatik.uni-erlangen.de/
- University of Georgia:
  http://lsdis.cs.uga.edu/
- University of Massachusetts:
  http://www-ccs.cs.umass.edu/db.html
- University of Twente – Anaxagoras Workflow:
  http://www.anaxagoras.com/

WAWM-related research projects:

- *ContAct* (see also p. 95):
  http://www.iwi.uni-sb.de/contact/
- *FlexWare*, *Workconnector* and *WAX* (see also pp. 87, 92, 96):
  http://www.wi1.wiso.uni-erlangen.de/wi1wiso.html

- *ORBWork* and *WebWork* (see also pp. 94, 95): http://www.cs.uga.edu/LSDIS
- *Phanta Rhei* (see also p. 96): http://www.ifi.uni-klu.ac.at/~herb/Overview.html
- *PRINCESS* (see also p. 84) http://www.iwi.uni-sb.de/research/princess/dfg_spp.html
- *VORTEL* (see also p. 94): http://www.isst.fhg.de/pages/projekte/1996/VORTEL.html
- *WorldFlow* (see also p. 97): http://www-ccs.cs.umass.edu/kamath/hpts97.html

CSCW and Groupware:

- CSCW Conferences – download of proceedings: http://www.acm.org/pubs/contents/proceedings/cscw/
- CSCW Linkpage, Technical University of Munich: http://www.telekooperation.de/cscw/
- CSCW Linkpage, University of Marburg: http://www.wiwi.uni-marburg.de/lokal/bwl06/interess/cscw/cscwengl.htm
- Tom Brinks' CSCW linkpage: http://www.crew.umich.edu/~brinck/cscw.html
  new: http://www.usabilityfirst.com/cscw/
- Groupware Competence Center, University of Paderborn: http://gcc.uni-paderborn.de

Miscellaneous:

- Center for Coordination Science, MIT: http://ccs.mit.edu/ccsmain.html
- *POLIKOM* project (see also p. 91): http://www.ba.dlr.de/md/it/iv/tk/polikom/index.html
- Further information on and download of the Wide Area GroupFlow System: http://gcc.uni-paderborn.de/wags
  http://www.springer.co.uk/comp/support/index.html
- The author's homepage: http://fb5www.uni-paderborn.de/winfo2/GeroldRiempp

11 Indices

11.1 Keyword index

S

T

U

V

W

X

11.2 Abbreviations

AI .... Artificial intelligence
ARIS .... Architecture of integrated information systems
ASCII .... American standard code of information interchange
BPR .... Business process reengineering
CAD .... Computer-aided design
CGI .... Common gateway interface
CIM .... Computer-integrated manufacturing
CIWP .... Complete integration of workflow parts
$\text{CLUSTER}_{\text{CEN,WAW}}$ .. Workflow cluster with centralized modeling for wide area workflows
$\text{CLUSTER}_{\text{PAR,WAW}}$ .. Workflow cluster with participative modeling for wide area workflows
CM .... Content management
CORBA .... Common object request broker architecture
CPI .... Continuous process improvement
CRP .... Continuous replenishment
CSCW .... Computer supported cooperative work
DCOM .... Distributed component object model
DDCF .... Distributed document component facility
DM .... Deutsche Mark (German marks)
DTD .... Document type definition
EC .... Electronic commerce
EDI .... Electronic data interchange
EDIFACT .... Electronic data interchange for administration, commerce and transport
Eds. .... Editors
eEPC .... Extended event-controlled process chain
ERM .... Entity-relationship model
GCC .... Groupware competence center
GIOP .... General inter-ORB protocol
GRI .... Global routing information
GRN .... Goods received number
GSD .... Group sales director
GUI .... Graphical user interface
HTML .... Hypertext markup language
IB .... International brewery
IBIT .... International brewery idea team
IBQOT .... International brewery quality optimization team
ID .... Identification
IDL .... Interface definition language
IIOP .... Internet inter-ORB protocol
IMAP .... Internet mail access protocol

IN/OUT ....Node for incoming and outgoing message objects
IN ....Node for incoming message objects
ION ....Interorganizational network
IOS ....Interorganizational information system
IP ....Internet protocol
IRI ....Internal routing information
ISDN ....Integrated services digital network
ISO/OSI ....International Organization for Standardization / open systems interconnection
ISO ....International Organization for Standardization
IT ....Information technology
JIT ....Just-in-time
LAN ....Local area network
LDAP ....Lightweight directory access protocol
LLM ....Large lighting manufacturer
MAPI ....Messaging application programming interface (standard)
MIME ....Multipurpose Internet mail extension
MIT ....Massachusetts Institute of Technology
MRC ....Material request card
N&A ....Lotus Notes names & address book (directory service)
NWP ....Nested workflow parts
ODBC ....Open database connectivity
OLE ....Object linking and embedding
OMA ....Object management architecture
OMG ....Object management group
ORB ....Object request broker
OUT/IN ....Node for outgoing and incoming message objects
OUT ....Node for outgoing message objects
PC ....Personal computer
PGP ....“Pretty good privacy” (encryption system)
POP ....Post office protocol
PWPS ....Parallel workflow parts with synchronization
QR ....Quick response
R & D ....Research and development
RAM ....Random access memory
RMI ....Remote method invocation
RPC ....Remote procedure call
RSA ....Public key encryption method (Rivest, Shamir, Adelman)
RSM ....Regional sales manager
S_ARROW ....Synchronization arrow
SCC ....Supply chain council
SCM ....Supply chain management
SCOR ....Supply chain operations reference
SD ....Sales director
SGML ....Standard generalized markup language
SMTP ....Simple mail transfer protocol
SQL ....Structured query language

SR .... Sales representative
SSL .... Secure socket layer
$SUBWORKFLOW_{DEC,WAW}$ ..... Sub-workflow with decentralized modeling for wide area workflows; also labeled *ordered subworkflow*
SWP .... Sequential workflow parts
SYNC .... Synchronization node
TCP/IP .... Transmission control protocol / Internet protocol
UNSM .... United Nations standard message
URL .... Uniform resource locator (WWW address)
US, USA .... United States of America
VIM .... Vendor-independent messaging (standard)
VO .... Virtual organization
VSTART .... "Virtual" start node
W3C .... World Wide Web Consortium
WAGS .... Wide Area GroupFlow System
WAN .... Wide area network
WAPI .... Workflow application programming interface
WAWM .... Wide Area Workflow Management
WFM .... Workflow management
WfMC .... Workflow Management Coalition
WFMS .... Workflow management system
$WORKFLOW_{SUB,WAW}$ .....Workflow, subscribed for wide area workflows; also labeled *external subscribed workflow*
WPDL .... Workflow process definition language
WWW .... World Wide Web
WYSIWYG .... "What you see is what you get"
X.400 .... Standard for electronic mail
X.500 .... Standard for directory services
XML .... Extensible markup language
ZBI .... Zwischenbetriebliche Integration (German for: interorganizational integration)

11.3 Figures

11.4 Tables

About the author and his team

The author

Dr. Gerold Riempp

has studied industrial engineering and business computing at the Technical University of Darmstadt. During and after his studies, he worked as an IT consultant for several companies in Germany and the USA. He is an experienced scientist as well as practitioner in the fields of database management systems, office applications, desktop publishing solutions, groupware platforms and workflow management systems.

From 1994 until 1997, he led a research and development team at the Groupware Competence Center, University of Paderborn. During this time, he and his colleagues developed the concepts and prototypic solutions for Wide Area Workflow Management described in this book.

Dr. Riempp is now working as an IT consultant for PricewaterhouseCoopers, Consulting Group, Frankfurt/Main, in the fields of workflow management, groupware as well as Internet and WWW solutions.

Feel free to contact him via e-mail: griempp@t-online.de

The "Wide Area Workflow Team":

Rear row, from left to right:
Michael Gross (*WAGS Gateway, XML converter*), Stephan Schniedermann (*case studies*), Matthias Hovestadt (*WAGS Modeler*), Christian Peine (*WAGS Modeler*), Stefan Simon (*literature research*), Helmut Finke (*WAGS External Directory*), Carsten Siekmann (*WAGS Workflow Viewer*)

Front row, from left to right:
Stefan Kremer (*WAGS WebConnect*), Gerold Riempp, Dietmar Saliger (*WAGS Engine*), Oliver Tunnat (*WAGS Gateway, WAGS Tracking*), Thorsten Temme (*WAGS WebConnect*)

Missing on this picture, in alphabetical order:
Stephan Bartholomé (*WAWM in virtual organizations*), Thomas Beyer (*case studies*), Dirk Deleré (*literature research*), Wolfgang Eilks (*WAGS Message Objects*), Jörg Dürre (*WWW integration*), Martin Geissen (*WAWM in virtual organizations*), Karl Gustze (*WAGS Tracking*), Alexander Haasper (*WAGS Gateway*), Olaf Hein (*WAGS Analyzer*), Frank Hundehege (*research on interorganizational BPR*), Barbara Ising (*case studies*), Gerald Kaufhold (*WAGS External Directory*), Markus Klocke (*WAGS Engine*), Michael Küthe (*WAGS Gateway*), Herbert Langhorst (*WAGS Message Objects*), Sven Lubek (*WWW integration*), Martin Manke (*WAGS Gateway*), Michael Marr (*case studies*), Karin Meierfrankenfeld (*WAGS External Directory*), Claudius Niebiossa (*case studies*), Michael Pauls (*WAGS Message Objects*), Christian Schulte (*WAGS Gateway*), Marc Sonnabend (*literature research*), Martin Stelbrink (*WAGS External Directory*), Jörg Touchard (*WAGS Modeler*), Klaus Wischmann (*case studies*), Martin Wolf (*WWW integration*), Thorsten Vogedes (*case studies*).

Kolibri 360 GmbH
Ferdinand-Jühlke-Straße 7
99095 Erfurt, Deutschland
produktsicherheit@kolibri360.de